Birth of the State

Birth of the State

The Place of the Body in Crafting Modern Politics

CHARLOTTE EPSTEIN

OXFORD
UNIVERSITY PRESS

OXFORD

UNIVERSITY PRESS

Oxford University Press is a department of the University of Oxford. It furthers
the University's objective of excellence in research, scholarship, and education
by publishing worldwide. Oxford is a registered trade mark of Oxford University
Press in the UK and certain other countries.

Published in the United States of America by Oxford University Press
198 Madison Avenue, New York, NY 10016, United States of America.

CIP data is on file at the Library of Congress
ISBN 978-0-19-091763-0 (pbk.)
ISBN 978-0-19-091762-3 (hbk.)

3 5 7 9 8 6 4 2

Paperback printed by Marquis, Canada
Hardback printed by Bridgeport National Bindery, Inc., United States of America

Contents

Acknowledgments

This book has taken a long time to write, a longer time still to read for and to think through. Several institutions have hosted me for writing visits along the way. I am grateful to my colleagues at the Centre d'Études et de Recherches Internationales (CERI/Science Po) in Paris, at the Wissenschaftzentrum (WZB), in Berlin and its wonderful librarians, and at the University of Sydney. Many friends and colleagues have helped the writing process, sometimes without knowing it, sometimes just with a well-placed word at a difficult moment along the way. I am grateful to Kate Johnston, Étienne Balibar and Frank Smith on that score. I would like to thank Jimmy Casas Klausen, James Der Derian, Paul Halliday, Fleur Johns, Alex Lefebvre, Nancy Luxon, Harry Maher, Jeannie Morefield, Ben O'Loughlin, Sarah Phillips, Kim Rygiel, David Schlosberg, Laura Shepherd, David Smith, Sharon Stanley, Rebecca Suter, Ditlev Tamm, Simon Tormey, Carolien Van Ham, and the Press's two reviewers for taking the time to read sections of the manuscript. Thank you to Harry Maher for his eagle eye, and to Angela Chnapko from OUP who has been a joy to work with. I am deeply grateful to Jess Whyte and Rob Walker for the thoroughness and the care with which they repeatedly engaged with the manuscript and with my ideas. For his grace, forbearance, and thoughtfulness; for the insights he has sparked throughout the writing, and for his unwavering support through my own doubts, I am grateful beyond words to Ole Wæver.

A Note on References

I have used the author-date system throughout to give the reference of quotations, and the reader will find the full references at the book's end.

Key works by Thomas Hobbes and John Locke have constituted, in addition, my primary textual materials. These are available in many editions. To make the quotations as readily identifiable as possible across different editions, I have cited both chapters and section numbers, in addition to the page of the specific edition that I have used, whose references are also at the book's end.

I have also abbreviated these texts' titles as I indicate in the list below.

For example, Hobbes (*L.*, chap.17[3]57) refers to *Leviathan*'s chapter 17, section 3, which may be found on page 57 in the Hackett edition. Or again (Hobbes, *L.* 3) refers simply to the political treatise's third page in the same edition.

Locke (*EHU*, II.chap.31[3]250), would likewise refer to the second book, chapter 31, section 3 of Locke's *Essay concerning Human Understanding*, page 250 in my chosen edition. When referencing his *Essays on the Law of Nature*, I indicate the essay number and citation page. Thus (*ELN*, iii, 95–96) refer to the third essay, with the citations to be found on pages 95 and 96.

Abbreviations for Thomas Hobbes's Main Texts Used

DC: *De Corpore*
DCi: *De Cive*
DH: *De Homine*
EoL: *Elements of Law*
EoLi: *Elements of Law, Part I: Human Nature*
EoLii: *Elements of Law, Part II: De Corpore Politico*
L: *Th\e Leviathan*

Abbreviations for John Locke's Main Texts Used

CU: *On the Conduct of the Understanding*
EHU: *Essay concerning Human Understanding*
EE: *Essay concerning Education*
ELN: *Essays on the Laws of Nature*
PL: *Essay on the Poor Law*
TT: *Two Treatises on Government*

1

Introduction

> The eternal silence of these infinite spaces terrifies me.
>
> Blaise Pascal, *Pensées* (my translation)

The body is the political object par excellence. It is the means by which states count, and, since the introduction of the biometric passport, account for their citizens to one another (see Epstein 2007, 2008b, 2016; Müller 2010; Gates 2011; Ajana 2013). It is what they aim to keep safe, and healthy. Global pandemics, where the body is especially acutely watched, scrutinized in its temperature and its movements, are forceful reminders of the extent to which the state's ontology is, and as I will show in this book, always has been, corporeal. The biometric technologies that enable this monitoring and measuring are thickly woven into the fabric of our everyday lives.[1] They help us unlock our electronic devices, access our workplaces and government services. They enable citizens to exercise their rights to vote, with the growing use of biometric voter identification systems. They also help states track demonstrators. And they open up new hacking opportunities. The widespread diffusion and swift normalisation of bodily-centred surveillance technologies has been enabled, I suggest, by the corporeal political ontology whose origins I lay bare in this book. It accounts for the ready embrace of biometrics by all states today, former colonisers and postcolonial states alike.[2]

To parse this political ontology, I return to the origins of modernity's body politic, the state. The state is the form of political association that first emerged in seventeenth-century Europe to administer a sovereign authority over a bounded territory, and the unit of the contemporary international political system. For all the promises of globalisation and of a borderless world that resonated so loudly but a few decades ago, today the desire for sovereignty that is tightly bound up with the state appears to be reasserting itself wherever we turn, with a vengeance. Can the return of the state be explained simply by a pathological politics; by, say, populism or the deceitful manoeuvrings of a few authoritarian rulers? Or is there instead, more uncomfortably, something to the ways in which we are intimately gripped by the state, in its very constitution, and in our own, as subjects or citizens who all live in states, that might account for a persisting attachment to the state, that is broader and deeper than the political contingencies of our times?

Birth of the State. Charlotte Epstein, Oxford University Press (2021). © Oxford University Press.
DOI: 10.1093/oso/9780190917623.001.0001

This book is about the co-constitution of the state and the modern political subject. By 'co-constitution' I mean that neither the state, nor a subject endowed with political rights guaranteed by the state, pre-existed the relation. The poles of the relation were instead established by the relation itself. I appraise the three fundamental rights—to security, liberty, and property—as the three knots where it was first sealed. Tracing the state and the modern subject of rights back to their origins in seventeenth-century England draws out the extent to which these two categories—the state and the subject of rights—that we tend to take for granted, because of the extent to which they structure our lives, are neither natural nor eternal. They are less fixed, less firmly in place than we assume and often experience them to be. What did pre-exist this contingent, constructed, original modern political relation was the body, in the straightforward sense that there have always been bodies; well before there were states and subjects. I must begin by specifying two directions I do not take in turning to the body. My purpose is not, on the one hand, to chart how the body was represented in the seventeenth century, but rather the other way around. It is to track where and how this body, as a 'natural' object, entered into the crafting of its two new political constructs, the state and the subject of rights, and into the strategies to legitimise and stabilise them. My aim is thus not, on the other hand, to pierce through the weft of words in order to finally, finally, attain the physicalness, realness, or materiality of the body, beyond its representations. As Gayatri Spivak once put it, this 'cannot be thought, and I certainly cannot approach it' (cited in Lennon 2014). Instead the body in this book indexes the *unconstituted*, the ultimate given. It marks the place from which I analyse the co-constitution of the state and the political subject.

My wager with this book is thus to turn the ipseity of the body, its 'thereness,' into a methodological starting point. An enquiry always proceeds and speaks from a particular place, whether it admits it or not. Attending to this epistemological situatedness has been a central concern of the contemporary practice of radical critique, insofar as concealing this standpoint is what supports the claims to occupying that of 'the Master, the Man, the One God whose Eye produces, appropriates and orders all difference', as Donna Haraway (1988, 57) has put it. My starting point here is the body qua given. This entails that I work with this given-ness. I do not attempt to cut through it in order to elucidate what would be 'really' there and might have so far eluded us. Or to compensate for this unknowability by turning to the physical sciences that, surely, must know what there 'really' is to the body; both of which index recent gestures in contemporary thought. To take up the corporeal standpoint I propose in this book, then, is to turn the unknowability of the body into a strength rather than a weakness; into the starting point of a self-assured scientific enterprise that is focussed on tracing historical processes of social construction and aware of its limits, rather than constantly trying to make up for them by chasing after other kinds of sciences that would be somehow better positioned to know the body, or indeed any other material reality. The body's workings may be better known to other kinds of sciences than they are to us, in the social sciences and the humanities; only, I ask, is this really our task? Mine here is to understand, first, how matter itself became thinkable to modernity, and thus to all sciences, in the first place. And it is, second, to grasp how a new matter, in turn, made it possible to conceive a new kind of polity that did not exist before the seventeenth century: the state.

A central purpose of this book is to analyse how the state was born of a revolution in the very understanding of nature; and of the concepts of matter, movement, and space that were previously enfolded in it. Two decisive effects of the scientific revolution that swept through Europe in the sixteenth and seventeenth centuries was that, first, it unmoored a distinctly *human* nature from nature at large. The state, I will show, was invented to grapple with the consequences of Europeans' loss of their anchoring in nature. Second, matter was decisively spatialized. The new concept of matter was 'extension'.[3] Every material object, every body, became a *res extensa*, a 'thing extended', in the sense of placed or positioned in space. The human body qua material, natural thing stood at the juncture of these two, literally earth-shattering, we will see, transformations. The piece of nature closest to hand, it afforded a last bond to a nature that was fast fading out of sight. Matter as a spatial category, in turn, meant that every thing could be considered on the same plane; the body, the machine, but also the body politic. For Hobbes the body is 'that which having no dependence on our thought is coincident or coextensive with some part of space' (*De Corpore*, II.chap.8 [1]102). I will show that this new conception of matter furnished the condition of possibility for conceiving a new political form that was extended yet delineated and contained, the state. The state was born in seventeenth-century Europe through the process of demarcating an 'inside', as the space of political rule and belonging, against an 'outside' (Walker 1993). This border-drawing is what distinguishes the state from, notably, medieval rule, where multiple forms of authority—political, civil, religious, or corporate—overlapped territorially, and vied with one another for control over the different parts of a person's life (see Bloch 1968; Harding 1980; Ruggie 1993). Just as 'extension' reduced all things to their positions in space, the state simplified political authority by 'territorialising' it (Agnew 2017); by containing it in a single territory centred upon a point that was coextensively geographical (the capital), and political (the sovereign). Border-drawing, and redrawing, is the hallmark and prerogative of the state to this day. In this book I parse the original spatialisation of political authority that begat this modern form. By 'spatialisation', rather than 'territorialisation', I mean to underscore how the invention of the state and of territory, understood as the spatial expression of the state, was enabled by the invention of modern space; by thinking in terms of lines, points, and planes of the geometry that Hobbes, Galileo, and also Louis XIV were so fond of. (Territorialisation is considered however, in chapter 4.) I bring the body into focus in three distinct ways. First, as the extended, moving thing that required being placed within this new political space. Second, as the natural thing that furnished the link to nature at large, in the context of a dramatically transforming human-nature relation. Third, and now shifting from the ontological to the epistemological level, the body affords me the lens that exposes the state's delineating as a process of excluding and including, of excluding to bound and to bind.

I undertake a genealogy of the founding modern political relation, between the state and the subject, under the optic of the body. A genealogy is a history of the present that shows, not just why history matters, but how and where it shapes contemporary configurations. I track how the state-subject relation, as the basic structure that is implicated in, and reactivated by, every demand that a political right be recognised and upheld by a state, was first crafted in seventeenth-century England.[4] To clarify my terms on both ends of this relation, my focus is 'the state', the modern political form that took shape in Europe in the seventeenth century, rather than 'the nation', which emerged a century later (see Anderson 1983). On the other end, it is 'the subject', rather than either 'the citizen', the figure born of the French Revolution, or 'the individual', which is a contemporary category often too hastily read back into the seventeenth century (see Macpherson 1962), although its emergence is also a strand of the story I tell. My focus is on how the state-subject relation came into being, rather than how it evolved. The scientific revolution forms a crucial backdrop to my enquiry, which is situated at the point where science and the modern political conjoined. Histories of science, science and technology studies, legal histories, as well as art histories have provided me important sources for staking out this juncture. England is my exemplary state. It was the first polity where the two lines of political and religious authority converged upon the sovereign, Henry VIII, when he divorced the Catholic Church in order to establish himself at the helm of a national religion. England was also the site of the 'legal revolution' that begat the subject of rights as a counterweight to the sovereign (Berman 2003). In this it was the crucible for the agonistic relationship that fashioned coextensively the state and the subject of rights.[5] England in the classical age, as it is known, affords me my main genealogical terrain, with some forays into France and Holland and into the Renaissance and Middle Ages. In centring my enquiry primarily on seventeenth-century England, my purpose is not to nail the definitive birthplace of the state, nor to argue that there is only one meaning to 'the state' for every discipline and every purpose. The state has been traced to multiple sites, historically and geographically. Each attempt reflects a particular understanding of what the state is, and carries its own disciplinary injunctions (see also Bartelson 1995). Mine is, rather, a circular argument, where I identify a formative period for the emergence of the bounded political entity I call 'the state', that has carried forward into the state as we know it today, and that has added biometrics to its border-drawing practices (Müller 2010; Epstein 2007; 2008). It does not invalidate (or validate) other arguments that have explored, say, Renaissance Italy, Ancient Greece, or the French Revolution to locate the state's origins in another sense. A multiplicity of perspectives is, rather, warranted by as complex a concept as 'the state'.

Because of the state's dual nature as a concept articulated by key authors at important historical junctures, and an institution shaped by the play of practices, my genealogical materials encompass practices as well as texts; specifically the law (in chapter 4), medicine and art (in chapter 7). My theoretical corpus comprises the classical cannon of early modern English political thought, particularly the writings of Thomas Hobbes and John Locke, corporeally reconsidered, and against the broader backdrop of natural rights theories (in chapter 6). This entails that I consider Locke, whose primary political concept is 'government', as a theorist of the state, for reasons I elucidate in chapter 5. While I draw upon the established scholarships to illuminate some of the traditional themes in these authors that are pertinent for my argumentation as it unfolds, my reading overall tracks closest to those, ever rarer in a time of increasing disciplinary specialisation, that consider together their political and philosophical writings, like Thomas Spragens's (1973) or Richard Flathman's (1993) readings of Hobbes, or, to a lesser extent, James Tully's (1980) reading of Locke. The latter two, in particular, have each foregrounded the centrality of constructing (or 'making', as Tully called it) to Hobbes's and Locke's thought, respectively. None of the secondary readings, to my knowledge, have parsed the role that the body plays for these thinkers, with the notable exception of Samantha Frost's (2008) for Hobbes.

In the remainder of this introduction, first, I locate my enquiry along the wide spectrum of approaches concerned with analysing processes of social construction, broadly known as 'constructivism'. I am interested not merely in 'the construction of', but properly in the *constitution* of the modern political, and in how the form of agency this implicates places it on the critical or radical side of the spectrum.[6] Second, I further elucidate my recourse to the body as an optic and situate it in relation to other somatic enquiries. Third, I present three key problematiques running throughout the book that help circumscribe the specific juncture of the scientific and the political I explore, before, fourth, explicating its structure and chapter contents.

Construction as Constitution

In the academic landscape of the second half of the twentieth century, constructivism afforded a compelling and productive meeting point for the social sciences and the humanities. It has led to fundamentally rethinking the 'givens' of some of these disciplines, and of our constructed social and political worlds more broadly. Questioning this taken-for-granted quality, by bringing instead into focus both how they came into being (their genealogies), and how they became constructed as 'givens', is a primary aim of constructivist theorising. A corollary to this critical commitment is a new mode of constitutive theorising that sheds the traditional model whereby X 'causes' Y, in favour of a more open-ended and humble effort that, beginning instead from 'Y', seeks to trace some of the processes that account for how it is shaped as it is, as opposed to nailing the full range of variables that make up the 'causing X'. 'The state' is the founding given of international relations, the discipline that has cast its focus upon the highest level of political analysis: relations between states. Hailing initially from philosophy and political theory, 'the subject' has furnished a productive juncture for disciplines across the humanities, such as literary criticism, postcolonial scholarship, and psychoanalytic theory. Wielded as a critical tool since its emergence in the seventeenth century, 'the subject' harbours less of this taken-for-granted quality than 'the state'. Opening up international relation's proverbial black box, in order to bring into focus the state-subject relation (and not merely inter-state relations) as the backbone of the political system it holds in its sights, has been one of the decisive consequences of the discipline's turning to constructivism since the 1980s. That I focus on the state-subject relation also entails that I set aside other political bonds—of nationhood, community, or kin, for example— that have been in focus in other disciplines. The co-constitution of the actors, from the state to the subject, and of the structures of international politics is the staple starting point for the constructivist, constitutive theorising to which this book belongs. However, a residual naturalism has hampered the so-called mainstream international relations constructivist efforts to fully unravel the implications of this co-constitution, as I have shown elsewhere (Epstein 2013a; 2013b). That I start from the body does not entail that I hold on to a 'rump materialism', to use the expression of one of its prominent representatives (Wendt 1999). That is, the body does not afford me a material or natural base, beyond the state-subject relation, in which it would be ultimately grounded. My analysis works exactly the other way around. I track how the body was used to naturalise the original modern political bond. My purpose is to analyse how the state and the subject were constructed all the way down, by going all the way back to their initial crafting in the seventeenth century.

The relations between 'construction' and 'constitution' have been explored the furthest, and by way of the body, within a radical constructivism. Judith Butler's (1993; 1990) deconstruction of the sex/gender distinction parallels the critique levelled at conventional constructivism in international relations for needing to uphold a material substrate for thought. Nature, in this book, functions for the state-subject relation in the same way that sex does for gender in Butler's analysis, as the ultimate construct that, in concealing its constructed-ness, purports to provide a stable basis for its crafting. Whether there really is a nature 'out there' is simply beyond the pale of a humanities and social scientific analysis, as all radical constructivists have amply emphasised. It is driven home especially saliently by the period I consider, where two drastically different natures come into view—the highly motile nature of the scientific revolution and natural law's stable one. Nature had not changed; the knowledge of it decisively had. This knowledge qua the site of its construction is my focus. Nature, then, like sex, is a 'constitutive construction' (Butler 1993, x). Through her engagement with constitution, Butler (1993) has shown how even something as material as the sexed (male or female) body is constructed all the way down, before it was even born.[7] With Butler, I understand constitution, not as a spontaneous or natural emergence, but as implicating a deliberate human agency, a construct*ing*. With radical (or critical) constructivists more broadly, I understand constructivism as a mode of critical thought concerned specifically with the constitution, or crafting, of structures—linguistic, political and social. I term the variant of radical constructivism I develop in this book a 'constitutive constructivism'.

Butler (1993, x), however, has also reduced constitution to a constraining force (a 'constitutive constraint'). It is the norming and normalising power that shapes or materialises bodies that are always already marked as either male or female. My concern in this book is instead to open it up to another kind of agency, that is enabling and not just constraining, that is creative, and collective. It is implicated in the legal instrument by the name, 'the constitution', in a declaration of independence (see Derrida 1986). The question I pursue, it bears repeating, is not 'how is the body constructed?' For this question beggars the next, 'at what point is it sexed?' which Butler has addressed: all the way down. Instead I invert the question. I take the body as the unconstituted in order to chart the constitution of the modern political. My unconstituted, however, is not Butler's (1993, xv) 'un-constructed', which works to conceal the dynamics of construction. A key implication of her analysis is that there is no such thing as 'the body', as a generic or a strictly biological entity, a blank page upon which cultural norms are written. In this, moreover, Butler merely buttresses a longstanding feminist and postcolonial focus on particular, gendered, and racialised bodies that has served to unearth the structures that gendered and racialised them in the first place (Fanon 1952; Said 1978; Spivak 1989; Stoler 1995). These scholarships have, each in their own way, amply emphasised the sticking power of structures—the weight with which, even though they are never fully fixed, they bear down upon individuals. Or exactly because of it. The structuring, constraining relation that interests me first emerged in the seventeenth century and still endures, notwithstanding its multiple historical and geographical variations, insofar as it underwrites the possibility of having rights in the first place. The state-subject relation furnishes us, I suggest, with political modernity's original 'exclusionary matrix' (Butler 1993, xiii). Yet I claim to analyse it *from* the body. How, then, am I to mobilise the body without committing yet again the fallacy of generalisation Butler has exposed, that only ever harbours a nostalgia for the unconstructed, and always curtails the force of the critique that has foregrounded the body in order to expose relations of domination? To explain in what sense I hold the body as the unconstructed, and as the place from which to parse political constructing, requires further unpacking the constitution-construction nexus and how it relates to the question of agency.

Problematising Agency, Constitution and the Body: Beyond Performativity and New Materialism

Butler (1993) rooted the problem of agency in the difficulty of conceiving a construction without a constructor. Having identified language as the medium of political construction, constructivist thought was caught between two unsatisfactory alternatives. It tended to either evacuate agency, by attributing a generative, 'godlike agency' to the structures of language (Butler 1993, xvi).[8] Or it reverted to a pre-discursive actor, effectively short-changing its discovery of the role of language in construction. In this case, the 'metaphysics of the subject' were kept intact, together with the presumption that 'where there is an activity, there lurks behind it an initiating and wilful subject', God or Man (Butler 1993, xviii). Butler (1993, xvi) articulated the conundrum as follows: 'how can there be an activity, a constructing, without presupposing an agent who precedes and performs that activity? how would we account for the motivation and direction of construction without such a subject?' Butler's solution was to shift the focus from the individual actor and their actions to the activity, to the *'stylized repetition of acts'* (Butler 1993, xvii; 1990, 191; and 1988, 519, emphasis in originals). These do not simply 'express' a pre-existing essence of gender, they 'perform' a gendered identity into being (Butler 1990). They produce very material effects, like sexed bodies. Butler has put forward a powerful alternative to the hyper-individualistic agency underwriting liberal thought and US political science that I have also critiqued elsewhere (Epstein 2013a). Her focus on performativity supplied an important way of understanding the collective agency of political construction. Only Butler (1993, xvi) also dismissed too quickly the 'divine performative', and metaphysics for that matter, with the result that God and the individual stand in strictly parallel positions in her critique. They are the sovereign, single constructor that require being discarded as the starting points for reconceptualising a constructivist, collective agency. I propose attending to the time in the history of Western thought when political agency shifted from the divine to the human. It brings into view another agency, that is neither divine nor heroic, that is collective, and especially pertinent for constructivist theorising.

A new and peculiar kind of agency was emerging in early modern Europe, that was no longer God's nor nature's, that was not natural but not unnatural either, that appeared to evince a distinctly human nature. It was not the agency of individual choice, notwithstanding its *post hoc* appropriation by liberal thought (to which I will return). It was, I suggest, the original, collective agency of modern political construction.[9] It was bound up with a new mode of thought that was taking shape at the juncture of a profound reordering of the relation between the word and the world in Europe. It was, I will show, the first form of constitutive theorising (see chapter 5; see also Tully 1980). 'Artifice' was the seventeenth-century term for this new agency. The quasi-iconic status of the machine in the Renaissance expressed the jubilation that it inspired (see Sawday 2007). For it augured an age of inventions, the possibility of genuine innovation, of creating something ex nihilo that was no longer a copy of a thing that already existed in nature. The state was one of these inventions. '*Art* goes yet further', wrote Hobbes (*Leviathan*, 3), who, I will show, was also the first radical constructivist (see chapters 2 and 3). Hobbes (*De Corpore*, Author's Epistle to the Reader) enjoined his reader to '[i]mitate the creation' in their quest for knowledge. Geometry was his favourite science because it supplied a method that most closely approximates 'Generation'.[10] Artifice, then, was not rooted in a 'heroic' individual will (Walzer 1965 notwithstanding). It is not reducible to interests and their maximisation; which is to miss entirely its creative, and destructive, as well as collective, dimensions.[11] In fact, it was bound up with a new and purposely nonindividualistic form of political rationality, raison d'état (see chapter 2). It does not originate in an idea (in, say, Hobbes's, or Jean Bodin's, or Henry VIII's, or Henri IV's mind) that would be then enacted. It is always already in the interacting, and in the interplay of thought and practices. That this agency does not lie latent in the mind (in a pre-existing idea) was why, for Hobbes, it was thoroughly corporeal; although this was his idiosyncratic way of making sense of something that was taking shape with and by him. Hobbes's performative act of naming the new political form he helped midwife 'the Leviathan', and of representing it (as a giant, crowned body composed of miniature bodies turned towards it)[12] are best understood in these terms. The invention would unlikely have caught if it had been his alone.

Artifice has largely fallen to the wayside in our late modernity, because of the extent to which it is bound up with modernity's project of mastery over nature, which is a central focus of this book. Yet artifice also troubles in interesting ways what have become established assumptions about agency in critical thought, that limit the possibilities of thinking through agency, power, and creativity. Butler's critique has yielded an implicit binary; whereby the act considered in insolation conjures a problematic figure of agency (God or 'Man'), and collective agency can only be thought of in terms of many acts ritualistically repeated. Yet this also forecloses the possibility of apprehending the single act as the site of the realisation of a collective rather than individual, of a disruptive and creative, rather than iterative agency. A declaration of independence is seldom a single actor's achievement, even when the text that enacts it has a clearly identifiable author (see Derrida 1986). Nor does its proclamation (the act) perform into being a preexisting structure that it thereby reproduces. It ruptures it. So does a declaration of war, which comprises another collective, non-iterative single act. The work of reordering instituted by a new constitution can seldom be ascribed to a single actor, even under an absolute sovereign.

The limits to Butler's re-theorisation of agency, then, are twofold. First, it misses the relations between constitution and the single act.[13] The acts she considers require being repeated to wreak their constitutive effects, *to construct*. Constitution emerges from iteration, for Butler; largely as a function of taking gender as her paradigm. Political construction is produced of repetition. Overlooked as a result is the single act that cannot be serialised, that dents rather than upholds structures. Crucially, this act can constitute a site of collective empowerment, as it was France's Third Estate at the eve of the revolution, who proclaimed themselves to be the new and properly representative 'National Constituent Assembly'. Second and relatedly, agency is too quickly collapsed onto power. Contrast Butlerian performativity with l'Abbé Sieyès's (a key architect of this Assembly), concept of 'constituent power' (*pouvoir constituent*), conceived as the power reclaimed by the people of France to enact their general will. Though Sieyès termed it 'power', he meant a properly political, popular agency (see Rubinelli 2019). Hobbes's 'power' which, I will show, is a reworking of the Aristotelian efficient cause, is a creative power—the power to bring something into being (see also *DC* II. chapters 9 and 10). By 'agency' Butler means a structural power. This constricting of agency is consistent with a project aimed at underlining the underappreciated and very real, very material, power of structures. For Butler, as for Foucault, we are far less autonomous than we tend to assume in the acts we perform and the discourses we speak. But it also derives, I suggest, from their focus on the body solely as the privileged site of the deployment of modern power. Instead I hold agency, power, and the body as separate in my analysis. This enables me to apprehend the genuinely creative and open, yet still constraining, non-individualistic agency of modern political construction. But it also allows me to reclaim the body for different epistemological purposes, namely, first, as a standpoint and a lens through which to track the co-constitution of the state and the subject of rights. Second, however, this also reconfigures the crucial radical constructivist concern with boundary-making.

Butler's corporeal focus enabled her to show how the body's surfaces and bound-aries are discursively constructed rather than given; and how this boundary-drawing wreaks both normalising and exclusionary effects, since it serves to determine who is to be considered as 'human' and who cannot. I too am cen-trally concerned with exclusionary delineations; only those that contour the state rather than the body (see also Campbell 1998). For example, I analyse, in chapters 5 and 6, how the body was utilised by John Locke to carve out the space of modern politics as an exclusive community of bourgeois, white, male, rational consenters. Hence whereas, for Butler (1993, 20), the border-drawing happens *on* the body, by securing its 'variable boundar[ies]', for me it is undertaken *with* the body to secure the borders of the body politic.

I do not, however, consider the agency *of* the body, which has been another direction taken by Butler's critics. Reacting to what was perceived as an excessive focus on construction, a new materialist feminism, as it is known, has called for reclaiming the body in its 'weighty materiality' (Grosz 1994, 21); 'reality', even (Jagger 2015). There is a need, according to these theorists, to better accommo-date for the force of matter, for matter as force, as agency in its own right (see also Bennett 2010); together with 'sciences studies'' understandings of this embodied agency (Jagger 2015). The reason, as explained by Elizabeth Grosz (in Ausch, Doane, and Perez 2000), is that 'we have, by now, been denaturalized as much as we need to be'. However, in this critique the 'somatophobia' at the heart of Western philosophy, to which I shortly return, is countered, I suggest, by per-haps an excessive somatophilia (Grosz 1994, 5). In turning to the body, I do not seek to 'renaturaliz[e] that which was taken away' (Grosz, in Ausch, Doane, and Perez 2000). Attending to how it was made knowable in the first place is instead my aim. I continue to dwell with construction and the work of the discursive (see Epstein 2011; 2013b) or more specifically here, concepts (rather than *a* dis-course, as in Epstein 2008). I consider the new concept of matter that rendered bodies thinkable by modern science in the first place. I do not consider that we have been denaturalised nearly enough; particularly in the intimate and exclu-sionary ties that bind us to the state and the system of states. Moreover, the era I analyse highlights the impossibility into which this new materialist thought has steered itself. For the claim is not merely 'to resuscitate' the body but properly 'a concept of the body' (Grosz 1994, 20); while at the same time turning away from the stuff of which concepts are made: language. Paradoxically, the rediscovery of Hobbes as a 'materialist thinker' set one of the milestones for this new mate-rialism (Frost 2008). Yet even for Hobbes, and for Locke, whose blind spots and exclusionary moves my bodily optic aims to draw out, all concepts, including 'the body', are constructed. In this book the body indexes the unconstituted, ontologically; while methodologically, it marks the place from which I ana-lyse the co-constitution of the state and the subject. I work with the historical givenness of the body, the fact that it has been the unnoticed, 'natural' thing that is always there, not in order to unearth what is really there, what there is to the body, but rather to turn this thereness on its head, as it were. I consider how it was mobilised at crucial junctures in the seventeenth century to craft the state-subject relation *and* its exclusions. The un-constituted in this specific sense sets the limits for my project. It does not require being dug into or filled with a positively reconstructed corporeality, only acknowledging the impossibility of doing so, and that this is not necessary to the task at hand, which is to appraise the founding relation structuring politics to this day.

Senses of the Body

The human body in this book functions both as the lens that brings into focus anew the founding modern political relation, and the material thing that played a crucial role in catalysing the scientific revolution. Its starting point was the publication of Nicolaus Copernicus's *On the Revolutions of the Celestial Spheres* and Andrea Vesalius's *On the Fabric of the Human Body*, both in 1543 (see also Whitehead 1954). While the body as optic affords me my main analytical frame, I also consider it in four additional ways throughout the chapters. First, the human body was, along with celestial bodies, one of the catalytic *objects* of modern science. Turning to this body to open it up was one the triggers of the epistemological revolution that yielded a new mode of knowledge. It instituted the subject-object structure that characterises modern science, and it founded the imperative of grounding knowledge in direct observation. The second sense in which I consider the body is as the privileged *organ* of modern science. The seventeenth century decisively shifted the starting point for knowing the world from ideas pre-existing in the soul to the body. Although this was especially pronounced in English empiricism, four of whose founding figures (Francis Bacon, William Harvey, Thomas Hobbes, and John Locke) feature centrally in my story, even in its rationalist counterpart, which sought to reconcile innate ideas with the new requirements of observation, the body was established as the place from which the thinking, Cartesian, subject apprehends the world. In this context, the eye, in particular, took on particular importance, as we will see in chapter 7. How the human body was established coextensively as the site of the experience of the knower and of the experiments that catalysed an empirical mode of knowing, and how this was bound up with the work of reordering, epistemological and political, that was under way, is at the centre of this book.

Third, I consider the body as a crucial historical vehicle for the work of naturalisation. I mean 'naturalisation' in the dual senses of, first, something becoming taken-for-granted and unnoticed, experienced as 'natural', but also, second, as referring to nature. The body qua natural thing, as a piece of nature, serves to bring into view the various natures that are implicitly conjured in processes of naturalisation. I restore these natures to naturalisation, as it were, for the purposes of charging the latter as an instrument of critique. The body featured in two very different ways in the seventeenth-century English political discourse. It tapped into a long tradition, exemplified by the medieval body politic, of drawing upon corporeal metaphors to anchor the polity in nature. At the same time, however, entirely novel argumentations were also being put forward, that decisively circumscribed the political as a discrete realm, distinct from ethics or religion, and that referred to the body per se, not as a metaphor, but in its realness, and to conjure its mechanical workings. The body that was being laid bare upon the anatomy slab for all to view had become very real indeed in the seventeenth century. The broader context, moreover, was one in which the relationship with nature was being ruptured or at least profoundly transformed by the scientific revolution. Nature was not what it had seemed to be, in the many ways I broach briefly in the following section. Nothing moved or behaved as they once had been thought to, including the human body, and even the blood coursing through it. A crucial consequence is that the human embeddedness in nature, which had been a taken-for-granted feature of Ancient Greek and medieval thought, was no longer as secure. The nature that was becoming the object of modern mastery and domination no longer furnished the stable dwelling-place it once had. Nature as a fixed referent for political construction was fading out of sight. In this context, the body qua natural thing afforded one of the few remaining sure joins to nature. A central interest in this book is how this piece of nature closest to hand was utilised to negotiate the changing human nature relationship in the classical age, and to re-hook the polity back to nature. How the body was drawn upon to legitimise the decisive reordering of political relations under way is at the heart of my analysis.

Fourth, I distinguish between *the* body and bod*ies*; between the oneness of the concept, and the many actual bodies. The tension between these two modalities of the body is one of this enquiry's main critical instruments. On the one hand, 'the body', qua concept, is a universal. In ancient and medieval thought, it was configured with another universal, human nature, in that having a two-legged body was a marker of being human. This body was the container of the human essence. The advent of modern medicine brought the promise of being able to locate this essence, no longer in a nebulous and elusive faculty of reason, but on the anatomy table and in this body. Human nature was decisively *corporealised*. Concurrently, in the English Revolution, another kind of political universal was being crafted that also implicated human nature. These were the rights found, and by the same token, founded in nature. This (constructed) naturalness would afford the vehicle of their generalisation to humanity at large. Exploring the points of juncture that took shape between these two, political and natural, universals, between rights founded in nature and an enfleshed human nature, is another core interest. However, specific bodies—poor, non-white, and female— were also excluded from the political and epistemic universalities as they were being crafted. Starting from these particular bodies, instead of the generic body, serves to reveal the original exclusions by which the universal 'human rights' was constructed, upon and by way of the body. A key organising principle in the chapters is my shift between these two corporeal lenses, between the generic and particular bodies. It enables me to chart who is included and who is excluded. For a central aim is to draw out the convergences between the epistemic and political boundary-drawings, and to show how both were implicated in crafting the state. To further explicate my body-as-optic, I now show where it maps onto, first, feminist theories of embodiment, and second, the works of Michel Foucault.

The Body in Feminist and Postcolonial Thought

The body has long indexed the unseen. Attending to it has been crucial to appraising how the seen and the unseen, who is rendered visible or invisible, is produced by historically specific configurations of power/knowledge. It has been history's unnoticed site for the operation of power, Foucault (1995) showed. Before Foucault, feminist thinkers first brought the body into focus as the place from which the world is experienced and known. As Simone de Beauvoir (1953, 29) put it, '[T]o be present in the world implies strictly that there exists a body which is at once a material thing in the world and a point of view towards the world'. They revealed what is at stake in denying or erasing this human 'situated-ness' (Haraway 1988). To be unsituated—*bodiless*—they showed, is to occupy the place of power, which functions most effectively as an eye that sees without been seen. Problematising embodiment has been at the heart of the feminist project (Lennon 2014), both in order to expose this work of disembodiment, *and* the excessive embodiment that sustains it. Feminist thinkers have analysed how Western thought's traditional binaries, of mind and body, form and matter, reason and the passions, double up as dichotomies of domination that have written women out of thought and practices for two millennia by casting them on the side of the body, the material, the irrational. 'Women are somehow *more* biological, *more* corporeal, and *more* natural than men', as Elisabeth Grosz (1994, 14) put it. By this singular conjoining of nature with one kind of human body, 'corporeality [has been] associated with one sex [. . .] which [has] then take[n] on the burden of the other's corporeality for it', Grosz (1994, 22) continues. Constructions of 'the second sex' have afforded the starting point for systematically unearthing the structures, epistemic and social, by which it has been locked into this secondary place, and the ways in which innateness has been mustered to naturalise it (Beauvoir 1953). Other bodies, nonwhite and poor, were rapidly brought into view, whose corporealities were also cast and configured on the side of nature, by being either laden with nature's productive and reproductive functions, or by being dressed with 'masks' of bestiality (Fannon 1952; see also Stoler 1995). Together feminist and postcolonial scholars have laid bare how relations of domination operate by allocating the burden of corporeality to some—most—bodies, but not others. The purchases of the classical age for this critical enterprise are that they hold one of the first sites where this division of dis/embodiment was initially delineated, the public anatomy theatre. They also contain one of the original concatenations of 'whiteness as property' (Harris 1992). The nature-body nexus is also a central theme of this book. However, I aim to broaden the lens to encompass, not merely how these bodies were held off from the public space by weighing them down with a diminished, demeaning corporeality, but how this space was carved out in the first place. Hobbes's common-wealth was made of nothing but bodies living in common. I therefore appraise the nature-body nexus as *both* a motor of naturalisations that served to universalise the subject of rights, *and* as the line-drawing instrument that was wielded to contain the state-subject relation within an enclosed space and, by the same token, to exclude some bodies from acceding to the status of subject.

There have been two ways of turning critically to the body. The first, which I call epistemological, to which this study belongs, has been to locate the body in the play of practices and in the texts that articulate them. How the body was constituted as the object of modern medicine (Foucault 2003), how it is fashioned by the gendered identities we inhabit (Butler 1990; 1993), and how it affords the site for the regulation of patriarchal structures (Bourdieu 1998) have all been appraised. The crucial purchase of this mode of enquiry for my purposes is to have short-circuited the strategy that consists in resorting to the body as the natural or physical, hence irrefutable, substrate for cultural constructs, by revealing how this strategy is itself a contingent historical construct, specifically, a product of the Enlightenment (see Laqueur 1990). The second, ontological, way is rooted in the phenomenological tradition, and has sought to counter the work of disembodiment by reinvesting the body as the place of the subject's being-in-the-world. Whereas in the first mode of enquiry, the body is envisaged from without, here it is reclaimed from within. It has been used to propose alternative histories of pain (Bourke 2014; Scarry 1985), of the city (Sennett 1994), and in order to rehabilitate the points of view that have been erased by traditional forms of historical narration, as well as the violences, real and epistemic, effecting these erasures. The subject's point of view is this scholarship's underlying assumption (see also Gallup 1988). In this book I return to the roots of phenomenology, to the moment when this point of view—when the self-conscious, thinking, feeling, ailing, subject—was first circumscribed by Descartes.

Reading Foucault against His Own Grain

Foucault first honed the corporeal lens in order to bring into focus a distinctly modern power, beyond the top-down sovereign power that punishes. This pervasive power works instead from the bottom-up, fashioning the subject from within, through discipline, and shaping entire populations, via biopower. The corporeal lens served to pivot the focus beyond sovereignty and towards 'governmentality', the umbrella concept Foucault (2009) coined to mark this break with the classical focus on the state. Moreover, the biopolitical scholarship, with which I engage in more detail in the chapters, has largely followed Foucault's cue in turning away from sovereignty and the state. In this book, I read Foucault against his own grain, as it were, by, first, using the object he brought into focus, the body, in order to turn the lens back to sovereignty and to the state. Second, I conjoin the epistemic and political angles that index his so-called early and late works, respectively. I build on Foucault's (2005) analysis of 'the classical episteme' to illuminate how the conditions of political thought and action were profoundly transforming in the seventeenth century and in ways that have been overlooked by disciplinary divisions of labour, notably between philosophy and political analysis.

However, bringing together the two parts of his work also leads me to shift time frames and genealogical terrains. Foucault's analyses of practices centred upon the body; medical (Foucault 2003), punitive (1995), or intimate (1990) began in the middle of the eighteenth century and focussed largely on the nineteenth. In the works where he did consider the seventeenth century, the body was not in focus (see Foucault 2003; 2005; and 2009). *Society Must Be Defended*, the series of lectures he delivered at the Collège de France in 1976, marks a pivotal point in his trajectory, and elucidates how these different foci hang together. Throughout the first half of the 1970s, Foucault's public lectures explored extensively the disciplinary practices that still relied upon repressive structures of statehood. This yielded *Discipline and Punish* (1975). The state, and Hobbes, still loomed large over his early 1976 lectures, which is where Foucault explicated the need to move the analysis of power beyond the state. The bottom-up forms of power characteristic of neoliberalism then concerned him for the rest of the decade. He briefly returned to the state and to the seventeenth (and sixteenth) century in the following lecture series (delivered in 1977–78); only this time, as an object of knowledge, that emerged coextensively with a new form of reason (raison d'état), rather than as the sole source of (a top-down) power (see Foucault 2009).

Taking the lens Foucault first carved to the period prior to the one where he honed it troubles Foucault's periodisation. Firstly, it reveals a key site of the making of modern science and the state, the public anatomy lesson (see chapter 7). Foucault, who began his modern power in the eighteenth century, overlooked it. Secondly, it shows that 'discipline' originated earlier than where Foucault tracked it to, in the seventeenth century and with Locke. Locke marks an intriguing (near) silence in Foucault's work, on account of the centrality of discipline to his analysis of power (see also Metha 1992). Downplaying Locke's role was part and parcel of Foucault's broader strategy to displace liberalism's monopolistic hold over the accounts of the formation of modernity, which is an ambition I share. Foucault restored the older language of 'the subject' to political analysis in order to counteract liberalism's 'individual' and the illusions of autonomy it helps maintain in place. This is also my language; and my focus on the co-constitution of the state and the subject is intended to underline their mutual dependence. The state cannot exist without the subject, and vice versa. Nevertheless, Foucault never fully clarified the relations between the 'governmentality' with which he pivoted beyond the state and the 'government' with which Locke made the same move three centuries earlier.[14] Third, the eighteenth century subject that furnished Foucault his starting point for his analysis of modern power was more fully subjected (*assujeti*), chiselled by this power, than its seventeenth-century English forerunner; if only as a function of the densification of the power relations that he tracked throughout his later work. My suggestion, to put it in another way, is that, although it was not the sovereign agency of liberalism's 'individual', there was still more agency to the seventeenth-century political subject-in-the-making than to the one Foucault set his sights upon. The 'subjection' that Hobbes (*L.*, chap. 17[5]107) conceives as a condition of possibility for achieving peace ('there would be [no] peace without subjection') was not Foucault's *assujettissement*, the mechanism of the modern subject's making, which presupposes some measure of political order rather than the complete disorder of war. In reconsidering agency, I aim to loosen liberalism's grip upon a crucial concept for political analysis. This entails, first, historicising the trope of individual choice onto which it has been collapsed by, second, finding new ways of re-engaging critically with Hobbes and Locke, whom liberal thought invariably claim as its two touchstones (see, for example, Walzer 1965; Berlin 1969; Goldsmith 1989; Spitz 2001; Manent 2012; Josephson 2002. For more critical accounts, see Grant 2003; Hirschmann 2008; Meiksins Wood 2012; Bell 2014). This serves to open up other ways of conceiving agency, in terms of creativity, of bringing new political forms into being, and indeed of destroying them.

Having introduced my bodily optic, I now begin the excavatory work proper, and turn the lens back in time. The break that begat modernity in the seventeenth century is at the heart of this book. In order to draw closer for the reader an era as foundational as it has become unfamiliar, I first introduce three problematiques that help stake out the nexus of modern science and politics that my enquiry explores. The first is the passage from the medieval to modern conceptions of space and matter. The second is how the task of knowing nature shifted, in the seventeenth century, from one of deciphering to one of *sorting*; and how this, in turn, opened up the problem of difference and equality for political modernity. The third is how the relations between authority, reason, and critique were reconfigured by these transformations.

Three Themes at the Nexus of Early Modern Science and Politics

From a Medieval *Place* to a Modern *Space*

Analysing the original spatialisation of political authority first requires locating the concept of space itself underwriting it. Space as we know it simply did not exist in medieval Aristotelian physics (see Jammer 1993; Leijenhorst 2002). It was a product of the scientific revolution. The first problematique running through the book is how a medieval-Aristotelian *place*, understood as a dwelling-place, gradually gave way to a de-anthropomorphised, geometric *space*. A closed, spatially differentiated, highly static and deeply hierarchal world, in which every thing rested in its assigned place, the *cosmos*, came to be replaced by a value-free, uncontained and infinitely open world of ceaselessly moving bodies held together merely by the laws of motion, the *universe* of modern science.[15] This change, which unfolded over two centuries, represented nothing short of a fundamental shattering of the understanding of the world we inhabit, can inhabit, and in which we can build polities; and of the very bodies, political and natural, we live in. Two scientific discoveries, both spatial, broke open the cosmos, infinity and the laws of inertial motion. Together they yielded space as we know it and matter as 'extension'.[16] This fully flattened out, homogenous infinite space, emptied of the values that had attached to it and, for that matter, of all human contents, populated with nothing but 'extended things', afforded both the conceptual horizon against which and the tools with which the state was crafted. Crucially, the undifferentiated space of 'extension' could no longer be relied upon *to contain*. In the absence of the notion of space as a container, the problem of how to hold together as one this human-made thing became a pressing one in the seventeenth century. To restate the problem differently, whereas the unity of the biological body is given, it must be constructed for the state. The old putting together function was lost, along with the sense of place. Charting the emergence of the state as a bounded, containing space, as a space that encloses by including and excluding, thus requires first understanding the prior spatial and conceptual imaginary that was upended by the scientific revolution.

From the Closed Hierarchies of the Finite Cosmos

The inhabitants of the cosmos conceived and experienced space as a container or dwelling-place. 'Place' (*topos*) was Aristotle's concept. His was a world where there is 'a place for every thing and every thing [is] in its place' as Alexandre Koyré (1966, 19, my translation) put it. In this topological space, every individual thing or body had its right place, towards which it innately tended, per the properties of its nature or essence. Per its heaviness a stone falls back to rest on the ground after it is thrown into the air. These sensible properties reveal its 'natural' movements, which Aristotle distinguishes from 'violent' movements; here, that of the throwing hand. At the centre of the ancient and medieval cosmos an un-moving earth nested within a series of celestial spheres rotating around it, each filled with one of the primary elements (water, fire, air, and ether) (Grant 1984a, 1984b). This non-mathematical space, this space-qua-place, was also non-uniform. It was a succession of variegated containers defined by their contents.[17] The spheres, for example, marked the different types of spaces the cosmos was made of, as determined by the primary element that filled each one and by its distance to the earth-centre. This highly differentiated space accounted for motion, since everything naturally moves so as to return to its right place and in order to rest. Nature achieved considerable epistemological work, explanatory and pre-scriptive, in a world where ethics was derived entirely from ontology. Individual natures, first, accounted for how things behave. The stone's heaviness elucidated its fall. That humans were political animals explained their tendency to come to-gether to form polities. How humans ought to behave (the ethical question), and the forms these polities should take (the political question), were also prescribed by their nature. Understanding its laws was the ethicist's task, so as to better align the latter upon the former. Second, nature at large was these political animals' dwelling-place. It afforded them the locus for collective life that held both the material resources required to live together and the symbolic structures ena-bling it. The natural and the social order were a seamless continuum. The order in the world (*Logos*) was decipherable by humans' natural capacity to reason (our *logos*), by which they, in turn, could partake in this ordered nature. Justice itself was a topological concept. It entailed ascribing 'to each their due' (*suum cuique tribuere*)', according to the place they rightly occupied within an order that was inscribed in nature itself (see chapter 6). This sense of place, together with the values invested in it, would be knocked off balance by the new concept of space that loomed large in the sixteenth and seventeenth centuries. Hence why Blaise Pascal (quoted in Koyré 1958, my translation) deplored: 'the eternal silence of these infinite spaces terrifies me'. How to continue to think politically in this value-free, perhaps indeed value-less, at any rate, homogenised space that no longer afforded humans the moral comforts of a dwelling-place was the challenge that Hobbes, for one, would take up.

Above all, the cosmos was finite. This entailed that it had no 'outside'. All that was existed within it, and was contained by the outermost celestial sphere, filled with ether. Beyond this limit, there was nothing; not even a void. Aristotle and Aristotelians actively rejected the existence of the vacuum (see Koyré 1957; 1966; Kuhn 1957; Jammer 1993). The void threatened the possibility of being contained. The world's very principle of coherence, what held it together as a world, was at stake. Hierarchy was this finite world's ordering principle. The cosmos was made of hierarchies all the way down, natural and social. Medieval rule was layered and differentiated, functionally and geographically (see Ruggie 1993). The provision of justice, for example, was distributed across the manor, the church, and the monarch. These hierarchies were also topological, anchored in places; like the field or the village (for the communal agricultural system which we will explore in chapter 5) or the parish, the town or the city (for the corporate structure we will consider in chapter 4). The 'city and the world' (*urbi et orbi*) were the emblematic twin pillars of this imperial spatial imaginary.[18] The earth, the *orbis terrarum*, was humanity's bounded, continuous dwelling-place, and the horizon of Christianity. Though the different forms of medieval authorities vied with one another, sometimes ferociously, this rivalry was contained by the cosmos's finite space and within an imperial horizon. This contained-ness is what infinity would tear open.

To the Discoveries of Infinity and Inertial Motion

The story of the twin spatial discoveries, of infinity and of the laws of motion, that shattered this finite and holding world begins in the skies and ends with falling bodies tumbling back upon the earth.[19] In ejecting the earth from the centre of the world in favour of the sun, Copernicus's *On the Revolutions of the Celestial Spheres* had opened up the prospect of an 'outside'. For the cosmos had none, we saw. However, Copernicus's system remained finite and centred, only on the sun rather than on the earth.[20] The world really began bursting through the seams of its enclosing spheres with Nicholas of Cusa (1401–64), the first to envisage a world with neither limits nor a centre (Cassirer 2000). Only Cusa's world was merely limitless, unfinished (*interminatum*) (Koyré 1957). He remained one step short of asserting the positive existence of infinity. This would be the achievement of Giordano Bruno (1548–1600), who was both the first to use the term 'universe' and to assert 'the infinity of [this] universe and of the world', per the title of a 1584 work (*De l'infinite universo e mundi*). Bruno embraced Cusa's centre-less world. Crucially, he inverted the negative connotations habitually associated with infinity. He turned a limitlessness into an abundance, an expression of God's magnificence. In asserting an infinite and centre-less world, Bruno paved the way for an undifferentiated space, where 'up' and 'down' were relative notions, not fixed properties that inhered in the natures of particular things, like the rising flame or the falling stone. His boldness had him burned at the stake. Moreover, he drew the Church's attention to the earth-shattering consequences of the astronomical experimentations that were under way, and led to both Copernicus's and Galileo's condemnations (in 1616 and 1633, respectively).

Aristotelian metaphysics had collapsed by the late sixteenth century, while the new physics that was to stand in its place—and in space—would be furnished, in its final articulation, in the late seventeenth century by Isaac Newton, who takes us back to England. The steps between these two stages of the scientific revolution are too numerous to detail here; hence I simply signpost the few that led from the discovery of infinity to the new laws of motion, insofar as they hold the crucial juncture in the story of how place yielded to space. Johannes Kepler, 'the man who made the Copernican system work', was also the astronomer who turned his lens from celestial to earthly bodies (Kuhn 1957, 131). Only, little noticed in the classical histories of science, and what interests me in this book, is how Kepler achieved this by bringing in focus the human body at the other end of his instrument—the eye, as we will see in chapter 7.

Galileo's work on the telescope further enhanced the understanding of planetary motions. But his crucial contribution was to generalise the focus to all moving bodies, by turning his attention to falling and projected objects. This is where he began to geometrize space. Hence Galileo's decisive move was methodological. He shed the causal account, the Aristotelian quest for *why* things moved as they do, which located the answer in their individual natures and their inherent properties. (The stone moved downwards because of its heaviness.) Instead, he simply described *how* objects with different weights, like a ball of lead and a ball of wood, fall when they are dropped from the top of the tower of Pisa. That is, he shifted from a causal account to a spatial description, an account of the objects' progression through space, for which he required geometry. Seemingly innocuously, he ushered in geometry into physics, and forever transformed the nature of physical explanations. For geometry's explanations are in fact descriptions. Geometers 'have explained the line by the movement of the point, and the surfaces by that of the line' as Descartes (cited in Koyré 1966,

321) put it. Descartes himself formalised the coordinate system (the x-, y-, and z-axes) with which the object's progression through space is plotted.[21] Galileo and Descartes thus developed the vocabulary and instruments of the spatial thinking that made the modern machine and the state possible.

The New Understandings of Movement, Matter, and of Nature's Causal Role

In addition to ushering in modern space, Galileo's methodological move bore out momentous consequences for the understanding of motion, of matter and bodies, and for the place of nature in causal explanations. I consider each in turn. By turning to space and its science (geometry) to parse motion, Galileo and his successors effectively exogenised it (to propose a new term). They dislodged motion from the nature of things, and cast it instead as an independent physical phenomenon that could be understood—described—on its own terms. Motion was one, they showed; it obeyed its own set of mechanical laws, whether it occurred in the body or in a machine. Second, the weighting of 'violent' and 'natural' movements was inverted. The main form of motion, for Aristotle, was those that could be accounted for by things' natures. All other kinds were unnatural, 'violent'. By apprehending movement as external to the object, our moderns flattened out this distinction. There is only one kind of motion, they found, the violent kind, since movement is caused by the action of force applied to an object. The concept of 'force' is what Aristotelian physics lacked (see Koyré 1966).[22] It decisively troubled established notions about natural agency.

Third, Galileo and his successors inverted the priority accorded rest and motion. The cosmos was at rest. When a thing moved, it was only in order to return to its resting place. Instead the universe of modern science is ceaselessly in motion, even when it seems at rest. Rest is simply an absence of motion, revealed Descartes, who discovered inertial motion in Galileo's wake.[23] His key move was to envisage motion as a *state*, rather than as an explanandum (as that which required being explained by a cause, by a thing's nature). This, in turn, further loosened the hold upon motion of Aristotelian causality.

This new motion, in turn, yielded the new category of matter qua extension. It was developed in two steps, taken by Descartes and by those who corrected him, respectively. This single, uniform movement brought into view a different kind of space, homogenous and undifferentiated, with no (absolute) centre and no limits, defined only by points, lines, and planes: the space that had always lain in geometry's sights. As Locke (*EHU*, II.chap.13 [11]115) put it at the century's end, 'motion can neither be, nor be conceived, without space'. Moreover, it furnished the mathematical demonstration for what had been intuited (and endlessly debated about) for the skies, of infinity's existence.[24] The new space, in turn, brought one, level plane upon which all things were 'extended'.

Descartes, who initially coined the category by turning to geometry, also went one step too far. He collapsed together 'matter' and 'space' (see Koyré 1957).[25] For Locke this amounted to losing the 'thingness' of the thing. It also erased space itself, that upon which motion and matter depend, by excessively materialising it. Locke carefully separated out matter, or the body, and space. 'Extension includes no solidity', he wrote (EHU, II.chap.13 [12]115). Indeed 'space' and 'solidity' are 'very distinct ideas'; the latter is 'inseparable [...] from body' (ibid.). He then used the Cartesian conflation of space and matter as an example of an erroneous proposition: 'he that with Des Cartes [sic] shall frame in his mind an idea of what he calls body to be nothing but extension, may easily demonstrate that there is no vacuum, i.e., no space void of body' (EHU, IV.chap.7 [12]400). Indeed, Descartes had rejected the vacuum, falling back onto old scholastic positions (see Koyré 1966). Hobbes's refusal to fathom a vacuum brewed one of the most famous controversies in the histories of modern science and led to the founding of an experimental (and not simply empirical) science by Robert Boyle (see Shapin and Shaffer 2011). Both motion and matter depend on space. Space is where matter exists and motions occur. It is pure extension, and matter, bodies, are 'extended things'. Geometry's space decisively replaced Aristotelian 'place' because it had become the epistemic condition of possibility (or condition of think-ability) of all matter and motion. The closed cosmos yielded to the infinitely open universe. In Locke's (EHU, II.chap.13 [10]114) words again, 'we can have no idea of the place of the universe', because we now need to talk in terms of space; whereas 'place' is instead 'a relative position of any thing'.

Last, nature was demoted, in its dual epistemological and ontological functions, as explanans and as an ordering principle. The natures of individual things were no longer required to do the explanatory work, once movement could be explained, or rather described, on its own, strictly spatial, terms. The cosmos's inherent order (the Logos) had furnished Aristotle with his theory of 'natural tendency' or striving (hormē or ὁρμή). A dog tends to bark; a stone, to fall; while a human, for Aristotle, inherently seeks to know and to live together with fellow humans. This 'tending' is a 'tending towards'; it implies a natural dwelling-place. Every natural being has an innate desire to first come into itself, by taking up this place; and to then persist in its being, by staying or always returning to it. Aristotle accounted for movement simply by generalising this model. His motion is purposeful and directed, caused by a thing's striving to return to its dwelling-place. This purposefulness was what Galileo and his successors flushed out. Movement became without purpose or reason, senseless, in the dual sense of the French sens, as a meaning and a direction. Thomas Spragens (1973, 63) nicely described this new infinite motion, holding no meaning outside of its mathematical inscription, that Hobbes and his contemporaries were wrestling with: 'Hobbesian movement is infinite. It has no order, no structure, no end or limitation. It is endless, aimless motion [...] an endless chain without a goal'. This led to an inversion of the valences that attached to orderly and disorderly motion. "*To automaton*" was Aristotle's term for spontaneity or chance, understood as being contrary to an ordered nature. The category extended to all forms of movement that do not spring from something's nature, disruptions or violent movements, but also accidents, which fall short of expressing a substance's essence, or anything that moves for no reason. It was the lesser kind of movement. This hierarchy was instead upturned in the age of artifice. To the extent that, for Hobbes (*L*, 3), automatic movement was the only kind of movement, inorganic or organic; and life itself 'but a motion of the limbs'. In Aristotle's world, 'that which is produced or directed by nature can never be anything disorderly: for nature is everywhere the cause of order' (cited in Spragens 1973, 99). For Hobbes instead, disorder *is* nature. No wonder, then, he found it far less hospitable to humans than Aristotle had. He saw a radically different nature.

This Aristotelian notion of a natural striving would morph into one of the defining categories of early modern political thought, self-preservation. It features through all the authors I consider. This investment in self-preservation was, in fact, I suggest, an effort to rescue it from the loss of relevance it incurred as a function of the new physics. For it had by then been displaced in physical explanations by the far less homely concept of force. The exogenization of movement significantly curtailed the traditional principle's reach, sealing it off from whole areas of nature, where new laws of 'physics' were replacing the old laws of 'nature'. A crucial consequence of these scientific discoveries is that the nature that self-preservation traditionally conjured had shrunken to a fraction of itself. It was reduced to the realm of human nature. Force and inertial motion drove a wedge between physical and human laws. However, far from being washed out, along with the elements of the Aristotelian ontology, like 'substance' (or 'essences'), this old nature was instead invested all the more intensely—including by the author who was otherwise most willing to embrace the rift taking shape before his eyes between the new worlds of science and of politics: Thomas Hobbes. Self-preservation became the early modern factory for naturalising the new political constructs that were being crafted, such as a modern concept of 'rights', which had little to do with medieval rights (see chapters 4 and 6). Another way to understand the founding problematique of political modernity, then, was how to salvage a substantially reduced first law of nature (in the Hobbesian terminology) from the epistemological wreckage wrought by the geometrization of space and the exogenisation of movement that Hobbes especially otherwise enthusiastically embraced.

To bring together the elements of this first theme, firstly, this infinite, mathematical space drove a decisive wedge between ontology and politics. The modern distinction between positive statements on the one hand, and prescriptive or normative statements on the other, is but the final consummation of this divorce. Upon it rests both the modern division of scientific labour between the natural and social sciences, and the defining injunction of moral ethics, to distinguish 'ought' from 'is', and to not derive the former from the latter. Modern political thought can be read as a long, drawn-out attempt to grapple with the fallout from it—including by denying it. This has been the enduring and highly successful gesture of modern natural law (see chapter 6). Secondly, this new space drove a wedge between nature and human nature. Modern natural law's nature, which the likes of Locke, Coke, or indeed even Hobbes upheld as a referent for law-making, was no longer, in fact, science's nature. Human nature was decisively set adrift from nature in the universe. One of the purchases of the corporeal lens is that it reveals how, in a context where the link between human nature and nature was far less assured than it had once been, the body furnished a conjunction, perhaps the last one, to a nature with which the chasm was constantly widening. Thirdly, this bore decisive consequences for the question of political order. The universe's nature no longer afforded the answers to the question of how to build an ordered polity, nor, for that matter, the right space for the enterprise. This physical system held together by mechanical laws devoid of purpose and of meaning was resolutely mute. Order was no longer yielded by nature. Instead it became a task of *ordering*: entirely voluntary, a matter of choice, to be carefully constructed, but also legitimised by reference to that indelible trait still persistently ascribed to human nature, liberty.

Hierarchy, Equality, and the Problematisation of Difference

How the epistemological problem of difference emerged coextensively with the political problem of equality is the second theme running in the background to this book. Foucault (2005) showed that difference was never given to the naked eye; that it was rendered visible to European cultures by the advent of the 'classical episteme' in the seventeenth century, at the point where knowledge turned back on itself, and took itself as its own object of knowledge – when, as I will show in chapter 7, the naked eye was opened up to the view. This was also the time where these cultures encountered difference on an unprecedented scale, with the discovery and appropriation of the new world that the corporeal lens draws out especially starkly (see Stoler 1995). In the medieval episteme, difference was built into the structures with which the world was known and organised. Aristotle's concept of 'substances' (or 'essences', *ousia*), paired with his topological space, accounted for the observable fact of difference. There were as many differences in the world as there were individual substances (or essences), each with their distinct set of qualities and kept in their assigned places (*topoi*). Hierarchy was the organising principle of these highly differentiated spaces, which functioned as a succession of containers. Every person, animal, or plant was in its own place and belonged to 'species' that was itself contained by a 'genus'. While difference was everywhere socially, it remained unseen epistemically, un-thematised, insofar as it was written into the structures ordaining both knowledge and political rule. The differentiated, closed space of the cosmos underwrote deeply hierarchical modes of social organisation. It legitimised and naturalised them by maintaining them unseen. Sexual difference, for example, was accounted for in a key of sameness. Thomas Laqueur (1990, 63) has shown how, prior to the eighteenth century, male and female bodies were understood as two versions of the same 'canonical body'. The male was simply the more perfect copy, the closest to the original.[26] The differentiation between 'man' and 'woman' was therefore much more fluid, in this 'one-sex' model of the body. It was not yet etched onto the body. Only once an episteme equipped to register differences was in place did the distinction harden. Laqueur (1990, 12) thus circumscribed the moment when the body became constructed as 'biological foundation of what it is to be male and female' in the eighteenth century. His history of the making of 'sex' illustrates the chasm between what is empirically given, and what is epistemically recordable, hence thinkable. In summary, the epistemic non-visibility of difference and naturalised hierarchies were the two sides of the pre-modern episteme.

Difference would instead be set off by the homogenised, flattened, and infinitely extending space, where it no longer blended into space itself. A mathematical space afforded the homogenous, neutral surface upon which, and the universal coordinates with which, all extended things, a ball of lead or wood, could be placed side by side. They could be measured in relation to another, but they could also be seized in their singularities. What the new space set into relief above all was the work of *ordering* itself that was wrought by each of these epistemological choices. Rendered visible in this way were both the *form* this ordering took, and its instruments. Hierarchy rests upon differences that work most effectively by remaining unseen. By contrast, equality requires an even plane upon which the items can be arranged alongside one another. This was furnished by modern space. It rendered hierarchies visible, and therefore questionable, as the exclusive mode of organisation. Different but equal was the solution the European sovereigns arrived at with Treaty of Westphalia in 1648. It begat sovereignty as we know it and the state system. The state emerged as a solution to the problem of how to accommodate difference without collapsing it back onto sameness. This occurred at the very point, I suggest, where knowledge itself was 'no longer posited as the experience of the Same but as the establishment of Order' (Foucault

2005, 80). The horizontal ordering logic of the taxonomic table that substituted, in the seventeenth century, the vertical hierarchies of Aristotelian being was the conceptual condition of possibility of the contemporary state system. This horizontality rendered equality thinkable, epistemically *and* politically. Equality is traditionally considered political modernity's founding value, liberty's twin. It was made conceivable, I will show, by the new space. Conceivable, but not necessarily realisable (see chapters 5, 6, and 7).

The Echo Chamber of Sameness: The Cosmos

Difference was backgrounded in the pre-modern world, where the like was arranged with the like, and the unlike, with another unlike that was more like it, so as to constitute another class of 'alikes', on another level. Sameness was the organising principle of a world of geocentric hierarchies. Its structuring work can be shown in two ways. First, it was built into the key trope of the medieval episteme, the similitude (see Foucault 2005). The cosmos was a vast echo chamber, where macro- and microcosms mirrored each other. Knowledge in the Middle Ages was, literally, reflection. The order of the world revealed itself to a human reason by being accurately reflected by it. The cosmos 'was folded onto itself', as Foucault (2005, 19) put it, 'the earth echoing the skies, faces seeing themselves reflected in the stars, plants holding within their stems the secrets that were of use to man'. In this endless play of mirrors, 'resemblance was the fundamental relation of being to itself, the hinge of the whole world' (Foucault 2005, 75). The unknown was accounted for by way of its degree of proximity to the known; and these gradients, in turn, established the ranks of the overarching order. Knowledge proceeded by assimilation, which is to say that it effectively did away with difference qua difference. Furthermore, the closed space of the cosmos guaranteed the feasibility of the task, since the number of unknowns to be assimilated was not infinite. The enterprise was contained by the cosmos's finiteness.

Second, Renaissance scholars came to chafe against the hold of sameness upon scholastic thought. The fifteenth-century theologian Nicholas of Cusa's search for a way to conceive the unlimited, the incommensurable, in order to appraise God, brought him up against the limits of the medieval episteme (see Cassirer 2000). He questioned the adequacy of the very notion of knowledge for this task; and in the process, he laid bare the assumptions underpinning Aristotelian knowledge. The knowable was necessarily commensurable, for Aristotle, which meant (for him) set into relation to other known, similar things. The unlike was not unimportant, since it accounted for change. Change was the actualisation of an opposite property that a thing also contained (Duhem 1913; Grant 1984b). Brown hair turning grey was explainable by the amount of white it contained in potentiality.[27] Aristotelian commensurability required reducing things to one another, since there was no form of measurement separate from the properties that inhered in the object, or from their assigned places by which they would be apprehended. There was no universal coordinates. This is what modernity would bring. It may have wrought other forms of reductions, or hollowing outs, but it afforded one space where bodies, natural and human-made, were simply 'extended', in all their singularity. Aristotle's instead required a specific form of comparison that rested 'on the union of the equal and the similar and upon the separation of the unequal and the different' (Cassirer 2000, 10). It presupposed, and imposed, homogeneity upon the objects compared. And it yielded hierarchies. Cassirer (2000, 12) described how the hierarchy emerges from this mode of reduction by comparison: 'by such a process of comparing and distinguishing, of separating and delimiting, all empirical being splits up into different genera and species that stand in a definite relation of super- or sub-ordination to each other'. Indeed, 'making this interlocking of the conceptual spheres clear and visible' was the aim of logical thought, for Aristotle, by way of the syllogism notably (ibid). Cusa turned away from the syllogism and to mathematics instead.

A World of Differences: The Universe

Difference was thus not an epistemological problem in the pre-modern world; merely a set of observable positivities that could be accounted for, and more or less done away with, through the play of sameness within the cosmos's closed confines. It began to be problematised at the point where, once order was no longer yielded by the world, Western knowledge turned back on itself, to *order itself*. The moment where knowledge held up a mirror to itself, whether the initial gesture was Cusa's (for Cassirer), or Descartes's (for the traditional story, which is also Foucault's), heralded a thought that sorts itself before sorting what it discovers in the world, which is the definition of modern critique (from the Greek *critein* 'to sort'). The problem of order and the problem of difference were born coextensively in seventeenth-century Europe, as two sides of a modern critical reason. Thought made orders visible because it grappled with its own instruments of ordering, namely, language and reason itself. The seventeenth century was the age of grammatical treatises (Foucault 2005). It was also the age of the invention of the analytic method, formalised by Descartes in his *Discourse on the Method for Conducting One's Reason* (1637). The method breaks complex wholes into their constituent parts, in order to determine what belongs to each part and what does not. It differentiates between what is identical to itself and what is not. Only the non-identical is not reduced to the identical, because resemblances are not sought at all costs. Instead a clear and distinct perception of the extended thing itself is, to paraphrase Descartes. No longer caught in a mesh of sameness, the non-identical is appraised on its own terms, *as different*.[28] 'The activity of the mind [. . .] no longer consist[ed] in *drawing things together*' in order to find resemblances between them, Foucault (2005, 61, emphasis in original) underscored, 'but, on the contrary, in *discriminating*, that is, in establishing their identities'. 'Of Identity and Diversity' is the title of one of the most commented upon chapters of John Locke's *Essay concerning Human Understanding* (chapter 27, book 2). In the pre-modern world, differentiations were yielded by space itself, and this effectively wrote differences out. In the classical age, to differentiate became to analyse, to correctly apply one's reason. It was an embodied act of human ordering whose political implications are at the heart of this book.

Classical reason did not remain folded onto itself however, far from it; it set out to master nature and to possess the new world. The seventeenth century was marked by a vast classificatory effort to record and to 'sort' the species identified by deploying the new method, that would culminate in the encyclopaedias of the Enlightenment (Locke, *EHU*, III.chap.6). The taxonomic table was the emblematic instrument of the classical age. Crucially, its logic was no longer vertical. It was not the slotting into a group of similar objects ranked above or below another within an overarching pregiven hierarchy, whose task it was reason's to reveal. Differences are arranged side by side in a table, allotted their own spaces. The table enables comparisons between the items, but it also allows for their incommensurability. Likewise, the Westphalian solution was a horizontal arrangement, an alignment of different but equal polities, which were also, by the same token, dislodged from imperial hierarchies. The flat, 'tabulated space' of the classical episteme was, I suggest, the space of the modern state system (Foucault 2005, 83). The cabinets of curiosities, that other emblematic fixture of the classical age, was the folkloric version of this epistemic encounter with difference, and one of the sites where the unease it triggered played out. It adorned the salons but also, as we will see in chapter 7, the public anatomy theatres. For the human body comprised one of the most curious terra incognita for the early modern audience.

To sum up my argument in this section, modern reason's problematisation of the relation of identity and difference was the epistemic condition of possibility for beginning to conceive an order founded in equality instead of hierarchy. Differences of opinion and religious beliefs were central preoccupations for Hobbes and Locke, I will show in chapters 2 and 5, respectively, and how to craft a political order that accommodated for them without destroying it. Though the degree of differences in play may seem narrow from a contemporary, postcolonial perspective, since they were variations within Christianity, they drove people to deadly battlefields for over a century. The Westphalian state system was the answer to the problem of equality engineered in practice. The state of nature was the emblematic artefact devised to think it through in theory. Or not, as we will see in chapter 5.

Varieties of Reason, Forms of Authority, Modes of Critique

The third and final theme is the reconfiguration of the relations between reason, authority, and critique, both in the period I consider, and with regards to how this yields tools for writing about our own. In the pre-modern world, reason was an instrument for deciphering the natural and rightful order of things, not for critiquing it. In nature inhered a reason *Logos*, an organic-cum-rational order, that was reflected in a human reason (*logos*) and through which it was decrypted.[29] Both reason and authority bore down from on high in the Middle Ages. Progressively investing the sorting task (*critein*) in the seventeenth century from a variety of different epistemic sites would yield critique as we know it, as the practice of deconstructing the age's taken-for-granted. What began as a questioning of the established epistemic and natural order (a geocentric cosmology) led to interrogating the power *to* order. It begat the autonomous reason of modern critique. Reason itself splintered, as it shifted from being the instrument of an authority ascribed to God and pinned onto nature, to becoming the individual's faculty to deconstruct, and reconstruct. The reason that emerged from this moment, moreover, modern reason, was never one, unified thing; the analytic method notwithstanding. Rather, a range of distinctions proliferated; between 'knowledge' and 'opinion', which I explore in chapter 2; Descartes's 'good sense', in addition to his 'reason' proper; and Locke's concepts of 'understanding', 'mind', and 'consciousness', in focus in chapter 5. To complicate matters further, the main distinction, between a reason lodged in the natural order, on the one hand, and in the subject's mind, on the other, did not overlap neatly with pre-modernity and modernity, respectively. The *Logos* continued to loom large in the early modern natural law that was centrally mobilised to naturalise the work of political reordering under way. Lastly, another kind of reason altogether was taking shape, that attached neither to nature nor to the subject but instead to the political object it helped carve out, a reason *of* the state (raison d'état). The non-unicity of reason is a central theme running through this book. Methodologically, it affords a key critical resource for questioning any kind of enterprise, past or contemporary, that mobilises reason to include and to cast out, to draw lines that determine who is 'in' and who is 'out'. Throughout the chapters I focus on how different kinds of rationalities were mustered as exclusionary border-drawing instruments. For example, I show in chapter 5 how the reasonable consent that Locke puts forward as the necessary and natural corner-stone of modern freedom works to reserve it for the exclusive few. I aim to hone the multiplicity of reason into an instrument for deconstructing any hegemonic enterprise that pins its hegemony upon one, modern reason.

The enterprise of denaturalisation I embark upon, in tracing the state-subject relation back to its origins, is a critique of those who invented critique. They author*ed* the instruments we wield to critique, together with the concepts that still structure political life, like the state and the subject of rights. They have become the established author*ities* of our times; hence why they have been ab-sorbed by its prevailing ideology, liberalism (in its various kinds). Who, then, author*ises* my critique of the critics? My own reason and those of my readers who would grace me with receiving it. Here, however, lies the fundamental double-bind that is built into modern reason itself, as a function of its having established itself as its own source of authority—of having chopped off the monarch's head. Reason has only itself to draw upon to critique. It is the tool of deconstruction and of reconstruction. Our times are marked, I suggest, by a virulent rejection of the deconstructive moment; or at least a tendency to want to fold it precipi-tously and to move on as quickly as possible to the next stage, of reconstruction. The multiple efforts to fill the void that deconstruction appeared to have opened up with all manner of re-naturalisings, or re-materialisings, are expressions of this rejection. The claim that the deconstructive work is done and dusted, which regularly resurfaces, for example, in the demands for an 'ethics' to be simply added on to a policy area—to surveillance technologies or artificial intelligence, for example—without needing to attend to its underlying structures, is a wor-rying one to me. Every time I look around me, I find modernity's basic, gen-dered, and racialised structures of domination that, surely, were meant to be fully deconstructed by now, still firmly in place. The body in this book is meant to function as an ontic provocation that, in its 'there-ness', its ipseity, prods on the deconstructive work. I intend it, not as the remainder to deconstruction, but as a reminder that it is not yet completed. If I have in some ways helped restore the old language of 'naturalising' and 'denaturalising' to continue to interrogate our worlds, then I will have achieved something. In closing, I now outline the book's structure and chapter contents.

Book Structure and Chapter Contents

Security, liberty and property were enshrined as the 'absolute rights' of the modern political subject in William Blackstone's *Commentaries on the Law of England* (1765), the first compendium of modern English law. The triptych then resurfaces, with slight variations, in two other constitutional reference points for legal modernity, the French Revolution's Declaration of the Rights of Man and the Citizen (1789) that was then enshrined in the first constitution of the modern French state (1793) and the United States's Declaration of Independence (1776).[30] Whereas Coke, over a century earlier, oscillated between the point of view of the sovereign and that of the subject (see chapter 4), Blackstone squarely espoused the perspective of the English (male) subject to catalogue his rights. This is what makes his *Commentaries* distinctly modern. His legal record thus evinces a subject clearly carved out in and by the law, and a state-subject relation securely in place by the mid-eighteenth century, which accounts for Voltaire's admiration for English law. For my genealogical purposes, this record functions like a rear-view mirror that brings the seventeenth century into focus. I take Blackstone's (1848, 92, 93) 'absolute rights [. . .] [of] every Englishman' as revealing the three original knots that bound the subject and the state to each other. Blackstone's text is worth rendering at some length, to show the extent to which (and still largely unnoticed) he rooted the three fundamental rights in the body and for its colourful language of state-building:

> These therefore were formerly, either by inheritance or purchase, the rights of all mankind; but, in most other countries of the world being now more or less debased and destroyed, they at present may be said to remain, in a peculiar and emphatical manner, the rights of the people of England. And these may be reduced to three principal or primary articles; the right of personal security, the right of personal liberty, and the right of private property
>
> I.   The right of personal security consists in a person's legal and uninterrupted enjoyment of his life, his limbs, his body, his health, and his reputation [. . .]
>
> II. Next to personal security, the law of England regards, asserts, and preserves, the personal liberty of individuals. This personal liberty consists in the power of loco-motion, of changing situation, or moving one's person to whatsoever place one's own inclination may direct, without imprisonment or restraint, unless by due course of law [. . .]
>
> III. The third absolute right, inherent in every Englishman, is that of property: which consists in the free use, enjoyment, and disposal of all his acquisitions, without any control or diminution, save only by the laws of the land. (Blackstone 1848, 93–94, 97, 100)

Security, liberty, and property furnish me the tripartite structure of my genealogy. I apprehend them as the primary knots where the bond of mutual constitution between the state and the subject was first sealed. Each of the three parts of the book develops an overarching argument across two chapters. Security is the focus of part 1, where I track how the body, in seventeenth-century England, was crucial to establishing security as the necessary and sufficient foundation of the state-subject relation. The naturalisation of security is thus the overarching focus of part 1. I introduce the corporeal ontology of statehood in chapter 2, where I show how it first emerged as a specific solution to the religious wars that were raging through Europe in the seventeenth century. Hobbes, who formulated it, and whom I approach as the original constructivist, is in focus in that chapter, together with, on the side of practice, the new political technology of raison d'état. Hobbes diagnosed the conscience as the cause of war. He established politics as a discrete domain of actions, distinct from religion and ethics, by restricting it to bodies alone. He cast the state's focus upon the bodies so as to turn it away from the conscience, which contained the deadly threat to peace. In this way Hobbes delineated the space of collective living, of the commonwealth, by cordoning off the conscience and restricting it to bodies. He defined what seeing like a state meant, in the seventeenth century and for today's contemporary surveillance state. This first chapter also serves to draw out the dialectic of secrecy and transparency that begat the modern state, which is one of the main threads running through the book. The two poles of the dialectic are indexed by Hobbes and the raison d'état on the one side, which I consider in this chapter, and by John Locke as a founding figure of the Enlightenment on the other, who comes into focus in chapter 5.

In chapter 3, I turn to the other pole of the founding modern political relation, the subject, to track how security was established as its first absolute and natural right, by reworking the very corporeal medieval notion of self-preservation. Hobbes remains in focus in this chapter, insofar as he articulated the furthest a right to being protected that rapidly became an established dogma of early modern thought, notably in natural right theories, and of nascent state practice. Early in the century Edward Coke, as chief justice of the Court of Common Pleas, had already succinctly captured the dynamic of mutual constitution that bound the state and the subject to each other in security: 'protection draws subjection, and subjection draws protection' (*protectio trahit subjectionem, et subjectio protectionem*). In this chapter, I also consider the different kinds of natures that troubled the naturalisation of this first modern political right. For nature was also appearing, as a result of the scientific revolution, as a source of disorder; and no longer simply as the stable referent for the task of political ordering. This new, epochal instability in the constructions of nature and the way it was addressed by Hobbes in his philosophical writings contains, I suggest, precious resources for short-circuiting the naturalising work that Hobbes was engaged in. Hence my purpose in this chapter is to parse the initial naturalisation of security as the modern subject's constitutive right, for the purposes of denaturalising it. The main architect of security as the natural, hence unquestionable, right that warrants the state stepping in at any cost to 'keep us safe' also furnished us the tools to question this original construction. These resources include Hobbes's nominalism, which marks him as the original constructivist, and his critique of universals, which include what he termed 'paternal dominion', or patriarchy.

From texts, I turn to practices in chapter 4, which is the first of the two chapters on Blackstone's second absolute right, liberty. My argument across these two chapters in the book's second part is that the body served to *individualise* liberty. This occurred coextensively in the play of practice in revolutionary England (chapter 4), and in early modern English political theory (in chapter 5). Chapter 4 considers how liberty evolved in the law from being attached to a collective, metaphorical body, the medieval corporation, to being rooted instead in the individual body. I track this shift across an array of different sites in England and beyond. I analyse the early modern practices of toleration that developed from the ground up in Protestant Europe (Holland and Germany in particular) to address the problem of how to live together against a backdrop of religious wars, including the practices of 'walking out' (*Auslauf*) to worship one's God, and the house church (*Schuilkerk*). I show how these practices were key to delinking liberty from place, and thus to paving the way to attaching it instead to territory and the state. I also analyse the first common law of naturalisation, known as *Calvin's case* (1608), which wrote into the law the process of becoming an English subject—of subjection. This law decisively rooted the state-subject relation in the bodies of monarch and subject coextensively. I show how both of these bodies were deeply implicated in the process of territorialisation that begat the modern state in seventeenth-century England, and to shifting the political bond from the local authority to the sovereign. I draw out the corporeal processes underwriting centralisation. However, I then show how the subject's body also became, via an increasingly important habeas corpus, the centre point of the legal revolution that yielded the natural rights of the modern political subject. Edward Coke plays a central role in this chapter, insofar as he circumscribed both poles, of the state and the subject, as they were emerging. I also show how other revolutionary figures, like the Leveller John Lilburne and the common soldiers of Cromwell's army, who stood up to their Puritan generals at Putney in October 1647 to claim their right to partake in the new order they were fighting for, mobilised the body to claim their natural right to liberty.

Chapter 5, the second of the liberty chapters, parses the theoretical individualisation of liberty. I track the place of the body in Hobbes's and Locke's writings on liberty, respectively. I argue that, whereas Hobbes externalised political liberty, by rooting it solely in the body, Locke instead re-internalised it, by bringing instead into focus the mind and the body. At the heart of Lockean liberty stands a Calvinist conscience that, I argue, he durably established as a pillar of political modernity. Between them, Hobbes and raison d'état on the one hand, and Locke on the other, index the two poles of a dialectic of secrecy and transparency that lie in the foundations of political modernity. Amending Foucault's (2005) analysis of the classical episteme, I develop an alternative framework for reading Hobbes and Locke to liberalism's, whose monopolistic and anachronistic claim to these two authors turns on their understandings of its eponymous concept, liberty. Their concepts of liberty are better apprehended instead, I suggest, as part of two distinct *ordering* projects that were necessarily coextensively political and episte-mological, in line with the broader transformations of their times. The centrality of the conscience to Locke's liberty is what establishes him as the first theoretician of modern discipline. The conscience was both what was 'given', by God, and what required fashioning by way of reason. However, Locke was, in fact, recovering a notion that was being profoundly transformed at the juncture of a scientific and a religious revolution. To parse the under-appraised role of the conscience in his thought, I map the troubled history of the conscience, from Aquinas to Calvin. I show how Locke brought back together two distinct functions of the conscience, the moral and the epistemological, that were initially folded together in the theological notion, but had been separated out by Hobbes and Descartes respectively. Key to this recovery of the conscience, I will show, was another con-cept that Locke coined for modernity: 'consciousness'. I show how, together with 'the mind', it enabled Locke to negotiate a complicated relationship with the old faculty of 'reason'. This in turn reveals a key antagonism at the heart of Locke's work. He dispensed with 'reason' in his epistemological writings, yet he held on to it firmly in his political writings, where he wielded it as a boundary-drawing instrument to carve out the space of modern political subjecthood as an exclu-sive club of bourgeois male consenters. The distinction between Locke's 'disci-pline' and his 'punishment' draws out additional mechanisms of social sorting at work in his political writings. Locke's (TCE) discipline shapes the body and the mind, of the children of 'gentlemen' only. Punishment applies to the body alone, and of the poor. The constitutive role played by the criminal and by the death penalty in Locke's political ordering project also are also in focus in this chapter. The criminal functions as the figure of the other to the reasonable, free subject to whom he aimed his 'government by consent'. It marks the constitutive outside to the Lockean state. Civility and criminality, the law-abiding and the law-breaking subjects are co-produced in Locke's thought. They constitute modalities for sep-arating out the state's inside from its outside.

Chapter 6 is the first of the two chapters of the book's third part, which centres on the modern subject's third absolute right, to property. My overarching argu-ment in this part is that the body served to *privatise* property, and to establish the human subject, instead of the natural order, at the centre of the law. Whereas modern science expelled humanity from the world's centre, a second revolu-tion in the law, which is at the heart of this chapter, achieved the opposite. It begat legal modernity and the right to private property that supports its mode of production, capitalism. The site for this revolution was early modern theories of natural rights. Locke remains in focus in chapter 6, where I show how he located the original mechanism by which property is privatised in *the hand*, the characteristically human body part, *that grabs*. Locke, I will show, legitimised private property far more effectively than his fellow early modern natural rights theorists by corporealising it; and this, I suggest, is why he continues to loom large today. I begin by showing the extent to which private property required a complete re-ordaining of the structure of property itself which, in Europe, up until the Middle Ages, was attached to collective rather than individual bodies. I read Locke against the corpus of early modern natural rights theories and show how his mechanism of appropriation served to resolve an enduring tension underwriting it, regarding whether private property was natural, or socially constructed. Natural rights theory has emphasised the centrality of agency to the task of political construction. Yet this constructed-ness, and therefore contingency, of private property also weakens it, as a foundation for building the state. The appropriating hand affords Locke the means to resolve this tension, I will show, and to secure private property as the seemingly unshakeable foundation for political modernity. The body, then, performs decisive work to cover over the instabilities that inhere in a natural right to private property. I further explore these instabilities by shifting from the generic body to the particular bodies that were explicitly excluded from Locke's corporeal scheme, his slaves. The figure of the slave in this chapter functions in a similar way to the criminal in chapter 5. I show how slavery was not simply a practice he was deeply invested in personally, or an embarrassing but secondary feature of his political writings. It was, rather, part and parcel of the constitutive logic by which he articulated a racialised right to private property.

Chapter 7, the second of the property chapters, returns to the realm of practice, to analyse the public anatomy lesson, this unique early modern institution which, I contend, was a crucible of the state's making. I show how the body, this piece of 'natural' property that every human innately 'has', was being increasingly opened up and peered into, for the purposes of finally *seeing* human nature. I analyse the specific mode of seeing that begat coextensively modern science and the state. Bringing together visual studies and international relations I chart the scopic regime that established vision as modernity's primary ordered instrument and that was honed upon the body dissected in public. To map its contours, I begin with the writings of two of its first visionaries, the anatomist William Harvey and the scientist-statesman Francis Bacon. I then track how this scopic regime was institutionalised by the spread of the highly popular public anatomy lesson across early modern Europe. It was considered a marker of scientific advancement, and served distinct state-building purposes, notably in Holland, as it was breaking away from Spain. In England, science and state-making converged upon the sovereign Charles II, the Royal Society's patron. I analyse the work of epistemological and political ordering that was wrought upon the body in the public anatomy theatre. Tracking the dissected body as the quintessential object of modern science reveals a crucial tension at play upon the anatomy table, between the universality of the truths this body was thought to contain, and the particular bodies that, in practice, ended up on the dissection slab. For only the bodies of the poor qualified. To explore this tension, I analyse Renaissance and early modern representations of the public anatomy lesson, notably the frontispiece of the first manual of modern medicine, Andrea Vesalius's *On the Fabric of the Human Body* and the Dutch painter Rembrandt's Anatomy Lesson paintings. I parse the work of boundary-drawing and state-building wrought by these public performances by tracking the roles of the female and the poor body in their crafting.

Weaving together these multiple threads, I consider in the final chapter how together they designate modernity's defining problematique, ordering, understood coextensively as an epistemological and a political project. I conclude with the extent to which the body has operated as the great naturaliser of history, working to stabilise political construction, and notably the racialised and gendered figures that entered into the making of the modern category of 'the human' from the onset. I consider the two sets of processes, of putting together and of dividing up, that took the body as their referent and produced, respectively, the state and the individual who bears rights. I return to appraise the nature of the agency that is implicated in political construction, in this crafting. I parse the relations between construction, constitution, and another kind of corporeal agency altogether, generation (giving birth). I show how generation, as the distinctive agentic capacity that indexes only one kind of body, the female one, functioned throughout the seventeenth century as the other to constitution, to the agency that was being expended and experimented with to craft the state and the subject of rights. Generation loomed large, as that which constantly eludes constitution, and that it ultimately seeks to control and to emulate. Hence it serves to reveal a new knot of masculinist fantasies that underwrites the modern project. I end by returning to the duty of critique, understood as the work of denaturalisation undertaken in this book, and considering it in its relation to agency and to the urgency of taking responsibility for the world in which we live, and therefore for changing it.

PART I
SECURITY

2

The Corporeal Ontology
of Modern Security

[E]very sovereign hath the same right, in procuring the safety of his
people, that any particular man can have, in procuring the safety of
his own body.

—Hobbes, *Leviathan* (chap.30[30]233)

Human beings were not always organised into states. Rather, sovereignty and the
state are constructs devised in the seventeenth century to address the problem of
war. No thinker draws this out more starkly than Thomas Hobbes. Since war has
traditionally been considered the founding problem of international relations,
the discipline that emerged out the world's first global war, Hobbes has from the
onset held a prominent place in its pantheon—for better and for worse. The state,
Hobbes argued, was created to address the ongoing threat of conflict; hence security is its raison d'être. Security as the central purpose of the state, and war as the
discipline's founding problem, furnish me my starting points in this book. Only
in this first part, I widen international relations' traditional lens beyond states
and the international system and well beyond the present, in order to bring into
view the original security relation, between the state and the subject, that under-
girded the emergence of the system of states in the seventeenth century. By the
eighteenth century, security had become entrenched as the very first 'absolute
right or liberty' of 'the Englishman', in what was effectively the first compendium
of modern domestic laws, Blackstone's (1848, 92) *Commentaries*.[1] Moreover, the
lawyer defined this absolute right by way of the body, as 'the legal and uninterrupted enjoyment of [the Englishman's] life, his limbs [and] his body' (ibid.).
This corporeal articulation of the right to security originates in Hobbes. He
formulated the original way of 'seeing like a state' that keeps its population safe
(Scott 1998). That is, he articulated how states ought to see in order to achieve
their raison d'être, and that was to look only at their subjects' bodies, rather than
at their souls or at their consciences. I show in this chapter how turning to the
body was key to the solution Hobbes devised to the modern problem of war.

How the body was drawn upon in the initial naturalisation of security that
durably established the state as the form of the modern polity is the thread

Birth of the State. Charlotte Epstein, Oxford University Press (2021). © Oxford University Press.
DOI: 10.1093/oso/9780190917623.001.0001

running through this and the following chapter. The body serves to excavate the origins of one of the most enduring, politically efficacious, and taken-for-granted assumptions underwriting contemporary political life, that the human desire for security is 'natural'. The stakes in this construction are considerable. Understanding security as a natural need is what establishes the state's role as its guarantor beyond questioning. As a result, laws and policies need only be justified as being necessary to protect us to become very difficult to contest. To put it another way, it becomes especially difficult to argue against the numerous policies that tap into the notion that 'keeping us safe' is the state's foremost obligation, as a function of security having been successfully constructed from the onset as being what human beings innately want, in their very flesh, and above all else. This 'naturalness' is the reason that security systematically trumps all other political demands (Wæver 1995). For example, it accounts for why in over two decades of debates accompanying the relentless expansion of surveillance, security has more or less systematically prevailed over countervailing demands for privacy (see Epstein 2016). That private actors, and no longer states alone, now also tap into this security discourse is further testimony to the depth of its entrenchment. Historicising it serves to 'denaturalise the taken-for-granted' assumption that security is as natural as a bodily need (Weldes et al. 1999). The tools for both the original naturalisation of security *and* for deconstructing it were first honed by none other than Hobbes himself. Hobbes naturalised war, and in doing so, he de-historicized, and universalised, the particular solution he devised to the war he witnessed. That solution was the state. At the same time and somewhat paradoxically, he also denaturalised the state's right to kill. The body was central to both moves.

Hobbes wrote on the tail end of devastating religious wars that had swept through Europe for over one hundred years, claiming up to 30 percent of its population in some areas (Tully 1988). In England he witnessed political order strained to breakpoint by disagreements on religious questions. A war fuelled by these differences in 'opinions', to use his terminology, which had disrupted these European kingdoms' internal orders and their external relations, was the problem that both he and the diplomats who gathered in Westphalia in 1648 to negotiate the terms of peace, were grappling with. There the monarchs mutually agreed to look away from their respective subjects' souls and which creed ruled them, and at one another instead. To each monarch, their religion (*cujus regio ejus religio*). The Treaty of Westphalia separated out the realm's 'inside' from its 'outside', and, in doing so, it founded coextensively the state and the political system in which states interact (Walker 1993). To shift the focus away from the subjects' souls or consciences was to shift it instead to their bodies. This was the part of the solution Hobbes crafted. It is my focus in this chapter. My contention, then, is not that the ambassadors who met in Westphalia were following

Hobbes's rulebook; the *Leviathan* was three years from being published. It is, rather, first, that there was a broad convergence in Hobbes's rationale and in the form of reason that was emerging coextensively with this new political form, raison d'état (reason of state), and that established security in practice as its raison d'être. Second, there is a structural homology to the founding principle of modern sovereignty, the turning away from the state's inside, and the Hobbesian gesture to turn away from the subject's inner world in order to found a common realm—a commonwealth. Hobbes demonstrated why matters of the conscience and the soul were not for the state; indeed, that its appropriate 'matter', per the subtitle to the *Leviathan*, is the body. In this chapter I will show how the body emerged from this singular convergence of political thought and practice at the seventeenth century's midpoint as the site where the founding relation of modern sovereignty was sealed, and that somatic security is the original form that this relation took. This relation is what the state (and private actors) continues to tap into today when it promises to keep us safe. It also shapes the subject's expectations towards their state.

Although the motivation that led me down the path of history is to shed light upon our world, I aim to avoid the disciplinary pitfalls of instrumentalising Hobbes for a contemporary concern. I read his texts closely against their contexts and with the established scholarships in the history of political thought.[2] The central assumption upon which my own reading rests, however, is that Hobbes's ontology, his epistemology, and his political prescriptions are tightly imbricated. Hobbes's decisive gesture, I will show, was to have addressed a political problem, that of securing peace, by way of an epistemological solution. This solution achieved nothing short of founding a modern science of politics.[3] This crucial parallelism, whereby Hobbes's political project doubles up as an epistemological enterprise, and vice versa, underpins my analysis of security through this and the next chapter. My reading of Hobbes is therefore closer to the scholarship that has been concerned with thinking together these three dimensions of his thought, and with underlining that the insecurities that Hobbes sought to contain were not merely those entailed by the latency of war, but also the epistemological insecurities bound up with our being embodied, sensorial and sense-making creatures (Ball 1985; Blits 1989; Watkins 1989; Flathman 1993; Williams 1996; 2005; Prokhovnik 2010; Abizadeh 2013). It is also less close to the traditional scholarship that has picked out discrete political theoretical themes from his system (like his conception of natural rights; see Strauss 1963 and 1965; Tuck 1979; Manent 2012; or his theory of obligations; see Warrender 1957). Moreover, the body achieves considerably more work in Hobbes's thought then has been recognised even in the scholarship that has been careful to render the Hobbesian system, as I will show. It has, however, began to receive attention in political theory (Esposito 2008) and beyond (Frost 2008; Cohen 2009).

The body in this book is both the 'extended thing' (*res extensa*) whose place I map in the making of the state-subject relation, and the lens that reveals the founding modern political relation in a new light. In addition, to hone my own corporeal lens for this and the following chapter, I consider the body primarily as the organ of modern knowledge, the medium through which the world is known. Some philosophical context is necessary to clarify what I mean. Modernity began the moment the knowledge turned back upon itself, in order to consider not only what could be known in the world, but how such a knowledge was possible in the first place (see Cassirer 2000). It brought into focus the experience of the knower. It begat the figure that stands at the core of modern philosophy, the thinking, doubting 'I' that René Descartes first circumscribed, and that would lay the foundations of the contemporary 'self' (Taylor 1989). It would also eventually bring into focus 'the individual', except it is one of my central contentions in this book that casting Hobbes as the founder of 'the possessive individualism' that defines our age is to retrofit upon Hobbes a figure that was far less contoured, in both Descartes and Hobbes, than has tended to been assumed, both by liberal thought and its critiques (see notably Macpherson 1962). Holding off the figure of the individual from his thought is what focussing on the body enables. Descartes had discovered this 'I' (or *ego*) in setting out to find what constituted adequate grounds for knowledge, and he had worked through the thinking process itself, the *cogito*. Only Descartes had found it in his soul. This is precisely what Hobbes cast out. He rejected the immateriality of the soul, and thus the dualism of a body and soul that underpinned Descartes's discovery. For Hobbes (*L.* chap.46[15]459), 'the whole mass of all things that are [. . .] is Corporeal'. However, the experience of the knower was also a central concern for this quintessentially modern philosopher, as was the quest for adequate foundations for science. But, for him, knowledge originates exclusively in the body; the experience of knowing is embodied through and through. Hence in this chapter I apprehend the body as the organ or the means though which the world is acceded to and known. This is distinct, first, from the body as the object of the modern sciences, which will come into focus in the book's second part. The sciences of the body were fundamentally transformed by the scientific revolution. The body as the epistemic object produced by these transformations is not yet my concern in this chapter. It will be in chapter 4. Second, focussing on the embodied experience of the knower is also distinct from attending to the experience *of* the body, for example, that of 'the body in pain' (Scarry 1985). The particular conjunction of the body and the activity of know*ing* is my focus here. Hence in this book's first part, I seek to understand what it means to consider the body, as Hobbes did, as the sole medium through which the world is known.

The place of the body in the crafting of the state as the security guarantor is this chapter's topic. It is divided into five parts. After considering in the first part how Hobbes articulated the modern problem of war, I will show how he came to diagnose the causes of war in the conscience and in the soul, in the second and third parts, respectively. These were the sites of private beliefs, which, in the seventeenth century, was to say, of religion. Consequently, casting the conscience and the soul off-limits for the law were the two prongs of the solution Hobbes crafted to achieve peace. Doing so was necessary to being able to accommodate differences of opinion within the polity, and thus to carving out a common space where living together despite these disagreements became possible. For Hobbes, only bodies, their movements, and their deeds, must stand in the state's sights. A strongly delineated sphere of private opinions shielded from the sovereign's scrutiny (an inside) was the necessary counterpoint to building a peaceful public sphere (an outside). Whereas in the chapter's second and third parts, the body is simply what is left once the conscience and soul have been cast out in Hobbes's argumentation, in its fourth part I show what it enabled him to build, namely, a singular right to stand up to the state. This right, which is unique to him among early modern theorists of rights, yielded a staunchly dialectical state-subject relation, that properly posited either as discrete yet complementary poles of the interactions. It also established around the subject's body a space for a political agency qua resistance. Hobbes's right of resistance is what marks him as the necessary starting point for parsing the dynamics of mutual constitution. The classical Hobbes scholarship on rights and the biopolitical literature are also engaged with here. Shifting to the realm of practice in the chapter's final part, I show how Hobbes's turning away from the inner life of the subject paralleled European states turning away from their internal affairs and towards one another in the mid-seventeenth century. I parse the convergence between Hobbes's geometrical, line-drawing reason and the spatial rationality of raison d'état that crystallised at Westphalia. They carved out, in theory and in practice, respectively, a strictly political, a-religious sphere of action for the modern state.

1. The Problem of War and Embodied Peace as Its Solution

Peace as Modern Sovereignty's and the *Leviathan*'s *Telos*

Peace was the primary pull to Hobbes's entire political thought. His wish, as he wrote in the dedicatory epistle to his *De Cive* in 1642, was 'that mankind should enjoy such an immortal peace, that [...] there hardly be left any pretence for war'. *De Cive* was a second draft of the ideas he would revisit throughout England's revolutionary decade, which was bookended by his *Elements of Law* (1640) and the *Leviathan* (1651). The latter was drafted with a new urgency in the wake of Charles I's beheading (1649), and was published in English. Sovereignty is its main topic; indeed, it is only the second treatise on modern sovereignty after Jean Bodin's *Six Books on the Republic* (1576), also written in a vernacular language (French). The two works were written against a backdrop of violence fuelled by religious differences; in both cases, sovereignty is a means, peace is the end. [4] In both, the compulsion to abandon the traditional Latin in favour of the vernacular in response to disintegrating political orders spurs extraordinary conceptual invention.[5] Bodin first coined the term 'sovereignty' in French (*souveraineté* from *le souverain*, the sovereign), which did not exist in Latin. Hobbes (*L.* p.3) conjoined the 'sovereignty' with 'the state' for the first time in the opening pages of this political treatise, establishing as its object the 'great LEVIATHAN called a COMMONWEALTH, or STATE (in Latin CIVITAS)'.

Peace, then, is both the *telos* of Hobbes's Leviathan and a central motif of the *Leviathan*'s. It regularly resurfaces throughout the treatise as 'the end for which the sovereignty was ordained' (*L.*, chap.21[15]142). Its subtitle establishes this structuring role: 'The Matter, Forme [*sic*] and Power of a Common-wealth' is a play on Aristotle's four causes, in which the first two causes (matter and form) are held intact, the efficient cause morphs into 'power', and the final cause is disappeared altogether.[6] The attack on the Aristotelian final cause (*causa finalis*) was a hallmark of the scientific revolution (see Hacking 1987; Bartelson 1995; Casirer 2000; Foucault 2009). Early in the century Francis Bacon (2000, 102), in his programmatic vision for a new science, had written that 'the final [cause] is a long way from being useful; in fact, it actually distorts the sciences'. Only Hobbes was the one who took the battery of new epistemological instruments to the realm of human affairs, thus founding a science of politics. He played a key role in both 'demythologiz[ing] power' and in undoing its moorings in Aristotelian causality, as Jens Barteslon (1995, 163) has underlined. In eliding the final cause, Hobbes opened up the plane upon which that artificial, peace-building machine that is the modern state could be constructed. He substituted a naturalist final cause with a human-made one: peace. Moreover, this collective *telos* is both mirrored and supported by an individual one, self-preservation, which is properly the 'final cause, end, or design of men' (*L.*, chap.17[1]106). The naturalist overtones of this second *telos* constitutes a key focus of the following chapter. Let me note for now that it too is orientated towards 'a more contented life'. Together they locate the two poles of the founding relation of modern sovereignty, the state and the subject, that is sealed by having peace as their common end.

Peace is, for Hobbes, both the purpose of the modern state and what the subjects desire for themselves. But how did the body become the site of this primordial modern political relation? This was far from self-evident in an age where that other part of the subject, the soul, was considered the more significant part; when salvation in the afterlife was more important than a long or comfortable life in this world. The immortal peace Hobbes was after ran up against promises of immortality in the afterlife which, against a backdrop of protracted religious wars, regularly entailed taking up arms to defend one's creed. The soul was the great battlefield upon which these devastating wars were waged throughout Europe in the sixteenth and well into the seventeenth century (see Tully 1988). It was precisely because 'their felicity in the present life' was not, or was so little, upon his contemporaries' horizon that Hobbes (*L.*, chap.13) so deliberately sought to draw attention to it, including in all the colourful ways in which he depicted this life in its felicity or rather, mainly, its misery.[7] Hobbes's task was to bring this life onto what the historian Reinhardt Koselleck (1985) has called their 'horizon of expectations'. The body provided a crucial means to achieve just that. Doing so, however, was also to turn inside out an entire structure of values and sense-making that is worth considering a little more closely if too briefly in order to take the measure of the task Hobbes set himself.

The Soul and the Conscience as Causes of War

The afterlife of the soul ordained the medieval Christian life spatially and temporally, historians have shown. The pilgrim, a key figure of the medieval society, underscores how this life was conceived as a passage through to the afterlife and beyond the 'weft of appearances' (Bloch 1968, 130, my translation). The afterlife of the soul was invested with an ideological charge that is difficult to fathom today precisely because the structures of the modern state system to which we are heir were begat by the solution to the religious wars it unleashed. In the Middle Ages, the afterlife of the soul provided what Koselleck (1985, 277) termed a 'structure of anticipation' that sutured together in specific ways its 'space of experience' with its 'horizon of expectations'. It worked both as pull upon this life and as a place where the scriptures' unrealised prophecies could be relegated. These two spaces of the Christian life were simultaneously discrete (spatially) and staggered (temporally).[8] This created an equilibrium, which, for Koselleck (1985), modernity would rupture, whereby spiritual hopes and worldly experience stood in tension but not in contradiction with one another.

Periodically, as in the seventeenth century, the distance between the two spaces was collapsed and the scriptural prophesies activated to go to war, generating specific forms of violence from actors who understood themselves to be called upon to hasten the realisation of these habitually deferred promises. Philip Buc (2015) has underscored the central role that martyrdom and Christian notions of the holiness of war have played in shaping the history of 'the West' in the long view. These ideas, and the sense of standing on 'a cosmic threshold', as Charles Webster (1975, 6) put it, and of the imminence of the kingdom of God—even 'Britton's God', for Milton—were crucial motives for the English revolutionaries who went to war against their king convinced that they were precipitating a preordained plan (cited in ibid., 4).[9] Charles Webster (1975, 5) has underlined the importance of the figure of the apocalypse, of providential histories and of millenarian ideas in fuelling the sense of urgency and in garnering support for Long Parliament in the 1640s, 'which was represented as God's agent of reformation'. The new order they toiled to bring about, the Puritans were certain, would, in Milton's words again, 'raise the Britannick Empire to a glorious and enviable heighth [sic], with all her Daughter Islands about her' (cited in Webster 1975, 4). The first visions of a modern British nation-state were suffused with this religious ideology.

The conscience was the centre point of this potent and bellicose religious ideology. It had acquired a singular value because of the role it played in the movement of religious reform known as the Reformation that swept throughout Europe in the sixteenth and seventeenth centuries, and specifically as the place from which to question the existing order. In 1520, when asked by Emperor Charles V to recant his theses before the Diet in Worms, in the wake of a papal Bull that threatened him with excommunication if he did not, Luther, before an authority that was at once religious and political, replied that he would retract none 'since it is neither safe nor right to go against conscience. I cannot do otherwise, here I stand, may God help me, Amen' (cited in Strong 1993, 135). This refusal to obey by 'the first modern theoretician of the conscience' has been called the 'birth certificate of modernity' (Büttgen 2014). Yet as the religious wars wore on, the conscience became weaponised with increasing stridency, notably in England.[10] Sermons pronounced in a Puritan-dominated Parliament in the 1640s testify to the extent to which whipping up the conscience into a bellicose frenzy was an integral part of the war that was being waged, and won, against the old order. For example, in a 1642 Fast Day Sermon its members were urged by the preacher Stephen Marshall to be unflinching in their violence against Charles I's supporters, and to 'take [their] *little ones* upon the *speare's point*, to take them by the heeles and beat out their *braines against the walles*' (quoted in McQueen 2017, 117). Following from Paris the tensions that were building up in England, Hobbes concluded as early as 1642 that 'there are no Warres so sharply wag'd as between Sects of the same Religion, and Factions of the same Commonweale', adding that the 'the Contestation [. . .] concerning Doctrines' is one of its bitterest causes (*DCi* chap.1[5]).[11] For Hobbes, the seeds of war had been planted in the conscience.

From the Outside-In: Carving Out the Scientific Point of View

Wary of this feverish politicisation of the conscience, Hobbes drastically inverted the direction of thinking of his times. 'Unlike his contemporaries' writes

Koselleck (1998, 29–30), Hobbes 'did not argue from the inside outwards but the reverse, from the outside in'. He deliberately eschewed the traditional early modern starting point for treatises on ethics or moral philosophy inherited from Christian doctrine, the confessional soul subjecting itself to the judgements of its conscience, where the ultimate judge was God. To this 'foro interno', or innermost court, Hobbes (L.,chap.15[36]99) preferred instead the 'foro externo', the outer forum of actions and deeds, which he established as the proper locus of politics. Before the intensifying acrimony between the various factions of the civil war who all argued in the name of their consciences, Hobbes sought to elaborate, as Koselleck (1988, 27) put it, 'an extra-religious, supra-partisan position which in turn enabled him to analyse all parties together, as parties to a common process' that had yielded the civil war that he would seek to cure.

My argument is that this neutral standpoint was the scientific point of view. Hobbes set out to develop a new science with which to diagnose the body politic's disorders and to develop the remedies to heal it. Hobbes admired the kings' physician William Harvey, whom he established in a prominent place in his personal pantheon. Harvey was, for Hobbes (De Corpore, dedicatory epistle), 'the only one I know that, conquering envy, hath established a new Doctrine in his lifetime' (concerning blood circulation, see chapter 4).[12] Appraising how the ceaseless and intensifying quarrelling between these inward-looking doctrines of faith had strained the body politic to break point, nothing short of a scientific doctrine was needed in order to step out of the conscience and analyse the effects of its productions upon the body politic. This is how Hobbes came to address a political problem, regarding the causes of war, by displacing it onto an epistemological terrain, which I will now explore. In the next section I will show how, for Hobbes, shifting the focus away from the conscience and finding new foundations for knowledge constituted the two sides of the same coin, and how turning to the body was necessary to achieving both.

2. Corralling the Conscience to Secure Peace: The Strategic Purposes of the Hobbesian Epistemology

From Differences of 'Conscience' to Differences of 'Opinion'

The problem, for Hobbes, was not the conscience as such. In fact, corralling the conscience would serve as much to protect it from others' meddling in our private matters as it would to prevent these from spilling over onto what also needed to be preserved as the public space for collective living. The problem, then, was people's vain and inordinate infatuation with their own. 'The conscience', wrote Hobbes (L., chap.7[4]36), was 'that reverenced name' that 'men vehemently in love with their own new opinions (though never so absurd)' gave to these opinions and are 'obstinately bent to maintain them'. They revered them to the point of going to war over them. Substituting 'the conscience' with 'opinion', a pre-Christian term devoid of theological connotations (the Ancient Greek *doxa*, the Latin *opinio*), was the linchpin to Hobbes's strategy to loosen its grip upon his contemporaries.[13] Hobbes began by offering a diagnosis of how the confessional metaphor of the conscience as an inner court became progressively corrupted. The error stemmed from confusing the cognitive fact of 'being conscious of' something with the metaphor 'being a witness to'. 'Afterwards', Hobbes (*L.*, chap.7[4]36) continued, 'men made use of the same word metaphorically, for the knowledge of their own secret facts and secret thoughts; and therefore it is rhetorically said that the conscience is a thousand witnesses'. Metaphors are powerful devices. Hobbes would know; it was he who invented one of the original metaphors for the modern state (the Leviathan) (Springborg 1995). People became so engrossed with their own inner witnessing, per this rhetorical emphasis, what with so many voices clamouring within, that they began to elevate their 'private consciences' over 'the public conscience [which] is the law' (*L.*, chap.29[7]212). 'Whereby the commonwealth is distracted and *weakened*' (ibid). This was how the otherwise laudable moral impulse to act according to 'the plea of [one's] conscience', which 'has been always hearkened unto very diligently in all times' was turned into a 'false doctrine' that must be weeded out in order to preserve the possibility of living together in peace, given the 'diversity as there is of private consciences', notes Hobbes (*L.*, chap.29[7] 212), adding wryly that 'the conscience may be erroneous'. Hobbes counted the conscience amongst 'those things that Weaken or tend to the *Dissolution* of a *Commonwealth*', which are the object of *Leviathan*'s chapter 29. The only way to guarantee a stable political order, then, was to move the inner workings of the conscience beyond the pale of politics.

The solution Hobbes crafted to achieve this went to the heart of his entire scientific-cum-political enterprise. That is, understanding how Hobbes neutralised the conscience requires fathoming the extent to which, for Hobbes, the political task of establishing the polity upon sound bases and the epistemological task of laying down scientific foundations for its study were coextensive. Moreover, they first required understanding the stuff that humans are made of—literally, corporeally. To ground these tasks in an account of the body was to guarantee their scientificity. Indeed, to be unscientific, as so many scholastic 'philosophers' before him had been, was to leave pretence for war.[14] Conceptual and political confusion were, for Hobbes, two sides of the same problem. The stakes in founding a science of the polity were political as much as they were philosophical, and they were nothing short of peace itself. 'Conceptual-cum-political chaos', as Terence Ball (1985, 754) nicely termed it, was the ailment

Hobbes diagnosed and that he sought to cure by turning to the body. Hence Hobbes disarmed the conscience by way of the body, which was both at once the source of true knowledge and of all errors. I now consider this dual nature of the body in the Hobbesian epistemology.

'Knowledge of Facts' vs 'Knowledge of Consequences'

The purpose of clarifying the slippage between 'being conscious of' and 'the conscience' was to recover the former, which constitutes a source of knowledge, from the latter. Being conscious of something is a form of knowledge that Hobbes (*L.*, chap.7[3]35) terms 'knowledge of facts'. He distinguishes it from 'knowledge of consequence' for which he reserves the term 'science'. Knowledge of facts is an 'absolute knowledge' that originates in 'sense [...] and memory' (ibid.). It is 'absolute' in that it has the stubborn, irrefutable quality of that which is imprinted upon our senses. In Hobbes's thoroughgoing materialism, sense-impressions are necessarily the starting points of all knowledge. Science is its end point. It comprises chains of reasoning or 'reckoning' grounded in and carefully developed from 'definitions'. It is conditional in the sense that it depends on these operations having been performed. 'Knowledge of facts' on the other hand trades in 'opinions'.

Hobbes sorts opinions according to their origins. The first form of opinions 'beginneth at some saying of another' (*L.*, chap.7[5]36). Whether one adheres to this first type of opinion hangs on how much one trusts this person's authority. Most religious beliefs are opinions of this kind, since, Hobbes observes, the use of the first person 'I believe' is generally reserved for persons in positions of authority ('divines'). For the majority of the believers, these opinions take the form: '*I believe him, I trust him, I have faith in him, I rely on him*' (ibid.). By analysing the structure of these mediated (in the sense of communicated) opinions Hobbes uncovers a basic structure of authority, at a time when the very bases of political authority are being contested. A key purpose of the *Leviathan* is to propose a new kind of political rather than religious authority that rests not upon the faith in another's opinions, but upon one's own act of *authorising* another— the sovereign—to act in one's name (*Leviathan*, chapter 16). The agency of this founding act contrasts with the passivity of believing. Where religious authority interpellates believers, this political authority constitutes the subject qua political actor. It founds the modern political subject. The second source of opinion is our immediate, embodied experience. Here lies the confusion between being 'conscious of' and 'witness to'. Indeed, knowledge of facts 'is the knowledge proper to witnesses' (*L.*, chap.9[1]49). Only '[w]hen two or more men know of one and the same fact, they are said to be CONSCIOUS of it to one another' (ibid.).

Hobbes's Theory of Error

Differentiating between types of opinion enables Hobbes to locate the sources of error in their formation. Two witnesses to the same fact will develop distinctive opinions about it. They may be unscientific, if they are simply statements of facts regarding what happened, as opposed to chains of reasoning that uncover its causes. But they are not erroneous, since 'natural sense and imagination are not subject to absurdity' (Hobbes *L.*, chap.4[13]19). That they should differ from one another is because they are rooted in each person's embodied sense-experiences, their singular biological wiring. Yet each opinion remains true to the opiner. Consequently there are two forms error for Hobbes; an epistemological and an ontological one. The epistemological error is an ill-composed causal chain. It pertains to 'knowledge of consequences' and will be considered more at length in the next section. The ontological error, which is specific to 'knowledge of facts', consists in believing that something exists which does not (Hobbes, *L.*, chap.9, 47). For example, for Hobbes, it is the soul, as we will see in the following section. This type of error takes shape when these opinions are conveyed to a third party, for whom it is no longer tethered to and verifiable by sense-experience. This source of error, then, is the communicative structure itself. Hobbes, in this way, exposes the fragility of the foundations of opinions and beliefs. This, in turn, calls for the recourse to definitions in order to stabilise the grounds for the formation and circulation of opinions but also of knowledge itself.

The importance of definitions for Hobbes is that, given the communicative structure that underpins the formation of opinions, which is also a source of error, they are necessary for individuals to develop common accounts, both between the two direct witnesses who, by recourse to shared understanding, move beyond their solipsistic, sense-based truths to a common truth, and so that this account may be broadcast more broadly. Definitions afford an alternative 'conditional' tether to immediate experience in the formation of opinions. They hook the opinion in the process of being formed (prior to it having become one or the other form of knowledge) into pre-existing 'knowledge of consequence'-type discourses. This enables it to become knowledge proper, rather than mere knowledge of fact. Hence this structure of communication, uncovered in the process of analysing 'knowledge of facts', also undergirds the 'knowledge of consequences', which is properly the mediated form of knowledge (in the sense that it is less attached to the immediacy of experience). Definitions, then, are important for Hobbes (*L.*, chap. 5[20]26) because '[t]he light of human minds is perspicuous words, but by exact definitions first snuffed and purged from ambiguity; *reason* is the *pace* increase of *science* the *way*, and the benefit of mankind, the *end*. And on the contrary metaphors and senseless and ambiguous words are like *ignes fatui* [a fool's fire], and reasoning among them is wandering amongst innumerable absurdities; and their end, contention and sedition, or contempt' (Hobbes, *L.*, chap.5[20] 26).

Circumscribing and Regulating Opinions

Opinions are the linchpin of Hobbes's strategy to corral the conscience. He accommodates for its productions, and he ultimately contains them in a place that is both carefully delineated and minimised in his epistemological enterprise. From Hobbes's analysis of opinions in addition, several consequences follow. First, as we have seen, it reveals a basic structure of authority to reconfigure (see also Strong 1993). Second, circumscribing this form of knowledge enables Hobbes to define it in contradistinction to what a political science consists in. This 'knowledge of facts' is 'the knowledge proper to witnesses' (*L.*, chap.9.[1]49, Latin version). Its 'record' is 'history [which] is divided into natural and civil'. '[N]either of which pertains to our purpose', (*L.*,chap.9.[1]49 Latin version) Hobbes's purpose is rather to develop a 'knowledge of consequences from the accidents of *politic* bodies' (*L.*, chap.9[40]48). This new science modelled upon geometry 'places [definitions rather than experience] in the beginning of [its] reckoning' (*L.*, chap.4[12]19). Political analysis lapses back into mere opining either when it is not grounded in definitions, or when these 'definitions [are] not rightly joined together' (*L.*,chap.7[4]36).

By analysing the structure of opinions, third, Hobbes shifts the focus away from the veracity of their content to their effects; from whether opinions are true to whether they are believed, and with empirically observable consequences. In this way, he came to circumscribe opinions at large as objects for political analysis. This displacement, fourth, yields a practical prescription for regulating opinions. Distinguishing between knowledge of facts and knowledge of consequence enables Hobbes to locate the question of truth as belonging to the domain of science rather than opinions. In formulating it as a scientific question, however, Hobbes also brackets truth as a basis for adjudicating between opinions. Ideally, 'in matter of doctrine nothing ought to be regarded but the truth' (Hobbes, *L.*, chap.18[9]113). However, with the epistemological work he has undertaken in the first ten chapters of the *Leviathan*, he has effectively disabled this criteria for all but scientific doctrines.[15] The only valid criteria for regulating non-scientific opinions, like religious opinions, is whether they foster peace. In addition, Hobbes (ibid.) surmises, opinions that do not are unlikely to be true: a 'doctrine repugnant to peace can no more be true than peace and concord can be against the law of nature'. This second criteria is also valid for the scientific truths uncovered by the succession of discoveries that had profoundly upturned the epistemic foundations of his time, and had prompted a backlash by religious authorities, in the name of divinely revealed truths. Galileo's trial looms large. Hobbes (ibid.) adds: 'the most sudden and rough bustling in of a new truth that can be does never break the peace'. Unlike religious dogmatism, heliocentrism did not kill. Once the scientific criteria has been cast off limits, the practical criteria for the regulation of opinions is thus afforded by the polity's *telos*.

This is the basis for Hobbes infamous defence of censorship (chapter 18). Only the state's right to censor applies, not to the content of opinions, but to their outward compatibility with the polity's purpose: peaceful coexistence. 'The actions of men proceed from their opinions' (Hobbes, *L.*, chap.18[9]113). Yet actions, not thoughts, are, for Hobbes (*L.*, chap.37[13]300), where this alignment is verifiable, since 'thought is free'. The criterion he devised for state censorship is strictly limited to the tangible effects that opinions, religious or otherwise, bear upon the behaviour of subjects. And by tangible this 'materialist thinker' understands that they, quite literally, push buttons in their nervous systems that move them to act, in ways that I will consider more closely when appraising his physiology of action in the next chapter (Frost 2008). In fact, at a time when the political principle emerging at Westphalia established that every monarch had an exclusive hand in deciding on his realm's religion, Hobbes elaborated an a-religious, strictly political criterion that, in principle, afforded the monarch a way to *not* simply impose their own religion upon their subjects. It accommodated for the diversity of opinions and faiths coexisting, albeit tightly contained, in ways we will see in the next section. Hobbes, I suggest, is often misread because of the sentence that follows: 'and in the well-governing of opinions consisteth the well-governing of men's actions, in order to their peace and concord [*sic*]'. Yet he also establishes bodies only as the site of this well-governing. Hence though the Hobbesian state has a right to 'examine the doctrines of all books before they be published', the actions, of taking pen to paper and the paper to the public, remain the criteria for censoring (Hobbes, *L.*, chap.18[9]113). A book may be banned because of its effect on its readers, but not, say, in order to establish the author as a heretic. That is, censorship should pertain not to the content that is being expressed, but to the embodied effects of this expressing upon its readers, and how it drives them toward conflictual behaviour. What is significant for our purposes is how Hobbes casts the state's sights upon actions and bodies in designing censorship criteria.

Regulating Actions, Not Consciences: Delineating the Space of the Law

Hobbes's treatment of opinions reveals the parallelism upon which his project rests, whereby his epistemological enterprise, to found a science of the polity, doubles up as a political undertaking, reordering the constituent components of the polity to secure peace in this life. Opinions are circumscribed and accommodated within the system of knowledge he designs, but ultimately cast aside since they provide inadequate foundations for his new science. But this epistemological work also yields a political prescription: these productions of the conscience ought not be legislated upon by the sovereign either, since 'thought is free' (Hobbes, *L.*, chap.37[13]300). Opinions are doubly cordoned off, from the remit of science and from that of the law.

To turn to the political project, holding off the conscience served to delimit the law as the place of collective living, the common-wealth. Hobbes conceives his reordering task in topological terms. He undertakes a series of line drawings to stake out this space. To begin with, he drew a sharp line between the conscience and actions, and he limited the law's purview to the latter only. 'No human law is intended to oblige the conscience of a man, but the actions only,' he had already reflected in 1640 (*EoLii*, chap.6[3]114).[16] At the other end of the turbulent decade he reasserted that 'the power of the law [. . .] is the rule of actions only' (*L.*, chap.46[37]466). Extending the law 'to the very thoughts and consciences of men', as the practices of 'examination and inquisition' sought to do, was as unnecessarily intrusive as it was ineffectual, an 'error' all around (ibid.). To do so was to be confused about the respective remits of the law and the conscience, in precisely the way that are those idolaters of the conscience who 'would have it seem unlawful to change or speak against their opinions' misunderstood that opinions and the law belong to two discrete spheres, a private and a public one, respectively, a within and a without (*L.*, chap.7[4]36). Moreover, reworking the conscience yields one of the first metaphors for the modern public sphere: Hobbes (*L.*, chap.29[7]212) coins the oxymoron of a 'public conscience' that requires being separated out from the infinite diversity of 'private consciences'—a deliberate pleonasm, since the conscience is already private—to accommodate for their peaceful coexistence.[17]

'There would be no peace without subjection', for Hobbes (*L.*, chap.17[4]107). The public space is the space of this subjection to the law. Only Hobbes's subjection concerns actions only, not the conscience. In fact, Hobbes (*L.*, chap.21[18]143 and chap.31[12]239) carved out a private space marked by 'the silence of the law' and for the conscience to dwell 'in secret free'. Moreover, his private sphere is not reducible to the loneliness of a single conscience. This is perhaps one of the most widespread contemporary misreading of Hobbes, and the explanation for the persisting assumption of his individualism. However, the private sphere that was taking shape in the seventeenth century against a backdrop of religious conflicts was not coextensive with the individual conscience. It included the household and even the congregation. 'Private' was still 'collective' in the seventeenth century, the communal structures of which I examine in more detail in chapter 4. Arash Abizadeh (2013), who parsed the spatial logic of Hobbesian 'systems' (chapter 22) and his theory of representation, has shown how Hobbes tolerates private assemblies so long as they do not claim to speak in the name of the public conscience. Speech falls on either side of the Hobbesian divide between actions and the conscience, depending on their effects. Talk within this private assembly is private, whereas any talk that bears effects beyond it (because, say, the assembly's speakers claim to speak for all of humanity) is public. Hence in the Hobbesian topology of modern sovereignty, the public space of common living is counterbalanced by a just as strongly delineated private space that is removed from the law. In fact, holding off a sphere of privacy shielded from the sovereign's scrutiny is a necessary condition for constituting the public space of the law in the first place, as Koselleck (1988) has underscored. These two spaces function as each other's counterpoints in the Hobbesian spatial logic. They establish the two poles of the sovereignty relation, the state and the subject.

To summarise, Hobbes disarmed the conscience because 'instead of being a *causa pacis*' (a cause of peace), its authority had become a 'downright *causa belli civilis*' (a cause of civil war), as Koselleck (1988, 29) put it. He displaced a political problem onto an epistemological terrain by shifting the focus from 'the conscience' to 'opinions'. Hence Hobbes's epistemological project to found a new science also served his strategic purpose of putting the conscience back in its place, by making a limited room for its productions. Having shown how he contained the conscience, I will now show how Hobbes neutralised that other non-corporeal human part, the soul. In aiming at the soul, Hobbes's target was twofold. He aimed at his contemporaries, first, at a time where, in context of doctrinal warfare, the 'belief in ghosts' was actively encouraged in order to uphold specific theological bedrocks, like the immortality of the soul (Douglas 2014). The second target was a broader medieval ideational ontology and its form of reason, which was lodged in the soul. The body would emerge as the locus of modern politics at the outset of these ontotheological wars.

3. Materialising and Mechanising the Soul

Hobbes's strategy to unseat the soul is manifold and deployed on several levels. The first is a broad and indirect ontological undermining. Hobbes's materialism undercuts the possibility of nonmaterial things existing altogether. In this context, the immaterial dimensions of human existence require either being deliberately recovered within his materialist ontology, or they are flushed out altogether. Developing such materialist accounts is Hobbes's undertaking in the first part of the *Leviathan*, notably for opinions and knowledge, as we have seen, but also with language (chapter 4). He makes no such attempt to retrieve the soul.

Moreover, early on in *Leviathan* Hobbes (chap. 5[5]34) strikes down all 'imma-terial substances' as '*absurd, insignificant*, and *nonsense*'; their names being but empty words 'whereby we conceive nothing but the sound'. While he does not mention the soul, he names a closely related notion that belonged to the idea-tional ontology he was targeting and that presumed the soul as its seat, the free will. This attack is indirect in that, at this level, Hobbes simply loads up his mate-rialism and lets it do the work.

Furthermore, when he does mention the soul, it is to evoke its substance-less-ness: 'the soul of man [is] of the same substance, with that which appeareth in a dream, to one that sleepeth; or in a looking-glass, to one that is awake' (Hobbes, *L.*, chap.12[7]65). The soul is of the same stuff that dreams or optical illusions are made of. He then compares it to 'spirits', 'thin aerial bodies', and 'invisible agents' that are 'feared' unnecessarily (ibid.) Lastly, the soul, for Hobbes (*L.*, chap.12[7]65) is a '*spirit incorporeal*'. In the Latin translation Hobbes undertakes of the *Leviathan* in 1668, Hobbes (*L.* chap. 46[9]470) takes a step further, writing that '*what is incorporeal is nothing*'.[18] Hence it follows in the logic of his argu-mentation that the soul does not exist. Hobbes himself does not take this last step, from the textual evidence I have been able to garner, perhaps because to pronounce the soul's death sentence was to take a step too far for his time.[19] Yet he was not shy of embracing the implications of his thoroughgoing materialism with regards to that other immaterial reality with which the soul was closely bound up, God. After being pressed on this question by his contemporaries, he added an appendix to the *Leviathan*'s Latin version to confirm that 'God, too, is a body' (*L.*, p. 540). Of the soul he says nothing similar. Hobbes's materialism thus flushed out the idea of the soul, while retaining that of God, by materialising it. It paved the way for the solution that his younger contemporary Spinoza would proceed to develop, albeit to eschew this thoroughgoing materialism and ulti-mately resolve the dualism of mind and body in a different direction altogether that need not concern us here.

The second attack on the soul is prepared for by his work to separate out the apparatus of human knowledge from that cognate notion, the conscience. In shifting the focus to 'opinions' and 'beliefs', Hobbes opened up the possibility, radical at the time, that these might exist, and be studied, without requiring a conscience or soul as their 'substrate' (Balibar 2014a). Hobbes, here, was par-taking in the mounting assault through the seventeenth century upon the scho-lastic soul, a key pillar of the development of modern philosophy (see also Balibar et al. 2014 and Balibar 2013). The soul, since Plato, performed this foundational and containing function. It constituted a unifying substance that held together the properties of a natural being, the locus of its identity or essence (see also Cassirer 2000, 124–26). Locke's subsequent attack on innate ideas was equally aimed at the substrate purported to contain them. With Locke, at the end of the seventeenth century, this rejection of scholastic soul would ultimately yield the modern concept of 'consciousness' (see Balibar 2013). Hobbes, in the middle of the century, simply did away with 'the conscience', leaving its place empty.

Instead, third, Hobbes displaces the problem from an ontological one (is there something behind or under these beliefs?) to an epistemological one, how to account for religious beliefs *without* presuming a soul or a conscience. This leads him to consider the nature of this particular type of opinion, and to develop a theory of how they are produced. It is 'peculiar to the nature of man' to be 'inquisitive into the causes of the events they see' (Hobbes *L.*, chap.12[2]63). Humans, as we have already seen, naturally opine about the things they witness or experience. Only they are caught between their 'ignorance of causes' and their desire to know these causes (Hobbes *L.*, chap.12[6]64). This gnawing anxiety 'must needs have for objects something' (Hobbes *L.*, chap.12[6]64). Humankind's natural epistemological 'ill-condition' is, for Hobbes (*L.*chap.13[13]78), profoundly generative (see also Blits 1989; Williams 2005). It yields the products both of reason and of religion, and this is the great difficulty that must be sorted through ahead of building the 'Mortal God' that enables humans to live together (Hobbes, *L.*, chap.17[13]109).

Hobbes (*L.*chap.7[11]66) identifies four 'seeds of religion': 'opinion of ghosts, ignorance of second causes, devotion towards what men fear, and taking of things causal for prognostics'. This epistemological desire to know the causes of things leads men to discover God 'as the eternal cause of all things'. This is the first cause. But it also 'hinders them from the search of the causes of other things', or second causes. It derails them from the 'deep meditation which the learning of truth [. . .] requireth'; from the plodding path of reason and the careful computations it needs to undertake to uncover their real, which, for Hobbes (*L.*chap.30[14]225), is to say, material causes. This ignorance of second causes affords the breeding grounds for the 'creatures of the fancy' (Hobbes *L.*, chap.12[7]65). It is the wellspring of those 'ghosts', 'spirits', and 'thin, aerial bodies' and all those other 'invisible agents' dreamt up by a prolific human fancying factory, which people then take to have caused that which they do not understand, and revere out of an anxious and impatient ignorance.

This, then, is how people come to have 'opinions of ghosts', or to believe in things that do not exist, and to make prognostics about an unknowable future out of 'fear of what was to befall them in time to come' (Hobbes *L.*, chap.12[6]64). Religious opinions are entirely accountable as a function of humankind's natural epistemological condition. They require being accommodated for in the ways we have seen, because they spring forth from the same cognitive desire that also sustains the work of reason—the work by which it strings together chains of causes and uncovers the laws of nature, then creatively rearranges these laws to build those awe-inspiring machines that were appearing everywhere in the age of the scientific revolution, or indeed that great peace-enabling 'automaton' that concerned him, the state (*L.* p.3).

Fourth, Hobbes held up his mechanist reason against the form of reason that the scholastic soul was bound up with. Hobbes brought the great discovery of the seventeenth century, scientific reason, to the realm of politics. Hobbes's (*L.,* chap.5[2]22–23) reason is 'nothing but *reckoning* (that is adding and subtracting)'. He is quite insistent that '*addition* and *subtraction*' be considered the only two operations of reason: 'where these have no place, there reason has nothing at all to do' (ibid.). It is deliberately mechanical, indeed soulless, in the literal sense that Hobbes designed to be delinked from the scholastic soul. This was the reason that was meant to establish humans 'like masters and possessors of nature' in Descartes's (in)famous formula (*Discourse on Method*, part 6).[20] This same reason, for Hobbes, would enable them to develop the political technologies required to secure peace, starting with this 'artificial soul' that would make their living together possible, the *Leviathan*'s very first oxymoron for modern sovereignty. Or indeed the 'public conscience' (Hobbes, *L.* 3 and *L.* chap. 29[7]212). The scholastic soul, to the contrary, presumed humans' immersion in nature. Reason was its highest faculty, the *logos* that mirrored the cosmic *Logos*, the natural order, whose laws it could seize through this reflective relation (see chapter 1). It was a conduit to nature, not the instrument of its mastery. Moreover, it was the only faculty that distinguished a being human from all other forms of natural being, in this naturalist ontology where 'being' itself was coextensive with 'nature'. In the mechanistic worldview taking shape in the seventeenth century and that Hobbes (*L.,* p.3) carried over to this new realm, '[T]hat most rational and excellent work of nature' is still to be 'imitat[ed]' in creating that 'artificial animal' of the state; only at a remove, from that external, scientific, point of view that characterises the reason begat by the scientific revolution.

In sum, for Hobbes the soul is merely a creature of our fancy spawned by our anxious ill condition; our cognitive desire to find causes; and our haste to believe we have found them in the figments of our imagination thus (also materially) produced (see also *L*, chaps. 1 and 2). It is entirely reducible to and accountable by our material circumstances and our biological wirings. While the soul's nonexistence is the logical entailment of his argumentation, Hobbes's strategy was to not dismiss it outright, but rather to mobilise a notion to which his contemporaries were deeply attached, and to steep it in a mechanistic reason.[21] Hence he mechanises the soul to found modern sovereignty. In the last two parts of this chapter, I have shown how Hobbes corralled the conscience and mechanised the soul in order to neutralise two major sources of war, leaving only the body as the rightful foundations of modern politics. Having shown so far that the body is what remained after Hobbes's ground-clearing work, I now consider what it enabled him to build. In the following section I show that the body was not merely the site of a subjugation to the power of the nascent state for Hobbes. It also legitimised a singular right to stand up to it. In the chapter's final part I will show how, in separating out actions from the conscience by way of the body, Hobbes tilled the grounds for a new form of 'thought and action', raison d'état (Meinecke 1984, 210).

4. The Body in the Hobbesian Edifice of Rights

'[T]he common people's minds, unless they be tainted with dependence on the potent, or scribbled over with opinions of their doctors, are like clean paper', wrote Hobbes (L.chap.30 [6]221). Both the conceits of the conscience and the fanciful soul were such scribbles that Hobbes sought to erase. Stripping them back revealed a pure natural-cum-political motive, self-preservation. For Hobbes, in common with the other natural rights theorists of his time (see chapter 6), the urge to self-preserve is an unshakeable instinct and the engine of political construction. The desire to be safe is a natural desire that drives humans out of the state of nature to build the state, for these seventeenth-century thinkers. The construction of this desire as 'natural' is my focus in the next chapter. Here I consider how, for Hobbes, and only for him, these deeply embodied instincts also found a natural right to stand up against the state. The body thus also demarcates, for him, a site of political agency *for the subject* and not just for the state. The Hobbesian right of resistance establishes the state-subject security relation as a proper dialectic, where the two poles of the interaction push back against each other without collapsing into each other, and mutually constitute each other as a result. All the other early modern natural rights theorists, bar Spinoza, removed this right of resistance.

Hobbes's Singular Right of Resistance

'No man is oblig'd by any Contract whatsoever not to resist him who shall offer to kill, wound, or any other way hurt his Body' wrote Hobbes in *De Cive* (1642) (*DCi,*, chap.2[18]58–59). By way of the body he opened up a space within the sovereign law beyond which the subject's duty to obey ceases to apply. In the *Leviathan* (1651) this space is firmed up into positive 'liberty to disobey' the sovereign in a set of circumstances that are specified by way of the body:

> If the sovereign command a man (though justly condemned) to kill, wound or
> maim himself, or not to resist those that assault him, or to abstain from the use

of food, air, medicine or any other thing with which he cannot live, yet hath that man the liberty to disobey (*L.*,chap.21[12]142).

The sovereign maintains a corresponding corporeal 'power [. . .] of punishing' the resisting subject (Hobbes, *L.*,chap.18[14]115). While this may affect the right's realisation, given the asymmetrical power differential between the one (subject) and the many (the sovereign) that it is sovereignty's purpose to establish, it does not take away this right to resistance. The subjects' and the sovereign's 'liberties' or rights, to use a more contemporary vocabulary, stand in tension with and mirror one another.

This right of resistance to the state's command is an original and one of the most enduringly intriguing features of Hobbes's political thought. It set him apart both from his contemporaries and from early modern theories of natural rights.[22] While all hark back to the Thomist natural law of self-preservation, which I consider in chapter 6, Hobbes alone pushes it to the point that a person may seek escape punishment *even if* she is found guilty and 'justly condemned' by the law (Hobbes, *DCi.* chap.21[12]142). Already in his time Hobbes's contemporaries chaffed against the radical potential his right of resistance seemed to contain. The Church of England's archbishop John Bramhall saw it as laying the basis for a 'rebel catechism'. Though elements of it can be found in Hobbes's predecessor Hugo Grotius, they are short of amounting to a right (see Tuck 1979). This natural right to resistance was cast aside by subsequent contractualists including by John Locke, who drastically inverted this natural right to escape punishment into a natural right *to punish*, as we will see in chapter 5. Nor does it feature in Rousseau, for whom the citizen's submission to the general will is absolute, including when it prescribes the death penalty.

Contemporary Readings of Hobbes's 'Life as Right'

The Hobbesian right of resistance has constituted an enduring aporia for the classical scholarship that has primarily read him as a theorist of modern rights and obligations. It has been alternatively minimised and aggrandised. For Tuck (1979), it is a non-essential feature of Hobbes's thought, since it does not feature in the *Elements of Law* (1640). Yet for Jean Hampton (1986) it constitutes the weakness to the entire Hobbesian edifice of rights and duties (see also Finnis 2011; Gierke 1950). More recently and from within this Hobbesian rights scholarship, Susan Sreedhar (2010) has shown that this right is neither an anomaly nor a secondary feature of Hobbes's political thought. It is the exact counterpoint to a strong sovereignty, not unlike his private sphere, in Hobbes's binary mode of argumentation where what appears superficially in tension in fact makes for the enduring strength of his edifice.

Moreover, Hobbes's singular emphasis on life has been central to the identification of biopower as a distinctly modern power. Hobbes has loomed large over the problematisation of the biopolitical from the onset. He was the figure against which Foucault (2003, 18–41) was pushing back when he first articulated the need to develop conceptual tools better suited to capture the bottom-up, acephalic power that eluded the Hobbesian model. Georgio Agamben (1998) also charts to Hobbes the emergence of 'bare life' as the defining modern political object. Our first theorist of the state was also pivotal for Roberto Esposito (2008, 57), who drew out, more than Foucault did (but to develop the concept that Foucault had coined) Hobbes's role in establishing modern sovereignty, not as the counter to (which it still potentially was in Foucault), but instead as the 'first and most influential' biopolitical regime. 'In Hobbes', writes Esposito (2008, 57), 'not only does the question of the *consevatio vitaeo* [the preservation of life] re-enter fully in the political sphere, but it comes to constitute by far its most prevalent dimension.' Esposito underscores how, far from a naive celebration, the emphasis on life is co-eval with an emphasis on death, as two sides of a modern dialectic whose destructive potential has been born out by the genocidal projects of the twentieth century, here echoing Agamben (1998).[23] Third, Edward Cohen (2009, 3) tracks the emergence of the body that features at the core of modern medicine to Hobbes's right to 'self-defence'. Lastly, the interest in Hobbes's 'life as right' has continued to grow beyond both the biopolitical and the classical rights scholarship (Ribeiro 2011).

This sense of Hobbes's liminal role and of the importance of his singular emphasis on life is one I share with the biopolitics literature. Only the bodily optic brings two sets of caveats, contextual and substantial. First, Hobbes (*L.*, chap.15[6]192) emphasised life in order to de-emphasise the afterlife, since attempting to 'gain the perpetual felicity of heaven [was] frivolous'. The binary life-death has a third term in Hobbes, given the audience he is writing for. A closer attention to his historical context corrects a tendency to absolutise 'life' in this literature. Moreover, second, Hobbes's focus is not on all 'life' but distinctly on the human body. The distinction matters for two reasons. First, it matters in the context of appraising raison d'état, given the problematic vitalism that characterises some of the raison d'état scholarship (see Meinecke 1984, for example). Endowing states with an organic life is another illustration of the naturalisation of security I track. Second, it matters in view of the complex renegotiation of the relationship with nature that was underway. This will also be at the heart of the following chapter; for now, it is enough to note that that the human body was being foregrounded just as nature as a whole was being increasingly backgrounded, or indeed subjugated. This relationship between the human body qua natural object and nature at large is eclipsed by the biopolitical literature's focus on an under-specified notion of 'life'. Moreover, the central aporia that casts the sovereign and the subject's self-preservation in tension with each other, in focus in the rights scholarship, is largely lost from sight in the biopolitical one. In fact, the self-defence paradigm, to borrow Cohen's (2009) language, never fully yields a unitary self in Hobbes in the manner he assumes, since the body politic and the political subject are always 'defending' their 'selves' against each other. This ongoing, double movement of mutual constitution is my concern. My purpose is to return to this productive tension in Hobbes, while retaining from the biopolitics scholarship this emphasis on the aliveness of the human body, and, from the classic Hobbes scholarship, a focus on the initial transfer of rights that constituted political subjecthood in the first place.

Hobbes's 'Desperate Paradox': Negating Natural Rights to Found Political Rights

The starting point for Hobbes's (*L.*, chap.14[4]80) analysis of rights was a 'natural right of every man to everything, even to another's body'. To explore the effects of this unlimited, original natural right Hobbes imagines a discrete space: the state of nature. This trope, of his invention, would become the main vehicle of the universalisation of the right to security, well beyond the set of circumstances where Hobbes circumscribed it (the European wars of religion), because it rooted the problem that the Hobbesian state aimed to address—war—in a human nature.[24] Here, however, I am interested in another of the 'desperate paradoxes' that his state of nature contained, to borrow Skinner's (2008, 42) term. The consequence of beginning from an indeterminate right is that specific, determinate rights, including to security, must emerge from foregoing this limitlessness. It established natural and political rights in fundamentally antinomic terms. The first must be abandoned to generate the second. According to Richard Tuck (1988, 261), Hugo Grotius, who was an important influence for Hobbes, explicitly rejected the 'radical instability' that this antinomy bred (Tuck 1979). It was also, I suggest a profoundly generative tension.

The passage from an unlimited natural right to limited political rights hinges upon an original act of negation. Negating the universal natural right to everything, including another's body, yields particular political rights. Certainly, Hobbes lists a suite of natural laws (chapters 14 and 15 of the *Leviathan*) after which civil laws are to be fashioned. Only the possibility of doing so in the first place is unlocked by the contract. This negating is what makes possible the individual's inscription into a system of collective rights. 'The renunciation of the right to all things entails the recognition of the rights of others', as David Levine (1978, 201) has put it. It is the condition of possibility for the state to exist as the place of and the guarantor for collective political rights. Hobbes's paradox is profoundly fruitful.

The category of the negative thus accomplishes considerable if little-noticed (but for Levine 1978) work in Hobbes's state of nature. It also plays an important role in other parts of his thought, notably in what I term his method of 'privation' with which he develops his natural philosophy. In his *De Corpore* (the first of the two volumes of his philosophical system, published in 1656), Hobbes set out to redescribe all that exists in strictly corporeal terms. To do so he devises another thought experiment, that consists in negating, or 'annihilating' in his term, all pre-existing concepts in the mind, such as space and time, in order to consider what is left 'to reason upon' once these have been stripped back. Hobbes describes the method in the following terms:

> 'In the teaching of natural philosophy I cannot begin better [. . .] than from privation, that is, from feigning the World to be annihilated', and from there 'to as[k] what would remain for any Man (whom onely I except from this Universal annihilation of things) to reason upon'. (*DC*, chap.7[1]67)

In the Hobbesian state of nature, the body sets in motion the original renouncing that generates the polity. It is precisely because it is the right 'even to another's body' that the original natural right must be negated, since it runs up against that other person's natural duty to self-preserve (*L.*, chap.14[4]80). The body in this appositive clause is in fact what triggers the entire mechanism of transfer of rights that founds the state.

The body, however, also establishes the outer limit to this productive original renunciation. If renouncing one's unlimited natural right creates political rights, then the body, in turn, limits this renouncing. It ensures that, if the negation of the right to 'everything' is necessary to found the state, not 'everything' is given up to the state in the process of constituting it. Hobbes (*L.*, chap. 15[22]97) writes: '[a]s it is necessary for all men that seek peace to lay down certain rights of nature (that is to say, not to have liberty to do all they list), so it is necessary for man's life to retain some [rights]'. The body provides the benchmark for establishing what rights cannot be renounced. Hobbes (*L.*, chap.15 [22]97) specifies 'the right to govern their own bodies, [to] enjoy air, water, motion, ways to go from place to place, and [to] all things else without which a man cannot live'. The natural governance of one's own body affords the gauge as to which rights are to be withheld from political rule in the process of founding it. Moreover, the body, the 'thing' that everyone naturally has, sets the reciprocity condition for the contract, since it requires that no person may reserve for himself or herself a right which he or she is 'not content [that it] should be reserved to every one of the rest' (Hobbes, *L.*, chap.15[22]97).

Somatic Security as the Subject's Exceptional Right

The mechanism that generates the polity is thus a double movement, of renouncing an unlimited natural right, but then excepting the body from this forgoing. Several consequences follow from the central role Hobbes grants the body. First, it establishes security as the exceptional, unconditional right. All other political rights (including to property, as we will see in chapter 6) hinge upon this initial renunciation. Because it is about the body, because it is a somatic security, it is both the only pre-political right and, second, the right that, subsequently, the state most needs to attend to, since, third, the state's inability to guarantee it terminates the contract. Hobbes stipulates the conditions of the contract's annulment. They centre on the body:

> A covenant not to defend myself from force by force is void [. . .] no man can transfer or lay down his right to save himself from death, wounds and imprisonment (the avoiding whereof is the only one of laying down any right) (Hobbes, *L.*, chap.14[29]87)

Somatic security both dictates the terms of the contract's suspension and, fourth, it lays the basis of the subject's right to resist the sovereign. By way of the body, Hobbes ultimately posited security as the absolute right of the modern political subject. Moreover, he theorised what was also emerging out of the play of political and diplomatic practices in the late sixteenth and seventeenth centuries, where security was taking shape as the *telos* of this new political form, the state, and of the new form of reason it was bound up with, raison d'état. It is to these that I now turn.

5. Staking Out the Space of Modern Sovereignty

Raison d'État or the State's Political Technology

The monarch who embodied the constitutive role of the Hobbesian differentiation between a within and a without was to be found not in England, where, with Henry VIII, personal and religious motives were entirely folded together in the liminal phases of state-making, but in France and with Henri IV, the first modern statesman by this distinction. As king of Navarre, then–Henri III had led the Protestant rebellion in France. Upon stepping on the throne of a Catholic country in 1589, he laid down his arms and set aside his private 'opinions' to be able to create the conditions of its peace. He proclaimed the Edict of Nantes (1598), one of the war of religions' first peace settlements that established the terms of a Protestant and Catholic cohabitation within one realm. Only he did so after converting to the majority creed, so as to be better able to incarnate it. His conversion, perceived as a betrayal by extremists on both sides, is difficult to reduce to self-interest, given that he had sacrificed what mattered most to a believer in the religious wars and for which he had personally gone to battle, his conscience. Henri IV was murdered by a fanatic Catholic in 1610, in the name of his own conscience. Hobbes was twenty-two and in Paris them; perhaps the 'good king', as he was known, afforded him his model of a public conscience. In foregoing his beliefs, Henri IV enacted on his own person the distinction between a private sphere and a discrete sphere of the interests of the realm. He converted, not because he was suddenly more persuaded by Catholicism, but because, as a Catholic, he would be better able to represent the latter. Henri IV's conversion evinces, rather, another kind of interest altogether, that was political and collective rather than individual, and that would help define the modern sense of 'public' (see Meinecke 1984). These were the interests of a raison d'état.[25]

This new, highly rational, disinterested interest indexed a new empirical reality, a political 'thing' of genuinely novel kind that was not the old known 'thing' (*res*) of the traditional res publica. This new political object was the state. It emerged coextensively with a new form of reason, practical; decidedly un-theological; a reason *of* the state; of the 'France' Henri IV sought to unify and pacify, rather than of his private conscience, like Luther's. Raison d'état was nothing short of a new mode of 'thought and action' (Meinecke 1984, 210; see also Butterfield 1975; Foucault 2009). It was a product of the inversion of the schemes of time that we considered earlier, in that it brought into focus a secular temporal horizon proper to the state. Henri IV's motto, 'the two [France and Navarre, his own kingdom] shield the one', (*duo praetendit unus*) encapsulates, first, the process of unification by which the single state emerged out of the suturing together of multiple medieval kingdoms. Second, it renders the extent to which this king understood this process to be both inward- and outward-turned, at a time when the most powerful force shaping Europe was a Spanish Catholic universalism. Spain was unhesitant to stoke the fires of France's internal disorder by supporting the other creed (the Huguenots), both under Henri IV and after his assassination, to further its own imperial ambitions on France's eastern and northern borders. Henri IV thus embodied a logic that would be only fully born out half a century later, when this process of internal unification and the strengthening of external borders would come together at Westphalia as the two sides of state-making. Raison d'état was the line-drawing political technology that etched in the public-private distinction upon which this ordering work rested. The epitome of raison d'état was Henri IV's grandson, Louis XIV. In him the political and public interest coincided exactly by his establishing the exact equivalence between his reason(s) and those of the state, when he proclaimed *to be* the state ('*l'état, c'est moi*'). However preposterous it might seem today, the performance realised the distinction that was being drawn around the same time by Hobbes by way of the body, between public and private interests. The latter could still be collective, as we have seen (the interests of one faith); only they could be not those of a commonwealth, of a space of a living together, Hobbes would show, since nothing could guarantee that they not be ruled by the dictates of the individual conscience.

Raison d'état was a genuine invention, on par with the telescope. Nothing short of a new instrument was required to secure a peace that had eluded Europe for over a century. Like the telescope, it was a collective creation. It was honed over the late sixteenth and the first half of the seventeenth centuries by a series of statesmen and stateswomen—Henri IV and perhaps Elizabeth I; the Cardinal de Richelieu, who sought to steer Henri IV's less agile son, Louis XIII, through the pull of dynastic and personal interests upon him and who unified France in a far less gentle fashion than Henri IV; and Louis XIV, who achieved the monopolisation of the use of force begun by Richelieu. Raison d'état was also just as scandalous to its times as the discoveries to which the telescope led. A late sixteenth-century pope (Pius V) declared raison d'état to be *ratio diaboli* rather than *ratio status*, the devil's very own reason (cited in Foucault 2009, 241). 'Statolatry' was an term coined in 1637 by another opponent who recoiled before a new way of thinking that, in holding up this new thing, the state, and the defence of its interests above all else, threatened to empty out the skies (ibid., 242). It was seen as the practical counterpart to a just as morally bankrupt 'Machiavellism'. Raison d'état historian Friedrich Meinecke (1984, 345) observed how it 'forced itself in like a foreign body, and succeeded in breaking into a predominant mode of thought which was entirely opposed to it'. It was morally abhorrent, then and indeed still now, because it radically reconfigured the relations between politics and morality. It established politics as a discrete sphere of action, with its own dynamics and its own laws, which were not those of the individual conscience. It ruptured the automatic alignment of the universal, the rational, and the good in which centuries of Western moral philosophy were steeped. It repurposed practical reason, attaching it to a good that was neither fully universal nor completely individual, that was particular yet collective: what was good for the state. But raison d'état was also scandalous, I suggest, because it revealed that the body politic, which had long been considered natural, as we will see in chapter 4, was but a human-made object, and a fragile one at that. That it was human crafted was why for Hobbes (*L.*, 3), it could be injected with an 'artificial soul', like any other 'automata (engines that move themselves by springs and wheels as doth a watch)'. For what could such a mode of action without a conscience look like? Like the movements of a machine. With the mechanistic imagery by which he conjured this new, human-crafted object, the state, Hobbes was merely taking this conscience-less mode of action to its logical if extreme conclusion.

The Treaty of Westphalia scaled up to the relations between European sovereigns the public-private distinction that were being worked through by Hobbes within the conceptual space of the state. The sovereigns' *foro interno* analogised the 'inside' of their respective states, which were being cast beyond one another's reach, and delineated through a series of negotiations that were driven by the calculations of raison d'état. Raison d'état afforded a common language for this peace-making enterprise. It begat the first international relations discourse as a security discourse. Of the treaty that brought an end to Europe's religious wars Koselleck (1988, 42) wrote: 'By virtue of absolute sovereignty each State's interior was clearly delimited against the interior of its neighbours. The conscience of a sovereign was absolutely free but his jurisdiction was confined to the inner space of the state he represented'. Without lay the new 'unified plane' that would become the European state system (ibid.) This space too was deeply Hobbesian; not because of his so-called pessimistic view of human nature, as the tired textbook reading runs; nor because of his bellicose metaphor of the states as gladiators pointing their weapons at one another; but rather because of the far more decisive, properly constitutive gesture, that Hobbes theorised and Louis XIV fully realised, that cordoned off private interests to create a common space. In the following chapter I will show how Hobbes further untied the old knot of morality and universality by counterposing an ethics bound by sovereignty. However, in chapter 5 I will then show how Locke retrieved the conscience and the universality to which it lays claims for modern politics. These two forms of morality have stood at loggerheads in the international system ever since.

Responsibility without Guilt: The Structure of State Action

Hobbes's corporeal ontology furnishes a specific way of parsing the relations between politics and morality that were being reconfigured in the practice of politics by raison d'état. For Meinecke (1984, 210–16) Hobbes occupies an ambivalent status in the history of the development of the concept on account of his materialism. The latter largely flushed out any form of emotional attachment to that emergent political form, the state. Hobbes's mechanical state, for Meinecke (1984, 215), 'while it can call for blind obedience' from its subjects, 'cannot require from them that devotion founded on faith and that attachment to the State, which might be expected from them by the truly living and personal

State, even from the *virtù*-republic of Machiavelli'. Moreover, the right of resistance represents, for Meinecke, the weakest point of Hobbes's theory, since the Hobbesian subject is ultimately wedded to their life, not to the state. Yet could this author of a treatise on the passions (*De Homine*, 1658) really have overlooked the subject's affective ties to the state? Bringing together the two raison d'état historians, Meinecke (1984) and Koselleck (1988), and their readings of Hobbes takes us a first step out of this impasse. A second is afforded by attending to the role of the body in the Hobbesian edifice of rights.

Contra (what he sees as) the cold utilitarianism of the Hobbesian subject, Meinecke (1998, 216, 194) underlines the 'love of the thing itself' that animated the original crafters of the state, even the 'secret sublimity' that enabled them to set aside the qualms of their conscience. Koselleck (1988, 19–20), for his part, explores how raison d'état reworked the affective relation at the heart of the Christian notion of the conscience, 'the intrinsic relation between responsibility and guilt' (see also Balibar 2014b). He analyses the birth of the state as a transformation of the 'structures of responsibility' underwriting subject-formation in the seventeenth century (Koselleck 1988, 19). He showed how these evolved from a 'manifold if loose structure' where the subject had their place 'as a member of a Church, as dependent vassal, in the framework of their own political institutions or of the feudal order of estates' (see also chapter 4), into a single framework whereby the 'responsibility for peace and order' was taken out of the subjects' hands and placed into the absolute sovereign's (Koselleck 1988, 19). This, in turn, ruptured the knot tying together guilt and responsibility in the individual conscience, and enabled them to be reallocated across the state and the subject, respectively. Subjectively 'the ruler was freed from all guilt, but he accumulated all responsibility' (Koselleck 1988, 20). In this way, starting from the conscience, Koselleck identified the specific affective ferment in the actions undertaken in the name of raison d'état: a distinctly modern political, depersonalised, and a-religious form of responsibility-without-guilt. 'The innocence of power' is another Koselleckian (1988, 20) term for it. Such an objectified, guiltless sense of responsibility may seem alien, even troubling, seen from the conscience. But this viewpoint was precisely what was being replaced by another, that of raison d'état: a reason that sees from the state.

Hobbes's separation of embodied actions from the conscience supplied the philosophical justification for this redistribution of guilt and responsibility across the subject and the state, respectively. By way of the body Hobbes delineated the space of the commonwealth as a realm of accountable actions, hence as the site of political responsibility, from the private sphere of the conscience, where the subject is free to contend with his or her guilt. Moreover, this differentiation of responsibility from guilt carries over to Hobbes's scheme of representation. The subjects remain the authors of the actions they have authorised the sovereign to undertake in their names. Consequently, they bear the guilt for the long-term effects of the actions for which their state, not them, is responsible. This affective structure continues to underpin the allocation of agency and responsibility at play in the policies of contemporary states. For example, it is expressed in the schemes of recognition whereby states take responsibility for past wrongs to their subjects, but where the guilt continues to be borne by the subjects, and regularly resurfaces in contemporary cultures. The Australian state's 2008 apology to the 'Stolen Generation' of Indigenous Australians is a case in point. This is also what enables the delinking of symbolic apologies, proffered by the state, from monetary compensations, whose costs are borne by the subjects (as taxpayers).

Raison d'état and Hobbes's political scientific reason were two spatial, line-drawing rationalities taking shape in the seventeenth century in theory and in practice. Louis XIV, also a man of his times, conceived his foreign policy in geometric terms, and specifically in the form of the hexagon he set out to shape his state into, in pushing back against Spain on its east and north. He largely succeeded, bequeathing France its modern borders and its nickname (*l'hexagone*). Hobbes-the-scientist conceived the body as a spatial object, a 'thing extended' or placed in space (*res extensa*). While he admired Harvey, the science of space was where his heart lay. Geometry was 'virtually the only precise science'; indeed, 'the only [one] that hath pleased God hitherto to bestow on mankind' and the one he was in charge of imparting to the future monarch Charles II (Hobbes was Charles II's tutor in geometry) (*L.*, chap.4[12]19). Geometry pared all bodies down to points moving along lines and across planes. In this way, 'the Earth is called a point, and the Way of its yearly revolution the *Ecliptick Line*' (Hobbes, *DC*, chap.13[12]81). A line, in turn, is 'made by the motion of a point' or body, and a plane or 'superfice' as 'made by the motion of a line' (Hobbes, cited in Shapin and Schaffer 2011, 149). Geometry thus afforded Hobbes the terms and the tools for the perspective he designed for the state, namely, to see the subjects from without and afar, and to see their actions only. It featured them as points moving across the plane of the polity. His geometrical reason sustained his corporeal ontology. His distinction between actions and the conscience worked like a compass to delineate the closed space of the law.

*

To see like a state, for Hobbes, was to see the challenges of holding together widely diverging opinions and allegiances into a political whole. In this chapter I have shown how, in setting out to address now long-gone wars, Hobbes formulated the defining problematique of political modernity, how to prevent differences in opinion from tipping into war. Such differences are unavoidable for Hobbes since they are rooted in the endless diversity of embodied human passions. The problem was not to prevent disagreements, with the state or with one another, but rather to forestall the risk of conflict that inheres in difference. To secure the subjects against this ever-present threat was to build a viable common space where disagreeing peacefully was possible. Hence to see like a state was also to look away from the subjects' inner sanctum, from the conscience and the soul; and to hold only their actions, hence their bodies, in sight. Hobbes spelled out the corporeal ontology that still underwrites contemporary border protection policies, which lead today's traveller through a maze of corridors swept through with sensors and biometric technologies in an ever-increasing number of airports (see Müller 2010; Epstein 2007; 2008b). 'For the use of laws (which are but rules authorised)', wrote Hobbes (*L.*, chap.30[21]229), 'is not to bind the people from all voluntary actions, but to direct and keep them in such motion as not to hurt themselves by their own impetuous desires, rashness or indiscretion, as hedges are set, not to stop travellers, but to keep them in the way.' The surveillance state, with its electronic personal data-gathering hedges, would hardly disagree. After all, the body-scanner at the security checkpoint is looking only at your body (see Magnet and Rodgers 2012; Hall 2007). But Hobbes adds something else; something especially precious for the critical study of surveillance. For him, the logic of transparency that has powered the relentless expansion for surveillance technologies through private and public spaces alike, at work in the airport scanner also reveals a key flaw. It ruins the necessary equilibrium between private spaces of retreat and public spaces of coming together. Especially unwise is how it encroaches upon the subject's deeply embodied, natural right to resist the state. Insofar as it is embodied and thus ineradicable, this is, for Hobbes, bound to backfire sooner or later.

By way of the body Hobbes drew a sharp line between the private (but not necessarily individual) space of the subject, and the public space of the state. He configured the bipolar spatial ordering of modern politics. On the side of the state, the Hobbesian distinction shored up the new form of reason that was taking shape, raison d'état. This was a line-drawing, practical political rather than philosophical reason; quite different to the medieval, Thomist reason, which had previously afforded the main guide in the realms all at once of ethics, religion, and politics. This new reason established politics as a distinct sphere of action. This reason *of* the state begat the state as both an enclosed space, with an inside clearly delineated against an outside, and as the object of security, that which requires being secured at all costs (rather than ruled in other ways). Moreover, by separating out actions from the conscience and casting only the former in focus for the state, Hobbes furnished the affective structure for the new type of rational action taken in the name of raison d'état. To the acting state attaches a responsibility-without-guilt, while the thinking subjects bears the guilt thus split off from these actions. The quality of ruthlessness we still associate with raison d'état is rooted here. Hobbes showed why securing the state as the site of peaceful coexistence despite differences of opinion required this unnatural—mechanical, even—certainly dispassionate, reason. Nothing short of an 'artificial soul' was required to hold at bay the passions that seemed invariably to stick to the natural faculty of reason (Hobbes, *L.*, 3). This unnatural soul was state sovereignty. Having shown in this chapter how Hobbes paved the way for raison d'état's distinct form of responsibility-without-guilt by separating out actions and the conscience, I will show in chapter 5 how John Locke then undid Hobbes's radical arrangement. He returned both guilt and responsibility to the individual conscience, which he moved back to the heart of modern politics.

On the side of the subject, in cordoning off the conscience Hobbes also reclaimed it as a clean space to be shielded from the relentless politicking over it that had run England into war. For Hobbes (*L.*, chap.30[30]233), indeed 'there is no natural court of justice but in the conscience only, where not man, but God reigneth'. Hobbes disarmed and depoliticised the conscience in order to restore it as the protected space of solitary reflection. By redrawing the line between this *foro interno* and the *foro externo* of collective life, Hobbes (*L.*, chap.15[36]99) returned the conscience to its original purpose in the Protestant tradition, as the space of both an unmediated relationship with God, but also of critical thinking; the place from which to critique existing orders, political and epistemological. But to establish the conscience as the natural court of justice was also to cast it beyond his concern, which was with the courts where humans adjudicated. These required being constructed. Lastly, with his right of resistance rooted in the body, Hobbes carved out a space within his legal edifice for a real political agency, qua resistance.

Hobbes, then, corralled the conscience and he materialised the soul by way of the body. Yet his solution to the problem of war raised new questions with regards to this agency. For, having cast out the traditional bedrocks of human agency, the conscience and the soul, what could this new agency rest upon? Moreover, how did Hobbes apprehend the will, the subject's ability to choose and act, that was traditionally considered to be lodged in the non-corporeal parts of a human being? I examine these questions in the following chapter.

3

Denaturalising Security

> The *pacts* and *covenants* by which the parts of this body politic were
> first made, set together, and united, resemble that *fiat*, or the *let us*
> *make man*, pronounced by God in the creation.
>   —Hobbes, *Leviathan*, pp.3–4

Hobbes was a theorist of the human ability to choose and to craft. The centrality
of choice to his thought has been underlined by two influential traditions on
either side of the northern Atlantic, rational choice theory, and a German political thought that has foregrounded his importance as a founder of political
modernity. Only, with regards to the former, the choice Hobbes honed was not
reducible to the rational actor's tossing up her preferences.[1] It was a foundational
choice, which established the space of modern politics as the place where natural and social determinations could be escaped, as a space that was not given by
nature but required being instead carefully constructed and therefore chosen.[2]
The German tradition, for its part, did capture this constitutive level at which
Hobbes's choice operated; in reading him, as Carl Schmitt did (1985; 2008), as
having laid bare the foundational 'decision' that undergirds the task of political
ordering. But Schmitt's will was of the state, of raison d'état. It was a strangely
disembodied will, emptied of the corporeal moorings Hobbes was at pains to
emphasise. Leo Strauss (1963; and 1965 to a lesser extent) also explicitly brack-
eted these embodied, subjective dimensions of Hobbes's thought (and his ontology at large), even while Strauss cast Hobbes as the founder of the rights of the
modern subject. Rational choice theory and Schmitt each focus, schematically,
on one of the two poles, the state and the subject, that I bring together under the
lens of the body in order to track how they were first constituted qua the poles of
the founding modern political relation.[3] In this chapter I retrieve the Hobbesian
choice from these two equally (though differently) problematic scholarships.
I resituate it within his core problematique of political constitution, of how best
to craft the state. What Hobbes sought to nail by way of the contract was the
agential fulcrum of life in common. It was the distinctly human political agency
that makes constructing this collective life possible at all, and that is also needed
to improve it. I read Hobbes as the first constructivist, in that his writings contain
constructivism's founding and most precious insight, that politics is collectively

Birth of the State. Charlotte Epstein, Oxford University Press (2021). © Oxford University Press.
DOI: 10.1093/oso/9780190917623.001.0001

constructed, and therefore always, at some level, chosen, such that it can also be unchosen. The agency that concerned Hobbes was that of the new a-religious, distinctly political sphere of actions that he helped stake out (see chapter 2).

Humans, for Hobbes, unlike other natural beings, craft their worlds. He broke with a long scholastic tradition in establishing the capacity for wilful, deliberate action, rather than reason, as the defining feature of being human.[4] The contract is its quintessential expression. Hobbes does not invent the device, but he carries it over into thought from the English battlefields.[5] Only human actions, for Hobbes, are also always *re*actions to embodied processes and stimuli. Humans, like all other bodies, are subjected to the laws of nature. How, then, can they escape the natural determinations of their physiology? How can they act in a wilful, chosen manner, if they are ruled by the rules governing their bodies? This is one of his 'numerous contradictions' I explore in this chapter (Strauss 1963, x). For Hobbes was just as committed to a thoroughgoing materialism, for the strategic reasons I analysed in the previous chapter, as he was to a voluntarism with which he drew out the genuinely creative potential of human agency. Starting from the body at the centre of his thought, I read this as another profoundly generative tension. Hobbes's efforts to reconcile a dedicated voluntarism with a materialist determinism helped produce the corporeal ontology of modern politics that I map in this book. Its crucial effect was to establish security as the first absolute natural right of the modern subject. I continue in this second chapter on security to parse its original naturalisation in the seventeenth century, by attending to the different kinds of natures, including human, by which it was wrought.

The chapter unfolds in four parts. In the first part, I show how Hobbes carved open a space beyond nature for modern politics. Politics is unnatural for Hobbes; the product of what he termed 'artifice'. His work of *de-naturing* is the focus of part 1. I will show how, in Hobbes's political thought, two natures—the old nature of natural law, and the new nature of modern science—stood in tension with each other. Politics, for Hobbes, requires, first, humans to pull away from nature and its determinations in order to make room for choice. But the Hobbesian choice is primarily embodied, not rational. It requires, second, a peculiar form of human agency that is 'not *un* natural but that is nevertheless distinguished from or discontinuous with all other kinds of natural agency', as Annabel Brett (2011, 3) nicely put it. I show how Hobbes's corporeal ontology functioned, in fact, as an anti-naturalism that carved open a space beyond nature for building the state. Artifice is the focus of the chapter's second part. I chart how Hobbes set out to circumscribe the human agency of political construction in the creative act of naming, and in the collective act of contracting. I show how, unlike Aristotle's 'art', Hobbes's 'artifice' captured a capacity to create fictions and machines.

Whereas in the first two parts I apprehend his work of denaturing, in the third part I consider Hobbes's epistemological efforts to *denaturalise* the taken-for-granted assumptions that supported the dogmatisms of his age. Hobbes's own critical undertaking comes into focus, together with his main instrument, his nominalism. I illustrate the critical resources it contains, in two ways. First, I show how Hobbes deconstructed universal norms. In this, his mode of thinking holds significant promise for contemporary critical scholarship, and specifically for postcolonial thought. Hence whereas in the previous chapter, Hobbes's most successful universalisation, the state, was in focus, here I show how he also equips political thought for de-universalising universalist projections. Hobbes also takes us back to the linguistic origins of constitutive theorising. Second, I analyse his proto-feminist critique of patriarchal ordering, where he showed. not only how this form of ordering one out of many possible kinds, but that it was not nature's; that it was a matter of construction and thus ultimately choice. Hobbes reminds us that to show that an existing political structure is constructed is to underscore that it is both willed and contingent; not necessary, unavoidable, or indeed stable. It is to draw out that it could have been—and still can be—configured differently. Hence returning to Hobbes serves to reinvest the radical potential that inheres in underlining the wilful dimension at the heart of political modernity. It serves to recharge the responsibility that comes with recognising the role of the human hand in creating its entrenched inequities. It helps short-circuit two contemporary reflexes: of either denying this choice, in order to shed responsibility for these structural inequities; or instead of individualising it, to further entrench these—or both. In the fourth part, however, I show how Hobbes ran up against his own limits in his deconstructive, critical enterprise, and that limit was the body. I show that, ultimately, Hobbes, too, naturalises security by way of the body, that is, with the very same vehicle of his denaturalising undertaking. Nonetheless, Hobbes is crucial to engage with because he draws out how the quintessentially modern commitment to critique was an epistemological project that doubled up as a political one from the onset. It aimed to release the play of choice underwriting political ordering.

Two methodological specifications before I begin. First, the relations between the scientific and the political subject are central to this chapter. Yet in the contemporary division of academic labour, the former has tended to be the purview of histories of science and philosophy, whereas the latter has been political theory's concern. Both figures of subjecthood are in fact central to Hobbes's thought. Bringing the two back together restores the force of his critique. Second, I consider the body, primarily, as a natural object, a piece of nature. I will show that the body qua natural object often stands in for nature at large in Hobbes's thought. The body became the synecdoche for nature at time when the human-nature relation was being thoroughly renegotiated. Third, the body is strictly the stuff that the polity is made of, for Hobbes, as we have seen. Finally and consequently, it is the location of the will, hence of the human ability to choose.

Unpacking the embodied nature of Hobbesian agency, exactly how our physiological buttons are pushed, is crucial to understanding where he wedges in choice. His physiology of action is therefore in focus in the chapter.

1. Denaturing Order: Staking Out the Space of Modern Politics

Hobbes opened up a *beyond nature* for modern politics. To be sure, and in keeping with his times, Hobbes invoked nature's laws as guidelines for building the state. The '*art*' that crafts the modern state 'imitat[es] that rational and most excellent work of nature' (Hobbes *L.*, pg.3). But he also broke with two millennia of political thought, and with the other natural rights theorists of his time, in demonstrating the necessity to leave nature behind to be able to do so.[6] For that art also 'goes yet further' (Hobbes *L.*, pg.3). Hobbes showed that the political 'nature' of Aristotle's animals is, rather, an artifice that requires being carefully and intentionally constructed. With Hobbes (*L.*, pg.3), the modern 'animal-machine' of statehood can no longer be built in nature, it has to be built *out of* it, in both senses of leaving it, and from its raw materials and forces. He carved open the plane upon which modern politics could take place as the product of choice. It is a 'distinctive sphere of being contradistinguished against natural being', in Brett's (2011, 7) words. This distancing is achieved by building failure into the workings of self-preservation, that natural impulse we considered in the previous chapter.

Human beings, for Hobbes (*L.*chap.18 [11]114), inherently desire security insofar as they have a 'natural and necessary appetite for [their] own conservation'. Crucially however, Hobbes renders this natural desire for security, by itself, ineffectual. Individuals' spontaneously coming together yields only chaos:

> And there be never so great a multitude; yet if their actions be directed according to their particular judgements, and particular appetites, they can expect thereby no defence, no protection, neither against a common enemy, nor against the injuries of one another. For being distracted in opinions concerning the best use and application of their strength, they do not help but hinder one another; and reduce their strength by mutual opposition to nothing: whereby they are easily, not only subdued by a very few that agree together; but also when there is no common enemy they make war upon each other, for their particular interests. (Hobbes, *L.*, chap.17[4]107)

This description of how attempted cooperation tips into war is a key moment in the Hobbesian logic. First, it underscores innate social impulses, derived from the natural *telos*, self-preservation. Humans in a 'multitude' are spontaneously drawn to cooperate by the prospects of enhancing their mutual 'defence' and 'protection'. Hence for Hobbes (and contra caricatures of his thought), humans inherently want cooperation. However, and this is key, these instincts are powerless, self-defeating even. They 'do not help but hinder one another'. Without a common compass humans remain 'distracted in opinions', 'directed' by the many 'particular judgments' spawned by as many consciences. A precursor to 'the mob', the notion of 'multitude', which would gain increasing currency throughout the seventeenth century and would be taken up by Spinoza notably, serves here to compound the destructive effects of these cooperative instincts. There is no natural path towards cooperation, for Hobbes. That road needs to be chosen and built.

Negating Nature: Desire as the Motor of Political Construction

Hobbes's crucial move is to have lodged the failure of cooperation in the very desire for it. This failure drove the initial wedge between an animal 'ill-condition which man by mere nature is actually placed in' and a political condition that is to be constructed (Hobbes, L., chap.13[13]78). It stretched the terms of Aristotle's oxymoron to a breakpoint, insofar as our animality becomes, with Hobbes, that which strains our ability to live together, rather than what naturally inclines us towards it. It punctured that uninterrupted weft of being that extended from nature to the polity, the great 'cosmo-theological continuum' as Foucault (2009, 234) called it, upon which the traditional oxymoron rested. It set in motion the pulling away from 'mere nature', a denaturing, in order to found the polity. Pushing against their own natural being tipped human beings into another kind of being that is not natural, but that is not unnatural either: political being. Building the need to move beyond it within nature itself opened up a new plane, contiguous with nature but discrete from it, upon which humans could construct themselves as political animals after all. It drew the original boundary between the two spaces, of nature and of artifice or politics, and their corresponding states.[7] This natural failing triggers the process of political construction.

Humans are wired to self-preserve, and this primordial instinct holds their other more aggressive instincts in check. A key question that has occupied the Hobbes scholarship is whether this natural law prescribing to humans 'the introduction of that restraint upon themselves' constitutes an adequate basis for developing a 'theory of obligation' that is robust enough to sustain life in common (Hobbes, L., chap.17[1]106; and Warrender 1957). In political theory, Howard Warrender (1957) defended it by showing that Hobbes's natural law obliges individual persons to seek peace first and foremost, and thus to self-restrain in order to achieve it.[8] Instead contemporary natural law scholars such as John Finnis

(2011, 208) see Hobbes's state of nature to be but 'a vacuum of law and obliga-tion' (see also Gierke 1950). What Hobbes's (*L.*, chap.15[2]89) nature does not feature, and that sets him apart from all other early modern theorists of natural rights (see chapter 6), is a duty to spontaneously abstain from that which belongs to another, since, for him, everyone has a natural right to everything. His place in the natural rights scholarship is contested on this score.[9] I invert the traditional readings of Hobbes that consider his state of nature merely as a set of background assumptions containing his views about human nature and focus on his political philosophy alone (as in Strauss 1963; 1965). Instead I begin from the Hobbesian conceptions of nature that begat it.

Considering this primordial instinct to self-preserve on its own terms, as a natural instinct, reveals a productive tension in Hobbes's nature. Indeed, how can instincts self-restrict, insofar as self-limitation is a reflexive, rational, and thus non-instinctual act? In rejecting the soul, which was also the seat of reason, Hobbes also deprived himself of the scholastic scheme for transcending instincts.[10] Hobbes's contradiction, or confusion in kinds, was rapidly picked up by other early modern theorists of self-preservation. Locke (cited in Lastlett 1988, 80) simply dismisses Hobbes, whose natural laws 'are not properly laws'. Spinoza builds on a Hobbesian concept, the *conatus*, to correct Hobbes's error. He extends the *conatus*, or drive to thrive, well beyond instincts (and notably to the mind), and has it carrying human beings (more or less) seamlessly from nature to the polity. By the same token, he sutured back together the smooth con-tinuum that Hobbes ruptured. Locke would do away with Hobbes's contradiction altogether by creating an additional state, the state of war, to which he relegated conflict, thereby rescuing instincts intact, and an innocent state of nature with it (see chapter 5). For Rousseau, Hobbes's error was to have mistakenly fitted into nature traits, such as competition or diffidence, that presumed intersubjective interactions, hence an already constituted polity. He did not contest Hobbes's dif-ferentiation of a political from a natural space. That, by the eighteenth century, the question had become a matter of determining which trait belonged to which illustrates the extent to which the Hobbesian dichotomy, of nature and the polity, had become entrenched.

Hobbesian instincts, then, must self-negate to self-realise. As in the previous chapter, I want to suggest another reading of what his contradiction achieves. These instincts must become something other than what they are. They must denature themselves. Otherwise, 'nature itself is destroyed' (Hobbes, *EoLi* chap.14[12]56). This is indeed a contradiction, and a profoundly productive one: it is a dialectic tension. Here again, Hobbes ushers in the negative—a cate-gory Spinoza was altogether uneasy with, as Hegel would show—at the heart of nature itself. Hobbes carved out a place for the negative at the heart of positivity, of the given, within the original realm of 'data' (etymologically the genitive plural of *do, das, dare*, to give). This natural self-negation triggers the moving out of nature, the process of denaturing that begat modern sovereignty. Pushing back against the immediacy of our natural, embodied experience opens up the plane of mediacy that makes culture and thus politics possible. Hence the negative, in Hobbes, is not simply the pessimistic or dark vision of human nature he tends to be reduced to in disciplinary histories. Fortunately, these textbook narratives go, the wheels of international relations could keep turning because other views of human nature were available; in particular, a Lockean one, which salvaged the prospects for cooperation, and a Kantian one, which rescued the possibility of a post-statist international politics (Wight 1992; Wendt 1999). Rather, the negative is an ontological category, a non-being (see also Epstein 2018). Here, it designates a lack in nature, an incompleteness, *what is not there but should be* for self-preservation to be able to realise itself. What the 'ill-' to Hobbes's ill-condition designates, I suggest, this lack in nature. This natural shortcoming makes room for, beggars even, the political.

Humans as Crafters

The natural desire for security, in failing, gives rise to a new natural-cum-political desire *to become* a subject. This desire is the motor of political construction. If 'peace without subjection' were conceivable, Hobbes (*L.*, chap.17[4]107) ends the passage I quoted above, then there would be no need to subject to a common power, no need for subjecthood, no desire *of* the political subject. Hobbesian 'subjection' is the condition of possibility for peace and security. He means the term literally, as the crafting of political subjects. Becoming a political subject is a purposeful project, a deliberate self-creation, and it is grounded in desire. 'Humans' make themselves into 'subjects' by wilfully subjecting to the state, that 'gimcrack contraption', to borrow Richard Flathman's (1993, 8) juicy term, that they also fabricate by joining together their natural powers. 'Thomas Hobbes is first and foremost a theorist of individual human beings as the *Makers* of themselves and their worlds', as Flathman (1993, 1) put it. The Hobbesian subjection is this double crafting, of one's self into a subject and of the state. It is preferable, Hobbes continues (*L.*, chap.17[4]107) to 'being subdued' by the 'few that agree together'. This is not because it yields more equal power relations than other forms of submission; Hobbes is capturing the constitution of modernity's most unequal of power relations, pitting the individual against the state. It is, rather that it engages the will. This gripping of the will is what the device of the contract captures.

My caveat regarding the figure of the individual is worth repeating at this point, so common is the tendency to project the individual back onto Hobbes (see Macpherson 1962).[11] In fact, he does not once use 'the individual' in noun form, hence to designate a fully dividuated (as Deleuze would call it) entity, in the *Leviathan*.[12] There were undoubtedly individual bodies for Hobbes, indeed there were many; 'the individual' was a biological reality, an undivided organism—a body. However, as a sociological, a political, or indeed as an epistemological category, it did not exist (see also Shapin and Schaffer 2011). The purchase of using the body as an analytical lens is that it separates out this biological from these extra-biological categories. Holding off the anachronism that has cast Hobbes as the founder of contemporary individualism helps better circumscribe the emergence of this figure. How the body became invested politically and socially on account of its biological 'oneness' is one of the key questions I explore with this book. However, Hobbes, read closely, shows that, still in the middle of the seventeenth century, and in that crucible of state- and subject-making processes that revolutionary England comprised, the individual was far less delineated than is often assumed. In the following chapter I will also consider some of the areas where it was being adumbrated in the law and by way of the body. However, to dwell here with Hobbes, 'human' ('man', rather) and 'subject' constitute, with the body, the main categories of his political thought.

The Modern Subject of Knowledge and Hobbes's Two Natures

At the heart of subjection is a wilful act, contracting. The will, for Hobbes, is an embodied faculty regulated by the laws of nature. Subjecting, by contracting, is what nature's primary law prescribes; it is the natural-cum-rational thing to do (see Hobbes, *L.*, chap.14). The trouble is that, for Hobbes and his contemporaries, there were other natural forces, equally lodged in the body, that were also incessantly tugging upon the will: the passions. The new interest in the passions indexed the emergence of the other crucial figure of modern subjecthood, the scientific subject. Three factors conjoined to cast the body in the seventeenth century in a new light entirely: the passions, the new conception of matter, and the objectification of nature. I consider each in turn. First, those who were committed to advancing modern reason were also interested in parsing the passions, as reason's obverse and the source of its derailment.[13] Reason versus the passions is the defining binary of the seventeenth century. The passions brought the body decisively into focus, on both sides of the divide that was taking shape between modern rationalism and empiricism. Whereas the location of the will was extensively debated by, on the one hand, rationalists like Descartes and Aquinas before him, who placed it in the soul, and, on the other, empiricists like Hobbes, who saw it in the body instead, that of the passions were not. They were unanimously ascribed to the body. Only this was no longer the body as 'flesh', in the theological conception; as the locus of a sinful human nature and the source of the sensual temptations that impaired the soul's natural-cum-rational inclination towards a peaceful order, in the Thomist account. For, second, a decisive consequence of the new definition of matter as *res extensa* was that the body could be conceived strictly as an 'extended thing', on its own terms, as a natural object regulated by its own, physiological rather than theological, laws. Hobbes explicitly discarded biblical accounts of a sinful human nature. 'The desires and other passions of men are in themselves no sin', he wrote (*L.*, chap.13[10]77). Moreover, he ruled out sin as pregiven or a natural basis for legislation, since, for him, no 'law can be made, till [the legislated] have agreed on the person who makes it' (ibid.). Consequently 'the actions that proceed from those passions [are not sinful] till they know a law that forbids them' (ibid.).

Third, the body qua natural thing, rather than sinful flesh, emerged from establishing nature as the object of modern science. From where we stand today, at the other end of the catastrophic consequences, ecological and po-litical, it set into motion four centuries ago, this objectification now appears a deeply ambivalent process at best. It set sin at a remove as a basis for accounting for human nature, but it also disembodied the human-nature relation. Charles Taylor (1989, 160) has defined the objectification of nature as a dual gesture of distancing nature and of emptying it of the 'normative force' it had held as a guide to human affairs. It enabled critique and modern reason on the one hand. On the other, it durably established the white man 'like the master and possessor of nature', in René Descartes's (2006, 51) original articulation of the modern scientific subject-position (see Merchant 1980; Haraway 1991 for crit-ical perspectives). This subject-object structure will come into scrutiny under the lens of the body in chapter 7. I posit it here simply to index the emergence of the other subject that Hobbes was also deeply invested in, the modern sci-entific subject. For him, just as for Descartes (ibid., translation modified), a new science was eminently 'desirable insofar as it supports the invention of an infinity of artefacts that enable us to enjoy trouble-free the fruits of the earth'. How to bring this new appetite and capacity for artifice to the realm of human interactions was the question Hobbes set out to address. Descartes, for his part, largely steered clear of it.[14]

My argument is that two natures stand, in fact, in tension with each other in Hobbes's thought, an ethical and a scientific one. He carried the former over from medieval natural law, along with the task of political ordering. It was a stable and decipherable nature that yielded 'precepts or general rule[s] found out by reason' to guide human behaviour of human beings embedded in it (*L.*, chap.14[3]79). This ordered nature had afforded the long-standing model for political ordering. The moral philosopher or lawyer's task was to transpose these laws. 'The science of [nature's laws] is the true and only moral philosophy' (*L.*, chap.15[40]100).

But another nature was also being laid bare by the scientific revolution, in which Hobbes, uniquely among the heirs to the medieval natural law tradition in the early seventeenth century, was extensively engaged in. This nature was instead constantly in motion, and deeply unstable.[15] Reconciling the two would prove a difficult if not an impossible task. No wonder Descartes avoided it. To the extent that, for the natural lawyer John Finnis (2011, 208), Hobbes simply ended up 'deprive[ing] the notion of rights of virtually all its normative significance'. Conversely, political theoretical scholars who read him as a 'critic of nature' for turning away from nature (to found the state) underestimate his dedication to its scientific study (see, for example, Manent 2012, 56–61). It is instead more fruitful, I suggest, to consider how he sought to hold together, by way of the body, two very different natures—each prescribing their own sets of behaviours, normative and physiological, respectively. Nature was simultaneously for Hobbes, the traditional source of order it had traditionally been in political thought, and a new source of disorder, the fount of tumultuous human natural forces that ceaselessly tugged upon a precariously constructed political order. Understanding Hobbes's juncture requires us to consider the new nature that was being revealed, and how.

Modern optics had revolutionised the way nature was seen. Galileo's telescope (1609), enthusiastically embraced by Johan Kepler (1610), helped trigger the chain of discoveries that eventually ejected the earth from the centre of the world. The cosmic coordinates were being scrambled. 'The sun is lost, and th'earth', bemoaned John Donne (First Anniversary 1611), 'and no man's wit/can well direct him where to look for it'. New worlds, infinitely large and small (per the telescope and microscope), were appearing before the scientific eye. Old laws and certainties were being shattered. This disappearing earth was the centre-point of the medieval ontology; the ordered, static, and geocentric nature upon which the system of natural laws rested. This was the era of the 'loss of certainty' (Hacking 1987, 25). It unleashed a profound crisis of scepticism. 'The new philosophy calls all in doubt', Donne concluded.

The 'universe' of modern science was progressively replacing the 'cosmos' of natural law (see chapter 1). Hobbes, however, had stakes in both. The realisation that nature was not what it had appeared to be to the naked eye, that it required these optical artefacts to discover its laws, complicated, for this modern scientist, the habitual reliance upon nature as a normative resource for ordering the polity. Like Descartes, he was deeply invested in the science of optics, and he had frequented Galileo in the 1630s. He visited the topic three times, twice at the beginning of his writing career, including when he was involved in the scientific circles of father Mersennes in Paris, who published his second treatise on optics in 1644, and again in his last philosophical writing, De Homine (1658). His intellectual trajectory was thus framed by his interest in optics. The laws of optics and the phenomenon of optical illusions with which the seventeenth century at large was fascinated raised a fundamental philosophical question, whether the senses could be relied upon to know nature. It was especially acute one for a stance, like Hobbes', that had rejected the soul (see chapter 2), and for which the body was therefore all there was.

For rationalists like Descartes the soul was the repository of innate ideas. Humans are born with an idea of infinity, for example. The path to knowledge proper was a reactivation of these ideas pre-inscribed upon the soul. Insofar as these natural ideas afforded a non-sensorial foundation for knowing the world, they left the rationalists better equipped than their counterparts, in what was shaping into the 'rationalism versus empiricism' debate, scepticism (see Tuck 1988). For Hobbes (*L.*, chap.3[11]14) instead 'the only act of man's mind that I can remember [is] naturally planted in him . . . [is]. . . to live with the use of his five senses'. The body was the only possible source of knowledge. The problem, then, for these modern empiricists, was how to build a science *out of* this embodied knowledge, while correcting for the unreliability of the senses, and cordoning off the scientific enterprise from the sceptical despair at the impossibility of knowing anything altogether.

Moving Bodies and Causes All the Way Down

When, after wading through the '*absurd, insignificant* and *nonsense*' of innate ideas, and the ordered, still cosmos they had promised, Hobbes (*L.*, chap.5[5]24) was finally able to see nature, a maelstrom of moving bodies was what he found. Hobbes (*DC*, Author Epistle) invites the 'courteous reader' of his *DC*, his penultimate work where he set out his complete philosophical system, to think of his undertaking as 'Natural Reason of Man busily flying up and down among the Creatures and bringing back a true report of their Order, Causes and Effects', rather than as a traditional metaphysical (and rationalist) enterprise. Perhaps it was a function of beginning it when he was fifty-two, but Hobbes was remarkably consistent across the philosophical system he elaborated over the eighteen years between his *Elements of Law Natural and Political* (1640) and his final *De Homine* (1658). 'Only one thing is real, but it forms the basis of the things we falsely claim to be something' and that was motion (Farrington translation, cited in Falthman 1993, 21). This is how Hobbes described his initial discovery that set him on his philosophical path when he looked back upon his life at the age of eighty-four to draft an autobiography in Latin verse. Even his 'natural reason' was motile. To the study of 'matter, motion', he continued in the next verse, he thereafter applied himself. 'What motion is, and what motion can do' (Hobbes 1994, pg.lvii).

This, then, is the universe Hobbes saw:

> [T]he universe, that is, the whole mass of things that are, is corporeal (that is to say, body) [...] every part of body is likewise body. [...] And consequently, every part of the universe is body, and that which is not body is no part of the universe. And because the universe is all, that which is no part of it is nothing (and consequently nowhere). (Hobbes, *L.*, chap.46[15]459)

Hobbes's world is full of bounding bodies, big and tiny, and it is causally determined all the way down. To the extent that Hobbes rejected the existence of vacuum, a space void of matter and motion, his adversaries called him a 'plenist' (Shapin and Schaffer 2011; or 'fullist' in Flathman's transcription of the insult). Movement is this world's primary determination for Hobbes, since 'motion cannot be understood to have any other cause besides motion' (cited in Gaskin 1994, xxvi). An airtight causality was his response to the spectre of scepticism, to the challenge of having to rely upon these unreliable senses to know the world. Causes, and causes as far down as one can go, were a way of guarding the scientific enterprise against an uncertainty that could never fully be shaken off, given his corporeal epistemology. Indeed, all that lay all the way down, at the beginning of cognitive process, which I will unpack in detail in the next section, were these very senses. Short of being able to do without them, a tight reconstruction of the causal chain, one step removed from this unreliable sense data, was the next best option. It was a way of both containing the sceptical doubt and of compensating for the problem of epistemological insecurity begat by wielding the body as the organ of knowledge.

This is why, for Hobbes, knowledge is a strictly causal enterprise. To define 'science' or 'philosophy'—like Donne, Hobbes uses the two interchangeably—as a 'knowledge of consequences' is, in fact, a way of establishing causes *in lieu of the senses* as the foundations of knowledge (*L.*, chap.5[17]25; see also *DC Politico*, chap. 1[2]186). To put it differently, it is because knowledge is necessarily embodied and its grounds are so thin that Hobbes is adamant about establishing causal chains as the basis for the new kind of knowledge he seeks to develop. This is also why Hobbes rejected the emergence, in the second half of the seventeenth century, of the experimental sciences. These were founded, not in tight chains of causality, but in a new logic altogether: probability (Hacking 1987). Hobbes ferociously contested the empirical demonstrations by which Robert Boyle of the Royal Society set out to demonstrate the existence of the vacuum using an air pump (see Shapin and Schaffer 2011). Of *this* negative, Hobbes wanted nothing. What was being threatened, to his eyes, was scientific knowledge itself. Armed with their applied experimentations and their artefacts, like the air pump, the new experimental sciences were displacing causal certainty with probability as the basis for generating knowledge. This was enabled by the rise of probability from the 1660s onwards. It provided a new form of non-causal, 'logic for contingent events', as Ian Hacking (1987, 90) put it, that Hobbes the strict causalist simply could not abide by (see also Tully 1988).[16]

Consequently, there is strictly no room for accident or contingency in Hobbes's saturated causal universe. 'All contingents have their necessary causes'. Taking a swipe at the nascent probabilistic reasoning Hobbes (*DC*, chap.10[5]95) continues, even 'those future things, which are commonly called contingents', which is to say probable, events are simply a category of 'things' whose causes have simply not yet been uncovered. '[F]or men commonly call that casual or contingent, whereof they do not perceive the necessary cause' (ibid.). Everything, for Hobbes (*DC*, chap.1[2]3)—whether a thing, an occurrence, or even an act— has a necessary 'cause or generation'.[17] '[E]very act, that shall be produced, shall necessarily be produced' (*DC*, chap.10[5]95). Hence, Hobbes understands this 'cause or generation' in the strongest possible sense, as, literally, *that which causes something to be generated*. It is what philosophy or science's aims at, insofar as it lies at the beginning of the causal chain that 'ratiocination' seeks to work up (*DC*, chap.1[2]3). In the case of 'natural things', their 'causes [. . .] are not in our power, but in the divine will, and . . . [we] . . . do not see them' (*DH*, chap.10[5]146).

What, then, of those non-natural things that are to be generated by humans, such as, and especially, the 'artificial animal' that is meant to enable collective life (Hobbes, *L.* pg.3)? More broadly, is there room, in a world of causes all the way down, for a genuine, undetermined act of generation? And if not, if human behaviour is ultimately entirely prescribed by our biochemistry, what are we to make of the subjection which, as we saw earlier, Hobbes envisaged as a self-making, a crafting of one's self into a subject? How can humans be the causes of their own generation, of their becoming-subjects, if they are subjected to the causal laws of physiology? To explore these questions I now turn to consider how Hobbes apprehends the agency of political construction.

2. Artifice: The Agency of Modern Political Construction

The Natural vs. the Willed: Demarcating the Space of Artifice

Notwithstanding—or rather, in direct tension with—his commitment to a materialist causality, humans are also, for Hobbes, the actors of their own lives and the shapers of their own worlds. They bear a creative capacity for agency that 'resembl[es] that *fiat*, or the *let us make man* pronounced by God in the creation' (Hobbes, *L.*, pg.4). Richard Flathman has aptly rendered this complex and paradoxical Hobbesian obligation humans have, not merely to choose, in the

hollowed-out so-called 'rationalist' sense of 'preferences', but much more fundamentally, to carve out their own path:

> the 'givens' bequeathed to humankind by God and Nature, while necessary to
> the possibility of human "being" and potentially contributive to human well-
> being, are insufficient for the former, radically so for the latter, and often recal-
> citrant to human purposes. [...] [Humans] must themselves give form and
> course to the opaque and often resistant materials that are their experiences
> and their lives. (Flathman 1993, 3)

Hobbes's two natures, I suggest, help us make sense of this perhaps ultimately
irresolvable yet deeply generative tension between a thoroughgoing materialist
determinism, and a consistent commitment to the choice that always potentially inheres in human agency. On the one hand, nature, for him, still harboured
its traditional political ordering functions. After all, the *Leviathan*'s two most
studied chapters (14 and 15) read as a guide to the natural laws after which the
polities are to be patterned. On the other hand, access to these normative resources is deferred and it is conditional. It hinges on wilful act, contracting. This
opened up the prospect, so unacceptably threatening for his fellow modern natural rights theorists like Grotius, Spinoza, and Locke, that the rational and natural path towards cooperation may not be chosen after all. Nature does not evolve
seamlessly into the polity; the latter must be deliberately chosen. What this deferment or break instituted by the contract achieved is that it drew a boundary
between a realm of the natural, of these 'givens bequeathed to humankind', on
the one hand, and that of the willed on the other, of the to-be-constructed. Hence
it also delineated the space where humans can become their own 'cause or generation'; of themselves as subjects and of the strange machines that make living
together possible (*DC*, chap.1[2]3). The contract thus drives a wedge into nature
itself. It opens up a plane for human agency that begins in nature, since it continues to hold the resources, both normative and, as we shall see, affective, with
which the polity is built, but it also extends beyond it. This is the plane of artifice.

'Artifice' or 'art' are Hobbes's terms for this distinctly human capacity to invent, to craft something that did not exist before, and is not merely patterned
after nature (see also Prokhovnick 2005). In that it both creates and constitutes,
it is like 'the art whereby God hath made and governs the world', in ways I will
further explore below (Hobbes, *L.*, pg.3). But artifice is also what enables humans
to exceed their natural determinations and to realise their natural-cum-political
desire for security after all. It is the agency of political constitution and construction. It tips humans beyond nature and sets them apart from all other natural
beings. What was new was not the sense of human distinctness. Even in in the
medieval scheme of the human embedded-ness in nature, they alone possessed

a rational soul, the container of innate ideas, with its corresponding faculty in the realm of action, a rational appetite. This was the scholastic definition of the will, which Hobbes rejected.[18] For it was located in the soul. Hobbes's provocation was to shift the will to the body instead. Descartes (1988, Art.18, 167) had maintained the will in the soul. What was different, then, was his idea of a distinctly human agency grounded in choice *without* needing to presume the 'nonsense' of a free will (see Hobbes, *L.*, chap.5[5]24). Not because humans are unfree; they are highly agential for Hobbes, as we have seen, whose conception of liberty is also the focus of chapter 4. But choice is not a hollow idea. It is both a creative capacity, the expression of human ingenuity, and it is embodied, the outcome of physiological processes.

The Agency of Modern Political Construction and Its Models: Language and Geometry

The 'most noble and profitable invention of all', for Hobbes (*L.*,chap.4[1]16), language, is useful for apprehending this agency of political construction.[19] In a prefiguration of what Ferdinand de Saussure would later call 'systems of signification', words consists for Hobbes (ibid.) in the '*names* or *appellations* and their connexions' that are contingently assigned to 'things'. Hobbes, like the Suisse linguist three centuries later, rejects the correspondence theory of language, which was mired in innate ideas, and presumed a necessary and automatic relation between a word and the thing it represented. In this classical scheme, a word represented a thing; it rendered it present to the mind as a cognitive object, hence an idea. Knowledge, as we have seen, was a reactivation by this representation of an innate idea (of goodness, for example) that contained some of the essence or real nature of the thing (the Good). These innate ideas were a property of human nature, expressive of humans' unique, among natural beings, access to a transcendent order of knowledge (their ability to know the essence of the God). Along with innate ideas, Hobbes (*L.* chap. 4[1]16) rejected any automatic or necessary connection between the word and the thing it conjures: 'I do not find anything in the Scripture out of which [. . .] can be gathered that *Adam* was taught [by God] the name of all figures'. Recovering instead the biblical grist for his mill, he continued: '*God* [. . .] instructed *Adam* how to name such creatures as he presented to his sight'. Thereafter Adam went on to 'add more names' by himself (ibid.).

Language, for Hobbes, does not reflect, it *names*. Names are attributed to, or 'arbitrarily imposed upon', things (*DH.*,chap.5[2]35). This arbitrariness is another expression of the human will, of the capacity for choice that is also engaged in political construction. By contrast, communication amongst non-human species falls short of constituting language. While they may use 'similar animal cries' to humans, they do so as a function of the 'unavoidable course of their nature' rather than because 'their free will' has ascribed the meanings of 'fear, hope, joy and the other passions' to these sounds (*DH*, chap.10[2]143, my translation). The relation of the name to the thing is thus conventional and contingent. It is not determined by the nature of the thing. It is human-made. Adam invented the words that he added. Speech, in turn, is simply the 'right ordering of names' (*L.*, chap.4 [12]19). Natural necessity does feature in Hobbes's (*L.* chap 4[2]16) account, as the human 'need (the mother of all inventions)' to register, recall, and communicate things to one another. Names, then, are constructs crafted to address the human need to communicate.

Having driven a first wedge between the word and the world (and consistently with his times, as I will show in chapter 4), Hobbes recovered the representative function of language to perform a major role in his project of political ordering. He re-engineered it into a scheme of political representation that combined the 'making' (of artifice) and this rendering present (of the classical function). Humans initially *author* the concept for and proper locus of political *authority*, the state, by mobilising an original, embodied individual act of *authorising* the contract (see also Strong 1993). This artefact, in turn, re-presents, renders present—but does not make—its authorisers, who instead make themselves into political subjects by engaging in this scheme, in the now familiar circular Hobbesian logic of co-constitution. This is also the mechanism generative of laws, 'which are but rules authorised' (Hobbes, *L.*, chap.30[21]229). What properly constitutes a law, for Hobbes and unlike for his fellow natural rights theorists, is not its degree of alignment onto one of nature's, but this authorising circuit. With it, Hobbes, in fact, tethers the law directly to a human agency, via the subjects' authorship (and potentially their ingenuity), and untethers it from the natural order. He unplugs law-making from a natural agency. He loosens the link between human and natural laws, to open up a space for humans to construct and indeed create.

The referent, or what is named, either already exists out there 'in nature'; such as the biblical animals that Adam (but not, apparently, Eve) encounters. Or it is invented, 'feigned by the mind of man' (*L.*, chap.4[18]20). *This* act of naming, of constructing 'fictions' (the noun corresponding to 'feigned') is the quintessentially creative, human act. It distils 'the *art* of man' (*L.*,pg.3). It is where humans come closest to God. These constructs, in turn, are of two kinds. They are either absurd chimera that refer to nothing real. Among these Hobbes counts the fanciful soul, in the realm of religion, as we have seen; or in that of science, the vacuum, which was one of the 'trifling wonders' his fellow scientists distracted themselves with at the Royal Society (cited in Shapin and Schaffer 2011, 112).[20] These fictions conjure sheer emptiness; they are 'fictions' in the derogatory sense. Or they refer to 'bodies that are, or may be conceived to be' (*L.*, chap.4[18]20).

Hegel would later term them 'concepts'. The body that 'may be conceived to be' in which Hobbes had a major stake in conceiving correctly and in helping bring into being was of course the unified state. 'Fiction' in this eminently rational, creative sense, is arguably the very purpose of the *Leviathan*, and in play throughout it. This naming is the act of constructing something in one's mind that precedes making it; the first step of craft—of statecraft. Hobbes multiplies these acts in a range of keys, in opening his political treatise: by attributing a proper name ('that great LEVIATHAN'), as an act of translation ('the STATE [in Latin CIVITAS])', or as a visual representation (the frontispiece) (see Springborg 1995). Naming, in this sense, then, is the creative act at the core of Hobbes's art, and of the notion of artifice he sets out to circumscribe. However, the properly collective act of contracting is, for Hobbes (*L*., pg.3–4) the ultimate human act that 'resemble[s] that *fiat* [. . .] pronounced by God in the creation'. Naming requires others for a successful communication (and for the construct to hold), but not in and of itself, whereas contracting does. Hobbes (ibid.) is careful to reserve this qualifier for 'the *pacts* and *covenants* by which the parts of this body politic were first made' (Hobbes, *L*.,pg. 3–4). His artifice was a collective agency, not the individualised agency of liberal thought.

This complete open-endedness underwriting artifice, the fact that it can turn either way and turn out both misleading, enslaving dogmatisms, *and* the contraptions and concepts that make cooperation possible, further explains the privileged place geometry holds in Hobbes thought, which I began to consider in the previous chapter. Here I consider how it relates to this work of naming. Geometry, for Hobbes, offered the perfect guide to artifice. It owed its precision to the fact that it proceeds, not from observation and thus from the senses, but rather from names themselves ('triangle') and their definitions (it is a form with three angles that equal two right angles (*L*., chap.4[9]18). Geometry is an artefactual knowledge since, in Hobbes's words, 'the lines from which we reason are drawn and described by ourselves' (cited in Shapin and Schaffer 2011, 149). Space is a human construct for Hobbes, as is the science of its study. In geometry 'we create the figures ourselves' (*DC*, chap.1[2]3 and *DH*, chap.10[5]146, my translation). Geometry is the science that properly enables humans to become the 'cause or generation' of their own worlds, and of a world in which they can cohabitate peacefully (*DC*, chap.1[2]3).

Hobbes's Anti-Naturalist Causality and the Role of Mechanism in the Crafting of the State

Geometry was mobilised in the service of a new kind of causality, artificial rather than natural, and anti-Aristotelian. This was the causality of the machine, that quintessential seventeenth-century product of artifice, and Hobbes's response to the naturalist figure of the political animal—another key marker of political hierarchies. For Aristotle (*Nicomachean Ethics* 6.6, 1140b30—35), knowledge or science (*scientia*) consisted in 'judgements about things that are universal and necessary'. I consider the necessity underwriting the Aristotelian-Thomist conception of knowledge in this section, and what he meant by universality in the following one. This necessity was not a logical necessity, as in the contemporary meaning of the term, where it is yielded by the reasoning process (see Hacking 1987). It was instead located in the nature of things, which was to say that it was lodged in nature itself, in a world where the former simply mirrored the later, and where causes performed ontological, and not merely epistemological functions (see chapter 1). The causes of a thing were, literally, its raison d'être, both why it is as it is, and why it is at all. Aristotelian-Thomist 'causes are necessary causes' (Hacking 1987, 22). Moreover, they are attained through demonstration.

Hobbes would not forsake demonstration. The tight chains of reasoning anchored to definitions were the bedrock of his knowledge of consequences, of the modern science he saw himself to be consolidating. But he also undertook to dismantle Aristotelian causality, as we began to see in the previous chapter. In addition to evacuating the final cause, Hobbes collapsed the material and efficient causes.[21] Hobbes was after a causality whose robustness would be guaranteed, not by its outward imitation of nature, but by the rigour of its own internal procedures. He searched for necessity located, not in the nature of things, but in the tight chains of reasoning themselves: a logical necessity. The machine was its embodiment.

Two factors made the machine thinkable and realisable: the new conception of matter, and debunking Aristotle's final cause. Matter as *res extensa* established a grand equivalence of all things and bodies, nature/God- or human-made. The default property of a 'thing' (*res*), in fact of physicality, indeed, for Hobbes, of being itself, was to be 'extended' (*extensa*). Hobbes (*L.*, chap.34[2]261) carefully stripped the body from any other attributes, defining it strictly as 'that which filleth or occupieth some certain room or imagined space, and dependeth not on our imagination, but is a real part of what we call the *universe*'. The machine was just another body. It was perhaps less well crafted than the human one (which was made by God), but not otherwise inferior to it. Hobbes's mechanistic materialism, in this sense, was an anti-naturalism designed to legitimise the products of human ingenuity. His was one strand of mechanism; that of Descartes, from whom he borrowed the imagery of the body as clockwork, was another (see chapter 7). This singular ontology of the seventeenth century, that all other ages since, including our own, have looked upon as peculiar at best, or outright destructive, was the imaginary that sustained the emergence of modern science's matter. My contention is that it also underwrote the invention of the state. In this, and in that it holds the seeds of the original agency of modern political construction, it requires being reckoned with.

Mechanism was instrumental in precipitating the demise of the Aristotelian final cause. Untethering bodies from their natural ends, from what they were inherently made for, enabled nature's purpose to be replaced with a human intentionality. Indeed, for Aristotle (1990, VI, 4 1140 1–20), 'art' was geared towards 'production', towards making something. The action was bound to the object and directed by its final cause. He contrasted it with 'actions', which are instead self-referential.[22] The difference between these two forms of agency lay in the final cause. In production, the artist or artisan merely realised a pre-existing model; they brought the artefact into being by carrying it to its final cause. There was little room for invention. The early modern machine collapsed this distinction. It was a production; only it was also self-referential. Even if it was made *for* something, like the telescope for magnifying, this purpose was designed by its crafters. It could be modified along the way. It was not locked in by a final cause. It could also be unnatural. Hobbes's artifice was not Aristotle's art. It contained something more, something that punctured the closed horizon of the final cause. Mechanism augured the open-endedness that was necessary to invent rather than imitate, including a new political form. Consider how Hobbes reworks the old metaphor of the body politic:

> what is the *heart*, but a *spring*; and the *nerves*, but so many *strings*; and the joints, but so many *wheels*; giving motion to the whole body, such as was intended by the artificer? (Hobbes, *L*. pg.3)

In mechanising the naturaliser of medieval hierarchies (see chapter 4), Hobbes also delinked it from a final cause pre-inscribed in nature. He opened up the possibility of another end, decided upon and designed by an '*artificer*' made of '*matter*' (humans), including the equality of all bodies within this artificial body. Only it first had to be chosen.

Passionate (E)Motions: Hobbes's Physiology of Action

In this universe of whirling bodies, there is a particular category of natural, animal motion, especially potent, that, if properly directed, has the potential to become the 'cause or generation' of that great machine, the state (*DC*, chap.1[2]3). Conversely, if they are left undirected, these 'powers natural of [the human] body and mind' will likely tear apart the space of living together (*DC*, chap.1). These motions are the passions. Under the razor of a materialism that pars all things down to their moving parts, the passions become strictly movements of and in

the body. 'Life is but motion' (*L.*, chap.6[58]34]). Even traditional political theoretical concepts, such as the virtues, become motions: the two 'natural virtues' for
Hobbes (*L.*chap.8[2]38) are '*celerity of imagining*' combined with a '*steady direction*'. The human life, Hobbes (*EoLi*, chap.9[21]36–37) suggests, is like 'a race'. In
what we might call his Russian doll picture of movement, human beings are ceaselessly chasing after the objects of their passions with, in turn, a myriad of minute
motions coursing through them. 'And to forsake the course is' well, simply 'to die'
(Hobbes, *EoLi* chap.9[21]37). Moreover, for Hobbes (*L.*, chap. 8[16]41), 'to have
weak passions is dullness' and 'to have no desire is to be dead'. In fact 'a man who
has no great passion' and is 'indifferent' 'cannot possibly have either a great fancy
or much judgement' (ibid.). Hence, for Hobbes, it is not a matter of quashing
the passions, which are 'essential to all effective thought and action' as Flathman
(1993, 20) underscored. It is, rather, a matter of understanding the play and sway
of these especially potent bodily motions, in order to harness them to the task of
political construction. To this effect, Hobbes envisaged a state of nature: this 'inference from the passions', as he described his thought-experiment (and political
science's first 'simulation'), was his space for analysing these human natural givens
(or 'data') in their raw, unbridled form (*L.*, chap.13[10]77.

For Hobbes, the passions, not reason, drive human behaviour. While it is not,
strictly speaking, his word, we might say that, for Hobbes, humans are moved
to act by *e*-motions, which he understands quite literally as both 'of' and 'out
of' (*ex-*) their bodies. Here, properly and literally—materially—lies the stuff that
human agency is made of. Hobbes distinguishes between two sorts of corporeal
movements: unintentional or '*vital*' motions that require 'no help of the imagination'. Examples are 'the *course* of the *blood*, the *pulse*, the *breathing*, the *concoc-
tion* [digestion], *nutrition*, *excretion*, etc' (Hobbes, *L.*, chap.6[1]27). Intentional
actions are '*voluntary*' or '*animal motion[s]*', such as 'to *go*, to *speak*, to *move* any
of our limbs, in such manner as is first fancied in our minds' (ibid.). The passions
are movements of this kind. But, and this is Hobbes's trick, the intention that
triggers the movement is itself an embodied stimulus. It does not take shape in a
discrete or generalisable faculty purportedly located in the soul, like reason.

What, then, of the will, the traditional site of intentions? It is nothing but
embodied movement, for Hobbes. It is a leaning towards, in which case it is an
'appetite' proper, or a retracting from an external object, where it is an 'aversion'.
Consent, for example, is the leaning towards one another of several wills (*EoLi*,
chap.12[7]48). Both the leaning towards and away from are reactions to the im-
pression the object has left upon our senses. 'The action of the things we see,
hear, etc' upon our senses triggers a 'motion in the organs and interior parts of
man's body', that Hobbes (*L.*, chap.6[1]27) calls 'sense'. This inner movement
leaves a 'relic' in our imagination that crystallises into an intention. All voluntary
motions thus begin in the imagination. It acts like a soundboard that reverberates

the vibrations of our embodied sense-impressions. Hence what is habitually referred to as the will is in fact but the point where the sway of appetites, the leaning toward and away from, stops. It is the 'last appetite in deliberating' before an action or decision is engaged (*L.*, chap.6[53]33 and *EoLi*, chap.12[2]47).

This ceaseless sway of human motions and emotions adds another dimension to the Hobbesian contract. It explains why, for Hobbes, unlike for Locke (see chapter 5), consent alone is not enough to found a polity. Considering the Aristotelian trope of the political animal in a passage in *De Cive*, Hobbes (*DCi*chap.5[5]87) reflects upon how Aristotle includes other species, such 'as the *Ant*, the *Bee*' amongst those animals that are naturally prone to collective life. 'Though they may be destitute of reason' they too 'direct their actions to a common end'. 'Yet is not their gathering together a *civill government*' Hobbes (ibid.) concludes 'because their government is onely [*sic*] a consent, or many wills concurring in one object, not (as is necessary in civill government) one will'. 'And therefore those animals not to be termed *politicall*' (ibid.). Simple consent is sufficient in the case of ants and bees, because, unlike among humans, 'the naturall appetites of Bees, and the like creatures, is conformable, and they desire the common good, which among them differs not from their private' (Hobbes, *DCi*, chap.5[5]87). The instability and complexity of human animal motions means that humans require something more to fix their leaning towards each other into a collective will, namely, a contract. It too is a wilful act begat by the same physiological process we have considered.

So far in the chapter I have explored the pulling away from nature, or denaturing, that Hobbes conceived to be necessary to build a peaceful, unified polity. I have charted in this second part how Hobbes found artifice, the agency with which humans build polities, in specific acts, like naming and contracting; and how he analysed its raw, human-natural component, the passions. Having considered his denaturing work, I now turn to his denaturalising enterprise, and show how he himself mobilised artifice towards critique. Hobbes's own critical undertaking illustrates how this quintessentially modern attitude first took shape coextensively as an epistemological and a political commitment that aimed to both reveal and reinforce the human ability to choose and to craft. His epistemological-cum-political project aimed to release the play of choice underwriting political ordering.

3. Denaturalising the Taken-for-Granted:
The Critical Roots of Modern Political Agency

In this section I explore the political implications of Hobbes's deconstructive enterprise by analysing, first, how he de-naturalised one of the most entrenched taken-for-granteds of his age, a universal justice lodged in nature itself. Hobbes counterposed an unnatural and non-universal justice. Justice, for Hobbes, was the product of the contract. Hence it was particular and constructed all the way down. There were as many forms of justice as there are contracts, and therefore sovereignties, for Hobbes. Second, I will show how he debunked the very idea of universals. Third, I consider the critical weapons he deploys to do so, his nominalism. In this part's final section, I analyse how he deconstructed an existing structure of domination of his times, 'paternal dominion'.

Denaturalising Justice to Found a Modern Sovereignty

With his contract Hobbes, in fact, broke decisively with the natural law tradition by grounding justice, and the entire system of normative coordinates that makes collective life, or indeed even just cooperation, possible in an original human act. '[W]here no covenant hath been made, there hath no right been transferred, and every man has the right to everything, and consequently', in nature, 'no action can be unjust' (Hobbes, L.chap.15[2]89). Justice, and the very possibility of normative ordering, is unlocked by the contract. It does not predate it. Justice is not natural, for Hobbes. Indeed as we saw in the previous chapter there is 'no court of natural justice' outside of the conscience (and that justice is not pertinent to the intersubjective space of politics) (Hobbes, L. chap.30[30]233). So strong was Locke's reaction to Hobbes's denial of a natural court justice that he short-circuited it altogether by asserting a natural power to enforce this justice, which he then takes as evincing it (see chapter 4). Yet for Hobbes, justice is socially constructed and deliberately chosen—or not. Conversely, injustice is not the violation of a universal natural moral rule, 'it is no other than the *not performance of covenant*' (Hobbes, L., chap.15[2]89). That is, it is the violation of a moral rule *only because* these standards have been previously set by the founding act that also begat sovereignty. It is not innately so, or by reference to a universal moral standard derived from nature. Hobbes invented, or conceived, sovereignty as an empty shell, as a pure normative void that is not 'pre-filled' by any innate notions of good or bad. What he was undoing was the deeply entrenched classical Thomist conception of nature as the repository of a universal justice, and its equally universal notions of good and bad.[23] Hence with Hobbes, nature could no longer afford the foundations for universal rights that it has long been taken to constitute in natural rights theories, both before and after him. Hobbes's nominalism, which is my focus in this third part, set him radically apart from this tradition, as his fellow early modern natural rights theorists, such as Grotius and Locke, were quick to realise.

Hobbes, then, rejects a universal justice grounded in nature. But he goes further. He recovers the notion of 'universal' in singular ways. For Hobbes (*L.*, chap.15[3]89) does posit a 'universal right': it is the negative natural right that must be rejected in order to create positive rights, as we saw in the previous chapter. Moreover, this universal right breeds only insecurity, since in the natural estate 'there can be no security to any man (how strong or wise soever he be)' (Hobbes, *L.*, chap.14[4]80). No Hobbesian natural right to security is to be found here. Hobbes's 'universal', in fact, designates a manner of conceptual empty stage. It *is* the rights vacuum dreaded by John Finnis (2011, 208). In fact, Hobbes's wielding of 'the universal' contained a two-pronged strategy of critique. First, he emptied it out, and charged it with the work of the negative. He transformed it in this way into an instrument of his ground-clearing enterprise.

Denaturalising Universals

However Hobbes's real target, second, was the original nexus underpinning the Thomist conception of a universal natural justice. This was the deeply entrenched construction of the still and static medieval nature, or unive*r*se, as the repository for all unive*r*sals. Unpacking Hobbes's strategy requires us to return to the place of the universal in the Aristotelian-Thomist conception of knowledge. Knowledge, since Aristotle (2000), was always of the universal. This is what distinguishes knowledge proper from sense-impressions. Hobbes's position in relation to Aristotelian-Thomist knowledge was complex. He actively partook in the attack on Aristotelian causality, on the one hand. On the other, his rejection of probabilistic reasoning harks back to a pre-modern stance (see Shapin and Schaffer 2011). He was also attached to the Aristotelian-Thomist distinction between 'knowledge' (*scientia*) and 'opinion' (*opinio* or *doxa*, see chapter 2), which was pre-probabilistic (see Hacking 1987). This differentiation is useful here too, I suggest, for circumscribing Hobbes''s target.

'Knowledge' and 'opinion' belonged to two different parts of the Aristotelian-Thomist rational soul, namely, the highest part, capable of knowledge proper or *theoria*, and the lesser part, which produced practical knowledge, relevant to the realm of actions or *praxis*. This was also the realm of ethics and politics. The problem, for this dedicated scientist, was evidently not the possibility of knowledge itself, nor the method of demonstration, which Aristotle had enshrined as the scientific method. The object of demonstration was universal truths. The geometrical axioms Hobbes favoured were truths. Only the truth they attained was a function of their internal cogency, rather than of their relation to the world. Hobbes's target, rather, was the blurring of the lines between forms of knowledge, between *scientia* and *opinio*, between *theoria* and *praxis*, by which a mere opinion sought to pass for knowledge. Such a line-blurring was precisely what dangerous dogmatisms rested upon. It was the means by which an authoritative opinion usurped an authority that did not belong to it – that of proper knowledge. The target of Hobbes's nominalism, then, was the conception of nature or the universe as the repository of the universals of practical knowledge, such as justice or the good.

Nominalism: Hobbes's Weapon of Critique

Language was the linchpin of Hobbes's strategy to debunk the taken-for-granteds of his time. Understanding his critical enterprise thus requires returning to his theory of language. Hobbes parses the process of 'accounting' by which particular things 'enter into account', become objects of speech ('accounts'), and are woven into reasonings ('reckonings'). A body has certain physical properties, such as 'hot, cold, moved, quiet' (L.,chap.4[15]20). We apprehend these qualities through our own 'conception[s]' or 'fanc[ies]', into which we also 'bring into account the properties of our own bodies'. Conceptions, then, are not the exact imprint of the object upon our senses, but rather the product of an encounter between two bodies, the object and our own, which brings into play the unreliable senses and the even more unreliable imagination (L.,chap.4[17]20). Comparing between conceptions then enables us to identify similarities between two or more objects, and to attribute the same (common) name to them. Having 'named' the object is what enables us to generalise about its properties, to 'reckon' (reason) about them and string them into affirmative or negative statements. This is the level where knowledge proper occurs. What we name, strictly speaking, are the conceptions, the cognitive products, not the objects themselves.

At this point, Hobbes adds a crucial distinction, between this level of generality, where reckoning occurs, and a further level up still, that of the universal. The differentiation was first devised by the 'nominalists' Duns Scotus and William of Occam against the so-called 'realist' followers of Aquinas in the debate around property that played out in the Church in the thirteenth century (see Villey 1975). Having separated out names proper from the fancies and conceptions they refer to, Hobbes posits that only the former, strictly speaking, are universal. '[T]here [is] nothing in the world universal but names; for the things named are every one of them individual and singular' (Hobbes, L., chap.4[6]17). Hobbes explains the common confusion as follows: 'The universality of one name to many things has been the cause that men think the things themselves are universal' (EoLi, chap.5[6]15). Now, the 'things named' do not refer to the real object out there, but to the conceptions we have of it, we have seen. The key to understanding Hobbes's nominalism is that, for him, these too contain some measure of particularism, since they are first produced by each person's complex of sense-impressions and imagination—by their bodies—,before they are conveyed from one person to the next. The name alone can be universal; not the idea it refers to, nor the object. Ideas are still particular, since they are formed out of our fancies and conceptions. However, they begin to effect some measure of generalising, of the kind that is needed to be able to associate two different four-legged animals perceived to the idea of 'dog', and then to communicate the thought to another. Hobbes, in this way, is able to separate out a level of general ideas, which still harks to the particular, from an additional level of universal names. To put it in another way, ideas mediate between the level of the particular and that of the universal, which is the plane of names proper. On the other hand, names are necessary to the work of generalising that begins at the level ideas. Both levels are implicated in the production of knowledge.[24]

What this distinction between a level of the general and of the universal proper achieved is that it undercut the traditional, purportedly 'realist' grounds upon which knowledge rested, in two ways. Firstly, the universal, for Aquinas, was the exclusive locus of knowledge. The mind accedes to the universal, whereas the body remains mired in the particular (see Aquinas I. Q86 Art.1). By separating out the general from the universal, Hobbes opens up a plane where knowledge, necessarily derived from the body and indeed still steeped in the particular, begins nonetheless to be produced. Second, in the scholastic scheme, universals have an objective existence; they are God's creation and thus rooted in nature itself. By locating them instead in names, Hobbes transformed them into human constructs: they are but the names that humans (since Adam) give to things. Their relation to any reality 'out there' is that of the signifier to the signified, to switch to contemporary terms. A third crucial epistemological consequence for our purposes is that, in recovering universals as names alone, Hobbes delinked universals from the scholastic conception of the universe/nature as a knowable totality they had been traditionally folded into. He prepared them instead for the task of knowing another kind of nature altogether. His was an endless dance of singular moving bodies.

The political implications of Hobbes's nominalism are, first, that it flushes out universal values upon which to model the polity that had been lodged in nature or the universe. 'The good' is a universal name without any content. It is an empty shell. There are only particular ideas of what is good or bad, specific to and constructed by particular, bounded polities. Fixing the name or the signifier 'good' to a common content or signified is a crucial function of the contract, the act that founds sovereignty. Prior to the contract, there are only as many goods as there are persons: 'whatsoever is the object of any man's appetite or desire that is it which he for his part calleth *good*; and the object of his hate and aversion, *evil* (. . .) there being . . . [no] . . . common rule of good and evil to be taken from the nature of the objects themselves' (Hobbes, *L.*, chap.6[7]28–29). Nature contains no universal good, the good being a human construction: 'there being nothing simply and absolutely so' (ibid.). Second, his nominalism explicates the function of sovereignty in the international system— one that has only waxed since it first took shape among relatively homogenous European states in the seventeenth century. It furnishes a structure for understanding how sovereignty can hold both a principle of universality (it is claimable by all states) and the idiosyncrasies of every state. Sovereignty, Hobbes showed at the dawn of the Westphalian era, affords an organising principle for the system of states precisely because the name alone is universal. It is an empty shell that can be differently filled by different states. It can accommodate both the universal principle required to coexist within one political system, while remaining distinct.

Of Paternal Dominion: Hobbes's Proto-feminist Critique

Once nature has been negated as the wellspring for universal rights, it no longer affords a source of legitimation for structures of domination deemed 'natural'— that have become entrenched and naturalised. This third political implication of Hobbes's nominalism has remained largely under-appraised for the critical resources it holds, and for which Hobbes himself shows the way. Hobbes's writing is not rid of the gendered prejudices of his time, we have seen. Nevertheless, he also deploys his nominalism to deconstruct step by step, in the *Leviathan's* twentieth chapter, one of the unequal and taken-for-granted structures of his time, 'paternal dominion'. Sovereignty is the linchpin that holds a political order in place. 'Patriarchy' (the term is already Grotius's) is only one kind of political order amongst many possible ones, and not even the one that is most closely patterned after nature. The steps of Hobbes's argument are worth unpacking, insofar as it offers one of the first deconstructive strategies in modern political thought, as Carol Pateman (1988) once noted.

Hobbes develops his proto-feminist analysis in the context of appraising sovereignty by generation, as opposed to by conquest. For Grotius (*De Jure Belli Ac Paci*, II, v, 1–7), patriarchy was simply the natural social structure into which the child is born. Hobbes (*L.*, chap.20[4]128) short-circuits this naturalism by introducing the necessity for the child to consent. While the child's consent has often been considered one of the more far-fetched moments in Hobbes's wielding of the contract, what it underlines, I suggest, is Hobbes's determination to privilege choice over the naturally given, to the point of straining his argumentation. It serves a critical rather than a plausible purpose, namely, to undercut naturalist assumptions and to underscore the constructed-ness of all sovereignties. Hobbes (*L.*,chap. 20[4]128) then proceeds by, first, unsettling another old naturalist assumption, noting 'there is not always that difference of strength or prudence between the man and the woman as that the right can be determined without war'. Nature offers no solid basis for differentiating gender roles, let alone for legitimising unequal relations that have been derived from these purportedly natural distinctions; not even physical differences between the sexes. Second, he examines the lay of the law. Considering patterns of adjudication in cases of contested child custody as a proxy for established legal orders, Hobbes (*L.*,chap.20[4]128) notes pointedly that if the courts have tended to come down 'in favour of the father', this is 'because for the most part commonwealths have been erected by the fathers, not by the mothers of families'.

Patriarchy is not natural, for Hobbes; it has been naturalised. In an exemplary gesture of critique, which consists in drawing into relief the contingency of established, naturalised orders, he then explores alternatives (*L.*, chap. 20[4]128 and 20[5]129). He looks in two directions: history and philosophy. First, the Amazons and their matriarchal mode of organisation affords Hobbes his historical evidence that other paths were possible.[25] For the philosophical route he returns to the laws of nature. He considers the child and its biological parents in the state of nature. From the law of self-preservation he deduces that, in view of the extreme vulnerability that characterises the human species at birth, and that the mother is more biologically suited to cater to its basic needs, in particular nourishment, the child's preservation prescribes the mother's rather than the father's dominion. Matriarchy, not patriarchy, is the natural order, he concludes.

4. Hobbes's Ultimate Naturalising Gesture: The Body, Again

So far in this chapter I have analysed Hobbes's work of de-naturing, by which he unsettled some of the old natural laws, or conceptions of nature, in order to clear the grounds for constructing a new, more viable and stable political order. I have also showed his de-naturalising enterprise, by which he shook some of the deepest taken-for-granteds of his time—philosophical, with universals, and social, with patriarchy. My purpose in doing so was to draw out the critical purchase of Hobbes's thought. It was also to show the extent to which the roots of modern critique are entwined with the enterprise of modern political construction. This enterprise, Hobbes shows, was first one of *de*construction. It requires wielding the key mechanism at work in critique, which I have called the 'jarring effect', that interrupts the naturalisation effects and unsettles the taken-for-granted (Epstein 2008). Still tracking the role of the body in his thought, in this final part I qualify my sympathetic reading of Hobbes and draw out some limits to Hobbes's usefulness for a critical enterprise. I will show how, despite these powerful denaturalising moves, with the body, Hobbes did in fact naturalise a desire for security after all. Ultimately, he too contributed to founding security as a natural right, and the most fundamental one.

Justice, Hobbes has shown, is not a universal derived from nature, nor from our human nature. It is constructed and it is particular. Although this was not his immediate concern, since, unlike Locke, Hobbes had his focus cast upon the constitution of the English state rather than its empire, the implications of his position for a postcolonial international relations is that it is not a one-size-fits-all whose norms and institutions are so readily diffused to all people (see also Epstein 2017b). Sovereignty is its condition of possibility; it is the linchpin that fixes a local and historically specific system of meanings and values. However, the very resort to the body that sustained his critical undertaking also undermines it in a few places. Hence for my purposes, the body now serves to draw out these limitations. First, in the context of articulating the sovereign's duties (chapter 30), Hobbes establishes a hierarchy of what people value most as a basis for determining what the sovereign must attend to in administering justice. Their 'own life and limbs' features at the top the list. It is also the only item that, Hobbes finds, can hold universal valence:

> Of those things [. . .] that are dearest to a man are his own life and limbs; and
> in the next degree (in most men) those that conjugal affection; and after them
> riches and means of living. (*L.*, chap.30[12]224)

The body, then, somehow suddenly becomes the criteria for a universal administration of a justice, after he has carefully demonstrated in earlier chapters the logical impossibility of there being any universal, beyond language. It is as though, having staked out the path of constructivist political theorising, he turns back at the last minute to the body to establish it as the pegging point for a natural universal value. Second, let us reconsider the right of the state of nature, the 'natural right of every man to everything, even to another's body' (*L.*, chap.14[4]80). With this corporeal clause bolted on to the original unlimited natural right, Hobbes lays down the criteria that will trigger the making of rights and the state (by departing from the state of nature): the claim to another's body. Since passionate humans are unlikely to abstain from making such a claim, the body, via the 'natural' impulse to defend it, is the guarantee of statehood (that state-making will happen). Without the body, the Hobbesian edifice crumbles. It is his ultimate natural universal.

*

To turn to the body, for Hobbes, was, above all, to turn away from dogma. It was to 'take one's instructions', not 'from the authority of books', but 'from natural sense', from embodiment. (*L.*, chap.3[13]19). With his thoroughly consistent—to the point of absurdity—corporeal ontology, he went the furthest in mobilising the body to break with a scholastic ontology of substances (or essences) and the mindless authority that was invested in it. In this, modernity is fundamentally Hobbesian; we, as critical subjects, are all Hobbesian. I have read Hobbes in this chapter as the original, albeit accidental, critical constructivist, in order to retrieve the origins of constructivism's most important insight, that politics is constructed and therefore fundamentally chosen. Across the chapter's four movements I showed, first, how Hobbes's state of nature encapsulated a widening chasm between two natures, two givens: the old, stable natural law that furnished the known models for constructing the polity, and the new laws of a highly mobile scientific nature. The givenness of nature no longer appeared so secure in the midst of the scientific revolution. Hobbes envisaged departing from it as being necessary to build a state that can keep its subjects safe. For my critical purpose of unsettling this structuring assumption of political life in the state, laying bare the several natures that were mobilised to naturalise security in the first place works to set our presumption of its naturalness into perspective. My hope, in drawing attention to history's great naturaliser, the body, is to loosen the grip of this sticky assumption that humans naturally desire security above all else, and to make room for other political demands put to the state.

Hobbes showed not only that modern politics is constructed rather than given but also with what particular kind of agency, which was the focus of the chapter's second part. Hobbes located his artifice first, in the act of naming. The name, or signifier in a more contemporary parlance, qua quintessential construct, condenses the human creative act. In this, the *Leviathan* itself is the political fiction, also understood in terms of construction, par excellence. Hobbes returns constitutive constructivism to its linguistic foundations. Second, however, he located the quintessential human *fiat* in a collective act. This is the significance of the contract. It is the first collective act required to make all others possible, and to sustain the capacity itself. The machine, with its open-ended, human-designed purpose, in lieu of a natural final cause, embodied this agency. I then considered its other crucial ingredient, the passions. These were, for Hobbes, the raw material of political construction, the formidable (human)natural moving force that must be carefully directed to be able to build the dikes to channel it.

Turning to Hobbes's enterprise of critique in the chapter's third part, I showed how he illustrates better than most how deconstruction is the necessary corollary to political construction, and thus the critical, as well as linguistic, roots of constitutive constructivism. I parsed how he picked apart two of the naturaliseds of his age, a universal justice and patriarchy. As the thinker of the body, Hobbes was the modern theorist of multiplicity, even endless multiplication. He saw nothing but moving bodies that were even further reducible to points and lines (Hobbes, *DC*; see also Leijenhorst 2002). His problem was how to hold together these endless singularities (see chapter 2). Epistemologically, he was deeply wary of any claims to the universal, the basis of all knowledge since Aristotle. He revived an old nominalist tradition in order to restrict the universal to the names we invent in order to group together like bodies. One name refers to many actual bodies. This scheme afforded him the solution to his problem: 'the Leviathan' (the name) refers to, and thus holds together, the many actual, embodied subjects after all. His nominalism wrought constitutive work. 'The Leviathan', as both name and machine, exemplified the human capacity for craft. But his nominalism also functioned as an anti-universalist scepticism, I showed. In this it affords a model for the practice of doubt in the face of all manner of claims to the universal that lie at the core of the theories and practices of international relations (see Walker 1993). I have suggested that it may be useful for those parts of the discipline, like postcolonial IR, that are invested in recovering the particular, the situated, and the localised, against the enduring epistemological tyranny of the universal, that is at play, for example, in IR's 'norms' (see Epstein 2017a). Last, however, tracking the body through his thought, and upon which he sharpened his critical tools, also served in the chapter's final part to draw the limits of his critique. Ultimately Hobbes played a central role, not only in theorising the state, but in securing what I seek to unsettle with this book: the body as history's great naturaliser.

In these two chapters I have sought not to resolve, but to reveal and to work with the productive tensions running through Hobbes's thought. His corporeal ontology achieved considerable critical work. Ultimately, however, paring down the human being to its material bits also left him ill-equipped to capture the element of creativity that necessarily exceeds materialist determinations, and that others had located in the soul. Yet Hobbes also had a prescience of what Hegel would subsequently term 'the negative', and this remains an intriguing and productive feature of his thought. The negative operates in his scheme of political constitution as the limiting mechanism that drives his humans to come together. As I have shown elsewhere, Hobbes had a keen sensitivity to the structural lack at the heart of human agency (see Epstein 2013). In his drama of origins, the natural need to compensate for this lack is the engine of human invention and the motor of politics. It is also what spurs on this never-ending modern desire to master nature and the body (see chapter 7). Having considered 'security' in this first part, I now turn to consider in the next two chapters Blackstone's second absolute right, liberty.

PART II
LIBERTY

4

From Liberties to Liberty

Crafting Territory and the Law with the Body

> It is the entrance of the state into the field of practice and thought
> that we should try to grasp.
> —Foucault, *Security, Territory, Population* (2009, 247)

After security, in this book's second part I chart the becoming-natural of modernity's second absolute right, liberty; or, in my perspective, the second knot in the relation that constituted the state-subject relation. Only, with liberty, I shift my focus from the state to the subject. Liberty as shaped by the practice of the law, or 'vernacular liberty', as Paul Halliday (2010) termed it, is my object in this chapter; whereas I return to a philosophical liberty and canonical texts in the next one. Here I trace the specific practices where individual liberty was constructed as 'natural' and as 'incontestable' by being attached to the body at key junctures in the English Revolution, which is widely considered to constitute the threshold of legal modernity (see Berman 2003; Kiser and Kane 2001; Comninel 2000; Lachmann 1989; Gould 1987). I analyse this practical liberty as a mode of attachment whose spatial referent evolved from a localised, medieval place to the abstract, modern space of the state. However, to understand liberty as something that ties rather than frees is to come up against one of liberal modernity's most enduring myths. Does a right Blackstone (1848, 92) was adamant was 'absolute' and belonged to 'all mankind' not foreclose attempts to apprehend liberty as something that *relates*, hence as specific to the relation it founds, which is to say, in relative terms? Not quite, I hope to show. These claims to absoluteness and to a human nature lie at the core of the myth's effectiveness. Historical practices serve in this chapter to set these claims into relief by showing how the liberty we know today simply evolved out of another form. Medieval liberties were plural and communal. Their referent was a collective and metaphorical 'body politic'. In this chapter I track how the body underwriting liberty shifted from the collective to the individual body, and how this transformation, in turn, begat coextensively modern liberty and the figure of the individual to peg it upon. 'The individual' was not a pertinent category of political and philosophical life in the Middle Ages. Its creation in the law as the linchpin of modern

Birth of the State. Charlotte Epstein, Oxford University Press (2021). © Oxford University Press.
DOI: 10.1093/oso/9780190917623.001.0001

liberty is at the heart of this chapter. I show how liberty was both naturalised and individualised by the body being de-collectivised and de-metaphorized, as it were; disentangled from the body politic and reattached instead to the biological body. This, at the same time that this body was being bared to the view in the anatomy theatre, as we will see in chapter 7. Here, I analyse how liberty changed from a collective to an individual notion as the law turned to the body.

The space between political incorporation and corporealisation, between the metaphorical and the biological body, is the one I explore in this chapter. My two-pronged argument is that an individual liberty was crafted by being attached simultaneously to the actual, non-metaphorical body and to territory, the state's spatial expression. First, I show how liberty evolved in the practice of the law from a set of localised, collective liber*ties* that belonged to a communal corpus, to a liber*ty* that attached instead to the individual, via his or her body. This transformation was bound up, second, with *territorialisation*, by which I mean the process of centralisation that yielded the bounded space of statehood, or territory. In the Middle Ages, a person enjoyed a certain number of privileges or 'liberties' as a function of the place he or she occupied in the social order. These liberties were indissociable from the social bond and from the communal mode of organization that is encapsulated by the corporation, that distinctly medieval political form. Only this collective body was experienced, not as an abstract entity, but as a tangible, lived thing—as just as real as we experience our bodies. Medieval liberties are my focus in the first part of the chapter. I explore the medieval corporation and the social imaginary it rested upon, in order to render familiar this figure of the collective-yet-concrete body that has faded from memory. Medieval liberties were deeply bound up with an Aristotelian 'place'. In the chapter's second part, I consider two sets of religious and legal practices by which liberty was progressively unmoored from place and re-moored to an emergent territory. The first are early modern practices of toleration that developed during the Reformation, *auslauf*, or 'walking out' to practice one's faith, and the *schuilkerk*, where, conversely, communities drew into their homes for the same purposes. The second is *Calvin's Case*, the first common law case of naturalisation. I mean 'naturalisation' here in the technical legal sense of investing a person with citizenship rights. But I am also invoking the other, critical, sense in which I have also been using the term so far, of 'naturalisation' as the factory of the taken-for-granted. The double entendre at play in the legal term reveals, I suggest, what I call a twofold practical intuition at work in the law itself, namely, first, of the constructed-ness of rights, but also, second, of the extent to which this constructing relies on a making-natural. With *Calvin's Case* I show how liberty was detached from place and tied instead to territory, by being inscribed by the king's judges in the embodied relation between sovereign and subject. Habeas corpus, the peculiar instrument of English common law that explicitly

foregrounds the body, is my object of analysis in the third part. I trace its transformation, around the figure of Edward Coke, from a tool of territorialisation
and state-building to the weapon of choice employed in defence of the subject's
liberty. Coke's evolution from a servant of the sovereign to the champion of the
subject's rights mirrors the shift, in this book's second part as a whole, from the
pole of the state to that of the subject that is effected by turning from 'security'
to 'liberty'.[1] The history of habeas corpus also contains the liminal moment of
the separation of powers that would eventually beget popular sovereignty and
the democratic state as we know it. The body of the subject, I show, comprised
the site of this original splitting constitutive of political modernity. In closing,
I analyse how both habeas corpus and birthrights, the form of rights rooted
in the body, were reclaimed during the English Revolution on the side of the
subject by, amongst others, John Lilburne and the soldiers in Cromwell's army.
Methodologically, I identify salient moments, processes, and actors in the shift
from the metaphorical to the biological body in the practice of the law, and how
it was bound up with the making of territory. Histories of the English Revolution,
legal histories, case law, historical sociologies, and the Putney Debates afford me
my sources and materials. Mine is genealogical rather than a causal history, in
that I circumscribe key junctures in the making of the liberty we know today out
of a very different kind that remains buried in the recesses of the past, not least
because it has been actively foreclosed by the liberal myth, which has tended to
emphase the break that modern liberty comprised (but not modern property,
see chapter 6). It is a history turned towards the present that aims nevertheless to
take history seriously, in its continuities and in its changes. This is the first of two
places where I move from texts to practices. The second is chapter 7, where, after
the law, I turn to medicine.

1. To Have a Collective Body (*Corpus Habere*):
Medieval Liberties

The Medieval Corporation

Understanding liberty in the Middle Ages requires first understanding the central role of the corporation in the organisation of medieval rule. The Church was
the original corporation. Corporation law developed out of canon law integrating
elements of the *Corpus juris civilis*, a body of Roman civil law rediscovered in the
twelfth century (Tierney 1982; 1997; Canning 1988). The term 'corporation' soon
came to designate any voluntary association of individuals brought together by
common purpose, whether religious (like the church), professional (a guild),
or geographic (a town or borough; Frohnen 2005).[2] Hospitals, universities,

and colleges were also corporations (Holdsworth 1922). On the model of the 'estate' initially donated by the monarch to the church, the corporation carved out a discrete territorial entity endowed with an 'immunity' from interference from other local jurisdictions, and thus a measure of legal and economic autonomy. Medieval England, while a single realm, comprised a patchwork of jurisdictions endowed with special privileges that were jealously guarded against one another's, but also against the monarch's encroachments (see Halliday 2010, 86). Examples included the trading powers of the City of London, or the semi-autonomous status of the so-called counties palatine (Durham, Lancaster, and Chester). These liberties composed 'a franchise', the term itself having been ushered into the language of liberty by the Frankish invasion of Gaul at the fall of the Roman Empire (Harding 1988). From the thirteenth century onwards, the urban corporation became a crucible for the development of vernacular liberties across Europe.[3] The town or city was an association of 'freemen' relieved from some of the legal, moral, and economic obligations that obtained in the web of allegiances to overlapping jurisdictions and authorities composing the agrarian feudal system (Berman 2003; Frohnen 2005; Frug 1980; Harding 1980). In England, this occurred against a backdrop of legal and administrative centralisation where, earlier than elsewhere in Europe, the monarch increasingly asserted the pre-eminence of his or her power over the feudal lords' local powers (Comninel 2000; Kiser and Kane 2001). Examples of the 'free customs' enjoyed by townspeople include unimpeded access to markets, exemption from toll or passage dues, but also marriage rights, and the right to control the office of sheriff (Frohnen 2005). The model of the grant by royal charter was formalised in the fourteenth century. In England the quintessential 'charter of liberties' was the Magna Carta, which, as Alan Harding (1988, 434) has underlined, was 'not a bill of rights for individuals' but rather 'the greatest charter of territorial immunity and communal privilege'; notwithstanding the ways in which it would be mobilised during the revolution to begin to assert these individual rights, as we will see further in the chapter. The corporation's autonomy became a source of tension with the centrifugal forces of the monarch, to the extent that they became the object of a specific category of 'Crown litigations'.[4] The structure nonetheless developed apace in England, spurred on by the forces of trade and indeed the Crown's own pecuniary interests (since the royal charters were purchased; Frohnen 2005). Eventually the Crown itself, then Parliament, endowed itself with corporate capacities (Holdsworth 1922; Kantorowicz 1957; Turner 2016).

This communal structure, then, underwrote medieval liberties. Legally, 'incorporation' was the act of bringing into existence in the law a grouping of many as one entity, which was thereby said to 'have a body', *corpus habere* (see Turner 2016). It was the creation in the law of a collective body within which a certain amount of liberties were apportioned to its members. This body was attached to a place—literally, to begin with, since, in English law, an act of incorporation required both a name and a location. But 'place' was also the primary locus of identification and belonging in the Middle Ages. Epistemologically, it was underwritten by the Aristotelian conception of space, as we saw in chapter 1. The medieval historian Allan Harding (1988) has traced how this place-based immunity was progressively extended, first, to the 'immunist', typically the English baron, then to the other kinds of corporations across the realm. The act also required a sovereign, this structure's linchpin. This franchise model marks the crucial difference with modern individual liberty: liberties were granted from on high and they were revocable. They were not 'naturally' given, as a mere function of an individual being born. Incorporation was also the process of an individual's integration into this collective body, for example, into a community of faithful, in religious conversions (see Corpis 2014). Having resided in a town for a year and a day without having breached its laws and its mores was the typical requirement for being admitted into its corporation and enjoying urban freedoms (see Babot, Boucaud-Maître, and Delaigue 2002). In sum, medieval liberties were a top-down, highly localised set of gradated privileges that were institutionalised over time and tied to a place, now in the sense of a position within a static and hierarchical order.[5] This place was also that to which a certain amount of justice was 'due', in the context of a conception of justice understood as an apportionment of 'rightness' throughout the natural-cum-social-cum-legal order, which I consider more closely in chapter 6. These liberties were also impersonal. They rested upon 'objective' rights, lodged in and legitimised by an external order, in contradistinction to our 'subjective' rights (Villey 1975; see also Douzinas 2000). In this topological and deeply communal logic, the social bond, not the body, was the locus of liberty.

The Realness of the Body Politic in Medieval Language and Custom

As the importance of the corporation in the Middle Ages evinces, the metaphor of the body politic was nothing new in the seventeenth century. The body had long afforded political thought a reservoir of tropes for grappling with its oldest problem, how to hold together the many as one, metaphor of which dates back at least to Aristotle.[6] It was adapted by Paul to invoke the unity of the Church by reference to Christ's body (*corpus Christi*). Yet this does not explain how incorporation, and therefore the body, became the prevailing frame for apprehending the problem of political unification in the Late Middle Ages. Roman law already possessed, in fact, another term, *universitas*, to designate 'that which is turned into one' (per its etymology) and is endowed with a legal personality distinct from that of its members (see Turner 2016). Moreover, this was the term that originally carried over into medieval law, as the generic category for a variety of associations of people brought together by a common purpose, such as *municipia* or *civitates* (towns or cities), *collegia* (universities), *societates* (societies), and *coloniae* (colonies) (Turner 2016, chap. 1). For example, the barons of England belonged to the *universitas regni*, the ruling body of the realm; the university of Paris was founded as a *universitas* (see Tierney 1982; Turner 2016). Moreover, *universitas* was still readily used in the mid-seventeenth century for a political association and as an alternative to 'politique corporation', and thus available to Hobbes (Skinner 2005). The ecclesiastical term, for its part, seeped into secular usage in the thirteenth century (see Kantorowicz 1997; Tierney 1982; Canning 1988). The central role of Thomas Aquinas in the development of medieval law (see chapter 7), the church as the referent for universality, and as the main client of corporation law account, to some extent, for the progressive generalisation of the term. Yet it was only possible, I suggest, because the structures underwriting the medieval social and political imaginary were non-individualist, literally without the figure of the individual; such that the individual body was *not* the default referent that 'corporation' conjured. The term wrought a *corpo-realisation* of the law, in the dual sense of making flesh and making real, or indeed realising by making flesh.

In the Middle Ages, the subsumption of individuals into a communal body—their *in*-corporation, or absorption into this body—birthed their liberties. The social bond was both a bind and the fount of liberties. This bond was no abstraction; the medieval town, no 'artificial entity', as the medieval urban historian Gerald Frug (1980, 1083–86) has emphasised. It was lived by its members as a thoroughly concrete, natural one; as, moreover, a microscopic reflection of 'the divinely instituted harmony of the universe' (Frug 1980, 1086). For his part Henry Turner (2016, 24) has parsed the many ways in which the medieval corporation was 'endowed with integrity and identity, understood as taking action and having force, recognized as possessing a physical and even an affective presence.' The premodern relation of the word to the world helps us make sense of this concreteness of language. Michel Foucault has shown how, in the Middle Ages, 'words' (*les mots*) and 'things' (*les choses*) were woven together in a single seamless weft of being. Signs and the objects they referred to were conjoined. They existed on the same plane. Consequently, metaphors, like the body politic, were tangible things and not abstract entities. Moreover, macrocosms mirrored microcosms, in this episteme founded in the similitude. This relation of imitation was the 'crease' running through the world (*la pliure du monde*): fold it together, and each would appear on either side. This reflecting was literal; it was distinct from the re-presenting, from the doubling up that makes something present a second time upon the plane of language. It was '[an] effect of nature' rather than of language (Foucault 2005, 78). Hence the medieval referent-object was always-already present in its sign, rather than re-presented by it. This ontological continuity and imitative relation are what modern science would puncture in the seventeenth century. It set words adrift, as it were. From then on, signs and their referent-objects evolved onto discrete planes, of abstractions and concrete things, respectively. Henceforth in the history of language, the world would merely 'touch upon the banks of discourse' but no longer flow onto them (Foucault 2005, 141). This distance is what enabled the new modes of abstraction that, in turn, made possible the modern forms of representation, linguistic and political. It sustained the scheme of representation Hobbes devised, of the many being abstracted into the one, and that he sought to make real for his audience by tapping into a familiar, corporealising metaphor.

The realness of the communal bond, the extent to which it was lived in the flesh, was also expressed in custom and ritual. A community was also a 'spiritual body' (*corpus mysticum*), whose unity was regularly re-enacted, and restored, through ritual. The processions that rhythmed the village or town life functioned as recurrent reminders to their inhabitants that Christian salvation was a collective, not an individual undertaking. Benjamin Kaplan (2007) has underlined how the church bells pealing through the countryside chimed these ties. Communal bonds were also reasserted in non-religious customs, like the 'perambulation' in the English country, whereby villagers would walk its outer bounds at significant moments in the parish's life (Thompson 1991). More than just an administrative or political unit, the village or the town remained an organic entity to which the individual was bound, spiritually and physically, well into the seventeenth century. The physicalness of the bond was manifest in conversion rituals. Duane Corpis (2014, 200–201) recounts the story of a convert who spat a needle and two nails to complete her incorporation into a new community of faith. Communion was perhaps the ultimate rite designed to regularly experience, reaffirm, and indeed repair communal ties. Parishioners would refuse to partake in it if they were at odds with other members of the parish, such that much of the priests' work consisted in repairing social relations in order to restore a community to its wholeness (see Kaplan 2007, 67–68). The realness of the communal bond accounts for the widespread early modern problematique of purity and pollution. Sin was experienced as a contagious disease that threatened to contaminate the social body as a whole. To commune with sinners or indeed heretics was tantamount to sharing in their sin. The danger was not just a moral one; the very integrity of the *corpus* was at stake. Excluding sinners from Communion was a necessary surgical procedure at times, akin to severing a gangrened limb. Since salvation concerned body and soul (per the Christian concept of personhood, see chapter 6), it was common, in Catholic and reformed areas alike, to refuse to let non-believers, or those of a different faith, be buried in the local cemetery, and to demand instead that they be left out on the gallows, like those of the criminals I will consider in chapter 6 (see Kaplan 2007, 95–96). In sum, in both language and in custom, the corporation was still a very real, natural entity in the seventeenth century.

2. Untying Liberties from Place, Binding Liberty to Territory

Liberty in the Middle Ages is inconceivable outside of its relation to place. In this second part, I will consider some of the ways in which liberty was dislodged from place in the seventeenth century, as a condition of possibility of its being attached to another kind of space altogether, that of the state. Liberty's abstraction from place is what enabled it to evolve from a set of practices to a concept, from liber*ties* to liber*ty*. It echoed the abstraction at work in the epistemological concept of space that begat 'territory' in the sphere of political. Here I analyse two key sites where liberty was detached from place: the practices that developed during the wars of religion to accommodate the coexistence of multiple faiths in the same place, and *Calvin's Case* (1608), the common law case that founded modern birthrights by tying them to both the biological body and to territory. While the former takes me beyond the geographical confines of my initial genealogical terrain (England), they provide the broader context that saw the link of community to place loosened during the course of the seventeenth century, as an effect of negotiating the problem of religious differences.

Early Modern Practices of Toleration: *Auslauf* and the *Schuilkerk*

How multiple communities could live together in one place was the great challenge posed by the Reformation. By producing a common authority and subjecting to it, was Hobbes's stark theoretical response, we saw in chapter 2; and it yielded the concept of the state. Early modern historians have recently shown how an array of arrangements were tried out during the wars of religion that laid down the practical foundations for the Westphalian peace (Kaplan 2007; Corpis 2014). I focus on two of these practices of toleration, *auslauf* or 'walking out' of the village or town in order to commune together beyond its walls, and the *schuilkerk* or 'house church', whereby, conversely, believers drew into the shelter of the home to worship collectively. Both were entrenched by the post-Westphalian legal framework designed to support religious pluralism in Northern Europe. Both were also ways of negotiating the boundaries of the *corpus*, spatial and spiritual, and ultimately of reasserting its unity; sometimes its uniformity. They enabled those who did not share the main faith of their town or village to carve out their own spaces of communal worship within and without, beyond the city walls or in the privacy of their homes. Benjamin Kaplan (2007) describes how the elaborate *schuilkerks* blended more or less seamlessly into the fabric of Dutch towns, and the formidable spectacle of vast processions of Protestants, up to ten thousand people, walking out into the countryside around Catholic Vienna every Sunday on foot, horse and wagon to the song of a Lutheran hymn. These practices were institutionalised in the aftermath of Westphalia in order to enable the peaceful coexistence of Calvinist, Lutheran, and Catholic collective bodies in one location. However, together with the Westphalian 'right of emigration' (*jus emigrandi*), they also supplied less tolerant rulers the tools with which to impose a stricter uniformity upon it, since the peace settlement equally upheld their right to dictate their territory's public confession.[7] Duane Corpis (2014) nicely termed these Westphalia's 'paradoxes of limited tolerance'.

Auslauf and the *schuilkerk* simultaneously reasserted and unsettled the coincidence of place with belief. This coincidence rested on the seventeenth-century distinction between public and private worship. The public worship was the ruler's and often the majority's religion. All other forms of worship were considered private. 'Private' was therefore distinct from 'individual'; the body it referred to was collective. Freedom of conscience was the primary form of liberty at stake in the seventeenth century, as we have seen. Yet while the conscience was where it played out, this form of freedom was not conceived as 'private' in the ways that it would be today. Even as personal an act as converting to a different religion was not considered 'private', as Duane Corpis (2014, 4) has underscored: 'few, if any Christian authorities in post-1648 Germany saw the freedom to convert as an inherent or natural right protecting the individual's inviolable private conscience. At stake was not the integrity and liberty of the autonomous individual'. It was instead, I suggest, that of the collective body. The distinction between public and private worship developed in practice, as a cultural rather than a legal differentiation that was gradually set in stone in the layouts and architectures of the towns and cities, Benjamin Kaplan has shown.[8] It was the product of the distinction between inward belief and its expression in rites being recast as one between public and private worship. It was not a provision for practising one's faith alone, which was meaningless in the seventeenth century (see also Abizadeh 2013). The line between public and private, then, ran 'not around the conscience but around the family house' (Kaplan 2007, 178). Crucially, then, the referent for the public-private boundary thus taking shape in the seventeenth century was the *corpus*, the collective, not the individual, body. On the one hand, by 'walking out', or indeed into their homes and out of the public space to commune, the believers helped maintain intact the boundaries of the communities whose forms of worship they eschewed. This was why they were (mostly) tolerated. On the other hand, these practices unmoored the freedom of conscience from place. They tied it instead more strongly to the collective body, albeit a peripatetic one. They strengthened the *corpus mysticum* while cutting it loose from place. They bred a different spatial imaginary for liberty, one in which it would become possible to envisage sailing for distant shores to practice one's faith.

Grounding Rights in the Body Natural and in Territory: *Calvin's Case*

Another key juncture in seventeenth-century England where political subjecthood was detached from a medieval place and attached instead to the modern space of a state-in-making was *Calvin's Case* (1608). Of its significance a judge in the case, Edward Coke (1932, 381[3b]), wrote: 'though it was one of the shortest [cases] that we ever argued in this Court [the Court of Common Pleas] yet it was the longest and weightiest that ever was argued in any Court, the shortest in syllables and the longest in substance [. . .], both for the present and for all posterity'. It is still considered the founding case for laws of naturalisation and for citizenship rights linked to territory (*jus soli*) as opposed to lineage (*jus sanguini*) (see Price 1997; Kim 1996). Upon Elizabeth I's death in 1603, the English Crown had descended upon the Scottish king James VI, who became James I and was proclaimed 'King of Great Britain' in 1604. James I's coronation had opened up the constitutional question of whether the union of the English and the Scottish crowns had generated a new body politic, Great Britain, or whether they remained two kingdoms with their respective laws, joined together at the crown only. At issue was the realness or substantiveness of incorporation, understood, with Eric Santner (2011, 34), as dual processes of 'constitution and delimitation of a recognizable body politic'. Unsurprisingly, the 'King of Great Britain' was strongly of the opinion that a new body politic had been birthed, and he sought this recognition from his subjects. Ending a speech to a reticent English Parliament he had declared: 'I hope therefore no man will be so vnreasonable to think that [. . .] I being the Head, should haue a divided and monstrous Body' (cited in Kim 1996, 155). The case afforded the opportunity to settle the thorny matter elsewhere—and for the king to sidestep a tetchy Parliament.

'Calvin' (not his real name) was a Scottish subject who had inherited a property title in England that was being contested by the English brothers Nicholas and Robert Smith. The legal issue under discussion was the status of the '*postnati*', individuals born after James I's accession to the throne. The judges were to determine whether a Scottish subject was to be considered a 'native' under English law, entitled to the same levels of protections as an English subject, or whether he was to remain an 'alien', which would invalidate the property title. The judges upheld the Scottish subject's right to inherit the title, thereby 'naturalizing' him into English-now-turned-British law. The case defined 'for all posterity' the legal act of admitting an alien into the rights of a native-born subject. It takes us into an early modern legal factory of subject-making, as it were; to the place where a British subjecthood was originally crafted out of an English and a Scottish one. Conversely, the determination by the judges that both nations were under the same laws of subjecthood effectively established England and Scotland as a single realm. I will show how the biological body was used instead of a meta-phorical one for resolving the constitutional question of the realm's unity.[9] The judges articulated the operation of incorporation in the law by reaching beyond it—for the bodies of the sovereign and the subject. In what follows I show how *Calvin's Case* lays bare the profound links between the two dimensions of incor-poration, that is, between the constitution of the modern state and its delineation within a territory.

The argumentation in the case turned on the theory of the 'corpora-tion sole', that peculiar branch of English corporation law that was born of its extension to the Crown in the sixteenth century, and that established the latter as a single member possessing two bodies, one natural and one 'politic' (Kantorowicz 1957; Santner 2011; Turner 2016).[10] The case for the king would have to emphasise these bodies' oneness. On the side of the Crown were two of the key architects of the modern state, historical enemies who, here, found themselves aligned; Francis Bacon, the founder of modern science (see chapter 6), who served as solicitor general in the case, and Edward Coke, who sat as a lead judge. Bacon had already a few years earlier conceived 'the in-corporation' effected by James I's accession to the throne in geometric terms, illustrating how the political imaginary was already being worked by the new geometric space: 'when the lines of two kingdoms do meet in the person of one monarch [they do so] as in a true point or perfect angle' (cited in Turner 2016, 12). Here, Bacon shifted his rhetorical grounds from geometrical to bi-ological and legal bodies. Deploying his argument in favour of a tight union, Bacon declared:

> Although his body politic of king of England, and his body politic of king of Scotland, be several and distinct, yet nevertheless his natural person, which is one, hath an operation on both. (cited in Turner 2016, 12)

Bacon's formulation is interesting on several counts. First is the extent to which contemporary usage has inverted the sense of 'body', as Turner (2016) has underlined. What we would today refer to as 'the body' (the actual, biolog-ical body) is 'the person' under these lawyers' pens; whereas their 'body' is the abstract construct, the body politic. Hence the primary meaning of 'body' for the law was metaphorical and thus collective, not individual and biological. Second, the biological body (their 'natural person') 'hath an operation': it conjoins the two bodies politics, England and Scotland, creating, as Bacon puts it, 'a privity [an intimacy] between' them (cited in Turner 2016, 12). This natural operation, moreover, trumped legal incorporation. It was the true meaning, Bacon continued, of the union of the crowns, whether or not the kingdoms had been formally 'united under one law and one parliament, thereby incorporated and made as one kingdom' (ibid).

The problem that the proponents of a tighter union faced is that the theory of corporation sole, in accommodating the monarch's multiple bodies, made room for maintaining the kingdoms separate. Corporation law laid the grounds for contending that each realm had its own 'politic body or capacity' in Coke's (1932, 388–89[10a]) terminology, even while these were held together by the monarch's 'natural person'. This was the route taken by the defendants, who questioned Calvin's right to inherit an English freehold. England and Scotland were undoubtedly attached to the monarch, these lawyers contended, only as to two different legal persons, such that the Scottish subject could not lay claim to the protections afforded English subjects, albeit by the same king. The two realms remained separate legal entities, and Calvin was an alien by English law.[11] The counterargument thus had to undo these claims to separateness. Bacon and then Coke shifted the grounds of the argumentation onto the king's 'natural' and away from his 'mysticall' person. Here is where a decisive shift from the metaphorical to the biological body occurred in the discourse of the law. Bacon effectively mobilised the 'natural person' against the 'body politic', in order to close the breach opened by the metaphorical body and stitch the two realms together. Only, as a solicitor, he could not leave the form of corporate law developed for the Crown to his opponents. In deploying his argument he played on both registers, and on the deeper, epochal rift that was taking shape between 'words' or the metaphorical, and 'things' or the real. The level of the metaphorical is where he reclaimed corporation law on the side of the Crown, by distinguishing its bodies' distinctness from their separateness. The king did indeed have two (metaphorical) bodies, only they were distinct, not separate, and to emphasise their jointness was not to conflate them. Conjuring Edward Plowden, a major theorist of Crown corporation law (see Kantorowicz 1957), he argued: 'though there be in the king two bodies, and that those two bodies are conjoined, yet they are by no means confounded the one by the other' (Bacon, cited in Turner 2016, 12). Meanwhile, the real body was achieving a different kind of 'operation' altogether, one that carried the argument beyond the law and the metaphorical, and grounded it instead directly in nature. It joined together the two realms in ways that even the law could not, which needed to hold the bodies distinct (but not separate). He was true to his king's word when he put to the Parliament: 'What God had conjoyned then, let no man separate (cited in Kim 1996, 155).

The substantive question that the case raised for the king's judges was whether the bond between the subjects and their monarch—between James I and Calvin, him and the Smith brothers—was specific to the laws of each realm, or whether it was grounded in something that superseded them. Significantly, Edward Coke, habitually 'the common law incarnate', chose this time to ground his analysis in natural law; though not without first specifying that 'the law of nature is part of the laws of England' (and not the other way around) (Maitland 1915, 113; Coke 1932, 383[4b]). Only the former was necessarily the same in England and in Scotland. Even for Coke, nature afforded a more solid, incontestable even, foundation for the relation between subjects and sovereigns, since natural laws are given (by God or nature), whereas the laws of the realm are constructed and (even for Coke) ultimately changeable. Coke begins by asking, what is the nature of the 'ligeance' or allegiance the two parties to the relation owe each other. 'Ligeance is the mutual bond and obligation between the King and his subjects', he writes (Coke 1932, 382[5a]). The king is 'the natural liege lord', for Coke (1932, 383[5b]) who mobilised the term's etymological roots in the old feudal 'liege', whereas his people are 'natural liege subjects'. 'This ligeance and obedience is an incident [a quality] inseparable to every subject', Coke (1932, 383[4b]) determines. It is what the subject owes the sovereign as a function of their being born into the relation (4b). '[F]or as soon as he is born', Coke (ibid.) continues, he oweth ligeance and obedience by birth-right [...] to his Sovereign'. Cokes thus locates the quality required for the political bond in the subject at birth rather than in the realm, since it is 'inseparable' from 'every subject'. Here is where he turns to the body. For this quality is not merely a moral one. Mustering the acoustic proximity of 'ligeance' and 'ligatures', Coke writes:

> As the ligatures or strings do knit together the joints of all the parts of the body, so doth ligeances join together the Sovereign and his subjects, *quasi uno ligamine* [almost as one bond]. (Coke 1932, 383[4b])

Compared to other social bonds, like that binding lord and tenant, Coke (ibid.) continues, there is, between sovereign and subject, a 'higher and greater', indeed physical 'connexion' such that the monarch guarantees the subjects' safety in exchange for their obedience. 'Protection draws subjection, and subjection draws protection (*protectio trahit subjectionem, et subjectio protectionem*)' is how Coke (5a) encapsulates the bond of mutual obligation.[12] The body looms large in Coke's report, where the law bears 'eyes', 'ears', and a 'stomach' (which is the legal record); it is 'tasted' and 'digested' by the judges (Coke 1932, 381[4a]). Other judges in the case also emphasized the physicality of the primordial political relation, moreover. Judge Flemming, for his part, determined that 'the deriva-tion of *ligencia* is from *liga*, a bond begun by birth, and ended by death' (cited in Halliday 2010, 70).

Incorporation as Constitution: The Constitutive Effects of Corporealising Rights

The sovereign-subject relation was *corpo-realised* in the law in *Calvin's Case*, realised by being rooted in the body. Only this time, the bodies at work were no longer collective ones. They were the monarch's and the subject's. In the context of the case, this served to undo the English defendants' claims to the distinct-ness of their bond and thus of their rights, and to adjudicate in favour of a closer union. If the bond of protection and obedience originates in their biological bodies rather than in the laws of the realm, it is the same for English and Scottish subjects. Beyond the case, birth acquired a new importance for the law. It was established as the site where the sovereign-subject relation is sealed. The king, Coke (1932, 389[10b]) writes, 'holdeth the kingdom of England' not because of his spiritual body, but 'by birth-right inherent', because he is born into a natural one.[13] The case wrought two crucial sets of constitutive effects, that played, re-spectively, on the old work of incorporation sustained by the medieval collec-tive body, and on another kind of naturalising effect altogether that was set into motion by invoking the individual, biological body instead. Both sets of effects came together in this case at the dawn of the seventeenth century. On the side of the state, the corporealisation of the primordial political bond helped incorpo-rate England and Scotland. On the side of the subject, first, locating this bond in the biological body served to generalise it across all of the king's subject. But, second, it would also serve to carry this bond beyond existing subjects, given the legal operation whose contours were being defined, namely, 'naturalisation', which establishes how a non-subject enters into the law to become a subject. The biological body was being established instead of the body politic as the locus of political rights, and as the vehicle for their diffusion.

In fact, this resort to the king's natural body in *Calvin's Case* inverted the more habitual recourses to the idiosyncratic legal artifice with which the English Crown settled many a constitutional matter, the theory of the monarch's two bodies (see Kantorowicz 1957). The monarch's mystical body functioned to secure the unity and perpetuity of the realm by casting it beyond the succession of actual monarchs. It was the symbolic place where to pin this perpetuity.[14] The theory reached its apex under the Tudors, which was also the high point of the process of centralisation that yielded the state. Tudor portraiture shows how Henry VIII and especially Elizabeth I actively cultivated the mystical aura that having such a body implied in the ways that they performed their sovereignty before their subjects.

The mystical body was habitually the one mobilized in juridical matters of the Crown. Here instead, at the dawn of the profound epistemic transformations I etched out earlier, James I's biological body was drawn upon to anchor the union of England and Scotland. The natural body that pre-existed it was conjured to institute this new body politic, Great Britain. Its biological oneness both guaranteed and helped stabilize political unification. English and Scottish subjects were naturalized into British laws, in the legal sense that was being defined by the case. Conversely, James I's body served to naturalise the new territory that was being carved out, now in my sense of using the body to make-natural.[15]

Incorporation as Territorialisation

Calvin's Case is the founding common law case for citizenship rights anchored in territory rather than lineage, or 'territorial birthright citizenship' (Price 1997). We have seen how it founded birthrights, only we remain one step short of comprehending how it attached them to territory, and thus why it has afforded the basis for *jus soli*. Coke seemed, in fact, to have dislodged the political bond from its embeddedness in place. By locating it in the body, he tightened the subject's bond to the sovereign; yet by the same token, he loosened their ties to being born in the realm, at a particular place in the dense web of localised relations that underwrote medieval liberties. Coke (1932, 385[7b]) insisted that, since 'ligeance [. . .] is a quality of the mind and soul', it 'cannot be circumscribed within the predicament of *urbi* (place)'.[16] The defendants in the case had argued that Calvin was an alien because he had been born 'within the kingdom of Scotland' and therefore 'out of his allegiance of the said lord the King of the kingdom of England' (cited in Price 1997, 82). Theirs was a place-based argument. Coke shifted the basis of this allegiance away from the place of birth, and rooted it instead in the subject's embodied relation with the sovereign. 'Ligeance', wrote Coke (1932, 388[9b]) 'cannot be local, or confined within the bounds thereof'. Instead it is 'due to the natural person of the king' (Coke 1932, 389[10a]). He pointedly dismissed the defendants' case that there was 'one local ligeance for the natural subjects of England', and another for those of Scotland as 'utterly insufficient' (Coke 1932, 388[9b]). Coke personalised the primary political relation and he de-localised it. This would seem prima facie to undermine a right (*jus*) grounded in the land (*solum*). In fact, abstracting liberty from place also prepared it for a different kind of space altogether: territory.

Unmooring liberty from place set it moving. 'The subjects of England', wrote Coke (1932, 386[7B]), are 'bound by their ligeance to go with the King, &c in his wars, as well within the realm, &c as without'. Moreover, the 'King of England sendeth his subjects out of England, and his subjects out of Scotland' so that their enemies 'may feel the sword of either nation'. Unfixed from place, ligeance was fixed instead to the sovereign, Bacon's 'true point' at the centre of the new space in the making. This space had several dimensions to it. The first, we have seen, was the delineation of a new space of 'Great Britain' through the suturing together of England and Scotland via the embodied sovereign-subject relation. Constitution and territorialisation thus appear as two sides of a coin. The second was the process of centralisation of the English legal and administrative apparatus, out of which the first modern state is considered to have emerged (see Berman 2003; Kiser and Kane 2001; Comninel 2000; Lachmann 1989; Gould 1987). This was coextensive, third, with the progressive concentration of military power, which occurred by either luring the great nobles or 'magnates' into Royal patronage or by defeating and dismantling their private armies, such that the sovereign's monopoly over armed force was achieved, in England, by the end of the sixteenth century (see Lachmann 1989). One of the courts Coke himself would come to chair, the King's Bench, illustrates how the creation of a legally unified territory centred upon the person of the monarch. This court 'hath the survey of all other courts' as Coke himself explained (quoted in Halliday 2010, 80). It was where the monarch sat, literally or in the person of their chief justice, and from where 'the king ordinarily dispenseth his supreme territorial jurisdiction' in the words of another chief justice and Coke's younger contemporary Mathew Hale (quoted in Halliday 2010, 141). It travelled around England with the monarch, legally and literally. Mobility, Paul Halliday (2010) has shown, was one of the key features of the judicial instrument deployed by the king's judges across the realm to consolidate this territorialisation process, habeas corpus, to which I turn next. In *Calvin's Case* the embodied relation between sovereign and subject is established as the touchstone for territorialisation, understood as the carving out, around a centre point (either geographic or symbolic, or both), of a uniform and legally unified space of statehood (see chapter 1).

The case reveals another, outward, movement at work. For Coke (1932, 388[9b]) adds: 'the King's power, command and protection extendeth out of England' (Coke 1932, 388[9b]). Building on the case Judge Hale would later add: 'Subjection is not only confined to those that are born in England only, not to those only that are born within the territories and dominions of the crown of England, but [extends] to those that are born under the same king, though in separate and independent territories' (cited in Halliday 2010, 71). Birthrights travelled with the monarchs' subjects. Two years before the case (in 1606), James I had granted the colonists in Virginia a bill of rights that afforded them the same rights as Englishmen 'as if they had been abiding and born, within this our realm of England' (cited in Price 1997, 75). Bacon, sure enough, had found the defendants' argument in *Calvin's Case* unsuitable 'for a warlike and magnanimous nation fit for Empire' (cited in Kim 1996, 158). Hence the other movement implicated in territorialisation was imperial expansion. Detaching liberty from place also unleashed colonisation (see Kim 1996). Hannah Weiss Muller (2017) has shown the distinctly colonial form of subjecthood that emerged out of this personalised, delocalised subject-sovereign relation. The farther from England they sailed, the more ardently colonisers reaffirmed their attachment to its monarch in celebrations and public events, she shows. They self-consciously cherished this bond as the fount of their liberties—and as a (more or less) implicit justification for not extending them to the colonized. 'Sovereigns consistently served as a crucial focal point for subjects as they dispersed across the expanding European empires', Weiss Muller (2017, 2) underlines. Bounding and expanding outwards, drawing boundaries at home and acquiring land abroad, thus appear closely entwined from the onset, the two sides to the making of the modern state. Our missing step, then, was the shift from place to territory, which, rather than the city, manor, or even the country or nation, is the spatial referent for modern citizenship birthrights.

3. From a *Corpus Habere* to the Habeas Corpus

In this chapter's third and final part I analyse the passage from the communal body of medieval law's *corpus habere* to the individual body, by way of the increasingly central role acquired by habeas corpus as an instrument for transforming the law itself in the English Revolution. During the course of the seventeenth century, habeas corpus rapidly evolved from an arcane instrument of common law to the weapon of choice for asserting the subject's liberty. The significance of 'the Great Writ of Liberty' as the touchstone of modern democracy and the guarantor of individual rights and liberties is well known (Halliday 2010, 2). Contra its mythologisation in liberal thought, however, Giorgio Agamben (1998, 124) has drawn out how it comprised the site where the bare body, not 'the free man and his statutes and prerogatives', was made the real subject of modern politics. However, Agamben has also reduced it to being the starting point of 'biopower', a distinctly modern, corporeal, bottom-up power geared to make-live rather than to kill, first identified by Foucault (2003). The biopolitical problematique more generally has led, I suggest, to an overemphasis upon an ultimately elusive notion of 'life', at the expense of the broader work wrought by the body in this foundational episode of modern politics. The writ's primary purpose was to assert the sovereign power of the law, not to keep the subject alive. Strictly speaking, the body needed not be alive, merely produced before the authority demanding it. I thus revisit the story of modern liberty's emblem to appraise the extent to which the state and the subject of rights mutually constituted each other. I track how habeas corpus was wielded first to sustain, then to contain, the state-in-the-making. For the writ also holds the story of the initial separation of powers that would yield its more democratic form, and a sovereignty (in England) divided across 'King and Parliament'. The subject's body, I will show, was the site of this original renting. Edward Coke, who spent the first half of his public career serving the two monarchs who ruled at the apex of the territorialisation process (Elizabeth I and James I), before dedicating the rest of his life to checking the concentration of powers he had helped engineer, takes centre stage in the story I tell. As a lawmaker, he articulated better than anyone the process of legal subjection we have seen; then he used his position to buttress this subject's political agency and their rights. I also consider other ways in which the body was drawn upon during the revolution to consolidate these rights, notably by John Lilburne and the common soldiers of Cromwell's army in the Putney Debates (1647).

A 'writ' or *brève*, in medieval law, was a short written command stamped with a seal that testified to the authority of the issuer. Writs of habeas corpus began appearing in common law in the thirteenth century (see Pollock and Maitland 1889, 586). They compel an authority who has performed an arrest to present the arrested 'body' before the authority who has issued it. They took many forms over the course of its history, but the most common was *habeas corpus ad subjuciendum et recipiendum* (Oaks 1965; Ekeland 2006). The body (*corpus*) is to be presented or 'had' (*habeas*) in order to be subjected (ad *subjiciendum*) to the authority of the law by 'receiving' (*et recipiendum*) the account of the subject's deeds. This corporeal encryption—inscribing the subject's body with the narrative of their actions—afforded, in turn, the basis for determining their guilt or innocence. The issuance of habeas corpus thus set in motion the due process of the law. But it also served to assert the authority of the issuer. In medieval England's complex patchwork of jurisdictions, it was jealously drawn on by all manner of courts to guard their legal privileges—their 'liberties'—from encroachments by other courts.[17] Habeas corpus was thus not originally intended to serve the subject's defence. The 'prerogative writ' was but an instrument in the ceaseless tug-of-war between jurisdictions that served mostly 'not to get people out of prison, *but to put them in it*' (Jenks 1902, 64, emphasis in original). In his careful study of the early modern habeas corpus archive, Halliday (2010) has shown that the writ's period of most intense use was not the English Revolution, with which it tends to be associated, but rather in the last decades of the reign of Elizabeth I, the high point of territorialisation. Habeas corpus was actively harnessed to the vast enterprise of legal and administrative centralisation, to the extent that it would become over the course of the sixteenth century the 'King's writ' (Jenks 1923). The King's Bench would use it to assert its prerogatives and, progressively, its pre-eminence over the other courts. The way this court wielded habeas corpus in relation to powers of arrest and imprisonment illustrates how the top-down structure of medieval liberties sustained territorialisation. These powers were local liberties bestowed by the monarch (upon abbeys, for example) on a case by case basis, as we have seen. Under the Tudors, the King's Bench increasingly dispatched writs of habeas corpus across the realm to these other courts to control how they were used. 'The jails', Chief Justice Hale explained, 'are all in the king's disposal [. . .] for the law hath originally trusted none with the custody of the bodies of the king's subject [. . .] but the king or such to whom he deputed it' (quoted in Halliday 2010, 74). The writ, however, was also used to expand the Bench's powers into areas in which it did not have recognised competences. This direct link to, and growing investment by, the sovereign's power is what gave habeas corpus its unusual force as a legal instrument in the sixteenth and early seventeenth centuries. This power was 'analogised outwards', first throughout the realm, but also later throughout the empire, as Halliday (2010, 72) has shown. Henry VIII's nationalisation of the church would render the resort to habeas corpus moot in the case of abbeys. They were both mustered in the making of territory.

From a Servant of the Sovereign to the Champion of the Subject's Liberty: Edward Coke

Edward Coke's appointment as chief justice of the King's Bench in 1613 crowned a shining career in two monarch's employ and across a dynastic change. Appointed by Elizabeth I as her attorney general in 1594, he helped her reassert her position at the helm of the first national Church by working to uphold Henry' VIII's Act of Supremacy (1543). In 1595 he wrote: 'by the authority of many acts of Parliament, the kingdom of England is an absolute monarchy' (quoted in Berman 2003, 238–39). He was retained as attorney general by James I, who rather agreed; before being appointed chief justice of the Courts of Common Pleas in 1606, where he adjudicated in favour of legal and territorial unification in *Calvin's Case*, as we saw. Coke then served as chief justice of the King's Bench from 1613 to 1616. His lifelong commitment, however, was to the laws of the realm, whose integrity he would defend at all cost, including against its other institutions, and even, when necessary, against the monarch. His confrontation with the Stuart king slowly ratcheted up over the first decade of his rule. In a series of cases decided between 1606 and 1616, Coke systematically asserted the prerogative of courts of common law, which included the ancient King's Bench, over the recently created royal courts (see Jenks 1902, 74). Here too he drew upon the habeas corpus, only, this time, to push back against the monarch's judicial power. Another

expression of the Tudor's intensifying judicial absolutism had been the establishment, by royal prerogative, of a series of new courts that were both better suited
to meeting new types of economic, social, and political problems, and indeed to
asserting the supremacy of royal justice over local jurisdictions. The Court of Star
Chamber in particular, the most efficient court under the Tudors, would come to
epitomise monarchical excess and arbitrariness with the Stuarts, as James I and
Charles I increasingly used it to prosecute their opponents, including reluctant
noble taxpayers who were too powerful to bring to trial in the lower courts (see
Berman 2003, 211–13; Jenks 1923). Dismantling the Star Chamber would be one
of the first provisions of the 1641 Habeas Corpus Act, passed after Coke's death
but bearing his thumb. The act delinked the writ from the monarch's historic
right to imprison, even for reasons of state, thus forcefully asserted the autonomy
of the due process of the law it had come to represent (see Cohen 1940).

   Coke initially picked his battle with the king where he served, in the judiciary;
more precisely at the juncture where the old courts, concentrating the essence of
'the old Law of the Land', in the words of one of his most ardent admirers, John
Lilburne (1645), met the newer courts that increasingly emblematised executive
overreach. His two weapons of choice would be Magna Carta and habeas corpus.
For Coke (*Ninth Report*, cited in Hostettler 1997, 151), 'the great antiquity of the
[...] courts of common law' handed down through the ages 'ever since the time
of King Arthur who reigned about the year of our Lord 516' condensed the true
character of the English nation. The law that had stood the test of time was, properly, the one that was condensed in the monarch's spiritual body, the repository
of the realm's continuity. Hence, to resume the terms of the reasoning found in
Calvin's Case, it would require being preserved against the excesses of monarchs,
like the Stuarts, who were swayed by the passions of their natural bodies. By way
of a substantive body of work (the four volumes of the *Institutes of the Laws of
England* and the thirteen books of his *Reports*), which moreover, were in increasingly wide circulation with the acceleration of printing that played a key role in
the English Revolution, Coke systematically dusted off and revived common law
principles and instruments to meet rapidly changing social, political, and economic circumstances. Indeed the 'laws of England' were the 'true touchstones
to sever the pure gold from the dross and sophistication of novelties and new
inventions', except of course his own (Coke, quoted in John Hostettler 1997, 153).
For 'out of the old fields must come the new corne' Coke (1932, 381[3b]) wrote.
He ploughed its old statutes and precedents relentlessly. After three years of what
appeared to the king as systematic obfuscation, albeit couched in the name of
upholding his Bench, James I dramatically dismissed Coke in 1616.

   Coke then took his battle to the institution that had custodianship of the law
and that, in the 1620s, would progressively rise up against the king: Parliament.
In England's (and Britain's) early seventeenth-century institutional landscape,

Parliament comprised the single counterpoint to an increasingly centralising and territorialising sovereign. The confrontation between England's 'Crown' and its 'Country' is the well-known story of the original separation of powers that would yield the first modern democratic state (Stone 2002; Hill 1980; Gould 1987). Coke himself personifies the extent to which the legal and the judiciary were still folded together at this point. The confrontation would catalyse around taxes that were perceived to be illegitimate, first under James I, who, in 1614, dissolved a Parliament that had denied him extraordinary 'impositions' (as they were known), then under his son Charles I, who was denied the lifelong taxes customarily granted to a monarch upon his accession to the throne in 1625. Edward Coke was elected to the House of Commons in 1621. Coke formed and chaired a committee of grievance, ostensibly to address the problem of monopolies that were created by the corporate structure underwriting the economy, but that rapidly came to tackle the matter of the House's liberties. On the basis of Coke's report, Parliament issued James I a 'Remonstrance to the King' in December 1621, who peremptorily rejected it, and threw its author into the Tower of London. Undaunted, Coke, who was seventy-three when Charles I acceded to the throne, and seventy-five when he was re-elected to the House of Commons in 1627 (at the same time as a thirty-three-year-old Oliver Cromwell), relentlessly spearheaded Parliament's revolt against the king.

Splitting Sovereignty on the Subject's Body

Habeas corpus features at every step along the way in the story of Parliament's rise. Upon stepping onto the throne the young Charles I, defiant like his father, proceeded to raise compulsory loans, sanctioning those who refused to pay with indefinite imprisonment. The already considerable debt Charles I had inherited from both James I and Elizabeth I was rapidly compounded by the need to finance the war England entered with France in 1627. Disastrous militarily, the war also dragged England into the Thirty Years War it had hitherto succeeded in avoiding, and placed a durable strain upon the Crown's coffers. Faced with increasing resistance, Charles imposed martial law, and billeted soldiers to homes, prompting Coke's most famous saying, 'the house of an Englishman is to him as his castle'.[18] Within a few weeks seventy notables, including some elected members of Parliament, were imprisoned. A legal challenge was mounted against the Crown to protest their indefinite detention in what is known as the Case of the Five Knights (1627), using habeas corpus. The case pitted new claims to the subjects' liberty against a nascent raison d'état we saw in chapter 2, which the Crown explicitly drew upon to justify the legality of the arrests.[19] Up until 1621, Coke too had defended state actions taken in the name of raison d'état

(Butterfield 1975, 17). At this point the modern political logics of subjecthood and sovereignty, both in their liminal phases, were being sharpened against each other.

The challenge to the legality of Charles's campaign of arrests and intimidation then shifted from the courts to Parliament. This, Coke saw, was essential to moving the battle beyond a few individual cases and onto the front foot. He immediately set out to draft a series of 'Resolutions', citing thirty-one precedents and seven statutes, which he promptly presented for their approval to the House of Lords, who prevaricated. Here is where habeas corpus first appeared in the language of lawmaking, and sections of Coke's text would feature in the 1679 Habeas Corpus Act. The resort to the writ was perhaps more necessity than virtue, since there were in fact few instruments Coke could draw upon (see Jenks 1902). Only his stroke of ingenuity was to frame habeas corpus together with the sacred Magna Carta. Already in 1621 after James I had rejected his Remonstrance, Coke had stood up before his peers in the Commons and declared:

> The privileges of this House is [*sic*] the nurse and life of all our laws, the subject's best inheritance. If my sovereign will not allow me my inheritance, I must fly to Magna Carta. . . .The Charter of Liberty because it makes me free. When the King says he cannot allow our liberties of right, this strikes at the root. (quoted in Hostettler 1997, 112)

His conjoining of Magna Carta and habeas corpus would be sealed by his sustained and eventually successful campaign to win over an initially recalcitrant House of Lords. Faced with the Lords' resistance to his Resolutions, he pressed his case, declaring that 'imprisonment in law [. . .] is a civil death'; that 'a prison without a prefixed time is a kind of hell' and that 'the greatest inheritance that a man hath is the liberty of his person, for all others are accessory to it' (Coke, quoted in Hostettler 1997, 130). 'The *Magna Carta*', he added, 'was not a matter of the King's grace but the subject's right and the common law of the land. [. . .] [It] and all the statues [. . .] are absolutes' (ibid., 131, 135):

> Take we heed what we yield unto: Magna Carta is such a fellow that he will have no 'Sovereign'. . . .We must not admit of it, and to qualify it is impossible. (quoted in Hostettler 1997, 135–36)

Instead Coke and his successors would wield the Magna Carta together with habeas corpus to 'qualify' or indeed contain the 'Sovereign'. Eventually adopted by the Lords, the 1628 Petition of Rights drove the initial wedge that began to dislodge sovereignty from the sovereign. It triggered the process that would yield a sovereignty divided across 'King and Parliament'. With it the subject's body became the site where this initial splitting of sovereignty that begat the first modern state occured.

Coke, who died in 1634, did not live to see the next two milestones in the crafting of habeas corpus into the emblem of the subject's liberty. The Act of 1641, which legal historians consider 'one of the greatest achievements' of 'the most memorable Parliament that sat in England', as Churchill called the Long Parliament (1640–59), was reaffirmed after the civil war by a second Habeas Corpus Act in 1679 (Jenks 1923, 526; quoted by Berman 2003, 216). As in the first, sections of the 1679 Act were directly lifted from Coke's Resolutions. Coke's argumentative strategy had tilled the ground for Parliament being able to assert itself against the king as England's sovereign lawmaking body. Via Coke, the arcane writ was successfully retrieved from the bowels of medieval law and charged with a new purpose. In fact, it was carried beyond Coke's beloved realm, the common law, by being entrenched as acts of Parliament. The Habeas Corpus Act became 'one of the three great documents of English liberty', along with Magna Carta, to which its fate was now locked, and the subsequent 1689 Bill of Rights (Hostettler 1997, 139; see also Dicey 1885). By the same token, the subject's body was established as the site where the separation of powers that underwrites modern democratic rule was originally sealed.

Revolutionary English subjects, like Coke; like the five knights; or indeed like the Leveller John Lilburne a little later, had shown their willingness to put themselves in the way of the monarch's expanding powers. In fighting to recover their own ability to move about unimpeded, they had succesfully called into question the legitimacy of the political order that impeded them. Their battle durably lodged liberty in the body of the subject, rather than in any of the corporate bodies to which he or she belonged. As in *Calvin's Case*, it brought individual rather than collective bodies into focus; only this time, and unlike in *Calvin*, the body in question was the subject's. Habeas corpus corpo-realised liberty in the subject's body exclusively.[20]

Claiming Habeas Corpus and Birthrights for the Subject: Lilburne and Cromwell's Soldiers in the Putney Debates

The original birthright articulated by the king's judges in *Calvin's Case* had defined a top-down subjection. During the revolution, this first corporeal right was reclaimed, together with habeas corpus; and not just by the highly ranked. In one of its (many) dramatic episodes John Lilburne, who was notorious for standing up in Parliament, a Bible in one hand and Coke's *Reports* in the other, confronted his gaoler, who, this time, was none other than the same Parliament whose rights the Leveller had fought for (Halliday 2010, 193; see also Berman 2003, 215). Lilburne, who pleaded his own council, argued for his release by ha- beas corpus. His argumentation (condensed in his *England's Birthright Justified*, 1645), grounded his right to the due process of the law in a God-given, natural birthright to an English liberty. The liberty 'freeborn John' invoked was a per- sonal rather than a corporate one, that he claimed to possess simply as a function of being born. He thus conjured a very different sort of incorporation than that in which were founded the claims of a member of a medieval guild or town. It was generated, not by a legal act, but the natural fact of embodiment. Although in this instance the judges remained deaf to his plea (but not to his 'shrill voice'; see Halliday 2010, 194), his argumentation evinced the broader transformation of vernacular liberty that was under way.

Birthrights were also appropriated by the revolution's common soldiers. The Putney Debates were a series of debates held within the ranks of Cromwell's army on London's edge in October 1647, when it was winning on the battle- field. They are widely considered to constitute a founding moment for modern democracy (see Hill 1989; Roots 1974; Macpherson 1962; Brailsford 1961; Mathiowetz 2011). These unusual debates were prompted by the soldiers presenting the army's general council with their Agreement of the People. This was a manner of constitutional document in which they had laid down their vision for the new political order to come, which included universal (male) suffrage. The debates feature discussed in practice and on the ground, by the soldiers who were putting their lives on the line, often without pay, to fend for a more equal political order, the defining themes and tropes of modern polit- ical thought, to which the likes of Hobbes and Locke would subsequently put their pens, like the contract, or the notion of consent (see chapter 5). They pitted common soldiers, on the one hand, most of whom had 'little propriety in the kingdom', as one of them put it, and their Grandee officers, on the other, in- cluding Cromwell himself and his son-in-law Henry Ireton, who hailed from the landed gentry. Maximilian Petty stated the case plainly: 'we judge that all inhabitants that have not lost their birthright should have an equal voice in the elections' (quoted in Woodhouse 1974, 53). Private Edward Sexby, sensing they were losing the argument, elaborated:

> We have engaged in this kingdom and ventured our lives, and it was all for this: to recover our birthrights and property as Englishmen. [. . .] There are many thousands of us soldiers that have ventured our lives; we have had little propriety in the kingdom as to our estates, yet we have had a birthright. But it seems now, except a man hath a fixed estate in this kingdom, he hath no right in this kingdom. I wonder we were so much deceived. If we had not a right to the kingdom we were mere mercenary soliders [*sic*]. [. . .] I shall tell you in a

word my resolution. I am resolved to give my birthright to none. (quoted in
Woodhouse, 1974, 69)

Ireton had flatly defended property as a basis for suffrage by declaring: 'no man
hath a right to an interest or share in the disposing of the affairs of the kingdom
[. . .] that hath not a permanent fixed interest in this kingdom' (Woodhouse
1974, 51). To these interests founded in property the common soldiers sought to
oppose a right founded instead in their body, birthright, as a basis for voting and
partaking in the direction of the realm: 'if we had not a right to the kingdom we
were mere mercenary soldiers'. Sexby again:

I do think the poor and the meaner of this kingdom—I speak in the condition of soliders [sic] in which we are—have been the means of the preservation
of this kingdom. [. . .] And now they demand the birthright for which they
fought. (quoted in Woodhouse 1974, 69)

His fellow soldier Thomas Rainborough concurred:

But I would fain know what the solider [sic] hath fought for all this while? He
hath fought to enslave himself, to give power to men of riches, men of estates, to
make him a perpetual slave. (quoted in Woodhouse 1974, 71)

The soldiers lost their case for universal (male) suffrage, but historically they won
the argument, specifically in the way they conjoined voting rights and the body.
Rights rooted in a body, whether born or naturalised into a political relation with
the state, are the basis for the 'one person, one vote' principle that underwrites
contemporary universal suffrage.

*

In this first chapter on liberty, I have traced the place of the body in the making
of modern law and territory across a range of sites of practice. I charted how the
liberty of the modern political subject emerged in the law out of a progressive
individualisation of a communal notion, as its referent shifted from a metaphorical to a biological entity. Both referents, however, were 'natural' for their times.
Only they implicated different modes of naturalisation, where the natural thing
in which liberty was vested comprised, respectively, a collective, metaphorical
and an individual, biological body. Apprehending the naturalness and realness
of the medieval communal body required understanding the way the medieval
word worked. For words made real in the Middle Ages. Signs and metaphors
were real, material things. They were as real as the afterlife we saw in chapter 2.
I then considered a first set of religious-cum-legal practices where these liberties

began to be detached from place in favour of other communal (religious) bonds, and where the collective body shifted, out of the bounds of the village or town in *auslauf*, or into shelter of the home, in the *schuilkerk*. With *Calvin's Case*, to which I turned next, I showed how this detaching from place enabled a new form of political attachment that implicated a different kind of spatial referent altogether: territory.[21] The case illuminated how the individualisation of liberty via its rooting in the biological body on the one hand, and territorialisation as the process constitutive of the modern state, on the other, were imbricated. It also drew out how boundary-drawing within, and imperial expansion without, comprised the two sides of the early modern territorialisation. Lastly, *Calvin's Case* marked the place in the history of British law when the subject-sovereign relation was lodged in their bodies. Upon these bodies birthrights and the law of naturalisation were first circumscribed. By the same token, these bodies naturalised the primordial modern political relation that was taking shape. The last chapter in this story of liberty's individualisation in the practice of the law via the body was brought by the history of habeas corpus. It cast the subject's body, rather than the sovereign's, decisively in focus during the English Revolution. Tracking the body through a broad range of historical practices has shown how it operated as the vector, not only of the liberty's individualisation, but also of the universalisation of this individualised liberty. This, I suggest, is the intuition that has been folded into the law all along. By being anchored in the body, liberty was located in human nature itself. This gesture crafted coextensively individual liberty and the figure it was pegged onto, the modern subject of rights. I have considered how this figure was constructed by the practice of the law. I will now trace it through foundational texts.

5

Externalising and Internalising Liberty via Discipline

> Let us place ourselves [. . .] at the other end of this immense process where the tree actually bears fruit. [. . .] [We] then find *the sovereign individual* as the ripest fruit on the tree [. . .] an autonomous, supra-ethical individual [. . .] we find a man with his own, independent, enduring will [. . .]—and in him a proud consciousness quivering in every muscle of *what* he has finally achieved and incorporated, an actual awareness of power and freedom, a feeling that man in general has reached completion'.
>
> —Nietzsche (1994)

Liberty, for Hobbes (*L*.chap14[2]79), 'according to the proper signification of the word', is 'the absence of external impediments to motion'. For John Locke (*EHU*, II.21[8]153), it is, in the broadest sense, 'the power to think or not to think, to move or not to move, according to the preference or direction of [one's] mind.' Both defined liberty in relation to motion; strictly of the body, for Hobbes; of the body and mind, for Locke. Freedom of the conscience, the form of liberty most starkly engaged by the wars of religion, loomed large over both. Hobbes's and Locke's concepts of liberty, I show in this chapter, were two different ways of positioning themselves in relation to the interiority of the conscience. Hobbes simply rejected it. He thoroughly externalised liberty by, over the course of his political thought, increasingly narrowing his focus to exclusively corporeal movements. Hobbes conceived liberty on the basis of 'shockingly reductionist observations about the geography of the human soul', as Quentin Skinner (2008, 34) quipped. Or, I suggest, by side-stepping it altogether. This shrewd diagnostician of the English Civil War set out to craft a liberty that was decidedly *not* of the conscience. He sought to establish a common rule for living together that was not founded in the subjects' *foro interno*, the private spaces he carefully sealed off from modern politics, as we saw in chapter 2 (Hobbes. *L*., chap.15[36]99). With the movements of the mind, John Locke retrieved this interiority, and established it as the cornerstone of modern liberty. His 'Freedom of Men under Government' consists in having a common 'standing Rule to live by' (*TT*,

Birth of the State. Charlotte Epstein, Oxford University Press (2021). © Oxford University Press.
DOI: 10.1093/oso/9780190917623.001.0001

II.chap.4[22]284). Only this rule, to work, must be consented to by the polity's members; it must be held within—in the *foro interno*. However, the conscience that Locke recovered at the end of the seventeenth century was quite different to the one Hobbes had cordoned off from the public space. It was a disciplined conscience. In this chapter I will show that Locke was the theorist of the 'disciplinary revolution' that begat capitalist modernity (Gorski 2003). Discipline was the handmaiden to his liberty. The seventeenth century was also the birthplace of disciplines, now in the sense of the ordering of the world into distinct analytical domains. This unique juncture where 'disciplines' as we know them on the one hand, and productive, docile bodies were crafted on the other, together with 'reasonable' (in the Lockean sense), consenting minds, is at the heart of this chapter.

I analyse under the lens of the body Hobbes's and Locke's concepts of liberty as the linchpins to their respective projects of epistemological-cum-political *ordering*. We have already seen in chapters 2 and 3 how, for Hobbes, the epistemic and the political were two sides of a coin. In Locke's thought too, I will show, a political and an epistemological ordering echoed and reinforced one another. To have an internalised standing rule to live by is what, for Locke, differentiates a political order grounded in our natural freedoms from rambunctious licentiousness. Ordering, 'the workmanship of the understanding', is the defining concern of his philosophical work (Locke *EHU,* III chap.3[14]276). Liberty, I will show, is where the two prongs of his ordering enterprise conjoined; specifically, in the space marked out by 'consent' and 'assent', the pillars of his political and philosophical thought, respectively. This work of ordering epitomized what Foucault (2005) first circumscribed as 'the classical episteme'. This singular moment, constitutive of modern science, where Western knowledge turned back on itself *to order itself* is at the heart of this chapter. It marked a radical break with its prevailing earlier concern to decipher nature's arcana and interpret its laws.[1] The epistemic angle displaces the debate that pitted Descartes-the-rationalist against Hobbes-the-empiricist that we encountered in chapter 3. It brings into focus instead their overarching concern with ordering; with discovering what Descartes (1998, 97) had termed the *mathesis universalis*, the matrix underwriting all orders.[2] Mathematics, for Descartes (1998, 95), was not just *a* discipline (see also Whitehead 1954). It was synonymous with 'disciplining', understood, not as the (self-)fashioning of individuals, but as the (self-)ordering of knowledge; although the former, and indeed the slippage between these two modes of ordering, is also a strand of the story I tell in this chapter.

Reappraising Hobbes's and Locke's conceptions of liberty within an epistemic framework and with the body serves, on the one hand, to loosen liberalism's hold on the new and distinctive agency that was taking shape in the seventeenth century. On the other, it corrects an excessive structural focus in the original framework that Foucault (2005, xiv) himself identified in the context of bringing *The*

Order of Things to English. Crucially for my purposes, it lays bare the historical origins of constitutive theorising. Foucault (2005, 80–84) termed 'genetic analysis' the distinctly novel mode of thought that took shape in the seventeenth century. With 'the idea of genesis' Foucault (2005, 77) aimed to capture the new concern it evinced, not merely with ordering, but with, in addition, the question of origins. Hobbes's trope of the state of nature (not considered by Foucault) typifies this concern. Yet Foucault fell short of differentiating between 'constitution' and 'genesis'. He explicitly defined the latter as the 'analysis of the constitution of orders', across, in his cases, natural history's taxonomic tables, grammars, and the structures of economic exchange (Foucault 2005, 80). Genesis and constitution are thus still folded together in his seminal analysis of the classical episteme, arguably as a function of the types of orders he considers in this early work. *Political* orders beggar folding them out. They require bringing into view, not merely their originating, in the deterministic, even naturalistic, sense that the idea of genesis still carries, but properly what I call in this book their crafting. The difference between genesis and constitution is the human hand. Crafting, or 'making' as James Tully (1980) termed it, is central to Locke's, as well as Hobbes's (see chapter 3), thought. It gives purpose to the work of ordering: having the models and tools to order is necessary in a world that humans have a hand in constructing.

Ideas are Locke's main ordering instruments. He sets out in the *Essay concerning the Human Understanding (EHU)* to analyse how the mind constructs them. He belongs, with Hobbes, to the pantheon of constructivism's precursors. He was what we might call its cognitive constructivist. He distinguishes between two kinds of ideas, or cognitive constructions, 'ectypes' and 'archetypes'. 'Ectypes' are the ideas we hold of natural phenomena. These, for Locke (*EHU*, IIchap.31[13]254), are mere 'copies' by which we seek to represent to ourselves the originals in nature: 'ectype' is an old term for the imprint left by a model upon a piece of wax or clay. We can, and do, adjust these ideas, as knowledge improves and we rectify our errors in constructing them, but we can never hold in our minds the originals to which they refer, merely our productions. Locke contrasts this mode of knowing with our knowledge of the social world, which is founded instead in 'archetypes'; the quintessential example of which, and the one at the heart of his *Two Treatises*, being 'government'. These ideas are 'not copies, nor made after the pattern of any real existence, to which the mind intends them to be conformable, and exactly to answer' (*EHU*, IIchap.31[14]254). They are instead 'originals' (ibid.) formed entirely in the human mind, and do not require being adjusted onto a nature that lies beyond them.[3] With regards to the quality of agency that goes into making these ideas, we could say ectypes hew closer to Aristotle's 'art' (see chapter 3), whereas archetypes are properly where the human creative potential lie. Norms constitute the other example. This distinction 'has provided the philosophical underpinnings for normative political theory', Tully

(1980, 33) has persuasively showed. It laid down solid foundations for a self-confident social scientific enterprise; at a time, moreover, where the invention of probability was prompting a reappraisal of certainty as the criterion for the pursuit of true knowledge (see chapter 3). Locke, however, was not always truthful to the distinctions he himself honed for constitutive-constructivist theorising, to damming effect for his political project, I show in this and the following chapter.

The chapter builds towards the political analysis in five parts. In the first, I will show how Hobbes externalised liberty by corporealising it, by making it strictly of the body. This liberty served an ordering project founded on a sharp delineation between the private worlds of the subjects, where the conscience is free and shielded from scrutiny, and a public space of subjection and peaceful coexistence. Understanding Hobbes's reasons for externalising liberty requires appraising the prevailing republican conception of liberty that he was pushing back against, which was inward-turned—towards the conscience. I show how, by way of the contract, he devised an inter-subjective politics without an interiority, that was rooted in the structure of the exchange itself. For this, the role of time and the promise were key. In the second part I use 'consent' to parse the similarities and differences between Hobbes and Locke and to pivot towards the latter. The Lockean project of political ordering is in focus throughout the rest of the chapter, where I consider successively the work of the conscience in part 3; his epistemological writings and his concept of 'consciousness' in part 4; and his political ordering project in part 5. Together the final two parts draw out a central antagonism at the heart of Locke's work, that play out between his epistemological and political thoughts, and that I continue to explore in the following chapter.

Parsing the spatial logics of Locke's writings, I show across these three parts that Locke internalised liberty by restoring the conscience to the heart of modern politics and retrieving the political ordering function of guilt that Hobbes had done away with. He repurposed discipline from a moral rule that affords internal guidance for how to behave, to a political technology that fashions rational, consenting subjects capable of rights. He helped craft for modern politics a sort of internal counterpart to the raison d'état that was taking shape between states, an inward-looking mode of practical reasoning or self-directing plugged into the conscience. In part 3, I show how Locke retrieved the conscience that Hobbes, on the one hand, had cast off limits for political ordering, and that Descartes, on the other, had turned into a strictly cognitive faculty. To understand how Locke reworked it requires first mapping the fraught history of the theological concept from Aquinas to Descartes via Calvin. Locke's rescue was two-pronged. With one hand, he ushered in the moral sense of the conscience as the foundation for modern liberty by way of his concept of 'consent'. With the other, he coined a new, embodied concept to capture the epistemic functions that were still folded together with the ethical one in the theological notion, 'consciousness'. I consider this concept, with its twin 'personhood', in part 4 where I show how these enabled Locke to sidestep the old dualism of mind and body, and to navigate a complex relationship with the scholastic (disembodied) faculty of reason. Understanding how Locke wields reason serves to appraise the naturalising functions it performs in his political writings, where all the cautiousness of his epistemological writings appears to vanish. These are the focus in the chapter's fifth part, along with the exclusionary, boundary-drawing effects his resort to natural reason wreaks.

Turning to his pedagogical and political writings in the chapter's final part, I show how Locke designed his polity as exclusive club of bourgeois male consenters by drawing a series of circles of gradated membership. His two instruments for doing so, that were geared to the mind and body, respectively, and that I consider successively, were discipline and punishment. The first fashioned, through education, the inner circle and proper constituency to which his 'government' was aimed: fully rational male subjects capable of express consent and internal assent. The second posited a constitutive outside of unreason where Locke's criminals and 'begging drones' (his term) roamed. Between these two circles lay a grey zone populated by women, children, and foreigners. These, for Locke, were tacitly consenting subjects, who were 'reasonable' enough to comply with the laws, yet with intellectual faculties insufficiently developed for this to constitute a wholehearted assent, fully cognizant of its own reasons (for assenting), and able to construct sound, unsuperstitious ideas. This is the Lockean capacity of the autonomous subject of rights. It would serve to write off many—most—potential subjects from access to political membership and to rights, including liberty, I show in this chapter, and to property in the following one. Here, against a historical backdrop where large numbers of people were being criminalised by the law itself in the age of capitalism's take-off, Locke's figure of the criminal indexes a first site of the series of constitutive exclusions with which he delineates his state.[4] In the following chapter, I will consider the figure of the slave.

1. Externalising Liberty: Hobbes

'This man deserves to be a perpetual slave' the clergyman George Lawson decreed (cited in Luban 2018,1). For the archbishop John Bramhall, Hobbes was engaged in little more than indulgent ramblings (see Skinner 2008, 33). He missed the human quality of freedom entirely. Nor was the wrath of clergymen the only scorn Hobbes attracted. For his republican adversary James Harrington, Hobbes had confused freedom by the law with a freedom from the law (Pettit 2005, 132; 1997, 39). Hobbes largely shunned the readily available conceptions of liberty of his times, such as the distinction between 'liberty' and 'licence', which Locke would take as his starting point. And yet as Skinner (1990, 122) has underlined, 'there is no case in which he is so anxious to insist on his own definition, and to argue that all others are dangerously misleading, as he is in explicating liberty'. That, notwithstanding its impact, his conception of liberty was—and still is—so ill-received is because he deliberately delinked freedom from the soul, by externalising it. Hobbes's *was* the liberty of the machine his critics were so wary of. Let us consider why it was important to him, and how he came to externalise liberty.

Hobbes's Corporeal Liberty

Properly circumscribing liberty mattered centrally to Hobbes, insofar as a contract that is not entered into freely is meaningless. Only, eschewing the traditional scholastic understandings, Hobbes, first, systematically undid the ties between liberty and the parts of the human being habitually conceived in non-corporeal terms; liberty and reason on the one hand, liberty and the will on the other. A free will is mere 'nonsense', for Hobbes (*L.*, chap.5[5]24). 'From the use of the word free-will no liberty can be inferred of the will' (Hobbes, *L.*, chap.21[2]136). Moreover, liberty 'may be applied no less to irrational and inanimate creatures' (ibid.). To delink liberty from reason was to deny its status as a human distinction. To then explicitly extend it to inanimate creatures, like stones, was to untie the traditional knot between liberty and the soul, which, for Aristotle, animals also possessed. Only Hobbes was not interested in stones so much as he was in machines. The last knot Hobbes (*L.*, chap.4[22]21) undid was between liberty the realm of speech and meaning that is 'peculiar to man', which, for example, would become once again central to Hegel's conception of liberty. Hobbes thus emptied liberty of any specifically human or indeed humanist content. He drew upon a repertoire of inanimates to metaphorize his liberty: water, iron chains, walls, stones (*L.*, chap.21). Along with the soul (see chapter 2), he materialised liberty '[w]hen the words free and liberty are applied to anything but bodies, they are abused' (Hobbes, *L.*, chap.21[1]136). Hobbesian liberty, then, is corporeal and literally soul-less.

Second, Hobbes backed his materialist liberty with his thoroughly mechanistic causality. Hobbes, we saw in chapter 3, carried the new laws of mechanism into the realm of politics. In doing so, he collapsed political onto physical laws. Perhaps this was the pitfall Descartes had foreseen.[5] Moreover, in 'blankly refusing to acknowledge' the established tropes of his time, Hobbes did little to soften the provocative edge to his liberty (Skinner 2008, 33). The conflation of political and physical laws was deliberate and systematic. Furthermore, it was sustained by an attack on the traditional, humanist understandings of the law. In his *Dialogue between a Philosopher and a Student of the Common Laws of England* he took aim at none other than Edward Coke. Scientists, Hobbes (cited in Cohen 1994, 195) finds, 'do not so often err as [do] the great professors of the law'. The law as an internal constraint was what he rejected. [6] The 'chains' of civil law simply 'fasten at one end to the lips' of the sovereign (an individual or an assembly) 'and at the other end to the ears [of the subjects] (Hobbes, *L.*, chap.21[18]143). And, like iron chains—here again, he favours the literal over the metaphorical meaning—their effects reach no further; or at least they are not to be sought any further, say, between the subject's ears. Any debate unfolding there, hence in the conscience, Hobbes has cast off limits for politics. Whether laws bind internally is irrelevant. Hobbes's laws, then, are the obverse of Foucault's norms.

Hobbes conceived political laws on the model of mechanical laws. The 'LAW determineth' for Hobbes (*L.*, chap.14[3]79). Civil laws determine human actions in the way that natural laws determine the movements of all bodies. A person's ability to perform an action in the polity is bounded by the law, like the water by the 'banks or vessels' without which 'it would spread itself into a larger space' (Hobbes, *L.*, chap.21[1]136). Hobbes's laws operate like natural necessity. '*Liberty* and *necessity* are consistent' (Hobbes, *L.*, chap.21[4]137). That political laws are the products of human artifice merely heightens the requirement to craft them properly. It does not, for Hobbes, introduce a meaningful difference between physical and political laws. This is perhaps the most jarring dimension of his conceptualisation of liberty. It were as though with his commitment to a mechanistic causality, Hobbes has cornered himself into having to par liberty right down to the minimalist sense of unimpeded movement. Only this was also counterbalanced by just as dedicated a commitment to human agency, creativity, and choice. This takes us back to the heart of the tension I explored in chapter 3. Hobbes *is* serious about the liberty that underwrites the contract; only this liberty, to be meaningful, must be corporeal. It is on this account, then, that his is the liberty of the machine.

Once he had methodically stripped it of the deceitful fancies it had long been loaded with, what liberty was Hobbes left with? Quentin Skinner (2008) has traced how Hobbesian liberty is progressively refined over the course of his political writings. Undefined in *The Elements of Law* (1640), liberty became the absence of impediments to motion in *De Cive* (1642). By the time of the *Leviathan* (1651), these impediments were specified, twice, as needing to be external to be pertinent. This specification was then reasserted in Hobbes's Latin translation of this treatise (1688). Hobbes was thus increasingly committed to reducing liberty to the subject's embodied ability to move unimpeded. Hobbes's (chap.14[2]79) definition of liberty in the *Leviathan*, then, is 'the absence of external impediments to motion'. In his mature political treatise he had pushed liberty as far out as he possibly could from the subject's inner world, and onto the body. He had externalised liberty by corporealising it. Having considered how, I now consider why Hobbes defined liberty as he did, by focussing on the two pillars of his definition successively, external obstacles and motion, and considering the role that the body played in Hobbes's argumentative strategy. I examine the political context to account for the first, and specifically, the alternative, republican conceptions of liberty that Hobbes was countering, and the social and cultural contexts for the latter. I will then analyse how this corporeal liberty plays out in the Hobbesian contract.

An 'Absence of External Impediments': The Political and Strategic Contexts to Hobbes's Corporeal Liberty

'The Commonwealth' was the political object Hobbes theorized. But England's first actual Commonwealth was founded by his republican adversaries, in the wake of the first modern regicide (1649). Liberty was central to their discourse. It offers a useful starting point for appraising what Hobbes was pushing back against with his corporeal liberty (Pettit 1997; 2005; Skinner 2008). The republican discourse's two main tropes were the figure of the free man (*liber homo*), which hailed from the Magna Carta, and the opposition of freedom and slavery. This binary was entrenched by the Commonwealth's founding act 'Declaring and Constituting the People of England to Be a Commonwealth and Free State' (1949), which starkly denounced the abuse of 'royal power and prerogative' to 'oppress and enslave the subject' (cited in Skinner 2008, 143). It would also be taken up at the end of the century by Locke to frame his *Second Treatise*. For these early modern republicans, a freedom that could not be exercised was no freedom to speak of. The mere presence of absolute power in the polity, regardless of whether it was deployed or not, was enough to turn free persons into slaves. It maintained ever-present the possibility of being arbitrarily dealt with, which was the condition of slavery.[7] To live under a king, as Charles I (and his father before him) had only too clearly born out, was to remain 'absolutely subject', as one of the Commonwealth's apologist put it. Monarchy was 'truly a Disease of Government', and only by eradicating it could the English people hope to return 'to their Pristine liberty and its Daughter happinesse [*sic*]' (cited in Skinner 2008, 147).

The psychological effects of unfreedom were thus central to the discourse Hobbes countered. The litmus test for a republican liberty lay within. In the terms of the time, it was bound up with the conscience. Asserting the degree of actual liberty in a political order required looking inwards, in order to gauge whether the subjects were free in any meaningful sense; free, that is, of the inner grip of power and of the shackles of dependence. This is the path down which contemporary analyses of power have since extensively travelled[8] It was exactly where Hobbes would not tread. 'Fear and liberty are consistent', he asserted instead (*L.*, chap.21[3]136). To be intimidated witless is not to be unfree, insofar as the impediment is internal. Only external obstacles qualify, since 'liberty in the proper sense' is 'corporeal liberty, that is to say freedom from chains and prison' (Hobbes, *L.*, chap.21[6]138). Hobbes (*L.*, chap.21[6]138) found that 'it were very absurd for men to clamour as they do for the liberty they so manifestly enjoy' as they strutted about unchained. To the republican conception convolved with the conscience, Hobbes opposed a liberty that was radically, provocatively, outward-turned. It was located in the body. Driving home his point against 'those democratical writers' Hobbes (*L.*, chap.29[14]215) described in minute detail the deleterious effects of their liberty upon the polity:

> [B]y reading these Greek and Latin authors men from their childhood have gotten a habit (under a false show of liberty) of favouring tumults and of licentious controlling the actions of the sovereign, and again of controlling the controllers. Hobbes (*L.*, chap.21[9]141)

This repetitious and violent cycle, in which every new controller controls the controller, in the name, not of an objective, common benchmark (which only the sovereign can set) but of some nebulous standard buried deep in the recesses of their individual consciences, and 'with the effusion of so much blood', is precisely what a conception of liberty tethered to an inward-turned notion, like the conscience, is bound to beget, to disastrous effect (Hobbes, *L.*, chap.21[9]141).

The 'Body-in-Motion': The Social and Epistemic Contexts of Hobbes's Liberty

Whereas the immediate political context accounts for Hobbes's focus upon external impediments, the importance of motion to his liberty owes to the epistemic transformations that 'literally set men [*sic*] moving' in the seventeenth century (Walzer 1965, 200). England saw the extraordinary conjunction of two revolutions, political and scientific. As Michael Walzer (ibid.) put it, '[T]ransformations in political experiences directly paralleled transformations in the reference-worlds which had previously provided the terms of symbolic expression'. Science did not just spill over into the realm of human affairs by itself; it did so because an entire repertoire of meanings and symbols that political actors had habitually drawn upon to make sense of their experiences was collapsing. The 'body-in-motion' was the new figure to emerge from these ashes (Walzer 1965, 202). Moving bodies were all around Hobbes. Two sorts, big and small, shaped his world. There was, first, the dance of the celestial 'heavy bodies' that had revolutionised the measurement of movement itself (Hobbes, *De Corpore*, Epistle Dedicatory). Hobbes placed his treatise *On Bodies* (1655), the first of the two volumes where he developed his mature philosophical system (the second was his *De Homine*, 1658) under the auspices of the inventor of the 'knowledge of the nature of motion', Galileo, and of Copernicus, from whom 'the beginning of Astronomy' is 'derived' (*DC*, ibid.). The second type of motion was the flow of blood *in* the body, which had been brought into focus by William Harvey, the third figure Hobbes conjures in this dedicatory epistle. These microscopic movements placed the human body as the heart of the scientific revolution in ways that I will consider more closely in the following chapter.

The Intersubjective Structure of the Exchange and the Mechanics of Contracting

How does this externalised liberty support Hobbes's contract? Contracting, we recall, is, for Hobbes (*L.*, chap.14[8]82), the original, 'voluntary act' that implicates the subject's liberty at a foundational level—at the level where natural beings constitute the state on the one hand, and themselves into political subjects on the other. In the previous chapter, I showed how Hobbes's contract tapped into a distinctly human agency to create and to choose; hence into something that necessarily lies beyond all determinations (naturalistic or mechanistic). Distinguishing between a simple decision and the type of choice that this contract involves is useful for understanding how Hobbes navigates this tension between his two commitments, to this creative human agency on the one hand, and to a deterministic materialism on the other. This distinction builds on the Hobbesian physiology of action we also considered in that chapter.

A decision precedes every action. It is the outcome of an internal process of deliberating between the various appetites and inclinations, in classical scholastic terms, or, in more contemporary terms, of weighing up one's preferences. Only for Hobbes, these appetites and inclinations are embodied, not rational. There is little room for rationality in the Hobbesian deliberating; recall that he explicitly rejected the scholastic definition of the will as a rational appetite. The will is simply '*the last appetite in deliberating*' (*L.*, chap.6[53]33, emphasis in original). However, since the contract is the foundational act by which individuals relinquish 'the estate of liberty and the right of all to all', as Hobbes (*EoLi*, chap.14[12]56) defines the state of nature, the decision that precedes this act is of an especially consequential sort. Hobbes 'is anxious to emphasise that the loss of liberty he is describing is not the result of our deciding to act in a particular way', as Skinner (2008, 46) underscored. Locking individuals into definitively laying down their unlimited natural liberty requires something more than a flimsy decision precariously poised on a particular turn of the appetites, possibly undone by the next turn. Hobbes's keen sense of the fickleness of human actions stems from his analysis of the will. Not only is deciding not a rational process, but it is not even necessarily stretched out in time, since some appetites, perhaps especially the less constructive ones, command their immediate execution. Hobbes has to address the question of how the founding political act can be transformed into something more than the reversible outcome of a fickle, embodied deliberative process. The contract, by which the individual chooses to limit their unlimited natural liberties, requires something more than a simple decision.

The Role of Time

Hobbes (*L.*, chap.14[101]82) builds a deferment, or time lag, into the contract by distinguishing between a situation of simple exchange, and that of the contract proper. 'There is a difference between transferring of right to the thing and transferring ([. . .]that is, delivery) of the thing itself', Hobbes (*L.*, chap.14[101]82) writes. Let us begin with the second case, which describes a situation of simple exchange. All obligations are met the moment the thing is delivered; none are left over to be fulfilled at a later date. The two parties to the exchange may happily never meet again; no injury has been committed. Nothing in the situation itself binds them to each another. Simple exchange is also, for Hobbes (*L.*, chap.14[12]82), the structure of gift-giving, where one party offers something to another without (in theory at least) expecting anything in return. Leftover obligations are what generate the 'BONDS by which men are bound' to one another (*L.*, chap.14[7]81). They characterise instead the structure of 'the PACT, or COVENANT' proper (*L.*, Hobbes chap.14[11]82). There, the delivery is postponed, and what is exchanged initially is only the promise of the thing, rather than the thing itself. This promise generates the right *to* the thing, including enjoying the benefits to be derived from it. The obligations of the promising party are stretched out in time.

While the analysis is compressed in *Leviathan*, Hobbes's original unpacking of the mechanisms of the contract in *The Elements of Law* draws out the importance of this time lag for differentiating the simple decision from the more fundamental choice the contract engages. 'For he that saith of the time to come, for example to-morrow: I will give, declareth evidently that he hath not yet given. The right therefore remaineth in him today' (*EoLi*, chap.15[5]59). This putative declaration stages the decision to give tomorrow, not the act of contracting. It features a present intention, which might be replaced with another decision tomorrow. On the other hand, 'he that saith: I give, presently, or have given to another any thing to enjoy the same to-morrow, or any other time future, hath actually transferred the said right, which he otherwise should have had at the time that the other is to enjoy it' (ibid.). In *this* declaration the act of contracting has been performed. It is, in John Austin's language, the speech-act that enacts

the transference of *the right* to the thing (rather than the thing itself) and binds
the two parties to each other.

Externalising the Promise

The decision that yields the contract is an especially consequential decision. The
difference between a simple decision that precedes an action, and the kind of ex-
istential choice implicated in the contract resides in the situation itself.[9] It lies in
the intersubjective structure of the exchange. Language and the promise are the
two pillars of the contract. Together they introduce the element of time that is
needed to transform this simple intersubjective act, exchanging, into the act that
founds the modern state. In the situation of the contract, 'both parts may contract now, to perform hereafter, in which cases' the 'performance' of the party 'that
is to perform in time to come (. . .) is called *keeping of promise*' (Hobbes, *L.*,
chap.14 [11]82). The promise acts as a token for the delivery to come. The recipient receives the promise in lieu of the thing itself. In the *Elements of Law* Hobbes
(*EoLi*, chap.15[9]60) defines the notion: 'Promises [. . .] are covenants and signs
of the will, or last act in deliberation, whereby the liberty of performing or not
performing, are taken away'.

What is remarkable is the extent to which Hobbes manages to short-circuit
any reliance on interiority in deploying his theory of obligation. Whereas Locke
relies upon consent, the inner 'sense of obligation' that implicates the conscience,
Hobbes mobilised the structure of the exchange itself (Josephson 2002, 279). In
fact, he manages to externalise even such a seemingly internal notion as the
promise. Must a promise to another person not require that someone first deliberate with themselves? If the promise has left no internal mark, in the contractor's
conscience, the person's *foro interno*, then is it not likely to be an empty promise?
Hobbes (*L.*, chap.14[11]81), moreover, was well aware of the problem of broken
promises, or 'violations of faith' as he called them. Yet his response was to bracket
the conscience altogether, and deploy a detailed analysis of the mechanics of the
exchange that relied exclusively on the intersubjective situation that the promise
created. He entirely elided the interiority of the promise, and shifted instead the
grounds for its analysis onto the outward plane of actions. To put it in another
way, he pushed the analysis out from between a person's ears and onto the space
between persons. This also explains why language is the second pillar to the
Hobbesian contract. Hobbes apprehends the promise as an act of external communication, whose traces are to be sought solely in the words exchanged in this
intersubjective space (whether written or oral). These become the 'signs' that a
contract has been passed between two parties (Hobbes, *L.*, chap.14[13]82). They
are either 'express' or 'by inference', in which case they consist in 'whatsoever sufficiently argues the will of the contractor'. Without language (in which Hobbes

includes silences) 'it is impossible to make covenant with those living creatures' with whom there is 'no common language', not because these creatures cannot first articulate promises to themselves—not because they do not have self-awareness, that is to say, a conscience—, but simply because 'we have no sufficient sign' of their wills (*EoLi*, chap.15[11]61). In Hobbes's (*EoLii* chap.10[2]147) final analysis, then, the covenant is entirely outward-turned; it is a 'declaration of a man's own will'. Via language, actions, and the will, Hobbes thus externalises the promise, as part of his broader externalisation of liberty.

To summarise, the conception of liberty that Hobbes settled upon in the *Leviathan*, as the absence of external impediments to motions, emerged from a trajectory of its increasing externalisation by way of the body. I have accounted for the Hobbesian liberty's increasing outward focus by reference to the political battles he was waging against his republican adversaries; and for the element of movement, with regards to the centrality of the trope of moving bodies in a profoundly transforming world. In chapter 2 I argued that, having closely witnessed the unhappy marriage of conscience and politics, with civil war as their sad progeny, Hobbes orchestrated their divorce. Here I have shown how, by rooting liberty in the body, he designed a politics without an interiority. The only natural court of justice is, for Hobbes (*L.*, chap.30[30]233), in the conscience, and there it should be held and preserved from the task of building a human one. Shifting the focus to the body enabled Hobbes to both cordon off the conscience, while retaining the liberty necessary to this task. I then showed how Hobbes located the source of the obligations that bind the political subjects-in-the-making to each other in the space between them, rather than in their *foro interno*: in the contract they pass with one another. Time and the promise, both factors that consolidate this intersubjective space, were key to achieving a solution that required liberty but no interiority, I have shown. Whereas Hobbes sought to hone a lens for modern politics that brought into focus only the outward alignment of the subjects' behaviours with the sovereign's laws in the spaces of communal living, Locke instead turned this lens decisively inwards. To introduce him, I begin by comparing Hobbes and Locke on the notion of consent.

2. Hobbes and Locke on Consent

The contract is the vehicle for the original limiting of natural liberty that yields political liberty, for Hobbes as well as for Locke. For both, it is a voluntary act that engages the individual will. They differ, however, on the matter of consent. For Locke, it captures the essence of the contract and is the expression of the subject's liberty (Laslett 1988; Josephson 2002). Locke (*TT*, p.137) opens his *Two Treatises of Government* by establishing 'Consent of the people' as the fount of 'all lawful Governments'. Yet he never defined the term, neither in the *Two Treatises of Government*, nor in *Essay concerning Human Understanding*, as Peter Laslett (1988, 85) has underscored. Hobbes does define consent, early on in his political writings, in the *Elements of Law* (1640). It does not, for him, afford sufficiently solid foundations for building a peaceful polity. Consent, Hobbes writes, is:

> When the wills of many concur to some one and the same action, or effect, this concourse of their wills is called CONSENT, by which we must understand [. . .] many wills to the producing of one effect. (*EoLi*, chap.12[7]48).

Consent is the opposite of 'CONTENTION', which is 'when the wills of two divers [*sic*] men produce such actions as are resistances one to another' (ibid). A legitimate civil government would be the crucial 'one effect' that, borrowing Hobbes's language to render Locke's purpose, this convergence of wills engenders. So what is missing, for Hobbes? The answer is yielded by his analysis of the will. For Hobbes, spontaneously converging wills are not enough to create the unity, the 'oneness', required to govern. Hobbes's wariness vis-à-vis consent resurfaces again in *De Cive*, which largely expands on the *Elements of Law*'s second part. Hobbes (*DC*, chap.1[14]51) begins by distinguishing between polities that are founded 'by constraint', in cases of conquest, or 'by consent', through contracting with one another. A few chapters on, Hobbes (*DC*, chap.5[5]87) parses the classic notion of political animality by considering the ant and the bee that, in addition to humans, '*Aristotle* reckons among those animals which he calls Politique'. These animals, Hobbes (ibid.) observes, do not 'contract, and submit to government' since (as Aristotle noted) 'they [are] destitute of reason', yet they 'direct their actions to a common end'. This common end is not a political end:

> [T]herefore [ants and bees are] not to be termed *politicall* [*sic*], because their government is onely [*sic*] a consent, or many wills concurring in one object, not (as is necessary in civill [*sic*] government) one will. (Hobbes *De Cive*, chap.5[5]87)

Converging wills by themselves, without the mechanics of the contract, cannot, we have seen, engender the single, unified will that modern sovereignty properly consists in. These converging fickle, a-rational appetites may diverge the next moment. Contention is the obverse of consent, and it leads to civil war.

The central problem Hobbes (*L.*, chap.17[13]109) set out to address is how to reduce the 'plurality of voices unto one will'. Only achieving 'the real unity of them all', he concluded, against a backdrop of civil war, requires 'more than consent, or concord' (ibid.). Securing a government by consent was instead Locke's core aim. By the time of Locke's writing the *Two Treatises* (1690) the English polity had been (more or less) cobbled back together around Charles

II, the son of the decapitated king. These historical circumstances may go some length towards explaining how the main problem to be addressed had shifted from unifying the polity to steering it consensually. But the differences between them are also fruitfully accounted for, I suggest, by considering how they wielded the relation between consent and the conscience. Whereas Hobbes looked to the movements of an embodied will to understand the workings of consent so as *not* to look to the conscience, for Locke, consent was unavoidably a matter of and for the conscience. The first bourgeois thinker, as Reinhardt Koselleck (1988, 53) once called him, shared none of Hobbes's concerns regarding the political dangers that inhered in the private conscience with regards to the possibility of constituting a public space for collective life. Locke, then, simplified the relations between the conscience and consent that Hobbes had complicated in foreclosing the conscience from politics.

Since he does not define consent, Locke's commentators have been left to fill out the blanks. James Tully (1980, 21) has underlined how his consent constitutes political society, in the strongest possible sense of 'being constitutive of'. It exemplifies Locke's constitutional mode of thinking that I will further explore in the following chapter. Peter Josephson (2002) for his part has parsed the intimate connection of consent and the conscience. It implies 'a sense of obligation' which is 'a feeling: we are obliged in conscience' (Josephson 2002, 279). Only in Locke, this feeling of being obliged does not follow from consent, but rather the other way around; 'it is itself a kind of consent' (ibid.). It is not a product of (consenting to) the contract, but rather its source, its subjective substrate. Locke thus founds the state in the individual conscience. By contrast, the Hobbesian obligation is generated by the intersubjective situation, since it is rooted in the promise. It requires the contract, *but not the conscience*. Unlike Locke, Hobbes does not need an inner foundation for his political system. Reinhard Koselleck (1988, 54–55) once underlined that Locke restored 'the space that Hobbes had exempted from the State', by which he meant 'the interior of the human conscience', thereby reinstating it as the bedrock of modern liberty. I will now show how the space he reworked to achieve this was the state of nature. In the chapter's final part I will show that the indeterminacy to consent is what enables it to perform key exclusionary boundary-drawing functions in Locke's political thought.

3. Re-internalising Liberty by Way of the Conscience: John Locke

John Locke shared with Hobbes the quintessentially modern, critical project of unsettling the dogmatisms with which the old orders, epistemic and political, had become naturalised. Innate ideas were his primary target, like Hobbes—or perhaps even more than him. The notions that were thought to inhere in our natures, as rational beings partaking in a broader weft of being, underpinned the pre-modern work of deciphering. Nature's laws were thought to be reflected in and revealed to us by these naturally held ideas. Like Hobbes's, Locke's was a major denaturalising enterprise. The task he set himself in the *Essay concerning the Human Understanding* was to demonstrate that all 'the ideas, notions, or whatever else you please to call them' that we hold are acquired, not given, by examining exactly how our minds 'comes to be furnished' with them (*EHU*, I.chap.1[3]34). Moreover, for Locke as for Hobbes, opinions were a crucial battleground. They are the locus of habituation, where these (acquired) ideas become sticky, unquestioned, such that we grant our assent to them without having a 'certain knowledge' of their 'truth' (*EHU*, I.chap.1[3]34). Knowledge and opinion, and delineating the 'bounds' between them, set the parameters for his *Essay* (*EHU*, I.chap.1[3]34). His two-pronged undertaking is to 'enquire into the original, extent and certainty of human knowledge, together with the grounds and degrees of belief, opinion and assent' (*EHU*, I.chap.1[2]33). *Assent* is the internal counterpart to the *consent* Locke established as the cornerstone for his Two Treatises of Government, which was published the same year (1690). Tilling the grounds of opinions and beliefs serves to establish the 'measures' by which 'we ought to regulate our assent and moderate our persuasions' (*EHU*, I.chap.1[3]34).[10] This, in turn, prepares us to be better equipped to grant our consent in the matters concerning the commonwealth.

Locke's denaturalising undertaking, however, rested, likes Hobbes's, on a series of naturalisations whose consequences are borne out, I will show in the chapter's final section, in his political works. They largely turn on his state of nature, the construct he borrowed from Hobbes (without so much as a nod towards him, as Peter Laslett (1988) has underscored). Locke introduced a decisive modification, however. He distinguished between a *state of nature* and a *state of war*. The ever-present possibility of violent disorder is just as necessary to him as it is to Hobbes; it remains the spur that drives individuals out of the state of nature to construct the state, and thus the motor of political construction. Only he locates it in a third state, that is neither the natural nor the political one. This enables Locke to de-link disorder and war from nature, and therefore to preserve the latter, far better than Hobbes could, as the unshakeable foundations for modern politics. This affords Locke (unlike Hobbes) his uncontested status in the canon of modern natural rights theories. Locke recovers nature on both ends of the state-subject relation, as the cloth out of which to cut out the state, and as the anchor for the political subject's liberty. That the conscience is the 'natural court of justice [...] where not man, but God reigneth', in Hobbes's (*L.*, chap.30[30]233) words, is precisely why, for Locke, it affords the right and necessary foundations for human courts. Only Hobbes's younger contemporary does not share his tragic sense of the impossibility of carrying this court over from the state of nature to the state, because, like Spinoza before him, he does not conceive the passage from one to the other as a radical rupture. His third state undoes the Hobbesian antinomy between the state of nature and the state. Locke's nature is a peaceful place regulated by natural laws onto which our reason inherently aligns, carrying humans towards 'Good Will, Mutual Assistance and Preservation' (*TT*, II.chap.2[4]269). It is a 'State of perfect Freedom' that is not lost by entering the polity, as it is for Hobbes (ibid.). Locke's is the harmonious nature where the Rousseauian natural man (and it was a man, as Mary Wollstonecraft was prompt to underline) would later roam, at peace with his solitude and with his conscience. Here I will show that, with nature and contra Hobbes, Locke retrieved the conscience's 'natural' dwelling place and, by the same token, he re-internalised political liberty. Locke recovered a notion that was being profoundly transformed at the unique juncture of a scientific and a religious revolution. I begin by considering the theological roots of 'the conscience' and how it evolved from Aquinas to Calvin. I then read Hobbes and Descartes as having carved out two different paths away from a dangerous overinvestment in 'the conscience' that had fuelled a century of devastating wars. Lastly, I show how Locke brought back together the two dimensions of the original conscience that Descartes, in particular, had separated out, namely, a moral or ethical function on the one hand, and an epistemological or cognitive one, on the other. Locke achieved this by coining a third concept, 'consciousness'.[11]

The Conscience, from Aquinas to Calvin

The epistemological and the ethical were initially folded together in the Christian concept of 'the conscience'. The term derived from *Scientia*, the Latin for knowledge or science. Charting its origins across theological doctrines and languages, Etienne Balibar (2013) has underlined how the 'with' added by the prefix '*cum*' contained from the onset both an outward- and an inward-looking dimension. It designated a community, a 'being with' other Christians. However, over the course of the concept's history, it would come increasingly to point within.[12] The epistemological and ethical dimensions contained in the conscience would be progressively folded out into distinct directions as a result of the double revolution, religious and scientific, that was under way in the sixteenth and seventeenth centuries. Prior to this juncture, Thomas Aquinas (*Summa Theologia*, 1a.Qu.79, Art.13), retuning the term *conscientia* to its etymological roots in *cum alio scientia*, had emphasised primarily its epistemological functions (see Balibar 2013). The conscience, for Aquinas, was the 'application of knowledge to activity' (cited in Langston 2015). It denoted acts (or a series of acts) of the intellect. It was a natural disposition, inscribed in our practical reason, that enables us to know innately right from wrong, good from evil. It was largely a cognitive concept, however. This is the path down which Descartes travelled, and I return to it shortly. The other path was carved open by the Protestant interrogation of points of dogma, in which the resort to the conscience played a central role. We have glimpsed how Luther wielded his in chapter 2. Since Locke was a devout Calvinist (see Dunn 1969; 1984; and Harris 1992), it is relevant to consider how Calvin circumscribed the conscience.

'Government' is the pillar of Locke's political project.[13] It is a central theme in Calvin's *Institutes of the Christian Religion*. Only Calvin understood it in the broad sense of a 'directing', as in 'God's government of the universe' (book I, chap. 5). In the realm of human affairs, Calvin (III.chap.19[15]847–848) sees humans as guided in their conduct by a 'twofold government', a 'spiritual' and a 'political' one. 'The former has its seat in the soul, the latter only regulates external conduct', the outer forum where we interact with others. Calvin uses 'soul' and 'conscience' interchangeably. The *for intérieur* or inner forum is properly where the conscience lies. It is the site of a personal, unmediated, and spontaneous relationship with God, but also of a natural instruction 'in piety and in reverencing God' (Calvin, *Institutes*, III. chap.19[15]847). But what exactly is the conscience, Calvin asks? The question arises in the context of enquiring into whose 'government' to abide by, God's or humans'. This in turn opens up the crucial question of the nature of 'Christian Liberty'—the very liberty that was at stake in the religious wars (*Institutes*, book III, chap. 19).

Calvin's starting point is Thomist. He begins his enquiry into the nature of the conscience with the activity of the mind. When humans, he wrote, 'apprehend the knowledge of things by the mind and intellect, they are said to know, and hence arises the term knowledge or *science*' (Calvin, *Institutes*, III.chap.19[15]848). Only the prefix *cum*, for Calvin, adds something more than knowledge. It denotes a distinctive form of 'knowing with'. It pivots the notion towards God, and, for Calvin, back towards its moral functions. In the same way that they have this knowledge, continues Calvin (ibid.), 'so they have a sense of the divine justice added as a witness. [. . .] That sense is called conscience'. God's presence in us, via this 'sense', illuminates the innate knowledge inscribed in us, the 'simple knowledge [that] exists in [humans], as it were, shut up'. To stage this internal presence, Calvin deploys the tribunal scenography that would cast such a long shadow over Locke and the capitalist modernity he helped found. 'The conscience' Calvin writes, 'is a thousand witnesses' (ibid). It 'does not allow [humans] to conceal their sins, but drags them forwards as culprits to the bar of God'. This natural tribunal 'stands [. . .] between God and man, not suffering man to suppress what he knows in himself' (Calvin, *Institutes*, III.chap.19[15]848</IBT). Invoking an ancient theological metaphor of the conscience as an inner light, Calvin (ibid.)

writes that it 'sits man before the bar of God' and 'is set over him as a kind of sentinel to observe and spy out all his secrets, that nothing may remain buried in darkness'. Calvin's conscience is thus both an internal watchguard and a natural light. It is primarily a moral notion. Crucially, it harked to the pre-classical ontologies of innateness.

Two Paths Away from a Charged Conscience:
Descartes and Hobbes

In the sixteenth century, the intensifying investment in the conscience by Reformist theologians and their followers who increasingly took to the battlefields in its name ultimately wove its epistemological and moral dimensions more tightly together than they had been at earlier points in the concept's history. There were two possible responses to what could only appear, by the seventeenth century, after decades of warring with no end in sight and on both sides of the Catholic-Protestant divide, as an overinvestment in the conscience. One was Hobbes's, who sought to put the conscience back in its place *within*, by sealing off the domain of politics he set out to delineate, as we saw in chapter 2. Descartes, for his part, retrieving the Thomist strand, carved out a strictly epistemological conscience. In what would come to be known as the founding gesture of the Enlightenment, Descartes (1998, 77) reworked the metaphor of the inner light in order to capture the 'conceptual act of the pure and attentive mind'.[14] Early in his trajectory, in the *Rules for the Direction of the Natural Intelligence*, where he defined the *mathesis universalis*, Descartes established intuition as the second pillar of the general science of order he set out to found, along with the rational method of deduction. This extra-rational, inner sense was properly for Descartes where 'the light of reason' shone:

> By intuition I understand neither the fluctuating testimony of the sense nor the deceptive judgement of an imagination which composes things badly, but rather the conceptual act of the pure and attentive mind, which [...] springs from the light of reason. (Descartes 1998, 79)

Only the 'inner light' that God had given us serves primarily 'to distinguish the true from the false' Descartes (2006, 14) pointedly wrote in opening his *Discourse on the Method*, rather than the right from the wrong course of actions. The inner sense of certainty in which Descartes sought to ground his scientific method was of a different quality altogether to that which had driven Luther to stand up to his questioners at Worms. It is a purely intellectual certainty rather than a moral conviction; what the subject experiences when he or she has 'clear and distinct' ideas, together with the sense of their incontrovertibility (Descartes, 2006, 33). To the conscience as *Gewissen*, ringing increasingly stridently with its 'certainties' (*Gewissenheit*) against a backdrop of religious wars, Descartes counterposed an epistemological conscience. [15] Descartes, then, reworked the conscience into the seat of the knowing rather than the acting subject. In doing so, he achieved nothing short of defining the modern problem of knowledge. However, he also turned away from the realm of human affairs—from the 'government' of Calvin's conscience.

Etienne Balibar (2013, 2) has 'knocked off balance a central orientating point of our understanding of the history of Western philosophy', as Stella Sandford (2013, xiii) nicely put it, by tracing the modern concept of 'consciousness' to Locke rather than to Descartes, where it is habitually located, as the founder of philosophies of the subject.[16] 'Consciousness' is the experience of the mind seizing itself thinking, the inner sense accompanying a thought, by which the thinking subject apprehends it as *this* thought.[17] My aim is not to enter into the debate on the origins of 'consciousness', not least because Locke explicitly saw himself as furthering the Cartesian enterprise (see Pringle-Pattison 1924). It is instead is to build on Balibar's argument, in two ways. In chapter 6, I will show how Locke's 'consciousness' operates as a crux to Locke's concept of property. Here, I further explore this inner sense that Balibar draws our attention to, and to how it plays out differently in 'the conscience' and in 'consciousness'. Both point to the thinking, acting subject, only in their moral and epistemological guises, respectively. Tracking these two concepts across Locke's political and epistemological writings, I will show how Locke sought to carve a third way, beyond both the Hobbesian and Cartesian responses to the seventeenth-century problem of the conscience, one that neither corralled the conscience, by relegating it to the private sphere, nor sidestepped its moral functions, by apprehending it as a strictly cognitive instance. Coining the concept of 'consciousness' opened up a third way. Tracing the role of these concepts, however, also requires parsing Locke's complex relationship with natural reason.

4. The Ambivalences of Reason and Locke's Embodied Consciousness

Reclaiming Reason's 'Naturalness'

'Governing conduct', to paraphrase James Tully (1988), was Locke's overarching concern, both 'in man' and between them, as Calvin (*Institutes*, III. chap.19[15]848) had laid out the terms of the problem. Between persons, in the realm of human affairs that Descartes eschewed, Locke, who was a man of his times, established natural law as the fount of human law-making.[18] Early on in his political writings, in his *Essays on the Law of Nature* (1663–64), Locke (*ELN*, vi, 120) wrote that political laws 'derive their whole force from the constraining power of natural law'. Moreover, we know these laws 'with certainty by the light of nature' (ibid.). Almost three decades later, in the *Two Treatises*, he reaffirmed that the '*Municipal laws* of Countries' are only fair and right when they are 'founded on the Law of nature, by which they are to be regulated and interpreted' (*TT*, II.chap.2[12]275). In negotiating his relation with natural law, another question was also in play for Locke, I suggest, namely, how to position the old conscience in relation to a new scientific reason.[19] In his classic introduction Peter Laslett (1988) has underscored that references to the conscience have all but disappeared from Locke's mature political treatise. Laslett (1988, 85) suggests that there Locke simply 'brushes aside the question of the conscience and political obligation, which had worried him as a young man as it had worried all his predecessors and contemporaries', more specifically, his fellow travellers in the natural rights tradition. In fact, Locke's gesture was a brushing aside of the most effective sort: the kind that preserved it intact for modern politics. I will show that the conscience looms large over his late political writings. It functions as an absent presence. By then he had largely succeeded in his epistemological work in subsuming it to another concept, 'consciousness'.

Natural law, which was also God's, was a pillar of the pre-modern episteme, as we saw in the last two chapters, and indeed of Calvin's world. The conscience, for Calvin, was both the place within the subject where this natural law was received and the natural instrument for deciphering it. How, then, did Locke peel this form of law away from the notion it was still tightly bound up within Calvin's writings, namely, that it was inscribed in the conscience prior to birth? For Locke (*ELN*, iii, 96) is adamant in these essays already that 'the souls of the newly born are just empty tablets'. In fact, 'there exists no imprint of the law of nature in our hearts', he plainly stated in the same essay (ibid.). With these *Essays* Locke (*ELN*, i, 84 and 86) sought to chart a path between upholding that 'there is a law laid down by nature' that 'can be derived from men's consciences', that, moreover, is independent of consent (fifth essay), while also establishing that it is 'not inscribed' in us (third essay). Yet Locke's position is never quite settled in these early writings on the law of nature. Moreover, he would later come to contradict himself, subsequently writing in the Two Treatises and by reference to scripture that the law of nature was 'so plain[ly] [. . .] writ in the Hearts of all Mankind' (*TT*, II.chap.2[11]274).[20]

The Lockean solution is provided by his mature *Essay concerning the Human Understanding* (see also Buckle 1993). There he draws a crucial distinction between *the natural* and *the pre-inscribed*. In his own words:

> There is a great deal of difference between an innate law, and a law of nature; between something imprinted in our minds in the very original, and something

that we being ignorant of, may attain to the knowledge of by the use and due application of our natural faculties. (Locke, *EHU*, I.chap.3[13]57)

The application of these 'natural faculties' is Locke's object in the *Essay*. He aims to show how humans, by their use, 'may attain to all the knowledge they have, without the help of any innate impressions' (Locke, *EHU*, I,chap.2[1]43). The problem was not the idea that human beings were natural knowers. Locke's (*EHU*, I,chap.1[1]33) creature was a 'sensible being'; like Hobbes, the body was the starting point for knowledge. It was, rather, the scholastic idea that there were principles already 'stamped upon the mind of man which the soul receives in its very first being, and brings into the world with it' (ibid.). Although Locke calls these 'innate principles', he could not dispense with innateness altogether, since natural laws are the source of political laws. What he cast out, in the *Essay*, was the notion that these principles were pre-inscribed in us. The law of nature *is* innate, for the older Locke, but not because it is already chiseled upon our consciences. Rather, it needs to be sought out by attending to the natural light God has placed in us. It requires being actively cultivated by our reason, the natural faculty we possess to discover this law. Locke (*TT*,chap.2[7]271) even comes to conflate the faculty with the law itself in the Two Treatises: 'Reason [...] is that Law'. This 'Rule of Morals', as Locke (*ELN*, i,81–87) also terms it in these political essays, owes its naturalness to its being discoverable by natural means, specifically, by our reason and our sense perceptions working in tandem (fourth essay). Differentiating the natural from the pre-inscribed thus did away with the need for this law to be priorly engraved in us, without undermining its naturalness.

In ridding the natural from the pre-inscribed, however, Locke also ushered in the moral 'sense' of Calvin's (*Institutes*, II.chap.19[15]372) conscience through the back door of modern political reason. Locke's bore very little resemblance to Hobbes's. The latter's instrumental, mechanical reason had also served to guard against the encroachments of the moral conscience. Locke sheds this mechanistic imagery entirely.[21] He *lets* the conscience encroach, notably in his metaphors. These are the sites of implicit dialogues with Calvin and with Descartes (but not with Hobbes, whom Locke ignores). In the *Essays on the Law of Nature*, Locke systematically reworks the Calvinist repertoire of light and darkness. In a succession of steps that replicate Calvin's enquiry into the nature of the conscience, Locke (*ELN*,ii, 90) asks, what might be this inner light that, if theories of innate knowledge held true, would simply illuminate 'the pandects [digests of law]' that 'man' has 'within himself and always open before his eyes, [containing] all that constitutes his duty'. Only 'doubts can be raised as to what this light of nature is', Locke (*ELN*, iii, 95–96) finds, 'for while like sunlight it reveals to us by its rays the rest of reality, it is itself unknown and its nature is concealed in darkness'. Locke (*ELN*,ii, 90), now echoing Descartes, contrasts this semi-clarity with the certainty afforded by the 'chief light of all knowledge', namely reason; 'right reason' being but another name for the law of nature itself (ibid.). Indeed, Locke (*ELN*, iv, 100) continues, 'what is characteristic of the light of nature' is instead 'that things otherwise wholly unknown and hidden in darkness should be able to come before the mind and be known and as it were looked into'. Locke's, then, is a critical recovery of the Calvinist conscience. He retrieves this natural inner light away from Calvin's somewhat nebulous conscience to tie it firmly instead to the bedrock of natural law: reason.[22]

Moving beyond Reason with the Body

The Mind and the Understanding

Locke, in good natural law fashion, rests his political writings upon the traditional faculty of reason, and I will return to some of the key political ordering functions it performs in the chapter's final part. Only, ultimately, natural reason was perhaps too irrevocably steeped in ontologies of inscription; at any rate, he departs from it altogether in his epistemological work. The *Essay concerning the Human Understanding* (1690) was Locke's response to Descartes's *Discourse on the Method of Correctly Conducting One's Reason* (1637), the established reference in the intellectual circles where the scientific revolution was unfolding. Locke's key move was to cast the understanding rather than reason as his core focus.[23] The opening lines to Locke's *Essay* weave a web of references to the *Discourse* that carefully position his epistemological treatise in relation to Descartes's. The different ways we have of 'directing our thoughts' is Descartes's (2006, 5) starting point, while Locke (*EHU*, I.chap.1[1]33) seeks the 'great advantage in directing our own thoughts'. Locke (*EHU*, I.chap.1[2]33) sets out to consider the 'discerning faculties of a man', echoing Descartes's (2006, 5) 'powers of judging correctly'. Only Locke calls these powers, not 'good sense or reason', like Descartes (2006, 5), but rather the 'understanding'. Locke then conjures the bodily organ Descartes and his contemporaries were obsessed with cutting open, as we will see in chapter 7: 'the understanding', Locke (*EHU*, I.chap.1[1]33) writes, 'like the eye, whilst it makes us see and perceive all things, takes no notice of itself'.

With 'the understanding' and 'the mind' (Locke uses these interchangeably), he recalibrated his epistemological work upon conceptual bases that were more tightly harnessed to the dynamics of action and to the body. This enabled him to reintegrate the sphere of *praxis* that Descartes had written out of his framework. For Descartes's reason was the product of two ancient dualisms. That of body and soul, first. The second, reflected in the two facets of the conscience, was of a theoretical reason (*theoria*) implicated in the production of science, and the practical rationality (*praxis*) that guided human actions, which was the faculty of government proper. By casting the focus onto the soul and its cognitive faculties in the *Discourse*, Descartes had directed it away from the body, *but also* from this practical, political sphere. These two exclusions—of the realm of *praxis* and of the body—were coextensive in Descartes's reason. I will now consider the twofold strategies, conceptual and metaphorical, by which Locke undoes them.

Conceptually, Locke recovers actions by way of 'the understanding', and the body with his 'consciousness'. I consider each of these moves in turn. Actions are at the heart of the dynamic, practical mode of theorising that Locke deploys against the backdrop of the discovery of the modern laws of motion. Locke (*EHU*, II.chap.19[4]148) directly inverts Descartes when he posits that 'thinking is the action, and not the essence of the soul'. Locke's central preoccupation in the *Essay* is with how 'the mind' acquires its ideas, rather than with reason's old revelatory process. 'The understanding', a nominalised verb, is a more active term; it is tightly tethered to the mind in motion acquiring its multiple 'understandings', which is Locke's (*EHU*, I.chap.1[5]34) other terms for 'ideas'. Warning against the confusion that the old talk of 'faculties has misled many into', Locke (*EHU*, II.chap.21[6]152) re-conceptualises the traditional faculties under the prism of action, in terms of agential capabilities. The understanding and the will are simply the mind's two powers. The understanding is its 'perceptive power' (*EHU*, II.chap.21[5]152). 'Willing' is the power deployed in 'directing [an] action or its forbearance'; and this includes 'an action of the mind', since thinking is also action, for Locke (*EHU*, II.chap.21[5]152). Thinking and moving are the two forms of conscious actions ('the two sorts of action of which we have any idea'; *EHU*, II.chap.21[4]151); the modalities of the perceiving Lockean mind always in motion.

The understanding is the pertinent power to appraise, in Locke's practical perspective, since it directs the will. It is our governing instance, the command-and-control centre of human conduct. It affords us the reasons for doing the things that we do, and every single thing we do. Locke uses 'reasons' mostly in the plural, to refer to motivations for actions, rather than to the traditional faculty. 'The understanding', Locke (*CU* [1]3) wrote, 'with such light as it has, well or ill informed, constantly leads; and by that light, true or false, all [of a person's] operative powers are directed'. For Locke (like for Hobbes, though for very different reasons) there is no such thing as a free will, since the will, 'however absolute and uncontrollable soever it may be thought, never fails in obeying the dictates of the understanding' (*CU* [1]3). Government, understood as the conduct of action, one's own in the *Essay* and others' in the *Two Treatises*, is the overarching concept of Locke's thought and it is inseparable from the sphere of praxis.

Consciousness and Personhood

With his 'consciousness', Locke counterposes a more carefully embodied concept to Descartes's disincarnate focus on the rational soul. He brings the mind back to the body.

> When we see, hear, smell, taste, feel, medicate or will any thing, we know that we do so. Thus it is always as to our present Sensations and Perceptions: And by this every one is to himself, that which he calls self. (Locke, *EHU* II.chap.27[9]210)

Locke, as an empiricist, retains the body as the starting point for all experience and knowledge of the world, but he does not dwell exclusively with it, in the way that Hobbes does. He does not 'meddle with the physical consideration of the mind', or with what we could call today 'the brain' (*EHU*, I.chap.1[2]33). Indeed 'the thinking substance in man must necessarily be thought immaterial', for Locke (*EHU*, II.27[23]216). With 'the mind' and 'consciousness', Locke thus avoids the dual pitfalls of Descartes's thinking but disembodied subject, and of a thoroughgoing Hobbesian materialism that cannot (and will not) handle interiority. Locke introduces his concept of consciousness, which he borrows from his friend Ralph Cudworth, to parse the problem of identity that is raised by his pragmatic focus on actions. It forms part of a broader conceptual register that Locke utilises to pivot away from the scholastic language of (immaterial) substances and souls, and that would be decisive for the modern psychological language of 'selfhood' (Taylor 1989; Balibar 2013): 'self', 'consciousness', and 'person', which I will consider extensively in chapter 6.

Locke begins by asking, what holds together the acting self? How are we to know that it remains the same self as it acts over time, and which actions to attribute to it, rather than to another? How can we be sure they are the actions of this same self? Locke (*EHU*, II.chap.27[6]208) rules out locating the principle of identity in the soul:

> If identity of soul alone makes the same man, and there be nothing in the nature of matter why an individual spirit may not be united to different bodies, it will be possible that those men living in distant ages and of different tempers, may have been the same man: which way of speaking must be, from a very strange use of the word man, applied to an idea, out of which body and shape are excluded.

The body, then, without which would make for 'a very strange use of the word man' is integral to the principle of identity Locke (*EHU*, II.chap.27[6]209) sets out to find. Locke's (*EHU*, II,chap.27[15]213) improbable example of a prince reincarnated as a cobbler drives home the point that the soul cannot be the sole locus of an identity and that 'the Body too goes to the making the Man'. [24] The same is true with all living beings. Take the plant kingdom, Locke (II, chap.27[4]208) writes, 'something is one plant if it has an organisation of parts in one cohering body partaking of one common life'. Locke (*EHU*, II,chap.27[5]208) rallies the common sense to underline the embodied nature of identity: 'it is not the idea of a thinking or rational being alone that makes the idea of a man in most people's sense, but of a body, so and so shaped, joined to it'. The body is what gives a plant, an animal, and a human their form and cohesion, not some immaterial substance or essence.

Having retrieved the body, Locke's next move is to distinguish, on the one hand, between *human* identity and *personal* identity. The former is, for Locke, the generic principle of individuation (*principium individuationis*) that humans share with all other natural beings (see Forstrom 2010). It is that by which a being is individuated or made distinct from another being, and thus constituted into an individual biologically; an undivided organised living being, whether plant, animal, or human. The simple and very corporeal notion of 'existence' furnishes him his generic principle. This enables him to draw a crucial distinction between 'human' ('man' in his language) and 'person'. 'Human' ('man') for Locke refers to the biological being, whereas 'person', that Locke borrows from theology, refers to the moral being. In the following chapter, I will show how he wields this distinction to establish humanity as the sole bearer of rights, at the exclusion of all other natural beings. For now, however, 'consciousness' is properly, for Locke (*EHU*, II,chap.27[10]211), what 'makes a man be himself to himself', in a non-biological moral sense, which is to say, as a person. He explains:

> As far as any intelligent being can repeat the idea of any past action with the same consciousness it had of it at first, and with the same consciousness it has of any present action, it is the same personal self. For it is by the consciousness it has of present thoughts and actions, that it is self to itself now, and so will be the same self [in the future]. (*EHU*, II,chap.27[10]211)

'Consciousness' is what the rational animal endowed with a conscience possesses exclusively. By way of 'consciousness' and 'person', Locke marries the Ancient Greek reason and the Christian conscience. By the same token, he decisively re-established the latter at the heart of the moral and political sciences. [25] To summarise, consciousness, which 'unites existence and actions [. . .] to the same person', is the locus of personal identity, but it is (generally) embodied. It takes a human to incorporate a person; the model here being the Christ (see chapter 6).

Lastly, in addition to ushering in a new term that makes room for the conscience in its midst, Locke restores the language of conscience in his rhetorical work. In the same opening lines to the *Essay*, Locke draws the metaphor of light back towards the moral lexicon Descartes had largely stripped from it. 'The candle that is set up in us, shines bright enough for all our purposes', Locke (*EHU*, I.chap.1[5]35) wrote. Only his 'purposes' included moral matters.[26] Locke metaphorized the cognitive phenomena and scientific artefact in a legal key, undoing the Cartesian separation of an epistemological from a moral-practical realm. For example, he moralised the *camera obscura*, the device with which Johannes Kepler had discovered the mechanics of sight, that also featured in Descartes's treaty on vision (the *Dioptrics*). Locke (*EHU*, II.chap.11[17]109]) compares the mind to 'a closet wholly shut from light, with only some little opening left', its pinhole. Only under his pen, the juridical meaning of *in camera*, in court and about to be judged, is also in play. In another example, he reconfigured the physiological organs that were being dissected to parse the mechanics of sight into sites of the conscience's interiority.[27] Simple ideas, like light and colour 'which have admittance only through one sense' are created, for Locke (*EHU*, II.chap.1[17]109 and II.chap.3[1]86), by the sense data conveyed by the nerves 'from without to their audience in the brain', which he also called 'the mind's presence room'. Jonathan Crary (1988, 32) has remarked that Locke 'adds onto the observer's passive role a more authoritative and juridical function to guarantee and to police the correspondence between exterior world and interior representation and to exclude anything disorderly and unruly'.

I have argued that, with the two prongs to his thought, epistemological and political, Locke sutured back together the two dimensions to the conscience that Descartes and Hobbes had separated out. He undid the Hobbesian solution to the problem of war, invented 'consciousness', and ushered the conscience back into modern political reason. I have also shown how Locke distanced himself from the faculty of reason in his epistemological work. And yet, as I will now show, the old equation of 'reason' and 'order' is at the heart of his political ordering project, and it serves as a boundary-drawing instrument to separate out those who qualify for political subjecthood from those who do not.

5. The Variegated Reasons and Exclusionary Logics of Locke's Political Ordering

Whereas the correct ordering of our understandings is Locke's concern in the *Essay*, in his political work it was with the creation of a human-made order. Constitution was the business of this state of nature theorist, or how to craft the polity from scratch, beginning on the blank pages of the mind at birth. Locke was the first to consider the child as the starting point to his project. Hobbes's natural being is given, in all its flawed, passionate nature. He seeks to study it and to arrange its communal living, but not to change it. Hobbes's thought is static; it juxtaposes two ultimately irreconcilable states. Education is a secondary concern, envisaged as part of 'the office of the sovereign' (*L.*, chap. 3). Hobbes (*L.*, chap.18[4]107) deems subjection a necessary condition for political order (since there is 'no peace without [it]'), but, forsaking interiority, he does not consider how it operates. Locke's thought is instead dynamic, at grips with action and with change. It is geared to 'government' rather than to 'sovereignty', and this encompasses education. 'The great work of a *Governour*', Locke (*Thoughts concerning Education* [94]156) wrote, 'is to fashion the Carriage and to form the mind; to settle in his Pupil good Habits, and the principles of Virtue and Wisdom'. Subjection is also at the heart of Locke's project of political constitution, only understood, I suggest, in the dual sense of a becoming-subject by submitting to collective laws, as in Hobbes, but also of his *own* role in crafting the modern political subject. Locke drafted two pedagogical treatises late in his life, *On the Conduct of the Understanding* (CU), initially conceived as an appendix to the *Essay* (published posthumously in 1706), and his *Thoughts concerning Education* (1693). He inaugurated a genre that would flourish the following century (under the pens of Rousseau, Wollstonecraft, or Condillac), and durably ushered in the figure of the child into modern political thought.

The difference between naturally given and socially constructed laws is central to Locke's ordering project. He distinguishes four types of laws—divine, natural, civil, and the 'law of fashion, or private censure'—; but the salient difference runs between the first two, given (by God or nature), and the latter two, political, laws (*EHN*, II.chap.28[13]239). The former are unchangeable; they require being understood in order to build an ordered polity, and this begins with appraising 'the State all men are naturally in' (*TT*, II.2[4]269). Political laws are where humans have a hand. Of the two kinds of human-made laws, the most effective is in fact the fourth 'law of opinion or reputation', as Locke (*EHN*, II.chap.28[7]235) also calls it. While someone may be able to escape civil punishment by successfully concealing his or her crime or misdemeanour, Locke (*EHN*, II.chap.28[13]239) points out, 'no man escapes the punishment of their censure and dislike, who offends against the fashion and opinion of the company he keeps, and would recommend himself to'. The 'condemnation of his own club' alone metes out the kind of punishment from which no one can hide, and that few ('one of ten thousand', by Locke's [ibid.] estimate) are 'stiff and insensible' enough to bear up under. Locke was a theorist of the power of norms and of the pressure to conform. He apprehends this as a properly political power, and of the most effective kind. It operates through the dual mechanisms of socialisation, through the desire to belong to a 'club', and through internalising the norms regulating this 'company'. A constructivist *avant la lettre*, like Hobbes, Locke underlines the extent to which these norms are constructed and contingent. In fact, the emphasis on human diversity is an important strand of his deconstruction of innate ideas (see Bernasconi 1992). Given the constructed-ness of norms, the only 'measure' of 'virtue or vice' is:

> the approbation or dislike, praise or blame which by a secret and tacit consent establishes itself in the several societies, groups and clubs of men in the world; whereby several actions come to find credit or disgrace among them according to the judgements, maxims or fashions of that place. (*EHN*, II.chap.28[10]236)

This un-self-aware tacit consent is the bedrock of sociality. To fashion the law of fashion by harnessing it to reason is therefore crucial to the task at hand.

Let me, at this point, assemble the building blocks of Locke's political ordering project. '*Political Power*' is 'the *Right* of making Laws' (*TT*, II.chap.1[2]268). Locke (*TT*, I.chap.5[48]174 and II. chap.7[86]323) distinguishes it from other forms of power, notably a natural power, which I will consider in the following section, and a man's 'Conjugal power' over his domestic sphere composed of a '*Wife, Children, Servant* and *Slaves*'. The law, 'in its true notion, is not so much the limitation, as the direction of a free and intelligent agent to his proper interest', for Locke (*TT*, II.chap.6[57]305). Political liberty consists in having a 'standing Rule' in our conscience to guide us to remain within the bounds of the law when we act (*TT*, II.4[22]284). Acceding to this collective right/power turns on having wilfully consented to relinquishing some parts of one's natural freedoms. Or rather, this is the stated rationale, and where the ideological function of consent in his thought resides. The conditions of entitlement to this right/power operate on several levels. Consent indexes the explicit one; it works to direct attention away from the others, where Locke builds a series of exclusions that short-circuit its purported generality, and the equality it appeared to promise.

Locke excludes in two key places, with his concept of property, which is my focus in the next chapter, and in the way he ties together reason and political subjecthood, which is my object here. Locke conceives this subjecthood in terms of an exclusive membership based on a naturalised capacity for rational and responsible behaviour. Building on a range of critical Locke scholarships, I analyse a central distinction running through his thought, between 'rational', 'irrational', and 'reasonable', by which he differentiates those who are entitled to full membership, and thus to political power, from those who are not.[28] Reason may be 'granted to all by nature', for Locke (1990, 109); in fact, it is not the same reason for all, and this has decisive implications for how he designs the polity. His typology of forms of reason operates in turn as a gradated system of inclusions and exclusions. It delineates the Lockean state as a three-tiered membership system, composed of an exclusive group of rational, full members; a larger group of reasonable, aspiring members; and the irrational, excluded rest. The distinction between the two Lockean outsiders, whom I term, respectively, the reasonable natural outsider and the irrational excluded, turns on whether their bodies are disciplined (the former) or punished (the latter).

Disciplining Consent

Tacit Consent and the Power of Habituation

The child is the future consenter. The importance of education to his thought has been amply drawn out by the scholarship on the 'disciplinary Locke'.[29] 'Freedom of thinking' is its aim, rather than perfecting the child's knowledge of 'any one science' (*CU* [19]44). This freedom consists, at its core, 'in a power of acting or not acting' (*EHU*, II.21[23]157). Not acting is where, for Locke (*EHU*, II.21[47]166), 'the source of all liberty' lies; in developing the mind's natural ability to reign in 'the execution and satisfaction of any of its desires'. It differentiates liberty from licence, which Locke (*TT*, II.chap.2[6]270) ascribes to the state of nature and the state of war, respectively. 'The great Mistake I have observed in People's breeding their Children', Locke (EE, [34]103) wrote, is 'that the Mind has not been made obedient to Discipline and pliant to Reason when at first it was most tender, most easy to be bowed'. Indeed, Locke (EE [36]105) continues, 'he that is not used to submit his Will to the reason of others when he is young, will not hearken or submit to his own Reason, when he is of Age to make use of it'. The problem is that, without a 'Mastery of his own inclinations', the 'true Principle of Virtue and Industry' will remain wanting and 'he is in danger never to be good for any thing', Locke (EE [45]111) explained. Training this 'power to govern and deny our selves in [our desires]' in the child so that it may 'be trusted to his own conduct', since liberty comes with the years, is therefore the purpose of a Lockean education (EE [36]105 and 10[90]).

The problem Locke faces is that consent is of more than one kind, and not all provide equally solid foundations for the polity. The consent expressed by the contract is the most active kind, that fully engages the will and the understanding. This 'express consent', as Locke (*TT*, II.8[119]347) terms it, 'makes a perfect member of that Society, a subject of that Government'. Locke's ideal political subject is a self-possessing express consenter endowed with a fully developed capacity to reason and to choose. What, then, of the tacit consent we considered earlier? It is a double-edged sword for Locke. On the one hand, it is the mechanism of socialisation. Though the lesser kind, it remains the form of consent at work in a range of 'liminal figures', to borrow Andrew Dilts's (2012) expression, who mark the threshold of Locke's perfect and fully rational political membership. This is where women stand in the Lockean scheme. Their semi-inclusion has been analysed by the critical feminist Locke scholarship (Hirschmann 2008;

Pateman 1988). I focus on two other tacit consenters, the foreigner and the child, in order to further circumscribe the nature of the consent that disqualifies an individual for full political subjecthood. The child is 'born a Subject of no Country or Government' (*TT* chap.8[118]347). By learning 'the long and familiar use' ascribed to words by the society of which they are becoming a member, these subjects-in-the-making progressively make theirs the collective reality it inhabits (*EHU*, III, chap.2[8]268). However, while this familiarisation is a necessary condition, it is not sufficient for political membership. The figure of the foreigner illuminates the difference. 'Submitting to the Laws of any Country, living quietly, and enjoying Priviledges [*sic*] and Protection under them', writes Locke (*TT*, II.chap.8[122]349) '*makes not a Man a Member of that Society* [. . .] a perpetual Subject of that Commonwealth.' Locke adds a key criteria, which is the quality of the society's grip upon the conscience that the 'standing Rules' have (*TT*, II.4[22]284). How solidly they stand there matters for a political ordering project founded in consent. To be simply 'bound' by these rules, 'even in Conscience', as is the foreigner, is to remain a step short of the active rational consent required for full membership (*TT*. II.chap.8[122]349). 'Nothing can make' any person a member of a commonwealth but his or her 'actually entering into it by positive engagement, and express Promise and Compact' (ibid.). The foreigner is reasonable and consenting enough, but he or she remains estranged from the established rules that individuals must abide by in order to be able to live together. These rules and norms command their tacit consent, but not quite the internal assent that do those one is born into. Only when this quality of assent is cultivated and attained do they properly become political subjects.[30] Hence the importance of education. This adherence is of course more difficult to fashion in an adult. Hence the significance of the child.

On the other hand, however, tacit consent is the bedrock of indoctrination. In it are also grounded 'those doctrines [...] derived from [. . .] the superstition of a nurse' (*EHU*, I.chap.3[22]60). Locke's systematic deconstruction of innate ideas in the *Essay* is war against indoctrination, and against the abuse of authority that establishes these (or any) ideas beyond the pale of questioning, by further entrenching, rather than reshaping, tacit consent. He takes aim at those 'affected . . . masters and teachers', who 'take [their followers] off from the use of their own reason and judgement' and put them in 'a posture of blind credulity', where they are 'more easily governed'—without questioning his own authority to establish himself as their teacher instead (*EHU*, I.4[24]74).

Habituation is both the source of the problem and its solution. For undoing innate ideas also revealed to Locke the malleability of the mind. If all notions are acquired, then mobilising the mechanics of habituation to correct an earlier ill-habituation is the only thing to do, in the critical, dynamic and practical perspective that was his. 'Custom settles habit of thinking in the understanding, and of determining in the will, and of motions in the body' he wrote (*EHU*, II.chap.33[6]261). Yet custom and habit can also be used to redirect these 'trains of motion' in the body and mind (ibid.). The 'relish[es] of the mind', Locke (*EHU*, II.chap.21[69]174) underlines, like those of the body, 'may be altered'. 'Men can and should correct their palates, and give relish' to things in which they find none but are good for them, and vice versa (ibid). 'Due consideration will do it in some cases; and practice, application and custom in most' (ibid.) A taste for bread, or tobacco, may not be automatic, but it can be carefully cultivated. 'Reason and consideration at first recommend [them] and begin their trial, because they are 'shown to be useful to health', wrote this physician, and then 'use finds or custom makes them pleasant' (*EHU*, II.chap.21[69]174).[31] Locke, then, set out to harness the political power of norms to shape reason, and discipline was the instrument he honed to achieve this.

Fashioning the Political Subject from Within: The Role of Education

The purpose of a Lockean education is to replace 'the Guard' put upon the child with one that one must 'put into his own mind by Good Principles and established habits' so that the child may be eventually 'trusted to [its] own conduct' and educated into its freedom, wrote Locke (*EE*, [10].90), with echoes of Calvin's sentinel. Only whereas Calvin's was already there at birth, Locke's first needs to be internalised. Discipline is the motor of this internalisation. With it the child musters the power of habit; it etches in its mind the grooves down which good thinking flows. For this mind, for Locke (EE, [2]83–84), is like water, 'as easily turned this or that way'. Shaping metaphors abound in Locke's (EE, [46].112) writings on the 'great Art' of education. The child is 'like white Paper, or Wax, to be moulded and fashioned as one pleases' (EE, [217].265). Locke's water is not without recalling Hobbes's liberty; only the imagery is brought within, by the mind and no longer just the body being in focus. Crafting 'a sound Mind in a sound Body' is Locke's (EE. [1].83) purpose. Discipline acts on the mind, even in physical exercises, since the mind directs the will (which moves the body). 'Carriage' or 'dispositions' are the target of Locke's discipline; they implicate body and mind. 'He that is a good, a virtuous and able Man must be made so within', hence in their consciences, Locke (EE, [42].110) writes. Here is how, for example, he describes the ideal of 'gracefulness' to be cultivated in the child of the gentry: it is that 'Beauty, which shines through some men's actions; sets off all they do, and takes all they come near; when, by constant practice they have fashion'd their Carriage' so that 'all those little expressions of Civility and Respect' seem 'not Artificial or Studied, but naturally to flow from a sweetness of mind, and a well turn'd Disposition' (Locke. EE. [66]123). This quality indicates 'a Mind free, and Master of itself and all its actions' that is yielded by the right sort of education (ibid.).

Locke's discipline is not the spectacular marking of the body through punishment, the lesser pedagogical instrument, for him. 'The Smart of the Rod, if
Shame accompanies it not, soon ceases and is forgotten and will quickly, by use,
loose its Terrour' [sic] (EE, [74].138). Corporeal punishment is effective only if
the physical pain gives way to shame, hence if it is internalised and moralised,
such that it can be readily reactivated. Locke marks the passage from 'punishment' to 'discipline' that Foucault (1995) identified as the threshold of political
modernity; although he shows it to have occurred earlier than where Foucault
located it (in the eighteenth century). Replacing the ruler smacked on the child's
fingertips or bottom (say) with reason's 'common Rule and Measure' is Locke's
(TT, II.chap.2[11]274) purpose. To this effect he recommends alternating 'a
strict hand' with a 'milder form of government' (EE, [42].110–11). For 'too strict
a hand' breaks these spirits; and 'dejected Minds, timorous and tame', lose 'all
Vigor and Industry' (EE, [46].112).

Locke favours shame and guilt, instead of fear, love or awe, as the primary
affects to be mobilised in the business of education. The rod alone makes for a
'slavish Temper' (EE, [50].113). It crafts someone who will obey out of fear of
being punished, rather than because she chooses to, because she adheres from
within to the reasons for doing so. For Hobbes fear is the primary ordering affect.
Locke prefers shame and guilt because they are more thoroughly internalised.
The problem with fear, for him, is that it can short-circuit this internalisation
process that he holds as the primary motor to his education. When habits are
beaten into a child, they remain 'a counterfeit Carriage, and dissembled Outside, put on by fear', rather than really 'put into him', and 'only to avoid the present
Anger of a Father' (EE, [42].110). Fear is ineffectual. It is also counterproductive,
since it weakens the bonds of love that attach a child to its parents, and that moti-
vate it to honour and obey them. The trick, then, to the 'great Art' of education, is
'to avoid the danger that is on either hand', in too much coddling and in too much
punishing (EE, [46].112).

Bodies have not been the primary focus of the disciplinary Locke scholarship,
since corporeal punishment is the lesser pedagogical tool for him. However, the
role of punished bodies in his thought, to which I now turn, has been brought
into focus in another strand of Lockean scholarship, which has focussed on the
essential, and essentialising, work that disorder, and punishment as the response
to it, achieves for Locke's ordering project (McBride 2007; Dilts 2012; 2014).
For this theorist of the social pressures to conform, one power is pre-social and
founds all others, the 'Power of punishing' (TT, I.9[130]353). This power applies
most directly to the body and presumes the possibility of its destruction since
Locke explicitly defines it as the power to kill. Crucially, containing this lethal
natural corporeal power is the main Lockean driver for founding the state.

Together Locke's discipline and his punishment draw out the internal and external dimensions of his state-making.

Disorder and the Death Penalty:
The Centrality of Violence and Punishment in Locke

Express and tacit consent together extend over the Lockean spaces where reason rules—fully actualised in the rational express consenter; still a potentiality in the reasonable tacit one. Beyond these spaces, unreason reigns. The figure of the criminal indexes the limit between the realms of reason and unreason. Appraising its central role in Locke's (*TT*, II.chap.2[15]277) thought first requires gauging the importance of his 'strange doctrine' of punishment. Punishment performs two constitutive functions. It founds the Lockean state, and it establishes humankind at large as the subject of natural rights. I consider each in turn. Violence is natural, for Locke. It is even perfectly legitimate in one, crucial instance: to retaliate. The compulsion to strike back after being hurt, far from being an unfortunate bend of our passionate natures, as in the Hobbesian logic, is a crucial mechanism by which the state of nature self-regulates. It is a natural ordering mechanism, the '*Executive Power*' that maintains order in the state of nature, and accounts for its orderliness (*TT*, II.chap.2[13]275). The instinctive knowledge that others will retaliate holds natural individuals in check. Locke conceives his state of nature as a system of mutual guarantees founded in the permanent threat of violence. This is another marked difference with Hobbes. In the Hobbesian state of nature, violence is everywhere realised as a function of our unbridled passions. It is not latent. It is the source of the disorder that pushes individuals out of this state. Instead Locke delinks disorder from nature, and returns to an older, scholastic conception of an ordered nature. In doing so he also preserves a much larger role for violence *within* the state, and in the form of a threat. He latentises violence. This is consistent with the dynamics of internalisation at work in his notion of discipline. Violence, like discipline, is at its most effective in latency. By rescuing an ordered nature, Locke recovers violence. He establishes it, not merely as the starting point for the state, which it also was for Hobbes, but also as the ongoing wellspring of its effectiveness. The Lockean state is born of a collectivised power, not to pursue the common good, but to punish, and indeed to kill.

The corporeal lens draws out the centrality to Locke's political project of upholding death as an arrival point for the deployment of this natural power to punish. Locke explicitly conjoins the execution of laws and of bodies, since he tethers the political power to execute these laws to the power to kill. Locke's political power is not merely 'the *Right* of making Laws'. A key specification is added: 'with Penalties of Death, and consequently all less Penalties' (*TT*, II.chap.1[2]268). The death penalty is a necessary rather than a contingent component of a violence that is not simply 'lawmaking', as Walter Benjamin (1986, 287) once termed, but more specifically with Locke, state-making. He illustrates more broadly the naturalisation of violence that Benjamin (1986) identified as one of the most effective and enduring effects of the resort to natural law. Death affords both the upper limit and the measuring rod for all legal penalties. The punishment Locke scholarship has underscored is the central role that reason's requirement of proportionality plays as a reason for founding the state (Dilts 2012; 2014; McBride 2008). I build on this scholarship to show how the body's biological limits afford the limiting principle of a constitutive project that has death at its core.

Nature's Limitlessness and Locke's Natural Executive Power

Proportionality affords the Lockean gauge for determining the right penalties and retributions to be applied to the transgressor. It is a rule of measurement furnished by our natural reason via our consciences. In the state of nature, 'calm reason and the conscience dictat[e], what is proportionate to the transgression' (Locke, *TT*, II.chap.2[8]272). Moreover, Locke (*TT*, chap.2[12]275) is at pains to show that this state contains very clear 'measures of punishment', upon which civil penalties are to be benchmarked: 'it is certain there is such a law, and that too, as intelligible and plain to a rational Creature and a Studier of that Law, as the positive Laws of Common-wealths, nay possibly plainer'. Indeed, human-crafted laws, or the '*Municipal laws* of Countries' are only fair and right when they are 'founded on the Law of nature, by which they are [also] to be regulated and interpreted' (*TT*, chap.2[12]275). The death of the body affords the upper limit against which all the 'less[er] Penalties' are to be set (*TT*, II.chap.1[2]268).

Why is this limitation necessary? For Locke's (*TT*, II.chap.2[8]272) state of nature lacks neither the instruments for gauging penalties, nor the means to impose them, since every one is an '*Executioner*' of its laws. What it lacks is the certainty that the rule of proportionality will be applied every time an offence has been committed. Locke's nature does, in fact, supply these kinds of natural-cum-rational limiting mechanisms. For example, Locke (*TT*, II.chap.5[36]292) shows, contra Hobbes, that a natural 'measure of Property' sets a spontaneous limit, such that in the state of nature no one appropriates for themselves more than they can use. Only he shifts the principle of illimitation that was already at work in Hobbes's state of nature (see chapters 2 and 3) from property to punishment; from an unlimited right to everything in nature to that of defending its laws. The problem, as he conceives it, is that this right, which is also a power, contains the risk of its own excess, of a limitlessness. Unleashed and left unchecked, the power to punish can spiral into a cycle of revenge. It risks becoming a disordering force, instead of that which upholds the natural order. This potential limitlessness is the other side to what renders Locke's natural laws effective, and gives them the bite that Hobbes's ultimately lacked. Effectiveness and illimitation are the two sides of Locke's natural executive power. Hence why, unlike the other natural power to self-preserve, this one must be 'wholly' forsaken (*TT*, II.chap.9[130]353). Although illimitation has changed places, Locke's solution to the problem it poses is structurally similar to Hobbes's. It is a renunciation. The very real possibility that calm reason and the dictates of the conscience may not be able to prevail are what trigger the need to exit an idyllic state which, unlike Hobbes's, human beings would have otherwise very few reasons to leave.

Locke's spur for exiting the state of nature, the proportionality requirement, is steeped in the mathematical thinking of his age. Like Hobbes, Locke stands with a foot in both worlds. His somewhat anxious insistence on the plainness and intelligibility of natural laws harks back to a pre-modern episteme. Like Hobbes's *read thyself*, Locke seeks the stable grounds that tapping into a familiar frame affords. The anxiety surfaces in what Locke casts off-limits for his argument, however. 'Though it would be besides my present purpose to enter here into the particulars of the Law of Nature' is how he prefaces the passage where he simply asserts the existence of these measures (*TT*, chap.2[12]275). As Peter Laslett (1988, 82) underlined, '[I]t seems that it was always "besides his present purpose" for Locke to demonstrate the existence and content of natural law'. Locke's posture denotes two possibilities. Either the laws of nature were so familiar to his audience that they required no demonstration. Or perhaps, like the old reason they were bound up with, they were no longer quite as stable, as certain, as they once were, and best not to venture there.[32] Either way, Locke's state of nature functions like a bridge between two worlds.

Delineating a Polity of Reasonable Consenters: Locke's Criminal

Whereas in Hobbes, the state of nature marks the limits of the state, in Locke's three-state scheme, the state of war serves this purpose. Consequently unreason, and where it rules, plays a key boundary-drawing role. It marks the outside of the state, but also and crucially as I will show, of humanity itself. A key effect of the three states is that it shifts the central operative antinomy in Locke's political thought from the state/state of nature to reason/unreason, via the state/state of war. For Hobbes, reason and unreason, or the passions, were but the two sides of human nature, and the reason why a state was needed in the first place. Unreason did not index the obverse of the Hobbesian state. It was contained within the state and what the latter was designed to contain. Instead, per Locke's equation of irrationality and war, unreason denotes what lies beyond the space of collective living and threatens to tear it apart.

However and significantly, Locke sees nothing unreasonable in the potential for excess and the violence that punishment holds. Indeed, he rescues punishment as a key instrument of government by locating irrationality else-where. As Andrew Dilts (2012, 61) has underscored, the creation of a political subject who freely contracts 'requires the production of a figure that carries the burden of danger and irrationality', the criminal. In the next section, I will con-sider who many of the criminals were in Locke's time. Here I show the twofold functions the figure performs for his constitutive thought, namely, boundary-drawing, and as an anchoring point for his notion of universality.

Punishing is a power and a right for Locke. 'The right of punishing is in every body' he wrote (*TT*, II.chap.2[11]273). It is the outward extension, in the inter-subjective space, of the right/power to self-preserve A crucial implication is that anyone is naturally entitled to retaliate if another's rights are violated, even if they are not directly injured. Locke's theory of punishment establishes humankind at large as the injured party in any violation of natural rights. In this it is consid-ered exemplary of the natural rights tradition (Simmons 1991). Consequently, any violation of any natural right is a 'trespass against the whole Species' (*TT*, II.chap.2[8]272). Everyone belongs to the injured party, even if he or she is un-hurt or even unaware, simply by virtue of being a member of the species; and this affords him or her the right 'to preserve Mankind in general' (ibid). Hence punishment is the generalising mechanism that carries Locke's natural rights to humanity at large, such that Locke has been read as a theorist of human rights (see for example Graf 2018). This claim to universality would even appear to be the primary purchase of having established retaliation, rather than another kind, as the state's founding violence.

In fact, Locke's 'universal' human rights are premised on an original exclu-sion. Everybody is entitled to retaliate, bar one: the first offender. This primordial exclusion is what establishes humanity at large as the subject of natural rights. A first offender is needed to claim this universality. Because they are rooted in the body, because the body is the anchor of their 'naturalness' in ways I will fur-ther explore in the following chapter, Locke's natural rights are individual. The initial crossing of the line of the (natural) law *by someone* is what triggers their collectivisation. Enter the criminal. In stepping across this line, the offender has 'renounced' his or her right to punish, and 'Reason' itself for that matter (*TT*, II,chap.2[11]274). By the same token, he or she has established *everyone else* as rightful punishers. Locke's is a universality minus one; it functions as the exclu-sion of the one that constitutes the many as a collective rights-bearer. Moreover, the transgression must be wilfully chosen. Locke requires the offender to bear exclusive responsibility for breaking the peace, and to carry alone, in their flesh and in their death, the consequences unleashed by their act. For they may legit-imately 'be destroyed as a *Lyon* or a *Tyger*, one of those Savage Beast with whom Men can have no Society no Security' (*TT*, II.chap2[11]274). Nor can they claim ignorance since the law of retaliation is 'plain[ly] [. . .] writ in the Hearts of all Mankind' (*TT*, II.chap.2[11]274). Since the transgression was achieved wilfully and in full conscience, the logic it manifests can only belong to another kind of (dis)order altogether: the state of war. It threatens 'the Peace and Safety of [. . .] the whole Species' (*TT*II.chap2[8]272). The issue is not the nature of the act, but the possibility of unreason it manifests. The trespasser, Locke (*TT*, II.chap.2[8]272 and [10]273) explains, has 'declare[d himself or herself] to live by another Rule than that of *reason*' and to have 'quit the Principles of Human Nature'. Thus any trespass is a declaration of 'War against all Mankind', because it augurs the reign of unreason and chaos (*TT*, II.chap.2[11]274).

In casting his focus exclusively on the crossing of the line of the law, rather than on the nature of the act and its context, Locke commits a fallacy of composition, by which he establishes the equivalence of all offences—stealing a coat or murdering one's brother. The consequences he draws are 'strange' indeed (*TT*, II.chap.2[13]275). 'This makes it' for Locke (*TT*, II.chap.3[18]279–80) 'Lawful for a Man to *kill a Thief*, who has not in the least hurt him, nor declared any design upon his Life, any farther than by the use of Force, so to get [. . .] what he pleases from him.' Locke (*TT*, II.chap.3[18]280) explains that, say, if the thief has held me up at knifepoint to steal my purse, 'I have no reason to suppose that he, *who would take away my Liberty*, would not when he had me in his Power, take away everything else', including my life.

A decisive effect of Locke's fallacy of composition is that it transforms an act, crossing the line of the law, into a type, the criminal. Rendering all offences equivalent shifts the focus from the nature of the transgression and the social context in which it was committed, which I will consider in the following section, to the qualities required to commit it. These boil down to one: unreason. The source of the justification for the resort to violence upon the criminal body has switched from the act to the essence contained in this body. As if forgetting his own critique of scholastic substantialist thought, Locke retrieves for his political project the old (innate) idea of reason as the human essence. Conversely, distilling the essence of criminality to unreason enables him to draw the line delineating a rights-bearing humanity right through the species itself. The criminal is on the side of the non-human, alongside the animal, Locke's other natural being with neither reason nor rights (see Wadiwell 2014). In renouncing their reason, the offender, for Locke (*TT*, IIchap.2[10]273), 'becomes degenerate, and declares himself [. . .] to be a noxious Creature' rather than a human being. They are no different to the lion or the tiger, and like them, they may be rightfully destroyed. Locke's degenerates thus perform crucial boundary-drawing functions. With one hand, he extends political membership potentially to humankind at large, the species endowed with natural rights and a reason to be shaped by discipline. With the other, by way of this very reason, he pulls up the drawbridge around his community of reasonable consenters and excludes specific categories of humans from political membership. Locke's essentialising moves are simultaneously universalising and dehumanizing, in the age when the criminal body was being offered up by the state to science, as I will show in chapter 7.

To Punish the Poor: Locke's 'Begging Drones'

This conjunction of irrationality and punished bodies features in another place in Locke's political writings, his "Essay on the Poor Law" (1697), a piece of legislation Locke drafted in 1697 in his capacity as chief director of the Council of Trade and Plantations, which was enacted in several towns around England (notably Bristol). This work contains Locke's second excluded: the poor. The 'disorder' Locke (PL[10]190 and PL 183) set out to address with this law was their 'multiplying'. Locke's law reinstated Elizabethan poor laws, which obligated parishes to tackle the rise of poverty caused by the profound transformations in the traditional modes of life in the wake of the emergence of capitalism. Locke (PL, [10]184 and PL190) prescribed a strict regimen of stringent physical labour and corporeal punishment for the children of 'these begging drones' with which 'the streets everywhere swarm', 'to the shame of Christianity'. From the ripe age of three onwards the children of the poor were to be put to work 'to the advantage of this kingdom', spinning and knitting for the English wool industry, the vanguard of capitalism (PL, [12]192).[33] Six days a week they were to be kept in these 'working schools', to which poor adults could also be sent 'to take away their pretence of want of work' (PL, [12]192 and [17]193). In addition, if a poor 'boy or girl, under 14 years of age, be found begging', they are to be 'soundly whipped' and punished with more physical labour (PL, [8]187). Locke had none of the qualms with these children that he had regarding the effects of corporeal punishment upon the gentry's offspring; his law explicitly aimed to shape them into productive and docile bodies, not well-rounded, disciplined individuals.[34] The only non-corporeal measure Locke recommends for this group of children was to keep them in the working schools on Sundays as well so that they may be brought to church, 'to some sense of religion' and out of their 'idle and loose ways of breeding up', since they 'are as utter strangers to religion and morality as they are to industry' (PL, [11]192). This estrangement from morality was also an estrangement from natural law and reason. The Calvinist conscience looms large. Poverty was not merely an economic condition, for Locke. It moulded characters, and crafted irrational types. From the age of fourteen onwards, Locke's law continued, the children came under the punishing regime the law also develops for the adult poor, which included a system of passes to control and restrict the movements of this category of population; a penalty of 'loss of ears', directly lifted out of the Elizabethan poor laws, for the first attempt at forging this pass; and the provision of free labour for the royal navy (*PL*, [8]187, [5]186, and [40]198). The ability to move about unimpeded was not for these 'idle vagabonds' (*PL*, [8]187).

The cause of this 'increase of idleness, poverty and villainy', for this trade commissioner who owned shares in the slave trade (see chapter 6), could not be the explosion of trade, nor the expansion of the market and its increasing encroachment upon traditional modes of living (Locke, *PL*, [10]190). Nor indeed capitalism, though in fairness the term for the profound transformation of the modes of production and of social relations that was under way had not yet been coined. It could be 'nothing else but the relaxation of discipline and the corruption of manners' (Locke, *PL*, 184). Vice was the companion of idleness, for this physician; it was to be treated like a disease that risked spreading moral decay (and unproductivity) through the social fabric. While his poor law rings with all the shrillness of the Puritanism of his time and milieu, Locke was fairly typical in his attitude towards poverty, though he was also in a position to do something about it. He helped wage what Michael Perelman (2000, 16) has termed the 'war on sloth' that was especially ferocious in capitalism's birthplace, England. Locke paved the way for the (not-so) laissez-faire theories that, while advocating hands off the markets, also recommended heavily hands-on measures that stripped people of their traditional means of support (see Perelman 2000). In capitalism's initial phase of 'primitive accumulation' a whole range of habitual behaviours were progressively criminalised (Marx 1992). People who engaged in practices they and their forebears had always engaged in were turned into criminals by the law itself. Hence capitalism was made possible by a violent dis-habituation that was orchestrated by the law. This process is entirely overlooked by our theorist of habituation, who treats the criminal, not as produced by the law, but as a natural type who roams his state of nature, alongside lions and tigers.

Criminalising Custom: The Shifting Boundaries of the Law in Locke's Time

The context in which Locke wrote was one where the boundaries between legal and illegal behaviours were in considerable flux as a result of the fundamental reorganisation of the traditional life-worlds required by the advent of capitalism. The late seventeenth and early eighteenth centuries saw the law harden significantly, such that some historians have characterised the Restoration (from 1688), to which Locke owed his own policy-making powers, as a 'thanatocracy' for its lavish resort to the death penalty (Linebaugh 1991, 50).[35] The 'Black Acts' of 1723 created at least fifty new offences punishable by death (Thompson 1990). This unfixing of the law, which would progressively establish a whole range of

customs and habits beyond the bounds of legality, was triggered by the privatisation of the Commons, which was well under way at the time of Locke's writing.
The 'Commons' was the collective mode of social, cultural, and legal organisation that characterised the Middle Ages, founded in the 'common-field system'
and centred, in England, around the manor and its vil (Firsk 1964).[36] Joan
Firsk (1964) has described the medieval mode of production and living in the
following terms:

> People all depended on common resources for their fuel, for bedding and
> fodder for their stock, and by pooling so many of the necessities of livelihood
> they were disciplined from early youth to submit to the rules and custom of the
> community. (Firsk 1967, 255)

The enclosure movement began as a series of individual initiatives to close
off land previously held and cultivated in common, that were increasingly
institutionalised as Parliaments around the country became involved. Four thousand Enclosure Acts were passed in England's Parliaments between 1760 and
1844 (Seebohm 1883), with the first one in 1710 (Thompson 1991). As a result the
age-old modes of doing were progressively overturned, such that the fodder and
peat gathered on the fallow strips running along the communal fields; the wood
collected in the surrounding forests; the birds and hares that were hunted on those
lands; the crab apples and cobnuts plucked off the hedgerows; the tansy, bramble,
and other wild herbs used for cooking—in short, a broad range resources upon
which people depended to feed and heat themselves became increasingly unavailable to them in the many customary ways they had been for centuries. Instead
these vital resources would need to be bought. Large numbers of land-labourers
with little but their labour to sell were forced onto the market and into the towns
Locke found teeming with 'begging drones'. Nor was this compulsory participa-
tion in the new ways of producing and living enthusiastically embraced, as many
historians have underlined (Marx 1992; Thompson 1990; 1991; Linebaugh 1991;
Perelman 2000; Dardot and Laval 2014; Neocleous 2014). A Lockean consent was
not forthcoming in a large section of the population.

With the Enclosure Acts the law was mobilised to redraw the country's life and
landscape. Moreover, when age-old customs and habits were not eroded sufficiently hastily, laws were passed that actively stripped people of their means of
subsistence and hurried them along down these changes. Hunting, for example,
was criminalised by the 1671 Game Laws (Perelman 2000; Thompson 1990).
Lastly, the law was used to bend any outstanding resistance. This was era of
Marx's (1992) 'bloody legislation', inaugurated by the Elizabethan poor laws that
Locke sought to revitalise. The transformations that ushered in capitalism were
thus simultaneously driven by the mode of production itself and by the work
wrought by the law to outlaw prior customs and habits. Capitalism's unrivalled

chronicler, Marx, painted the following picture of what emerged at the outset of this process:

> The advance of capitalist production develops a working class which, by educa-
> tion, tradition and habit, looks upon the requirements of that mode of produc-
> tion as self-evident natural laws. (Marx 1992, 898)

The self-evident 'natural' laws of the feudal system were forcefully rewritten into new, and somehow just as 'natural', laws; and those who could or would not comply fell into the category of criminals, by Locke's logic, since they placed themselves at war with the rest of humankind presumed to be enthusiastically embracing these new laws (and the profits they helped generate). Tracing corporeal punishment through Locke's political writings has thus led us to this blind spot in his thought. Locke made it his philosophical purpose to debunk the noxious habituation that lead to misunderstanding the nature of the mind, but he could not see another kind of violent re-habituation that was unfolding before his eyes. Or rather, he actively abetted it.

To summarise, Locke grounds his state in consent and in the conscience. Consent requires reason. Yet not all are able or willing to exercise it to the degree required to access their political freedom, which is guaranteed by a natural freedom all humans have. The problem, then, is that the limiting conditions he introduces, via the faculty of reason, thwarts the equality that founding modern political rights in universal natural rights appeared to promise. Consent works largely to conceal the boundary-drawing work by which he designs his state, that focussing on his disciplined and punished bodies reveals. Within lies an inner circle or club of rational and male express consenters. Beyond this 'gated community', as Koshcka Duff (2017) has called it, lies a zone of half-membership populated by reasonable-but-not-quite-rational, tacit consenters: foreigners, children, and indeed women. Without, the disposable bodies of the criminal and the poor roam threateningly.

*

This chapter has traced the place of liberty in Hobbes's and Locke's ordering projects under the lens of the body. Hobbes corporealised liberty in order to externalise it. The body served to dislodge liberty from a strife-fuelling conscience. Locke, instead, re-internalised liberty, by retrieving the conscience and establishing it as the cornerstone to his government by consent. Hobbes externalised liberty via the body, whereas Locke re-internalised it by broadening his focus to encompass the mind; and in the process, he invented nothing short of 'consciousness'. He bequeathed to modern psychology an embodied notion that transcended the ancient dualism of mind and body. This legacy explains how deeply Locke is engrained in the intellectual foundations of our world. We are all, I suggest, conscripts, not just of 'liberalism' at large, as Duncan Bell (2014) once put it, but more specifically of Lockean thought, and in ways that I continue to explore in the following chapter. Or, to put the point in another way, the individualist psychology underwriting modernity is deeply Lockean (see also Taylor 1989). Locke was the first early modern political theorist of an interiority and the inventor of discipline as an instrument of statecraft. By charting the evolution of 'the conscience' in early seventeenth-century thought, I showed how the theological concept previously carried many of the cognitive functions Locke pinned onto 'consciousness' instead. Only Locke never quite shook off the religious conscience from his newly minted concept. Indeed he never intended to; though he was never explicit about its origins. The modern individual, then, as the figure endowed with consciousness and with a conscience, was born with Locke. Between them Hobbes and Locke bring to light the founding dialectic of political modernity, which is a double movement of hiding and revealing. The first, Hobbesian, movement of hiding begat reason of state, and a political subject free within and subjected to the law without. It yielded the original topography of statehood as the differentiation of the public and the private. Transparency is the hallmark of the second, Lockean, movement of revealing. It indexes another kind of political rationality altogether, that lies in the foundations, not of the state, but of modern democracy. Secrecy and transparency remain the two poles structuring political life in the contemporary state system.

Through the remainder of the chapter I parsed a crucial antagonism at the heart of Locke's writings. Per his embodied, conscious and conscientious epistemic subject, Locke, in his philosophy, superseded the mind-body dualism that the old scholastic faculty of reason remained inexorably mired in. Yet for his political project, he retrieved natural reason intact in order to navigate a new and distinctly modern tension, between establishing humanity at large as the subject of rights on the one hand, and, on the other, the collectivised power required to realise those rights, the state. Locke's political thought reveals the constitutive exclusions underwriting the making of the category of 'the human' as the figure of rights at the dawn of modernity and as one of its cornerstones. 'The human' (or 'man') was not new; the category (and its gendered biases) is as old as Western philosophy. Subjective rights were new, as I will further show in the following chapter. They emerged from the singular conjoining of 'human' and 'rights'. Locke's political thought lays bare the universality-minus-one logic by which they were joined. It shows how human rights require as their condition of thinkability the prior delineation of a nonhuman 'outside', a place where to eject the inhuman (Walker 1993). It is figured in Locke's project by the criminal. Locke drew his lines of inclusion and exclusion by wielding reason as a natural capacity that everyone potentially has but that requires being trained to qualify for political subjecthood, hence to bear rights. This entails that it can be lost, along with one's rights, by crossing the line of the law and into this outside of unreason/inhumanity. Locke conceived political subjecthood in terms of a dynamic capacity for rational and responsible behaviour, of a qualification that requires training. By the same token, he made losing it a matter of individual responsibility. He psychologized political subjecthood. He turned it into a *subjectivity*. Locke's government by consent requires a closed, classed, gendered and, I will show in the following chapter, raced members' club.

PART III
PROPERTY

6

Privatising Property

> Words, English words, are full of echoes, of memories, of
> associations—naturally. They have been out and about, on people's
> lips, in their houses, in the streets, in the fields, for so many centuries.
> —Virginia Woolf, 'Craftsmanship', in *Death of the Moth and*
> *Other Essays*

When we talk of 'property' today we tend to assume an individual private property, so entrenched is the link between 'property' and 'the individual'. Collective
ownership is instead relegated to other, 'non-Western', more or less exotic, more
or less disappearing cultures. In this chapter I will show that the automaticity
of this link owes to the role of the body in the construction of private property
as the 'natural' or default form of property, and how it was actively used to displace the existent form of property in the West *as well*, which was communal
(see Coleman 1988; Comninel 2000; Pierson 2013; Dardot and Laval 2014).[1]
Medieval proprietors in the eyes of the law were largely collective bodies. They
were the Church, the commons, the corporations or towns I considered in
chapter 4. Seventeenth-century Europe saw a profound transformation in the
very meaning of 'property', to the extent that private property was already the
form the eighteenth-century English lawyer William Blackstone (1848, 100) had
in mind for his 'third absolute right, inherent in every Englishman', to which,
after security and liberty, I now turn in this book's final part. The intellectual
terrain for this revolution was early modern theories of natural rights, which
are in focus in this chapter. It was supported by a broader revolution in the very
meanings of 'justice' and 'law', that begat the defining concept of political modernity, individual rights. This conceptual revolution, in turn, is what enabled the
take-off and diffusion of capitalism as a distinct mode of production and of social
organisation (see Meiksin Wood 2012; Comninel 2000).

In this chapter, I follow a little-noticed strand in the well-known story of the
birth of capitalism to reveal how the human body in general, and the white body
in particular, were key to orchestrating the inversion in property relations that
yielded the modern subject of rights. This figure standing at the heart of political modernity was once termed 'the possessive individual' by C. B. MacPherson
(1962), in order to draw out its importance in constituting private property. This

Birth of the State. Charlotte Epstein, Oxford University Press (2021). © Oxford University Press.
DOI: 10.1093/oso/9780190917623.001.0001

constitutivity is also at the heart of my analysis; only I dwell with the 'the subject' rather than 'the individual', in order to maintain this rights relation and therefore the state in the frame, and to underscore their mutual dependence.[2] Nevertheless, regardless of how we name it, this figure is crucial to accounting for how private property became the primary organising paradigm of our world, to the extent that it is almost impossible to think, let alone act, beyond it. Etched deep into the subject of rights is the founding mechanism by which private property was successfully and durably legitimised. This was a labour theory of value, according to which a natural resource acquires value through the work by which it is transformed. This is what warrants, the theory continues, pulling it out of the pool of resources collectively owned, the commons, and depriving others from it. Here I take the familiar labour theory of value one level down, to the body at its heart. I start, not from labour as an abstract notion, nor from the produced goods that are often said to 'embody' it (Dooley 2005, 2), but from the toiling body itself; from the site where these abstractions were first produced and that remains the theory's referent and ultimate guarantor. Moreover, I parse the making, not of the commodity, but of the right to private property.

John Locke (*TT*, II.chap.5[27]288) understood the initial transformation of the natural resource as a thoroughly corporeal process, of its 'mixing' with the labourer; of their 'joining', 'annexing' even. Tracking the role of the body in the original crafting of private property reveals two crucial, contradictory conceits upon which the natural right to it was originally founded, and that have helped lock it in place. First, the body was key to casting the original act by which a resource is appropriated exclusively as 'natural', as a biological necessity. I will take for myself whatever I require to stay alive. Second, however, upon closer examination, not all labouring bodies qualified for ownership of their own labour, even if they were also striving to stay alive. Being able to claim its fruits required having a certain kind of body or skin colour. The body was mobilised as a naturalising device in the making of private property in two opposite directions. On the one hand, grounding the natural right to property in the body established a solid incontestable-because-natural basis for a universal right to private property. Everybody has a body and is therefore a potential rights bearer. Yet the body also set the outer limit of the scheme of exclusive appropriation powering capitalism. If the body is the anchor for the mechanism by which transforming a resource yields its exclusive ownership, because it is what we 'innately' own— who could contest that?—, then not owning one's body also delineates another kind of 'natural' limit, beyond which this exclusive ownership ceases, namely, in a 'natural' slavery. The argument is tautological, but that is precisely its point, or indeed its modus operandi. In the age of colonisation, whose take-off coincided with capitalism's, the only thing that could render the enslavement of the colonized 'natural' was their non-alikeness with the colonizer. Their bodies

furnished, along with the labour, the wellspring of this legitimising difference: non-whiteness. This wellspring is my focus in this chapter. My argument,
to be clear, is not simply that capitalism was cannibalistic; that its rise is littered
with many a chewed-out human and non-human body, although this is also true,
if well known. It concerns specifically the original privatisation of property, the
historical moment where property relations were turned upside down to enable
capitalism's and colonisation's take-off. The argument, then, is that, in this factory of private property that I pry open in this chapter, the body was carefully
drawn upon to erase the crafting of slavery—the fact that it was crafted. In this
factory, then, the body afforded the great naturaliser both at once of private property as the absolute right of the modern subject, and of slavery. They were the
two sides of one historical process.

This chapter unfolds in five parts. I begin by charting the emergence of the
modern language of 'rights' against, first, the broader transformation of a legal
framework that was once anchored in nature at large as the locus of justice, to
one that attached instead to a new concept of subjecthood. This took place,
second, at the juncture of two hitherto discrete lexical and legal spheres, that of
'laws' and 'justice' on the one hand, and 'property' on the other. I draw out how
the human body was key to stitching them together, via a concept that, I show,
has received far less attention in the natural rights scholarship than warrants the
role it played in its development, the *suum*. This is a natural sphere of 'one's own'
defined by reference to the body. It was the key with which the old notion of
'self-preservation' was narrowed down to the human body only in early modern
natural rights theory, and non-human bodies were written out of the sphere of
justice altogether.

Early modern natural rights theories of property, from Grotius to Locke via
Pufendorf, are in focus in the second and third parts, where I parse an original tension lying at their core. These theorists turned to a natural given, the
body, in order to legitimise the original act of privatization. At the same time,
this 'givenness' did not so readily sit with their voluntarism. For they all also
emphasised, by way of the contract, the need to establish the subject's wilful engagement as the proper founding stone of modern political construction. The
human body, I argue, provided the means to navigate this tension. I chart how
Grotius, Hobbes, Pufendorf and Locke, respectively, positioned themselves
in relation to the question of whether private property was natural or socially
constructed. Locke's labour theory of value, to which I turn in the third part,
decisively and durably resolved this tension, by rooting it in the labouring body.

I then turn to another key strength of Locke's labour theory of value in the
fourth part. Locke put forward the most effective and enduring legitimation of
capitalism, because of the ways in which, first, he conceived labour as an intentional agency rooted in the body. Second, he looped the original act of taking

back to the subject. He cast the exclusive appropriation in terms of the making, not just of (the right kind of) property, but properly *of the self*. This circularity turned on the distinction he drew between 'human' (or rather, 'man') and 'person', which is the concept he decisively coined for legal and psychological modernity. I show how the body triangulates the process by which, for Locke, a natural being becomes a 'self' endowed with consciousness, and therefore with political rights. In this way the possessing and self-possessing modern subject of rights was crafted.

In the chapter's fifth part, I consider the labouring bodies in Locke's political treatises that index the constitutive outside to his project of political ordering, the horse and the slave. They serve to reveal how the nexus of 'personhood' and 'property' that he lay down as the foundation for the state functions as an exclusionary mechanism and as a boundary-drawing tool. The work that slavery achieves for Locke's political project is the focus of his final part. I show that, far from being secondary or a blind spot of his political thought (but not for his purse), slavery was central to the making of the Lockean natural right to property. Locke, I contend, articulated the original, enduring conjunction of 'property' and 'whiteness' at the heart of capitalism (Harris 1993; see also Stoler 1995).

1. From Medieval Natural Law to Modern Natural Rights

Theories of natural right afforded seventeenth-century thinkers and political actors a powerful resource against the recourse to tradition and to customary law in an era of accelerating changes. It provided an alternative source of law to 'the ancient constitution' that could also claim the test of time: its constitution was written in nature itself (Pocock 1987; see also Schmidgen 2002). Because the body of early modern thought that has come to be known as 'natural rights theory' owes its force as an instrument of change to its lineage with a form of medieval law known as 'natural law', which I introduce in the following section, the natural rights scholarship has tended to emphasise the continuity between medieval natural *law* and modern natural *rights*, largely echoing natural rights theory's own legitimation strategy (see notably Strauss 1965; Tuck 1979; Tully 1980; Buckle 1993; and Finnis 2011). Yet these forms of law hold thoroughly different conceptions of property, reason, and even justice itself. Instead, in this chapter I emphasise the discontinuities between these two laws that claimed nature as their foundation in charting the passage from one to the other.[3] One of the changes underfoot in the seventeenth century was the transformation in the relations of production that enabled the rise of capitalism, which we began to see in the previous chapter. Natural rights theory supplied the theoretical score that accompanied the battle to privatise the commons, in England and beyond,

I will show in this chapter. It did so by setting out to answer the following question: under what circumstances can the act of depriving others from a collective resource by appropriating it for oneself, or evitalize it, be considered rightful? In line with their times, natural theorists, from Grotius to Locke, all start from an assumption of communal property— from an earth originally 'given to Mankind in common', in Locke 's(*TT*, II.chap.5[25]286) words. My contention is that this body of thought decisively inverted the default mode of property relations, from communal and collective, to individual and private. I will show that natural rights theory comprised coextensively the site of the legitimation of private property, and where human beings were established as the exclusive bearer of rights, and that these were the two sides of the making of the modern subject of rights.

Imitating Nature's Ordered Matrix: Medieval Natural Law

Medieval natural law was a legal-cum-theological framework that blended together Greek philosophy, Roman law, and Christian monotheism. Its twin pillars were nature and reason; only the latter was an instrument of authority, not of its critique. Thomas Aquinas (1225–75) was a major figure in its development, Thomist law being, as Michel Villey (1975, 168, my translation) put it, 'the product of reason seeking the just in nature'. God, the fount of creation and of all mastery (*dominus*), was also the source of all property (*dominium*). The gift was this framework's main paradigm. It expressed the relation between the creator and the created and humankind's ontological dependence on God. It accounted for both the origins of property and for the work of reason, granted to humans alone for the purposes of deciphering nature's laws. In a context where political ordering meant aligning human or positive laws onto natural laws, private property was only one of reason's many means for doing so. It was not, as it would become for Locke, the source and end of political order and the wellspring of liberty. When Aquinas (*Summa Theologia*, 2a 2ae 66.2 *responsio* a1) broaches the topic of individual ownership, he considers it as a derivative, a useful 'addition' devised 'by human reason' (ibid.) to avert the 'quarrel and laziness' that common ownership may sometimes breed. Natural law's default mode of property relations was communal, whereas private property was the product of positive law and of human ingenuity. I am not suggesting that people in the Middle Ages happily shared all their possessions with one another and that theft was left unpunished. Natural law had a mechanism for accounting for how communal property had been divided up, and theft was punished accordingly.[4] This mechanism was supplied by the definition of justice encapsulated in the opening line of the *Institutes of Justinian*, the sixth-century manual of Roman law that Aquinas helped evitalize, 'to attribute to each their due' (*suum cuique tribuere*).[5]

Only in property's evolution from communal to private, this formula was progressively untethered from its broader structures of being and meaning and attached instead, I will show, to the human body.

Medieval nature was a hierarchical matrix in which human nature was embedded through and through, both because humans were woven out of the same fibre as other beings, but also because of the human privilege of being able to apprehend its laws. Here is how Aquinas rendered the human embeddedness in the hierarchy of being:

> The order of the precepts of the natural law corresponds to the order of our natural inclinations. For there is in man *[sic]* a natural and initial inclination to good, *which he has in common with all substances*; in so far as every substance seeks its own preservation according to its own nature. Corresponding to this inclination, the natural law contains all that makes for the preservation of human life, and all that is opposed to its dissolution. Secondly, there is to be found in man a further inclination to certain more specific ends, according to the nature *which man shares with other animals*. [. . .] Thirdly, there is a certain inclination to good, corresponding to his rational nature: and this inclination is *proper to man alone*. (*Summa Theologia*, 1.2. Qu.94, Art.2, concl., p.123, emphasis mine)

Nature's laws are reflected in the laws of our natures and incline us towards three kinds of 'goods', which correspond to three levels of a human's being. The first holds the laws of self-preservation not yet collapsed onto a human 'self'. It is the essential part of ourselves that we share with all other living beings, including with the lion or tiger that Locke (*TT*, II.chap.2[11]274), with the criminal, would readily see 'destroyed' (see chapter 5). For Aquinas, they too would qualify as having 'selves' to preserve, but also for the 'more specific ends' that 'man shares with other animals' on the second level and that are bound up with having an affective life, like the anger triggered by the sense that one is attacked. Reason indexes the third level 'proper to man alone'. While it establishes the human species at the helm of the hierarchy of beings, it does not single it out as the exclusive and exclusionary subject of rights.

In fact, the subjective language of 'rights' did not exist in medieval law. The term was *jus* (*jura* in the plural) and it meant a law or what is just.[6] Justice (*justicia*), derived from *jus*, was the broader natural-cum-social order constituted by these laws. In the classical formula, 'to attribute to each their due' (*suum cuique tribuere*), this 'due' (*suum*) is what the law aimed to render, insofar as it defined what was fair for 'each'. Only it was not limited to humans; it applied to animals and even to inanimates (see Brett 1997). The narrowing of the recipient of justice to the human species, together with the shift in the sense of *suum* from 'one's due' to 'one's own', was what natural rights theory would wreak, crafting the modern subject of rights in the process. The interpretation of the Roman formula constituted the key site where 'law' became 'rights'. Up until the Middle Ages, 'one's due' indexed a place within a just order in which humans and other beings partook on all levels of their being. Like liberty (see chapter 4), justice was topological. It was the apportionment of a certain amount of just-ness or fairness. '[T]he aright' is the term with which John Finnis (2011, 205) captured this right-ness tied to a place rather than to a person. Annabel Brett (1997, 3) explains the medieval understanding of 'rights' as 'the just portion that is due between persons, rather than something belonging to the person herself'. Medieval natural law, then, was relational and impersonal. The figure that would trigger the dual process of its absolutisation and of its subjectivisation, the individual, was yet to be crafted.

Embodying the Modern Subject of Rights: The *Suum*

Individual rights were born of a revolution in the very meaning of *jura*, which shifted from rights that were 'objective', lodged in the natural-cum-social order, to 'subjective', anchored in the subject instead (Villey 1975; see also Douzinas 2000). This inversion in the point of view from which justice was done is what ushered in legal and political modernity. The writings of the Spanish Jesuit Francisco Suarez (1548–1617) and the Dutch lawyer Hugo Grotius are traditionally considered the 'watershed' (Finnis 2011; see also Villey 1975; Tuck 1979; Tully 1980; Haakonssen 1985; Brett 1997; Tierney 1997). Suarez and Grotius orchestrated two fundamental shifts. First, they injected an agentic dimension into the law (*jus*). Its 'true, strict and proper meaning' wrote Suarez in 1610, is 'a kind of moral power (*facultas*) which every man has, either over his own property or with respect to that which is due to him' (quoted in Finnis 2011, 206). Under Suarez's pen rights, *jus* became 'something someone has' in a moral sense (Finnis 2011, 207). The right-bearer's place began to shift from the passive recipient of a 'due' to the owner of an active faculty or even, by Locke's (*TT*, II.132) time, a 'power'. Contemporaneously, Grotius opened his magnum opus *De Jure Pace et Bellis* (1625) by first nodding to the Aquinian sense of *jus* as 'that which is Just' (Grotius, I,1,iii), only to add that 'there is another signification of the word Right [. . .] which relates to the Person', which is 'its proper or strict' meaning (Grotius, I.1,iii and I,1,iv). This right is 'a moral quality of the person enabling (*competens*) him to have, or to do, something justly' (ibid.). The notion of right had thus shifted from the object of justice to its subject as 'the beneficiary of the just relationship', and its ability to act. From there, rights then extended outwards to the 'beneficiary's doings and havings' (Finnis 2011, 207). Suarez and Grotius thus inaugurated the active rights that would bring the individual into focus as the political actor and the subject of rights.

The second shift, attributed mostly to Grotius and to Pufendorf in his wake, turned on reworking, by way of the body, the *suum* of the Roman formula, *suum cuique tribuere*.[7] It would trigger the transformation, which Locke would complete by the century's dusk, from the human species being one amongst many passive recipients of a just 'due' into becoming the active and exclusive appropriators of their rightful 'own'. The *suum*, in Hobbes's (*L*.chap.24[5]160) words, is the third person of the possessive '*mine*, and *thine* and *his*; that [. . .] [constitutes] *propriety*'. Only for Hobbes, the *suum* and the body are held separate. Property, communal and private, is unnatural. It is a product of the contract that enacted the break from nature required to constitute the state (see chapter 3). 'The introduction of *propriety*' is 'the act only of the sovereign', not of the individual (Hobbes, *L*., chap.24[5]160).[8] It follows from, rather than founds, the state. After invoking the Roman formula Hobbes adds:

> And this they well knew of old, who called that *nomos* (that is to say, *distribution*) which we call law, and defined justice by *distributing* to every man *his own*. (Hobbes, *L*., chap.24[5]160)

For Hobbes, then, the socially constructed realm of property and the natural realm of the body remained distinct. Moreover, although he was not explicit on this point, his strong law of self-preservation (robust enough to found a right to resist the sovereign, see chapter 2) entailed that that which is consumed to satisfy bodily needs effectively eluded the institution of property. Moreover, private property ('absolute propriety in [one's] goods') is a potential 'cause of dissolution of the Commonwealth' (*L*., chap.29[10]213). Hobbes, then, holds separate the sphere of justice and the *suum* on the one hand, and the body on the other. Hobbes, the theorist of the body, did not corporealise the *suum*.

Embody the *suum* is what Grotius achieved. He did this, not by redefining it, in the way that he did so decisively with *jus*. Neither Grotius nor, uncharacteristically, Pufendorf after him, defined the *suum* (see Olivecrona 2010; Mautner 2010; Mancilla 2015). Instead they simply catalogue its contents. The list is more or less exhaustive; the moral items it includes differ from one author to the other, but it always starts from the body. In Grotius:

> A Man's life is his own (*suum*) by Nature (not indeed to destroy it, but to preserve it) and so his Body, his Limbs, his Reputation, his Honour and his Actions. (Grotius, *De Jure Belli ac Pacis*, I.17.2.1)

Likewise, Pufendorf's (1934, III.1[1].314) list of 'things which nature herself has immediately granted us' includes 'our life, our body, our limbs, our virtue, our reputation, our liberty'. Under this author's pen the *suum* comes to delineate an immediate and natural sphere of one's own. It sets up an 'invisible fence' that marks is it off 'against others' (Olivecrona 1974b, 212). It owes its naturalness, I suggest, to the unnoticed human body at its core.[9]

This under-determined yet corporeal *suum* would come to play a central role in natural rights theories of property. First, it provided the benchmark for a form of property that was exclusive and private (*proprium* or *proprietas*). 'The essential characteristic of private property', writes Grotius, 'is the fact that it belongs to a given individual in such a way as to be incapable of belonging to another individual' (cited in Buckle 1993, 13). Grotius's decisive move was not to ground ownership in use. Use rights were widespread in medieval law and they often afforded the basis for property titles.[10] It was to tie the claim to the fact of using the thing *up*, and here the body was key. It afforded the measure for those things that cannot be shared with another because they are 'converted into its very substance':

> There are some things which are consumed by use, either in the sense that they are converted into the very substance of the user and therefore admit of no further use, or else in the sense that they are rendered less fit for additional service by the fact that they have once been made to serve. Accordingly, it very soon became apparent, in regard to articles of the first class (for example, food and drink), that a certain form of private ownership was inseparable from use. For the essential characteristic of private property is the fact that it belongs to a given individual in such a way as to be incapable of belonging to another individual. (Grotius, cited in Buckle 1993, 13)

This *suum* founds a natural right to use those items necessary for self-preservation. This use right, rearticulated by reference to a body that uses up items such as food and drink, legitimizes, in turn, a right to carve out for oneself a piece of property (*proprium*, *proprietas*) out of what originally belonged to all (*communio*). The notion of a natural consumption supplied by the body enabled him to rework the old communal use-right into an individual and exclusive right to private property. The importance of this consumptive model has borne out Grotius's defence of the freedom of navigation (*Mare Liberum*, 1609), one of the founding doctrines of international law. Grotius rested his case on the notion that the sea could not be occupied or claimed by any one state, because water could not be used up. By way of the body Grotius decisively inverted communal ownership from a belonging to all, into belonging to no one, and therefore open to all for navigation.

Second, the function of the *suum* was generalised, because it supplied, with the body, a simple gauge for defining 'a wrong' (*injuria*). The two core prescriptions of natural law, for both Grotius and Pufendorf, were, first, the duty to hold off from that which belongs to another, known as the principle of *alieni abstinentia*, and second to fulfil one's promises. This negative duty to abstain established the notion of a wrong or injury at the centre of the modern edifice of natural rights. It is a 'trespass across the boundary of another' (Olivecrona 2010, 211). In the chapter's third part I will consider how Locke's theory of property transformed this negative duty into a positive right to appropriate, but that is not my purpose just yet. It is to show, first, how modern natural rights theory rests, at its core, upon a mechanism for separating out a self from an other. The *suum* performs these crucial boundary-drawing function.[11] Second, it provides a ready criteria for determining what innately belongs to someone, and thus for clarifying the principle of *alieni abstinentia*. The duty to abstain presupposes that one inherently knows what does and does not belong to another (*alieni*). But how does one actually know where this line runs? Natural law said very little on the matter (see Olivecrona 2010). This left the old command 'lack[ing] in content unless it was determined, by agreement or positive law, what belongs to whom', as Olivecrona (2010, 210) notes. Yet early modern natural rights theorists, in particular Grotius and Locke, were unwilling to pin property only on an initial agreement, for reasons I will explore in the following section. The *suum* supplied them 'a theory of what belongs to the individual, independently of laws or agreements' (Olivecrona 2010, 210). It ensured that the old principle was 'not vacuous in the state of nature' (ibid.).

Narrowing Self-preservation to the Human 'Self' and Moving Property to the Core of Justice: The Embodied *Suum*'s Effects

The *suum* is the untheorised, corporeal core at the heart of natural rights. In the history of their emergence, it underwrote two profound transformations that I consider successively. It altered the notion of self-preservation and it established property at the heart of justice.

Natural right theory's main principle, self-preservation, was lifted out of natural law, with one crucial modification. The reworked *suum* recalibrated it onto the human body and away from all other natural bodies. In Aquinas, we saw, the desire for self-preservation coursed through all of nature—through humans, animals, and things. All beings sought to persevere in their being, to persist in being who (or what) they were, for as long as they were. The drive to thrive was lodged in their very essences. Self-preservation as a desire or momentum pulsing through all of nature was captured in early modernity by Spinoza's *conatus*. Spinoza, however, was an outlier. He was not a philosopher of the subject, nor a theorist of rights. His rights were still objective; nature's rights. Elsewhere, in Descartes's wake, early modern thought had turned to the subject. The *suum* was where this turn was taken in legal theory. The traditional focus on self-preservation was maintained, only redirected onto the subject. The human 'self' became the primary object of the desire for self-preservation by way of this peculiar, under-theorised investment in this embodied notion, the *suum*. Significantly, for Pufendorf, neither animals nor inanimates have a *suum* (see Olivecrona 2010). The distinctly human faculty of reason became the operator of the reduction of the *suum* to humans alone. 'Man is permitted to use creatures which lack the power of reason and to possess them', writes Pufendorf (1934, IV.chap.4[5]538). Or again 'man has by nature a faculty to take for his use all inanimate objects and animals', for Pufendorf (1934, III.chap.5[3]391–92), but the animals and objects do not. In sum, whereas nature at large remained the referent for medieval natural law, for modern natural rights that referent had become, by way of the body, the human self.

The *suum* helped stitch together two hitherto discrete conceptual clusters, that revolved around 'law' (*jus, justitia*, and *lex*) on the one hand, and around 'property' (*dominium, proprietas*) on the other. It helped move property to the heart of justice, to decisive effect for political modernity. In medieval natural law, property relations composed but one area of a legal system made up of multiple subsystems or spaces only loosely connected to one another, and each regulated by its bundle of norms. As Annabel Brett (2011, 79, emphasis in original) explained, it constituted 'neither an individual right nor a commanding law, but an *inter*-subjective rightfulness or lawfulness, or the body of norms that governs a particular domain of such inter-subjectivity'.[12] *Lex* was a specific rule within one such domain, created by an act of legislation or command (see also Mautner 2010). Nor was property an especially important part of medieval law, and it was not, as it would become for natural rights theorists, 'the first and most essential element of justice' (Buckle 1993, 3). Like the Roman law of occupation (*occupatio*), it affords an example of a previously minor part of an older law that the seventeenth century recalibrated for new purposes (see Fitzmaurice 2014). Property enters into Aquinas's considerations only as part of a broader examination of the proper human relation to material things, which must merely support the attainment of felicity through the deployment of reason. Property itself is defined in the chapter on the sinful nature of theft (see *Summa Theologica* in 2a. 2ae.66). Moreover, Roman law had in fact an extensive array of terms denoting many different sorts of property relations (*dominium, dominium directum, dominium utile, proprietas, possessio, proprium, communio, usufructus, jus utendi*). These were ordered in medieval law into a hierarchy of forms of property pegged onto God, who had full *dominium*. At this level, for this suprahuman form of property, mastery and ownership were coextensive. The question of whether it was exclusive or shared was moot, since it was God's, who is one. For Aquinas:

> God has supreme dominium over all things; and, according to His providence, He has ordained certain things for the support of man's body. For this reason,

man has natural dominium over things with regards to the power to make use
of them (Aquinas, *Summa Theologia*, 2a 2ae 66.1)

The mastery and ownership over natural things befalls God alone, whereas the
'natural dominium' humans may claim is merely over their use. Moreover, it
must be tethered to reason, the human faculty to exercise (a lesser form of) control, and geared to a higher good, which for him is also necessarily rational, as we
have seen. Medieval property, then, was 'not an end in itself nor [was] the right to
it unlimited' (Coleman 1988, 624).

Individual private property, capitalist modernity's property, required 'something that was *not dominium*' to emerge, as Richard Tuck noted (1979, 18). It was
supplied, I suggest, by the new investment in the *suum*. *Dominium*, as the conjunction of mastery and ownership, did carry over into early modern thought,
notably in the defence of the sovereign's absolute right to rule, Locke's target in
the *Two Treatises*. The property that his adversary Robert Filmer set out to legitimise by recoursing to it was absolute and exclusive. For Filmer the sovereign,
as Adam's direct descendent, was created in God's image, and his rule over his
subjects therefore mirrored God's absolute command. 'At the creation one man
alone was made', wrote Filmer (1949, 204), 'to whom the dominion of all things
was given, and from whom all men derive their title'. Filmer's property, however,
was not individual and private. It pertained to the pole of the state rather than
to the subject, and in this, Filmer draws out perhaps more directly then Locke
the original conjunction of property and statehood. The property at the heart
of capitalism was natural rights theory's distinctive innovation. Locke perfected
it in contending with Filmer, but Grotius had prepared for it by unmooring the
suum from its roots in medieval law and from the sense of 'a due' as a place in the
natural order.

Grotius attached the *suum* to the individual by infusing it with the agentic
sense of rights as faculty or power that we saw earlier.[13] After defining 'rights'
as 'faculties', Grotius (*De jure belli ac pacis* I.1.4.,25) introduces another distinction, between 'perfect' and 'imperfect rights'. The former are proper 'faculties'
(*facultas*), whereas the latter constitute only 'aptitudes' (*potentia*). In these the
power that inheres in the faculty is still underdeveloped, a potential. With this
distinction, Grotius drove a decisive wedge into the *suum* that has tended to remain downplayed, even in the scholarship that has emphasised its importance
for natural rights theory (see notably Finnis 2011; Buckle 1993; Tully 1980). For
Grotius 'a perfect right is a "faculty" over one's own, whereas an imperfect right
refers to one's due and, as such, is not a right, but an "aptitude", as James Tully
(1980, 83) explained. Yet contemporary scholars have also tended to minimise
the difference between the two uses of the *suum*, largely as a function of setting out to account for the Grotian distinction from a modern understanding
of 'rights'. My point is that it was crucial to establishing this point of view in the

first place. 'One's own' and 'one's due' are undeniably two grammatical forms of the *suum*. However, in Roman and medieval law, something is one's own because it is one's due, not absolutely. This semantic difference contains in itself the entire conceptual revolution that yielded the modern subject of rights. The *suum* is what one is 'attributed' (*tribuere*) according to one's place in the natural-cum-social order, rendered by the dative *cui*, 'to each'.[14] Yet for Grotius 'one's own' is no longer the outcome of an attributive apportionment. He absolutises the *suum*. As a result of redefining *jus* as 'faculty', the *suum* becomes something one innately has, like reason (that other natural faculty), or indeed like the body. This renaming triggered the progressive erasure of the function of the dative (*cui*), which was to place the legal subject within a just order where its due is determined.[15] It emptied out the *suum* of the broader ontological structures where its attributive functions were performed. It moved the human species to the centre of the legal edifice, transforming them from one among many passive recipients of justice into active rights owners. Enter the modern political subject.

I have traced in this section how human beings became the exclusive bearers of the natural right to private property. Beginning within medieval natural law, I showed how the *suum* of the old Roman law formula justice was untethered from its original structures of being and meaning by being rooted instead in the human body. This decisively reoriented natural laws' principle of self-preservation onto human rather than other beings, and it helped establish property as the core business of justice. The *suum* was the main operator of the differentiation between self and other, both between and within the human species. Between, it established the human species as the law's anchor. Within the bounds of the rights-bearing species thus constituted, it afforded the mechanism of individuation that separated out a possessing and self-preserving 'self' from the 'others' of communal ownership. With the *suum*, Locke inherited from his predecessors a notion that, though underdeveloped, had pegged a natural sphere of exclusive ownership onto the human body. As Roberto Esposito (2008, 65) nicely put it, Locke's theory of property 'unravels as concentric circles whose centre does not contain a political-juridical principle, but a biological reference', the body.[16] I now consider how these circles of appropriation unfolded from the labouring human body.

2. Between Nature and Consent: The Origins of Private Property in Natural Rights Theories

Locke scholars have extensively debated the question of whether he attributed natural or conventional origins to private property. C. B. Macpherson's (1962) classic reading of Locke as a pillar of late modernity's 'possessive individualism', on account of his natural right to private property, was persuasively challenged by James Tully (1980), who showed instead that Locke's property was socially constructed; and Tully's reading, in turn, has been critiqued by Jeremy Waldron (1988, 217), who convincingly restored Locke's place as 'the theorist par excellence of "the natural right to property"'. How can Locke be read as championing both the naturalness and the constructed-ness of private property? This drawn-out debate has shown that his writings yield grist for both mills. It reveals, I suggest, a deeper tension running through natural rights' theories of property at large, between the need to root private property in the contract in order to foreground individual consent on the one hand, and to ground it in nature to secure incontestable foundations on the other. I will show how Locke's theory of appropriation wrought a distinctive and decisive solution to this tension.

Consent is the core concept of natural rights theory, whose authors all grant a central role to the contract.[17] Property is where consent was mobilised especially acutely. This development culminated in Locke, who came to place 'the greatest weight of doctrine' on 'consent' and 'property' (Ryan 1965, 219). Locke established a grand equivalence between property and the essential human attributes of freedom, equality, and his natural executive power (see chapter 5), that operationalises consent as a core principle of political construction. 'It is because they can be symbolised as property, something a man can conceive of as distinguishable from himself though part of himself' that they can 'become the subject of [their] consent', as Peter Laslett (1988, 102) has underlined. I now chart the trajectory of consolidating consent that characterises natural rights theories of property, that culminated in Locke's *Two Treatises*. I show how natural rights theories navigated their contradictory requirements, to hold property as both naturally given, but also deliberately and consensually constructed by humans. Locke's predecessors were intent on demonstrating that property is born of an initial (in Grotius and in Hobbes) agreement or even several (in Pufendorf) agreements. Hobbes stands apart in the trajectory I trace, in that he marks the point where the tension is dissolved, in favour of consent. Hobbes pushed the role of consent the furthest by rooting all property in the contract, as we saw. But Hobbes was also the theorist who was willing to institute a radical rupture with a profoundly transforming nature. He took the greatest measure of the new nature that was being revealed by the scientific revolution (see chapter 3). All other natural rights theorists were intent on upholding a mythical nature as the fount of political construction, and here the body was key.[18]

The Social Construction of Property (I):
Occupation and Grotius's Extensible *Suum*

Grotius's is a developmental story that posits private property as simultaneously originating in nature and consolidated by post hoc agreements.[19] He grounded a private and exclusive property in the *suum*, which delineates the personal sphere around the body that a polity properly 'patterned after nature's plan' aims to protect (Grotius, *De jure praedae commentarius*, quoted in Buckle 1993, 13). 'It is easy to understand', he wrote, that society is designed to protect what belongs to a person 'even if private ownership (as we now call it) had not been introduced; for life, limbs, and liberty would [still] in that case be the possessions belonging to each, and no attack could be made upon these by another without injustice' (*De jure belli ac pacis* 1. 2. i. 5). 'The very source of the institution of private property' is, for Grotius (ibid.) 'an act of physical attachment' by which the individual takes and uses up what he or she requires to survive. Hence it is a natural, embodied act founded in and legitimised by self-preservation. However, crucially, Grotius rendered this pre-legal sphere extensible, potentially considerably so, by applying this natural right of first taking, not just to what individuals need to stay alive, but to everything they laid their hands on to prior to having entered into any agreement. Starting from the appropriating human body, Grotius thus stretched out the requirements of self-preservation to a point where even Pufendorf demurred.

Moreover, the body supplies the key for the initial individuation of a collective right. For Grotius the right to use the earth's resources was granted humankind in common, biblically and historically. To take something out of this communal gift is to make it unavailable to others. That this does not constitute a violation of a God-given communal right can only be warranted by the natural needs of the creature God created. This is why the 'attachment' to a thing must be 'physical'; and how it founds a person's claim to owning it exclusively. Grotius retrieved the Roman law of occupation to name and to generalise this deeply embodied process of attaching:

> The recognition of the existence of private property led to the establishment of a law on the matter, and this law was patterned after nature's plan. For just as the right to use the goods in question was originally acquired through a physical act of attachment, the very source (as we have observed) of the institution of private property, so it was deemed desirable that each individual's private possessions should be acquired, as such, through similar acts of attachment. This is the process known as 'occupation', a particularly appropriate term in connexion with those goods which were formerly at the disposal of the community. (Grotius, *De jure praedae commentarius*, quoted in Buckle 1993, 13)

Grotius posited the starting point for privatisation as a corporeal attachment. Moreover, he recalibrated for the land a law (*occupatio*) previously used primarily for wild beasts, as part of the broader game of claims European powers laid upon the New World (see Fitzmaurice 2014). His occupation is all at once natural, spontaneous, and where agreement enters into the process, since it often rests upon, and thus can be taken to express, tacit agreement:

> [Private property] happened not by a mere act of will, for one could not know what things another wished to have, in order to abstain from them—and besides several might desire the same thing—but rather by a kind of agreement, either expressed, as by a division, or implied, as by occupation. (Grotius, *De jure belli ac pacis*, quoted in Buckle 1993, 2)

Significant also is which part of the body Grotius brought into play to reinvest the Roman law, namely, the hand that can take, instead of the eye that can see. Grotius sided against a principle of discovery based in the simple act of seeing. Arguing in his *Mare Liberum* against the Portuguese claims to the Molluccas, Grotius contended that 'to find is not to see a thing with the eyes but to lay hold of it with the hands' (quoted in Fitzmaurice 2014, 120).

Pufendorf or the Social Construction of Property (II): Labour and Improvement

Although Pufendorf saw himself as refining and clarifying Grotius's views, a significant difference with Grotius takes shape around the *suum* in his *On the Law of Nature and Nations* that would strengthen the role of consent and thus the constructivist strand of the natural rights theory account of the origins of property. Pufendorf maintains Grotius's principle of 'first occupancy', as he termed it, or right first taking. Only he shifts it to the political sphere, and subjects it to the requirements of human agreement. It becomes a political rather than a natural right. For him:

> We cannot apprehend how a bare corporeal Act, such as Seizure is, should be able to prejudice the Right and Power of others, unless their Consent be added to confirm it; that is, unless a Covenant intervene. (Pufendorf 1934, IV.chap.4[5]539)

Taking something out of what belongs to all may be a natural act of self-preservation, but it can only become a moral act, hence generative of rights, through some form of mutual recognition, and thus by agreement. The natural equality of humans depends on it, Pufendorf (1934, IV.chap.4[5]538) underscored. Otherwise, without the need for others to consent to it, first taking is at risk of turning into a 'race to secure property' that well exceeds these natural requirements, and where some are innately swifter than others (1934,

IV.chap.4[5]539). 'In a state where everything is seized upon by the man who can get hold of it, it is staying much too little to wait till precisely the right moment' to limit first taking (IBT>1934, IV.chap.6[4]570</IBT>). It too must be founded in consent. With first taking, Pufendorf also kept Grotius's very physical *suum*, but he separated it out from the sphere of rights proper. For Pufendorf, 'the original notion of *suum* includes no right. It includes a natural faculty or power to take and use things [but] rights proper arise only through agreements between human beings', as Stephen Buckle (1993, 80) put it (see also Olivecrona 1974b; Waldron 1988, 183). Pufendorf's sphere of one's own extends as far as one's actions, but it stops at one's rights. The passage from this natural to a political sphere is properly what the contract institutes; it is necessarily the source of all rights.[20] Though Pufendorf rejects the Hobbesian state of nature in favour of the old belief in humans' innate sociability, he aligns with Hobbes's constructivism. 'It is idle to raise the question as to whether proprietorship in things is due to nature or to institution', Pufendorf (1934, IV.chap.4[1]532) concludes, 'for it is clear that it arises from the imposition of men'. Nonetheless the *suum* remains important, as a kind of pre-given, material substrate supporting political construction, since 'it must be supposed to spread itself thru' all those Institutions by which property rights are secured (Pufendorf 1934, III.chap.1[1]314).

For Pufendorf, unlike for Grotius and subsequently for Locke, property rights establish relations between persons, rather than between persons and things. Private property adds 'no new qualities' to those things that 'came under ownership'. What it introduces is a 'moral quality among men, of which the men [are] the subjects, and things only the terms' that link them together:

> When, indeed, certain things came under ownership, and the rest were still free from ownership, no new qualities should be understood to have been imposed on such things; but rather, upon the beginning of ownership in things, a certain moral quality arose among men, of which the men were the subjects, and the things only the terms [...] so, when ownership had once been established, each man was given the right to dispose of his own property, and among the non-owners there arose the obligation to keep hands off such property. The things themselves, however, obtained therefrom only an extrinsic denomination, inasmuch as they form the object of such a right or obligation. (Pufendorf 1934, I.chap.1.[16]16)

Property is a relation that runs squarely between persons, not between persons and things. This is what Locke would decisively alter by establishing, with the body, 'a primary intimacy between person and thing', as Wolfgang Schmidgen (2002, 54) nicely put it.[21] For Pufendorf instead property does not arise spontaneously out of an embodied interaction between a person and a thing, but instead it needs to be 'established' and mutually agreed to; and this, every time a new property claim is put forward. For the claim introduces a change, not to the thing but to the relation between potential claimants. Once the claim is acceded to, it imposes reciprocal obligations upon the non-owners, 'to keep hands off [the thing]'. The 'right to dispose of [one's] own property' is not natural but rather instituted through mutual consent. Pufendorf underscores more than Hobbes the communal dimensions of consent, which is to effect widespread buy-in. Insofar as Pufendorf's property rights bring into play the broader structure of intersubjective relations, he harks back somewhat to the Middle Ages' objective framework of rights and its relational conception of justice. With one key difference: his rights are resolutely centred upon the human subject, his exclusive claimant to the *suum*, as we have seen. Nevertheless, because it sets people in relation with one another, property affords appropriate foundations for community. Pufendorf's property, then, is constructed. Moreover, he grants a central role to communal, and not just individual, consent, regarding the forms and limits of ownership. Ultimately this bore out less brutal implications for colonisation than Locke's highly individualised consent, as Andrew Fitzmaurice (2014, 112–14) has shown.[22]

Pufendorf takes issue with the physical nature of Grotius's act of attachment. It is wrong to 'believe that a person who is the first to lay hands on a thing by some natural necessity becomes its possessor', since property 'arises from the pact', he writes (Pufendorf 1934, IV.chap.6[7]577). For Pufendorf is interested in the moral bases of property, in appraising how it affords the foundation for community. 'Taking', Pufendorf (1934, IV.chap.6[7]577) insists, 'must not presently be construed as *acquiring*: the former being a bare natural Action, whereas the latter includes a moral effect'. Interestingly, Pufendorf does not move away from the body to explore the moral dimensions of property; to the contrary. To take possession of something, for Pufendorf (1934, IV.chap.6[7]577), 'begins with the joining of Body to Body, immediately or through a proper instrument'. Joining must be either 'with the Hands' in the case of movable goods, or 'with the Feet' in the case of lands, and 'with the intention of cultivating it and of establishing boundaries'. Furthermore, Pufendorf agrees with Grotius and against the right of discovery that 'merely to have seen a thing' is not enough to justify a claim to owning it. Instead, he injects the moral dimension into Grotius's principle of first occupancy by bringing into focus a different kind of body: the labouring, rather than the consuming body. 'Many Things stand in need of human Labour and Culture, either for their Production, or to fit and prepare them for Use', writes Pufendorf (1934, IV.chap.4[6]539–40). If first taking entails that someone has put their labour into, say, tending to colts or calves, then it would be 'very inconvenient' that another, 'who has contributed no labour', 'should have a right to [them] equal [to the person] by whose industry [they were] raised or rendered fit for service' (ibid.). Whereas the ingesting and digesting body had afforded Grotius his model for transforming a right to use into a right to appropriate, for Pufendorf this model was the labouring body. By the same token, by shifting his corporeal referent to the body that gives, rather than the body that takes, Pufendorf moralises the privatisation process that Grotius had paved the way for with his first taking. Depriving others from a communal resource can only be justified by enhancing it, rather than merely using it up. Conversely, 'not to recognise the role of occupancy would be to ignore the [natural] right that use and industry bestow in our relation to things', as Fitzmaurice (2014, 111) put it. Pufendorf's notion of improvement would become central to Locke's theory of appropriation.

In sum, for Pufendorf the right to private property is not natural, and privatisation is a social process, but the labouring body affords a natural starting point. Grotius and Pufendorf posit between them the two poles, naturalist and constructivist, of the constitutive tension running through natural rights theories' accounts of this process. I now consider how and why Locke returned to nature.

Re-rooting Property in Nature: The Case against Robert Filmer

Locke held up private property as the bulwark that protected the rights of the subject and limited the power of the state. The argumentation he deployed in his *Two Treatises* against Robert Filmer, who advocated for the divine rights of sovereigns, re-gripped private property in nature more tightly still than his predecessors'. Filmer (1588–1653) had presented a serious intellectual challenge to the attempts to find, and to found, in nature a right to private property for the subject, insofar as his case for the sovereign's unlimited power rested entirely on an individual's natural right to private property: the sovereign's. [23] It was rooted in '*the natural and private dominion of Adam*', the proper 'source of all government and propriety' (Filmer 1949, 71, emphasis in original).

Hence for Filmer too private property was 'natural and primeval' (Waldron 1988, 148). It was also fundamentally unequal. This idea of a natural equality was, for Filmer (1949, 262), but 'an error which the heathens taught'. Furthermore, Filmer poked holes in Grotius's notion of an initial, tacit agreement. He underlined, first, both its implausibility, and the impossibility of empirically verifying it. 'Certainly it was a rare felicity', Filmer (1949, 273) mused sarcastically 'that all the men in the world at one instant of time should agree together in one mind to change the natural community of things into private dominion'. Rousseau would take up this line of argument in his *Social Contract*. Locke himself did not disagree. Second, Filmer questioned how the subjects' descendants could be bound by an agreement they had not signed on to. 'How the consent of mankind could bind posterity', he wrote, 'is a point not so evident' (Filmer 1949, 65). Consent, then, provided shaky grounds for private property.

Filmer had thus laid a forceful claim to the naturalistic justification of private property to legitimise the rights, not of the subject, but of the sovereign. He had shown that the work of naturalisation could be powerfully mobilised against the subject. Ironically, his natural rights best exemplified the 'power' (*facultas*) with which Suarez and Grotius had redefined the concept of rights. Furthermore, he exposed the tenuousness of consent as a foundation for political construction. And, along with consent, the bases of an equality between the subjects were also undermined. Filmer, then, had attacked the two pillars of natural rights theories of private property, the conventional and the natural one. He had called into question simultaneously consent, and the possibility of founding equal rights to private property for the subject in nature. Pufendorf had sought to guard against the instability that this questioning had revealed to lie at the heart of consent, by strengthening the role of the contract at every step along the way in crafting private property rights. Yet he also sought a second guarantee, on the side of nature, in Grotius's principle of first occupancy, which he otherwise found sufficiently lacking that he set out to enhance it with the notion of improvement. The threat of instability was serious enough, for Locke, that it led the thinker of the 'Consent of the People' (one of the most used expressions throughout the *Two Treatises*) to forsake the contract as the basis for individual right to private property.

Filmer's attacks aside, the institution of slavery had also revealed the fragility of consent as a basis for building subjective rights. If they were founded in consent, the subject's rights could also be given away, by this consent. To ground them in nature was to institute instead inalienable rights. This, ironically, was the argumentative route Filmer had paved. Locke sought to reclaim it in order to establish natural, inalienable rights for the subject. To do so he retrieved Grotius's *suum*, in order to root these property rights in the subject's *own* nature. That 'every Man has *Property* in his own *Person*', that is to say, with the *suum*, in their body, provides the unshakeable foundation for all ownership. Stephen Buckle (1993, 168), whose history of natural rights theories of property does draw out the role of the *suum*, underlines that for Locke, as for Grotius, 'this most fundamental of properties, like all property, does not depend on consent, neither can it be lost or alienated'. Hooking private property into nature anew by way of the subject's own body enabled Locke to resolve the persistent problem of self-enslavement that the very emphasis on consent had raised, 'an issue which had proved awkward for Grotius and Pufendorf' (Buckle 1993, 169). It enabled him more broadly to 'establish private property [as] the bulwark against slavery [and] the keystone of political freedom', Buckle (1993, 183) concludes. In fact, slavery performed a far more constitutive function for Locke's political thought, as I will show in the chapter's final part.

3. Appropriating Nature: Locke's Labour Theory of Value

Locke set out to reclaim nature as the surest foundation for the individual's right to private property, contra Filmer but also to counter the frailty of consent. His concept of appropriation is a synthesis of Grotius's first occupancy and Pufendorf's improvement, the parts of their respective theories where they too had turned to nature. It addressed a question raised by the *suum* that ultimately remained underdeveloped in both Grotius and Pufendorf, namely, how does something become naturally one's own; how does it come to form part of one's *suum*? Grotius had attempted an answer with his first occupancy, whose limitations Pufendorf had drawn out and sought to correct by way of 'improvement'. Pufendorf's critique pushed a wedge through the old use right, of the kind that would firm up eventually (with Hume) into the modern distinction between 'fact' and 'value'. He separated out the thingness of the thing, so to speak, from the morality of the act, which were still folded together in the old natural law (see chapter 3). The effect of Pufendorf's distinction for his concept of property was twofold. It foreclosed the circulation of 'substances' between things and persons that Grotius's first occupancy relied upon, and, consequently, it shifted the framework of property to the relations between persons, and away from persons and things. With his consumptive model Grotius had justified first occupancy by things being 'converted into the very substance of the user'. By contrast, when Pufendorf came to define private property late in his treatise as 'a right by which the very Substance of a thing, belongs to a Person in such a way that it does not belong in its entirety to another person in the same manner', he had taken care to set up a barrier between persons and things that disqualifies this kind of transfer of substances—or transubstantiation—that Grotius had laid down as the basis of his natural right to private property (Pufendorf 1932, IV.chap.4[2]533). Indeed, property imposes 'no new qualities' upon the thing, only an 'external denomination' (Pufendorf 1934, I.chap.1.[16]16). It does not alter its substance, only the relations between the persons around it. The thing's substance *belongs* to the owner, it does not *become* him or her. For Pufendorf, the substance of the thing and of its owner do not mix. He uses 'substance' in a strictly physical sense, to refer to the realm of the body.[24] He physicalises substances. This was his contribution to the thoroughgoing questioning of the keystone concept of the Aristotelian ontology ('substance' or 'essence') of his times, and it was supplied by the *suum*. It left unresolved the question of how something comes to be part of the *suum*. Only, in casting it on the side of nature, he also established it beyond the scope of what he had set out to undertake in *On the Law of Nature and Nations*, which was to stake out the other realm instead, of morality.

Locke's Mixing and Fixing

A mixing of the substances of the owner and the owned is exactly what occurs in Locke's labour theory of value. Locke collapses back together the two ontological levels that Pufendorf had folded out, by way, first, of labour, the concept Pufendorf had introduced to modify Grotius's theory of property. Second, he shifts the conceptual frame back onto persons and their things, or rather onto one person. Interpersonal relations all but disappear in Locke's account of the origins of property, with the exception of that between masters and their servants and slaves, which I will consider in the next section. Ultimately Pufendorf's relational framework afforded insufficiently stable grounds for the right to private property. Locke's first appropriator is the solipsistic and already highly mythologised, in seventeenth-century Europe, figure of the American Indian who roams alone through the wild lands of the new world as he—and it is a he—hunts deer, plucks apples, and gathers acorns under the oak trees. Yet between the many of communal property and this self-sufficient, and indeed already mythical individual (see Arneil 1996), there is (almost, as we will see in the chapter's final part) no one. Locke establishes the terms of the problem he set out to address as follows. While 'no body has originally a private Dominion, exclusive of the rest of Mankind, in any of [the fruits of the earth]', 'there must of necessity be a means *to appropriate* them'. Otherwise the old use right, by which they were 'given to Men for the Support and Comfort of their being' is moot. Appropriation is the Lockean mechanism by which something is drawn into the sphere of the self, or 'propered to' oneself (to use an old English word) through one's labour. 'Whatsover he removes out of the State that Nature hath provided, and left it in', writes Locke (*TT*, II.chap.5[27]288), 'he hath mixed his *Labour* with, and joyned to it something that was his own and thereby makes his *Property*'. Mixing a resource with something of oneself, with one's 'labour or Substance', justifies the act of appropriation (*TT*, II.chap.16[183]391). The 'something that is his own' is not quite the body, however.

Locke combines the two corporeal models at work in Grotius's occupancy and Pufendorf's improvement, respectively. Grotius's consuming body, and his extensible *suum*, afford Locke his starting point:

> [T]he fruit or venison which nourishes the wild *Indian*, who knows no inclo-
> sure, and is still a Tenant in common, must be his, and so his, *i.e.*, a part of him,
> that another can no longer have any right to it before it can do him any good for
> the support of his Life. (*TT*, II.chap.5[26]287)

However, in this instance, while the effects upon the other commoners (who are deprived of the resource) are the same, the Indian is only exercising the old use-right. The property title that completes the appropriative process is conferred by his labour. 'No Body can deny that the nourishment is his' writes Locke (*TT*, II.chap.5[28]288), uncontroversially. Only he adds:

> When did they begin to be his? When he digested? Or when he eat? Or when he boiled? Or when he brought them home? Or when he pickt [*sic*] them up? And 'tis plain, if the first gathering made them not his, nothing else could. That *labour* put a distinction between them and common. That added something to them more than Nature, the common mother of all, had done, and so they became his private right. (*TT*, II.chap.5[28]288)

Labour properly bestows the 'private', exclusive right by 'add[ing]' to nature. It '*begin[s] a title of Property* in the common things of Nature', writes Locke (*TT*, II.chap.5[51]302). What the labour that is 'fixed in' nature adds *to* it is value (*TT*, II.chap.5[28]289). This value-adding paves the way for his theory of money, to which most readings of Locke hasten forward at this point, overlooking the deeply corporeal processes by which, for him, this value is created in the first place. This 'adding' is nothing short of a mixing of the owner and the owned. The fruit and the venison do not simply belong to the Indian as they did for Pufendorf, they have become 'part of him'; Locke is careful to specify that he means it literally, bodily. The Indian is not the same before and after ingesting the fruit and the venison, which are also changed by the Indian having 'mixed his *Labour* with' them, and 'fixed' his property 'in' them (*TT*, II.chap.5[27]288 and *TT*, II.chap.5[35]292). Person and thing are 'joyned' to one another (Locke, *TT*, II.chap.5[27]288). They *have* acquired some of each other's 'Substance' (*TT*, II.chap.16[184]391).[25] The 'distinction' that 'labour put' is not between appropriators and their possessions, but between 'them and common' (*TT*, II.chap.5[28]288). Locke thus corporealises the appropriative process. Appropriation is an incorporation, not just literally, but *instead of* metaphorically, since it is the mechanism by which communal rights (that attach to a collective body) are individuated. Moreover, the question of whether the labour expended is physical or intellectual is indifferent for Locke, for the reasons I will shortly turn to. Owner and owned are transformed—in their bodies, hence materially; and socially, by being constituted as owner and owned. Crucially, private property is stabilised, 'fixed', through this mixing.

Labour as Property

The reason that this 'something that is his own', which is Locke's (*TT*, II.chap.5[27]288) definition of the *suum*, is not, strictly speaking, the body is that the latter properly belongs, along with all other natural bodies, to God alone, their creator (see Tully 1980). Instead this 'something' is the labour this body expends. Locke's (*TT*, II.chap.16[184]391) 'labour or Substance' radiates out from the appropriator and draws into their personal sphere that which it has touched. Labour 'annexes' that which it comes into contact with (*TT*, II.chap.5[27]288). Locke's (*TT*, II.chap.5[27]288) key move is to have defined the *labour itself*, and not merely its products, nor the body, as 'the unquestionable Property of the Labourer'. Labour is both a specific form of property, exclusive and private, and the mechanism of its making. It is the outcome of the process, its products, *and* the process itself. Expanding his definition to the process that produces property is what enables Locke to encompass the broad range of resources that sustains it, including life and liberty (*TT*, II.chap.9[124]350). This dual nature of labour (as products and process) enables a refinement of the *suum* in two ways.

First, the body is still maintained as the referent and anchor of the appropriation. However, second, considering labour, and not just the body, as part of the *suum* accommodated for the new, and distinctly human form of agency, artifice (see chapter 2). This mattered, first, in the age of the machine where the distinction between natural and artificial bodies was becoming central. What was the status of God's creatures' creations? Do humans own the machines they make in the same way that God owns them? This was also, second, for Locke as for Hobbes, the agency of political construction. Locke eschewed the Hobbesian route, of envisaging the state as a machine, we have seen (see chapter 5). But he was just as interested in this new form of agency, which, in the seventeenth century, was deeply implicated in the question of liberty and the prospect of breaking away from the old orders, political and epistemological. Instead he retrieved it decisively on the moral side, and here his concept of labour was key.

Labour is a moral agency for Locke, as indeed it was for Pufendorf. Moreover, Pufendorf's (1934, III.chap.1[1].314) *suum* already contained moral elements, like virtue, reputation, or indeed liberty, we saw. By firming up this aspect that was present but underdeveloped in the *suum*, Locke undermines the basis of Pufendorf's critique of Grotius's first occupancy. The ethical dimension, he shows, is not added on the edges of the *suum*; it inheres in it. The distinction Locke draws between labour proper and the body expending it enables him to bring the differentiation between the physical and the natural on the one hand, and the moral or political on the other, that Pufendorf had pinned onto the contract within the natural sphere of the *suum*. 'The *Labour* of his Body and the *Work* of his Hands, we may say, are properly his', writes Locke (*TT*, II.chap.5[27]288), but not the body or the hands, strictly speaking. Labour, even intellectual, is embodied; yet it is not the body. This distinction is what differentiates labour from theft. No doubt the thief is sweating profusely as he or she scrambles off with his or her bounty. This extracorporeal element opens up the moral dimension, the space of actions and intentionality. It is the doing or making proper, the series of actions that transforms the resource into property. The sweat makes not the labour (or the theft), the intentionality of the act does. This is why the work is indifferently physical or intellectual; both are inherently moral (see also Tully 1980, 109). It is also why machines cannot be proprietors.

An important consequence of honing in on the single labouring body at the centre of the sphere of the *suum*, and of distinguishing between the body proper, and the labour it adds in expending itself, is that Locke does away with the need to be recognised by others which, for Pufendorf, as for Hegel after him, comprises the very structure of moral life. Hence why, with Locke, private property decisively switches from a negative duty to abstain from that which belonged to others, to a positive right that requires no one to validate it. The fruit and the venison become the Indian's immediately 'without the assignation or consent of any body' (*TT*, II.chap.5[28]289). In sum, Locke's labour is the quintessentially human, natural-cum-moral intentional agency of political construction. It answered both questions, of what inheres in the *suum* initially, and how something comes to be part of it. Locke (*TT*, II.chap.5[30]289) illustrates: 'The Law of reason makes the Deer that *Indian's*, who hath killed it'. His example does beg the question as to why the lion or the tiger that kills a human should not qualify for this type of ownership, or rationality, for that matter (see chapter 5). At any rate, Locke's labour supplies the line-drawing instrument for delineating the contours of the *suum*, and for redrawing them as often as required by its natural, outward expansion.

The most far-reaching implications of Locke's equation of labour with property are borne out in his discussion of the profound reorganisation of property relations that was unfolding around him, the privatisation of the commons (see chapter 5). It is key to understanding how he founds labour as the universal and natural engine of property's privatisation, by doing away with the requirements of consent that Pufendorf had emphasised. Locke draws on the English commons as his real-world model of a conventional, collective property. 'In *Land* that is *common* in *England*, or any other country', he writes, 'no one can inclose or appropriate any part, without the consent of all his Fellow-Commoners' (*TT*, II.chap.5[35]292). The English commons well illustrates the role of consent Pufendorf had emphasised. However, 'though [this land] be Common in respect of some Men, it is not so to all Mankind; but it is the joint property of this Country, or Parish'. Consent cannot yield a universal mechanism of appropriation. In true constitutive mode (see chapter 5), Locke then makes a return-to-the-origins move to retrieve the original biblical-cum-natural 'Law Man was under' in 'the great Common of the World', the original, pre-contractual commons God gifted to humankind. The law he finds here was 'rather for *appropriating*': 'God commanded, and [man's] Wants forced him to *labour*. That was his

Property which could not be taken from him where-ever he had fixed it', he writes (*TT*, II.chap.5[35]292). What humans own in such a way that it cannot be taken away from them, even if consent is withdrawn or withheld, is their labour, he has shown. Locke (*TT*, II.chap.5[28]288) pushes his point, asking whether one could really call 'Robbery' the Indian's taking the acorns 'because he had not the consent of all Mankind to make them his' (*TT*, II.chap.5[31]290).[26] His Indian was not his criminal; these figures perform quite different functions in his thought. With labour, then, Locke has unearthed the natural motor of the privatisation of property, and for the diffusion of private property as a mode of organising social relations around the world. He has found the basis for a natural and universal right to private property. It owes its naturalness and its universality to the body.

4. Locke's Self-Possessed, Possessing Person

In mixing their labour with the object and fixing something of themselves in it, humans make property; but they also make themselves into autonomous subjects of right capable of consent. Locke's 'making' doubles up as a self-making. In appropriating, humans ('Man'), for Locke (*TT*, II.chap.5[27]287), make themselves into persons ('Person'). In this section I will show how this natural-cum-moral agency of political construction constitutes the subject at the heart of modern law. The labouring body is the instance that mediates between the *human being* and the *person*, the two pillars of his concept or property. This mediating function is what the latter concept, which he carries over from theology, affords him. I will begin by showing how Locke reworked a theological term for the law by way of the body, creating in the process modernity's concept of 'legal personhood'. I will then parse the Lockean making that double backs on itself to yield coextensively private property and the subject of rights.

Inventing 'Personhood' for Legal and Political Modernity

Locke's concept of personhood hinges together his political thought and his philosophy. It features centrally in the second treatise's chapter 'On Property'. Locke further expounded it in the chapter on 'identity and diversity' (book II, chap. 27). He added this chapter to the second edition of the *Essay*, published five years after the first edition (in 1694), at the prompting of his interlocutors, who were keen to better understand his principle of individuation (Forstrom 2010; Pringle-Pattison 1924). The concept thus took on a growing importance in his thought. Locke in fact peeled it away from its two established meanings. The first was the theological concept of Christ as person (*persona ecclesiae*) that hailed from the doctrine of the Trinity, and underscored the three-pronged nature of God (Father-Son-Holy Spirit). The second was the *persona ficta* of the thirteenth-century canon jurists, who proposed the term to designate corporations (see Balibar 2013, 233–35; see also Canning 1988). The latter had afforded the device Hobbes harnessed for his theory of representation. Turning away from theology and to the stage, Hobbes (*L.*, chap.16[3]101) conjured the mask actors wore in antiquity to emphasise the fictional and performative dimensions of a term that was used 'in tribunals as [well as in] theatres'. Hobbes, however, also mobilised the triangulation at work in the theological concept, where Christ mediates be-tween the two realms of the immanent and the transcendent. The representa-tion of the subjects by the sovereign, who constitute for Hobbes the 'authors' of sovereignty and its 'authority', respectively, is made possible by this triangulating instance, 'persona'.

However, Hobbes's was a decidedly outward-orientated, performative con-cept. Moreover, the body it invoked was still a collective one. This outward-ness and collective dimension is what Locke inverted. He reconfigured the concept by attaching it to another part of the law, and to the individual human body. Drawing upon the arcane terminology of legal proceedings, he defined 'person' as a 'forensic term' that captures the retroactive attribution of actions to, or in-deed appropriation by, an embodied self (Locke *EHU*, II.chap.27[26]217). Locke continues:

> *Person*, as I take it, is the name for this self. Wherever a man finds what he calls *himself*, there, I think, another may say is the same person. It is a forensic term appropriating actions and their merits; and so belongs only to intelligent agents capable of a law, and happiness and misery. (Locke, *EHU*, II.chap.27[26] 217)

From Hobbes to Locke, the concept of personhood shifted from capturing the outward performance that produced the political 'subject' by projecting on a public stage to represent it, to the interiority of what we now call 'the in-dividual'. Locke's 'person' is coextensively a psychological and legal principle. Psychologically, it affords the self its principle of coherence; and legally, it indexes the centre to which responsibility for one's actions attaches. The term 'appropriate[s] actions and their merits'. Locke defined the concept for modern law. Etienne Balibar (2013, 106) has underlined how he marks 'the exact point of a reversal through which, leaving a "theological age" and entering a "psycholog-ical (or anthropological) age"—while preserving a significant number of the in-tellectual instruments forged by the first for the use of the second—the "modern" question of multiple personalities has been substituted for the ancient question of the persons of the Trinity in the elaboration of the notion of the subject'. The theological concept of personhood was the trope by which Western thought had articulated together the one and the many, parsing the one becoming many (and vice versa). Moreover, the body already played a central role in it. God's becoming flesh as Christ conjoins the divine and the human. This trinitarian and corporeal structure is what Locke mobilizes at the heart of his theory of property, where, in labouring, 'humans' become 'persons', possessing *and* self-possessing subjects of the law.

Human Self-Making: From Individuation to Individualisation

By 'person' Locke, in the *Two Treatises*, means a free actor undertaking deliberate actions. I showed in the previous chapter how, for Locke, 'human' ('Man', in his language) and 'person' refer to a biological and a moral being, respectively. The effects of this distinction are borne out most decisively by his labour theory of value. 'Every Man has a Property in his own Person', writes Locke (*TT*, II.chap.5[27]287). The switch from 'Man' to 'Person' is not accidental since Locke restates the point the other way around. 'This no Body has any Right to but himself', he continues (ibid.). This 'Person', rather than his body, is properly what 'Man' comes to own. Only something has to happen between 'Man' and 'Person' to make good of what Locke conceives as an innate but latent property title the former holds in the latter. For Locke's (*TT*, II.chap.7[87]323) 'Man' holds a natural 'title to perfect freedom'; only it needs to be realised. This freedom, in turn, is a necessary but not a sufficient condition of personhood proper. That it is a necessary condition is borne out by the child, Locke's figure in-becoming. It is 'born to' this natural freedom but 'not born in it' (Locke, *TT*, II.chap.6[55]304). 'We are born free, as we are born rational', writes Locke (*TT*, II.chap.6 [61]308), 'not that we have actually the exercise of either: age that brings one, brings with it the other too'. What it brings is the development of 'the Understanding', which is the 'proper Guide' to human action and renders us capable both of freedom and of the law. For '*where there is no law there is no freedom*', for Locke (*TT*, II.chap.6[57]306). 'Capable of the Law' is precisely how Locke (*EHU*, II.chap.27[26]217) defines personhood in the *Essay*, we have seen.

However, second, Locke's personhood takes something more than just being capable of the law. This capacity needs to be realized, through actions. It can also be weakened by choosing the wrong course of actions, in which case the person-in-the-making veers closer to 'misery' than to 'happiness'. Or indeed it can be weakened by criminality, as we saw in the previous chapter, in which case they lose their capacity for legal personhood and their rights. This must be a real possibility for this initial natural freedom to be meaningful. Personhood is the end point of the developmental process that begins in the 'imperfect state' of childhood but is only fully realised by the individual's acting in the world (Locke, *TT*,

II.chap.6[58]306). Locke's concept of personhood rests at its core on an intentional agency: labour. This is the 'great foundation of property':

'Man (being the Master of himself and *Proprietor of his own Person*, and the Actions or *Labour* of it) had still in himself the great *Foundation of Property*; and that which made up the great part of what he applied to the Support or comfort of this being, when invention and arts had improved the conveniences of life, was perfectly his own. (Locke, *TT*, II.5[44]298)

That to which 'Man' has 'applied himself' becomes 'perfectly his own', his property. He becomes doubly 'Proprietor' of his '*Actions* or Labour', but also of the 'Person' he has crafted in expending himself. A human becomes a person in labouring. What happens, then, between 'Man' and 'Person' is the realisation through labour of the natural title to oneself as a subject capable of the law and endowed with rights that lay in latency in the imperfect state of childhood, before the child knew to exert himself or herself in the diligent and conscientious manners Locke aimed to discipline them into in order to prepare them for labour (see chapter 5).

Humans make property in appropriating, but also their 'selves', their personalities, which are 'annexed to' their consciousnesses in the ways I explored in the previous chapter (Locke, *EHU*, II.chap.27[22]215). Consciousness itself 'is not made', as Tully (1980, 109) has underscored; it inheres in our agency. Only it is engaged in the acting, by the appropriating. The acts double back on themselves to circle back to the appropriator, transforming the human into a person. The consciousness 'that always accompanies thinking' and acting is the linchpin to this self-making (Locke, *EHU*, II.chap.27[9]). Out of it a person emerges, a self distinct from other selves, to whom responsibility for his or her actions attaches. As in the trinitarian logic, a body is the effective principle of this self-realisation. The toiling body supplies the third term that triangulates the biological being ('human') and the legal and moral one ('person'). It is the motor of this developmental process that yields a legal subject endowed with 'self-responsibility' (Taylor 1989). Crucially, then, the labouring body affords the juncture between Locke's *individuation*, the biological principle that constitutes 'man' as an undivided organism, and his *individualisation*, by which 'he' properly crafts himself into a 'person'. This, I suggest, is the founding moment of 'the individual', the figure at the heart of political modernity. The stakes, then, are high indeed. They turn on the nature of the agency that inheres in Locke's labour.

Locke's labour implicates a genuinely creative agency that brings something into existence, that constitutes it. It is not the making of the machine. It is the very ingredient of constitution, understood in the strongest possible sense in which Locke (*EHU*, II.8[99]333) intended consent to 'actually *constitut[e] any Political Society*'. Locke's 'constitution theory', as James Tully (1980, 23) termed it, affords him the foundation for his case for demonstrating the superiority of the moral over the natural sciences. Humans make polities (and machines), whereas they can only know approximately the natural world. Consequently, certain knowledge is only possible in the moral (or political) sciences. 'Morality is the proper science and business of mankind', for Locke (*EHU*, II.chap.12[11]423). Tully (1980, 36) has explained how Locke reconciles his highly agential focus with the theological requirement to bow to the ontological dependency on God prescribed by his faith as follows. Humans, for Locke, are 'in a relation of continuous and intimate dependency on God in the way intentional actions are existentially tied to the agent who makes or performs them'. Having established this crucial caveat by way of his concept of person, whereby intentional actions, rather than God's creation ('Man'), is their property, the path is then clear for conceiving a very strong form of human making, though one that is carefully subsumed to God's. Locke, then, goes further than Hobbes in fleshing out the human agency of political construction that created the state in the seventeenth century. Unfortunately, this agency was also carefully reserved for some but not all human beings. It is to these active exclusions in Locke's thought that I now turn.

5. Locke's Self-less Labouring Body: The Slave

Having considered the nexus of property and personhood in Locke's thought, I now examine how he also wields it in such a way as to deny it to some kinds of bodies. The stakes are high, given the equivalence Locke (*TT*, II.chap.9[123]350) establishes between private property and life itself.[27] To withhold it from some is to negate nothing short of the most natural of rights, to live.

That Locke's labour is the 'unquestionable property of the labourer' raises the question as to why not all of the labourers that feature in his political treatises appear to qualify for this ownership of the work of their bodies (*TT*, II.chap.5[27]288). I consider in this section the three labouring bodies that do not: the servant, the horse, and the slave. Two of them appear when Locke illustrates his appropriative mechanism:

> The Grass my Horse has bit; the Turfs my Servant has cut; and the Ore I have digg'd in any place where I have a right to them in common with others, become my Property, without the assignation or consent of any body. The *labour* that was mine, removing out of the common state they were in, hath *fixed* my Property in them'. (*TT*, II.chap.5[28]289)

In these examples, the labour is automatically assumed to belong to an appropriator ('mine'); only in two of them, the effort is expended by another body, a servant's and a horse's. These bodies complicate the seemingly straightforward Lockean equation of labour and property I have been tracing so far. The servant does arguably own his or her labour, insofar as it is sold to his or her master with at least some degree of consent. The horse, however, does not. This figure begins to draw out the exclusionary effects wrought by Locke's 'personhood', and how it served to constitute the human species as the sole subject of rights, at the expense of all others. Locke's work of legal speciation, as I call it, will be in focus later in the chapter (see also chapter 8). My concern here is with 'another sort of Servan[t]' in Locke's (*TT*, II.chap.7[85]322) treatise who is actively excluded from ownership by the Lockean cojunction of 'personhood' and 'property', the slave.

The slave introduces in Locke's thought a human being that was not only not an owner constitutively, but is entirely owned, on par with the objects appropriated – often by way of his or her labour. The problem of slavery in Locke (*TT*, I.chap.1[1]141) has been treated as an 'embarrassing fact' (Glausser 1990, 191), where his life directly contradicts the theoretical commitments of this self-professed 'Lover of Liberty' (*TT*, dedication, 136), or as a blind spot in his political thought, an 'immoral evasion' (Dunn, quoted in Farr 1986). Regarding the facts, we know that Locke had an insider's knowledge of the role of slavery in the development of the English colonies in his capacities as secretary and treasurer of the English Council for Trade and Foreign Plantations (in 1673–74) and then as secretary to its successor, the Board of Trade and Plantations (1696–1700) (Armitage 2004). We also know that this theorist of the conscience had a personal interest in the slave trade, having invested 600 pounds in the Royal Africa Company shortly after its incorporation in 1672, following the lead of his close friend and patron, Anthony Ashley Cooper (later Earl of Shaftesbury) who, with 2,000 pounds, was the company's third-largest investor (Glausser 1990). Lastly, we know that he had a hand in drafting the *Fundamental Constitutions of Carolina* (1669) during his secretaryship to the five lord proprietors to whom Charles II had granted the piece of land that would become the state of Carolina, one of whom was Anthony Ashley Cooper. This actual constitution had laid down one of the most extreme legitimations of the power of slave-owners over their slaves, stipulating that 'every freeman of Carolina shall have absolute power and authority over his negro slaves, of what religion or opinion so ever'. It further outlawed the possibility of emancipation by securing that 'no Slave shall [. . .] be exempted from the civil Dominion his Master has over him', so that a slave may dwell 'in the same State and condition' of slavery (cited in Bernasconi 1992, 295–296).[28] An unlimited dominion of the kind that traditionally befell God alone, since it was a power of life and death, was properly the property in play on the ground in the slave trade. Critical postcolonial scholars have showed more broadly how natural rights theories supplied the site for the deployment of powerful legitimations of colonisation (Schmidgen 2002; Arneil 1996). The contradictions between Locke's life and his thought have thus puzzled many (see also Farr 1986, 2008). My argument explores instead the role that slavery plays, not on the edges of political treatises placed under the aegis of human freedom, but at their heart.

Slavery performs the same type of constitutive role for his theory as did punishment and the figure of the criminal (see chapter 5). Much more than a simple oversight or immoral evasion that takes us beyond his political thought, the slave functions as the minus-one that holds it together; not unlike the labour that fixes private property. I showed in the previous chapter how Locke's human rights are founded in an original exclusion. Humanity is constituted as the rights-bearing species by way of a double move. The individual right to punish, the natural executive power, is collectivised by withholding it from one person, the criminal. The responsibility for this primordial denial of rights is then inverted, by ascribing it to a transgressive act this person would have committed. In Locke's slippery-slope logic, moreover, this act condenses into a character trait to constitute a type. The figure of the slave marks the second constitutive exclusion underwriting Locke's scheme.

Slavery looms large over Locke's *Two Treatises*, performing several crucial functions. That 'so vile and miserable an Estate' appears in the very opening line, as that against which Locke (*TT*, I, chap.1[1]141) pushed back against wth his own political design. It indexes the opposite to the 'Freedom from Absolute, Arbitrary Power' that is 'closely joyned with Man's Preservation' and that therefore comprises the proper foundation for the state, for Locke (*TT*, II.chap.4[23]284). It draws the boundaries of his government by consent, since no one can '*enslave himself*' by 'his own Consent' (*TT*, II.chap.4[23]284). Slavery is also that '*State of War continued*' that the contract puts an end to (*TT*, II.chap.4[24]284). Equating slavery with the state of war is what establishes it as the antithesis to the political order he set out to design, and durably locks it in at the heart of the Lockean state. Just as Hobbes's state of nature holds ever present the possibility of what the state threatens to disintegrate into, slavery achieves the same for Locke. Hence slavery is constitutive, first, in the way that antitheses are. Locke needs the state of war and its slaves, in the same way that Hobbes needs the state of nature and its passionate and unruly humans: their political states arise from negating the state of nature and the state of war respectively. The latter two, then, function as the motors to their respective projects of political construction, and they delineate the outer limits to their political states.

The antonomy of freedom and slavery was, on one level, a well-established trope in Locke's time, that hailed from classical Rome and featured centrally in the earlier seventeenth century 'Republican' literature, as we have seen (see chapter 5; see Skinner 2008,). On another, however, the centrality of slavery to his project renders his blind spot regarding the slaves of his age in whose property he was materially interested in not so benign (or liberal for that matter). Did the Africans who were rounded up onto the vessels off the West African coast and robbed of their 'Lives, Liberties and Estates' really qualify as 'Captives taken in a just War', who 'are by the Right of Nature subjected to the Absolute Dominion and Arbitrary Power of their Masters', the English slave-owners? (*TT*, II.9[123]350 and *TT*, II.7[85]322). And if they did fight back against their own enslavement, why would their resistance to the slave-makers not qualify as the same kind of legitimate retaliation as those in the state of nature who rightfully punish a thief (see chapter 5)? Locke's trick is to have located slavery, not in the state of nature, but in the state of war. This leads to the second place in which slavery is constitutive in Locke's project: in its conjunction with violence. We have already seen the foundational role Locke accords violence. With his just war provision, Locke makes room, at the heart of his state, for the absolute, unlimited power over another's life or death it is otherwise designed to restrain. A war is just, for Locke, when it aims to punish an aggressor, in line with the primordial natural right. Locke's legitimation of slavery turns on a similar inversion of responsibilities to that underwriting the figure of the criminal:

> These Men having, as I say, forfeited their Lives, and with it their Liberties, and lost their Estates; and being in the *State of Slavery*, not capable of any Property, cannot in that state be considered as any part of Civil Society; the chief end whereof is the preservation of Property. (*TT*, II.7[85]322)

To call slaves servants by another name is to place them in a position similar to the servant's, who has contracted off his or her labour to the master; to then be able to imply that, unlike the servant (hence why the name is 'peculiar'), they have broken the contract. This breach is the original act of aggression that puts the 'Legislative Power of Life and Death' over them in the hands of the master (*TT*, II.chap.7[86]322). The device of the contract supports the inversion of responsibilities upon which Locke's just war theory rests. Morever, as if aware that he is perhaps taking a step too far, Locke then places careful limits upon the effects of this reversal of responsibilities, by way, once again, of his concept of property. Though the life of the original aggressor belongs to the rightful conqueror, those of their 'Wives and Children' who 'made not the War, nor assisted in it' do not; nor does that part of the aggressor's property-making 'labour or Substance' upon which they depend for their subsistence (*TT*, II.chap.16[183]390–91). The figure of the slave coupled with his concept of property enables Locke to distinguish between limited power for government within, and an unlimited, absolute dominion over another's life and labour without. They are logically constituted as the two complementary processes of political construction, at the time when England was throwing itself in the colonial enterprise, in which Locke had personal stakes and of which he had practical knowledge.

The slave and the criminal are thus the two figures of the original aggressors in the *Two Treatises*; the one innately belonging to the state of war and the other tilting human relations into it. They serve, on the side of the state, to found 'government by consent' in the terms of a rightful retaliation that is reserved *for some*. On the side of the subject, these figures complicate the scheme of self-making where the toiling body straightforwardly conjoined the 'human' and the 'person'.

The Lockean scheme of personhood had centred exclusively upon the lone subject and its objects who, in mixing, emerged as proprietor and possessions respectively. Intersubjectivity was entirely erased. Individualisation was instead a self-sufficient process, untroubled by any other. The body afforded the biological basis for an already naturally cohesive self, who could throw himself or herself into labouring to craft their personal identities. The criminal and the slave interrupt this smooth circuit of self-making. They mark the cracks in the dams where the other returns to haunt Locke's constitutive thinking. They lay bare another kind of constitutive logic, founded in the antagonism, whereby the self emerges in opposition to a series of others upon whom are pinned the negative pole of (often multiple) antinomies (see Laclau and Mouffe 1985; see also Epstein 2008). The first Lockean antinomy, between rationality and irrationality, that was revealed by the criminal in his conception of liberty, doubles up, in property, as an industriousness and idleness. These antinomies' boundary-drawing effects surface in the limiting condition Locke places upon the capacity for property that he otherwise attributes to all humans in the state of nature. Upon closer inspection, the property 'Title' that labour brings in things is reserved for 'the Industrious and Rational', and explicitly denied 'the Quarrelsom [*sic*] and Contentious' (Locke, *TT*, II.chap.5.[34]291).

Who are these idle and quarrelsome irrationals? The lion who attacks the human? The animal is hardly lazy since it hunts, as does the Indian. Yet the lion too qualifies for the same treatment as the criminal on account of the threat it poses to a rights-bearing, rational humanity (see chapter 5). The vanquished of a just war, who querulously rebel against being enslaved and robbed of their labour? The lion and the criminal serve to 'fix' humanity as the species endowed with reason, through the operation, in the case of the criminal, of the universality minus one logic. Through a similar negative constitutive logic, the horse and the slave secure labour and property as essential attributes of the human 'Substance' (Locke, *TT*, II.chap.16[183]391). The horse is the being capable of labour but not of reason, and therefore not of property or personhood. The slave is the being who is capable of labour, and who was capable of property and personhood, but who has lost this capacity, along with his or her rightful place in humanity, by forsaking his or her reason through an initial act of aggression. The horse is the non-human, the slave is the former human. As with the criminal, a primordial transgression constitutes a type, or indeed a permanent condition.

The slave remains an insistent if barely adumbrated, disincarnate figure throughout the *Two Treatises* who surfaces at key junctures. It helps accommodate for an unlimited form of private property, that escapes appropriation's natural limiting mechanism (take as much as you can use), and for a rightful power to kill that is not the state's. The slave is the other to the original appropriator, to Locke's naturally free human being (rather more) incarnated by the hunting and gathering Indian. The slave serves in Locke's thought to establish humanity as a community of naturally rational bourgeois proprietors though a logic of universality minus one. His theoretical elaboration of a natural right to private property for humanity at large rests on constructing a category of non-owning, non-human human beings. This denial of humanity is effected by the equivalence of property and personhood Locke had established by way of the body. The slave marks the place in the Lockean scheme where the labouring body fails to triangulate the human and the person. Becoming a subject recognised in the law is not the outcome of labouring, for the slave. This entails not only that they are not persons, but that they have no selves. The road to property, and therefore to legal personality and to selfhood was conceptually foreclosed to this category of humans from the dawn of modernity. These excluded few, then, are constitutive of the natural right to property for the many, and thus of (private) property as a fundamental human right.

Of Skin Colour and Boundary-Drawing in Locke's Thought

Locke's work of legal speciation threads through his epistemological and his political thinking in complex ways (see also chapter 8). Epistemologically, Locke, like many contemporaries, breaks from the Aristotelian notion of species where the boundaries are determined by nature. 'Species' is a human construct, like all concepts, for Locke, who, like Hobbes, is an epistemological nominalist. It is a taxonomic category crafted by humans in order to sort the world around them. 'The boundaries of the species, whereby men sort them, are made by men' (*EHU*, III.chap.6[37]302), Locke exemplifies the classical age's overarching concern with sorting as constituting the main business of modern knowledge (see chapter 1). In the business of knowledge that is his in the *Essay*, 'men make sorts of things', rather than the things themselves (*EHU*, III.chap.6[35]301).[29] In this context, the traditional definition of 'man' as a being with 'voluntary motion, with sense and reason, joined to a body of a certain shape' afforded an important place to interrogate the scholastic understanding of 'species' and ultimately to reclaim the concept for modern knowledge. Locke thus arguably played an important role in preparing the concept for the work of (biological) speciation that took off in the eighteenth and nineteenth centuries.

Locke's critique centred not so much on the concept's contents, on what are the essential attributes of the human species, as on its *limits*. The question of what constituted the limits of the human species was a pressing one, at the time where, in the wake of the discovery of the New World, Western knowledge was profoundly shaken up by the number of hitherto unseen creatures that were being uncovered during the course of appropriating these new lands. Moreover, how to classify the inhabitants whose labour was being mustered to the task no longer turned on the theological matter of whether they had a soul (as debated by the Spanish clerics in Valladolid), but rather on political issues of governance and rule. The ways in which, in this context, the question of species delineation would become suffused with questions about racial domination is illustrated by none other than David Hume, who wrote in his capacity as Under-Secretary of State, effectively for Colonial Affairs:[30]

> I am apt to suspect the negroes and in general all the other species of men (there are four or five different kinds) to be naturally inferior to the whites. There never was a civilised nation of any other complexion than white, nor even any individual eminent either in action or speculation. [. . .] Such a uniform and constant difference could not happen, in so many countries and ages, if nature had not made an original distinction betwixt those breeds of men. Not to mention our colonies, there are NEGROE slaves dispersed all over EUROPE, of which none ever discovered any symptoms of ingenuity; tho' low people without education, will start amongst us, and distinguish themselves in every profession. In JAMAICA indeed they talk of one negro as a man of parts and learning; but 'tis likely he is admired for very slender accomplishments, like a parrot, who speaks a few words plainly. (Hume, cited in Bracken 1973, 82)

The infamous footnote Hume added to this 1753 essay ('Of National Characters') is well-covered ground in the racism scholarship (Immerwhar 1992; Bracken 1973). My purpose is not to collapse too quickly Locke onto Hume, although they were both founders of modern science. It is rather to show how the concern with whether humanity comprised one or several species derived from the central question driving Western knowledge since humanism (in the 'anthropological age', as Balibar called it) was, what is 'the human' (or 'man')? The concept of species, which was tightly bound up with 'substances' (or 'essences'), was a pillar of the Aristotelian edifice that modern science was invested in dismantling. Yet it also was reinvested in ominous ways by those who saw themselves as pursuing its

quest. Hume's was a variation on, or indeed an answer to, the Lockean problematisation of the limits of the human species.

In fact, and unlike Hume, Locke urges epistemological carefulness. The
limits he is primarily concerned with defining in the *Essay* are of human knowledge rather than of the species. The human species is simply one of his favorite
examples for illustrating the constructed-ness of *all* concepts. Locke seeks different ways to do so throughout the *Essay*. The distinction between ectype and
archetype ideas was one way; it differentiates between concepts aimed at theoretical ('species') and practical ('government') knowledge, respectively. Locke
adds another, between 'nominal' and 'real essences', that he wields specifically
to parse the question of the limits of the human species. 'His Maker' alone, possibly also 'angels', know the 'real essence' of the species we name 'Man' (*EHU*, III.
chap.6[3]290). Should we have access to this knowledge we would have 'quite
another idea of his essence than what now is contained in our definition of that
species', Locke (ibid.) insists. Locke, then, is well aware of the difficulties that
inhere in delineating species. The limits we draw around the human species
are at best approximative, as with all of our (ectypal) knowledge of the natural
world, if not outright 'random' (*EHU*, IV.chap.4[16]383). Moreover, the *Essay*
is replete with borderline cases, like monsters, changelings, or indeed talking
parrots, that Locke deliberately deploys to challenge established assumptions
about these limits. His 'monsters' or 'misshaped' humans, and his 'changelings'
(simpletons) defy locating the essence of the species in our normal ideas about
the human form or about the ability to reason, respectively (*EHU*, IV.chap.4[13–
16]381–383). 'We cannot be too cautious that words and species, in the ordinary
notions which we have been used to of them, impose not on us' Locke (*EHU*,
IV.chap.4[17]383) concludes.

Whiteness, however, is an insistent theme throughout the *Essay* that spills beyond the examples where he broaches the limits problem, as Robert Bernasconi
(1992) has shown. This, coupled with the importance he grants colour for the
epistemological task of sorting ('it is the colour we most fix on, and are most
led by'; *EHU*, III.chap.6[29]299), and with the persistence of 'flesh colour' as
a favorite terrain for parsing questions of what to 'join together' and what to
hold separate, suggest that he too shared the racialised preoccupations of his
time, even if he was able to hold off from his theoretical considerations and indeed from his conscience his practical involvement in the slave trade (*EHU*,
IV.chap.7[16]402). This is the context in which 'the negro' appears in the *Essay*, in
one of the passages where Locke examines the sorting process by which complex
ideas are formed from putting together simple ones (*EHU*, IV.chap.7[16]402).
The African, then, does feature in Locke's epistemological work, albeit in a position whose relation to the human species remains undecided, but not explicitly excluded either (*EHU*, IV.chap.7[16]402). Hence Locke's is not the Humean

gesture that consists in finding sufficient differentiations 'in nature' to warrant breaking down the biological entity into distinct 'kinds', or indeed races.[31] The trouble is that, in the *Two Treatises*, where the African does not feature at all, this epistemological undecidedness becomes decisively settled by shifting categories to the slave. That the African is not explicitly mentioned matters little since there was little doubt as to whom the slaves were in Locke's time. With his slave, Locke effectively fixes the boundaries of the human species for the realm of practice in exactly the ways he cautions against in his epistemological work.

The problem is not simply that Locke throws his own warnings to the wind from one writing to the next—it is not reducible to (or explainable away by) inconsistency. It undermines the very business he is engaged in his political treatise, 'archetypal' in his own word, and with the properly constitutive, performative agency he embraces in undertaking it. Locke is well aware that he is fixing, and not merely copying, the state's boundaries, or its 'Extent', per the *Treatises*' subtitle. The state of nature is his ectypal raw material, but the state is what he sets out to design, his archetypal project. Here, it matters that he conceived a right to private property that implicitly excluded non-white bodies, not only from owning their labour, but from accessing legal personhood, from becoming subjects of rights tout court. In the human-person nexus that he seals with the labouring body, Locke, in fact, achieves the same aim theoretically as the Fundamental Constitution of Carolina provided for, to maintain the slave 'in the same State and condition', however hard each labours. The slave forever belongs to the state of war. It is the non-white body legitimately excluded from the state in order to constitute it. This most effective theorist of the natural right to private property paved the road for the 'whiteness as property' underwriting settler colonial states (Harris 1993).

*

Whereas scientific modernity was born of ejecting humanity and its planet from the centre of the universe, legal modernity emerged from a revolution that achieved the exact obverse. I have shown in this chapter how the body that everyone 'has' was key to founding a form of rights tethered to the individual, rather than to the natural order, and thus to establishing the human being, instead of nature, as the centre-point of the law. This decisive inversion begat the modern subject of rights, the figure that underwrites both universal human rights and capitalism. The right that underwrites this distinctly modern mode of production, to private property, was my specific focus in this chapter. The two-legged body that is innately 'one's own' served to delineate a 'natural' sphere of personhood from which others must abstain. This embodied, individual sphere afforded the starting point and 'natural' referent for a right that was conceived from the onset as a keeping out; as a holding out of everyone else to found the modern 'self' as a rights-holder. This sphere of privacy was firmed up by Locke's original mechanism of appropriation, which also furnished the 'natural' mechanism for its expansion. Moreover, Locke's theory of appropriation stabilised the right to private property by resolving an enduring tension in natural rights theories, between a voluntarist commitment to modern political liberty on the one hand, and a deterministic resort to a natural given, the body, to found this liberty on the other. John Locke legitimised private property the furthest by casting it, with the labouring body, as a somatic self-making. The right to private property, however, also reveals a structure of exclusion built into natural rights. The exclusions are twofold. The first founds the universality of these rights, on the basis of the body. The second denies them to some, also on the basis of their bodies. The body thus serves to reveal the two boundary-drawing gestures. In the first, it affords the site of individuation where the self is separated out from the other and established as the subject of rights. This exclusive, corporealised selfhood, in turn, is the vehicle for generalising these rights to humanity at large. Every human being has a natural right to private property, just as he or she has a body, in the rationale articulated the furthest by John Locke. Tracking the labour of the body in his political writings also served to lay bare the second exclusion. It turns on whether the labouring body that everyone naturally has also owns the fruits of its labour, or not. The first boundary-drawing gesture is exclusive. It delimits a universalisable self. The second is exclusionary. It denies some access to selfhood. It foreshortens this right's reach. It therefore institutes the universality-minus-one logic that underwrites the Lockean space of natural universal human rights. The figure of the slave revealed how the concepts of 'self' and 'personhood' that he tailored for modern law operates as line-drawing instruments that differentiate between those who are entitled to becoming subjects of rights and those who are not; simply as a function of their embodiment, of their whiteness (see also Glick 2018). It shows how these exclusions do not simply slip in in practice, because of the ways the concepts are misapplied, but instead were built into them from the onset. Having charted the troubled genealogy of the right to private property in this chapter, I now turn to analyse a different set of foundational early modern practices that also centred upon the body that everyone naturally 'has' and considered it as holding the key to the mystery of human nature.

7

The Public Anatomy Lesson

Know'st thou but how the stone doth enter in
The bladder's cave, and never break the skin?
Know'st though how blood, which to the heart doth flow,
Doth from one ventricle to th'other go?
And for the putrid stuff which thou dost spit,
Know'st thou how thy lungs have attracted it?
>   —John Donne, An Anatomy of the World. Of the Progress of
>   the Soul. The Second Anniversary (1612)

This book alone declares the blood to course and revolve by a new
route, very different from the ancient and beaten pathway trodden
for so many ages
>   —William Harvey, *On the Motion of the Blood* (1628)

There was, in early modern Europe, an unprecedented avidity to peer into the
human body. It was expressed in that singular institution of the sixteenth and
seventeenth centuries, the public anatomy lesson. This was a significant cultural
event; in some cases, the city's most attended. People of all social ranks flocked
to the anatomy theatres that were being built across Europe, in order to be able
to catch a glimpse of 'what nature has enshrined in all of us' on the body of the
criminal or the outcast displayed across the dissection table, in the words of an
invitation dispatched by a performing anatomist to his peers (quoted in Hansen
1996, 667). There was little of the prior proscriptions that attached to opening up
the body, and not the squeamishness or simply the reservations that doing so in
a public performance might provoke today. In the unique 'culture of the body'
that straddled the Renaissance and the classical age, even poetry turned anatomical (Sawday 1996). 'I have cut up mine own Anatomy, dissected myself', wrote
John Donne. Reflecting on a period of illness, Donne contrasted his own moral,
'anatomic' enquiry with that of his doctors who 'have seene me, and heard me,
arraigned me in these fetters and reciev'd the evidence' (*Devotions* 45). Moreover,

Birth of the State. Charlotte Epstein, Oxford University Press (2021). © Oxford University Press.
DOI: 10.1093/oso/9780190917623.001.0001

this fascination with these anatomical mysteries was coextensive with the discovery of the New World and the early stages of colonisation. The body was the terra incognita of early modern science. When Descartes articulated the project of mastery and possession of nature ('as it were'), he looked, not to the broader nature out there, but to the piece of nature closest to hand, the human body. 'The innumerable diseases of both body and mind and perhaps even the decline of old age' were the areas Descartes (2006, 51) identified as most set to benefit from this mastery, which was to be the medium of humanity's emancipation—of its liberty. Peering into the body was the first step to achieving it. Descartes (2006, 39) recommended dissections as a key component of a sound scientific education. Dissections were instrumental to the discoveries of the laws of blood circulation by 'Physician Extraordinary' and close friend of Hobbes's, William Harvey, who marked the threshold of the new science whose method Descartes (2006, 39–46) set out to design in the *Discourse*.[1]

Descartes's and Donne's 'I' represents two very different ways of relating to the new anatomical interior that was being revealed by scientific progress. The body fascinated both; only Donne divined, Descartes dissected. Donne grappled with the terms of a new science to make sense of the ailments of his own body. Descartes staked out the point of view of the modern scientific subject, external, removed from the object to be studied. The former spoke from within the body, the other from without, at a purposeful distance, that which would found modern science's ideal of objectivity. Hobbes, by this distinction, was the archetypal modern scientist in his refusal to apprehend the moving bodies that loomed large in his concept of liberty from any but an external point of view. But this also accounts for how Locke was caught between his commitment to a scientific reason on the one hand, and on the other, the pull of interiority, given seventeenth-century England's 'institutionalisation of the "inner anxiety" of Calvinist doctrine', which Donne's sermons also rendered (Sawday 1996, 20). Yet of the two theorists of the nascent state, Locke was the physician who, as an Oxford medical student, would have early on looked into the body. Peter Laslett (1988, 86) sees 'empirical medicine' as affording Locke his model for addressing the political problems of his time.[2] One body part in particular exerted increasing fascination in the age of optics: the eye. Indeed, the workings of vision itself was one of modernity's biggest discoveries. The means of this discovery were the camera obscura, a little black box with a pinhole and the quintessential artefact of the seventeenth century, and the opening up of the eye. In his treatise on optics Descartes (2001, 91) advised his readers to 'tak[e] the eye of a newly deceased man, or for want of that, of an ox or some other large animal' and that they 'carefully cut through to the back to the three membranes which enclose it' in order to see the mechanics of seeing itself.

In this chapter I trace the emergence of a mode of seeing that was honed upon the publicly dissected body in the seventeenth century. This mode of seeing furnished, I argue, the epistemic condition of possibility for the making of both modern science and the state. The classical era's problem of order heralded the demise of the text as the exclusive site of epistemic authority. Scripts handed down through the ages were no longer sacred; in fact questioning their authority was modernity's founding act. This problem of order decisively shifted the locus of epistemic authority from the text to the subject, who was thereby established coextensively as the subject of modern science and of liberty. This bore out two decisive consequences. First, in the wake of the renting of words from the world, words were mustered towards the new task of ordering. This explains why, in a context where words were no longer enmeshed with and securely fastened to things, Hobbes-the-scientist should be so anxious about their correct ordering. That the text was no longer the unquestioned locus of epistemic authority did not diminish the importance of words, however; to the contrary. They became crucial instruments for ordering a new 'space of knowledge', forever now distinct from that of 'things' (Foucault 2005, xi). They were scientific tools in this sense. The second decisive consequence was the preeminence of sight. *Nullius in verba*, take no one's word but what you see for yourself, was the founding motto of the Royal Society. This 'age of observation' was marked by what Svetlana Alpers (1983, 32) has called 'the art of describing', with the take-off of Dutch realist painting in the arts, which echoed the empirical turn in the sciences. Both set out to capture the world exactly as it appears to the naked eye. Sight also mattered in another way, as point of view. The task of ordering presupposes a viewpoint set at a remove from the world, from which it can be both undertaken and taken in. The sovereignty of sight is captured in an emblematic painting of the classical age, Velázquez's *Las Meninas* (1656). Foucault (2005) has shown how the painting encapsulates the seventeenth-century problematique of representation, understood as the cognitive act of rendering the seen present again (re-presenting) upon an ontologically discrete plane, of the canvas or indeed of thought itself. The painting features, on the left, Velázquez himself in the act of painting the Spanish emperor Charles V and his wife, who are reflected in the small mirror positioned at its centre; and to the right, the monarch's daughter being presented to her parents with her retinue. The viewing positions of the sovereigns who take in their daughter while they are being painted and that of the spectator coincide exactly. This point of view is also what binds the otherwise rather disparate elements of the painting; they are ordered by it and for it. Velázquez thus renders sovereign the act of seeing that does not see itself seeing. Locke (*EHU*, I,chap.1[1]33) compared the understanding to the eye that, 'while it makes us see and perceive all things, takes no notice of itself'. Velázquez's underscored that this point of view is the new locus of an authority that is *both at once* epistemic and political, although the latter was not Foucault's concern in *The Order of Things*. This overlap is precisely mine here. The painting's superimposition of the sovereigns' and the spectator's viewpoints captures the two facets of the sovereignty of sight that I explore in this chapter. On the one hand, the authority to see shifted from old texts to the epistemic-cum-political subject, thus founding modernity's autonomous 'self' (Taylor 1989). The ability to see for oneself is the pillar of this subject's autonomy and of her liberty. On the other hand, however, and less considered, is how this authority shifted to the nascent state. It yielded a distinct mode of viewing, and controlling, the subject from without, via her body. In the double movement I trace here, this visual mode was born upon the body by dissecting the eye and it held the body in its sights. The public anatomy lesson affords the second place for apprehending how, and where, the state began to see, after the Hobbesian articulation of the solution to the problem of war.

The scopic regime that established vision as modernity's primary ordering instrument, epistemic and political, is this chapter's topic. I analyse how it was crafted in the public anatomy theatre by slicing open the eye. This mode of seeing underwrites modern science's axiomatic distinction between the (seeing) subject and the (observed) objects of knowledge. This epistemological structure has, however, from the onset, operated as a structure of domination, where 'the objects' have readily ranged from nature, to outcasts or foreigners, to women, to the people of the new world. This epistemological-cum-political structure that privileged 'vision as the master sense of the modern era' is, I will show, the state's very own founding matrix (Jay 1988, 3). I borrow the concept of 'scopic regimes' from visual studies (Jay 1988; Feldman 1997), and bring it to international relations' long-standing attention to the state. Visual studies have shown how, in every culture, specific things are rendered visible or invisible, hence foregrounded or backgrounded, by historically specific frames and grids that ordain and regulate its 'seens'. One scopic regime, however, has consistently remained 'dominant, even totally hegemonic', the 'modern scopic regime', as Martin Jay (1988, 3–4) once labelled it; notwithstanding identifiable 'moments of unease' in its development, 'competing ocular fields' and efforts to unsettle it, including visual studies's own. Since it was first circumscribed in the 1980s, the 'ubiquity of vision' has been amply confirmed by the exponential rise of surveillance; including by the new, rhizomatic practices that no longer merely radiate from the state (Jay 1988, 3). While these horizontal modes of surveillance have turned the gaze sideways and onto one another, or back up to the institutions of power, they have but further consolidated the primacy of vision.[3] The source and enduring operator of its hegemony is this visual regime's claim to *not* be one; to be un-situated, such that it can claim instead the timeless place of 'natural vision' (Crary 1988, 30). This, despite its vision being resolutely monocular, not-so-natural; the single eye at the heart of the panopticon. My purpose in this chapter is to return to the original site where the proverbial naked eye at the heart of this modern scopic regime was constructed by dissecting the eye.

The state, however, has not been visual studies' primary focus. It has been that of international relations, where scholars have of late increasingly underscored the importance of understanding 'how visuality produces and shapes the international as a site—and sight—of politics' as Kyle Grayson and Jocelyn Mawdley (2018, 2) nicely put it. Critical security scholars in particular have mapped how this scopic regime ordains practices of contemporary warfare, producing 'the eye as weapon' (Bousquet 2017). Antoine Bousquet (2017) has underscored how the proliferation of cameras in weaponry is not merely a case of the weapon imitating the eye. Rather, the eye itself has turned into a deadly machine as vision has become 'disembedded from its originary biological substrate' through the increasing 'mechanisation of its functions' (Bousquet 2017, 63). In line with this scholarship's focus on the broader scopic regime that enable these developments, I will show that modernity's 'absolute occularcentrism' is not so readily relegated to the absolutist state of Europe's past (Jay 1988, 17). It is how the state continues to see today.

I draw, in addition, upon two of Foucault's early problematiques (from the 1960s). First, the body and how it was rendered visible in medical discourses was already in Foucault's sights in *Birth of the Clinic* (1963), where he mapped the emergence of clinical practice at the end of the eighteenth century. While anatomical practices serve to reveal them, my focus here is instead, second, on the deeper epistemic structures underwriting them, to which Foucault then turned his attention with the *Order of Things* (1966). This is also the only work where he considers the seventeenth century at some length, but not the body.[4] While I take his groundbreaking analysis as my starting point, I loosen Foucault's (2005) periodisation. Because representation is his focus in that work, he sees the classical age (the seventeenth and eighteenth centuries) as bookended by the Renaissance (from the fourteenth to the sixteenth centuries) and the nineteenth century. Because I start instead from the body, sight itself is my concern—the mechanics of the eye, and the desire to understand them. I apprehend the classical episteme as the decisive break in the structures of knowledge that ushered in modernity. In this longue durée perspective I consider it, not as a marker of one era in a long succession, as Foucault does, but as the matrix, epistemological and political, of the world we still live in. Hence I read the Renaissance as harbouring elements of both a pre-modern textual epistemology of deciphering and of a modern emphasis on seeing. My periodisation thus tracks closer to Martin Jay's (1988), who, in characterising the modern scopic regime as a 'Cartesian perspectivalism', locates it at the juncture of the Renaissance's discovery of the rules of perspective and of the Cartesian rupture.

The dissected eye draws out two additional differences with Foucault. First, the body Foucault held in his sights in *Birth of the Clinic* was the ailing body; the clinical discourse aimed at *keeping it alive*. This would become the focus of his mature concept of 'biopower', which illuminates the bottom-up powers geared towards making live rather than killing. The dead body is instead my focus in this chapter. It is the body put to death by the emergent state, then crafted into an object of knowledge by the early-modern anatomist.[5] Second, Foucault did not consider the public anatomy lesson, this singular institution that, I will show, reveals the extent to which science and the state were born hand in hand. The chapter charts thus the constitutive entwinement of modern science and the state. I show how together they created, in death, the anatomised body in early modern Europe as all at once an epistemic, a cultural, and an artistic object. Nevertheless, the principle purchases of Foucault's *Discipline and Punish* (1975) for my purposes lie, first, in the way it identified the relation between the body and the state as founded in the latter's power to kill. Second, it underscored the role of the spectacle in its dispensation. In this chapter I circumscribe a historically specific form of spectacular somatic violence that begat the state itself.

This mode of seeing the body from without, detached and deadly, is the enduring epistemic-cum-political structure I analyse here, in order to appraise how it continues to ordain political life, or indeed life tout court. Signature drone strikes are enabled, not just by technological improvements (by an unmanned areal vehicle capable of carrying both a high-resolution camera and a missile), but by this very specific, desensitised, modern mode of visuality that was born on the dissection table. 'The practical insensibility acquired in the dissecting room' is how the editors of the *Lancet* medical journal described the anatomist's stance in the nineteenth century, at a time where the avidity to see inside the body had become so acute that England was gripped by waves of graveyard robberies (1829 editorial, quoted in Richardson 1988, 75). A similar practical insensibility is also required from the soldier sitting in the military operations room in Utah who presses the button that releases the drone's lethal load upon the body identified by the drone camera in Yemen (Chamayoux 2015). The origins of this detached, external, techno-scientific-cum-military mode of viewing bodies is my object here. I trace the line that runs from the surveillance state's mechanical eye in the sky that registers the targeted body, to the scientific revolution's 'artificial eye' (the telescope), to the mechanics of the eye that were bared upon the dissection slab in the seventeenth century.

The chapter unfolds in four parts. To map the contours of this new mode of seeing I begin by considering the visions of two Englishmen who helped found it, the anatomist William Harvey and the scientist-statesman Francis Bacon. I then examine in the second part the site where it was progressively institutionalised across Europe, the public anatomy lesson, thus moving from the actors that helped design it to the structures that helped entrench it. I analyse the role that this early-modern institution played in helping establish a new empirical science in England. This alignment of science and the state, while not specific to England only (which was in fact a latecomer to the new sciences), became especially visible in the country where a political and a scientific revolution conjoined. I then analyse more closely the epistemological and political orderings that this ritualised performance of sovereignty achieved, in the third and fourth parts, respectively. I show how the production of the human body as modern science's object was underwritten by a crucial tension that played out in the anatomy theatre. On the one hand, the body on the dissection table was the site for the construction of a universal human nature. This was its epistemological function. On the other hand, the legitimacy of the dissection turned on the distinctive identity of the dissected subject, which was ritualistically publicised. The body that was opened up was required by law to belong to an outlaw or a foreigner. The work of political ordering was wrought by drawing a series of lines across (or through) the body on the dissection table that had two sets of functions. First, they served as a graphic reminder to a broad audience of modern subjects-in-the-making of where the lines of the law ran, and what were the consequences of crossing them. But these also operated, second, as a series of boundary-drawings of a moral and social, rather than strictly legal, kind. They served to delineate, in the Lockean terms we considered in chapter 5, a bourgeois polity founded in a lethal 'standing Rule to live by' that was *also* the bedrock to its members' liberty (*TT*, II.chap.4[22]284). The anatomy theatre afforded an important site for the line-drawing that delineated the bourgeois community of consenters that, for Locke, comprised the proper constituency of the modern state (see chapter 6). Women and the poor, I will show, 'naturally' fell on the wrong side of the line. I utilise two sets of visual materials to analyse this new regime of visuality, engravings drawn from one of the first textbooks of modern medicine, Andrea Vesalius's *De Fabrica corporis humani* (1543, 1st edition) (see fig. 7.1), and the Dutch painter Rembrandt's anatomy lesson paintings.

Methodologically, this chapter, first, develops the distinction I began to draw in chapter 2 between the body as an organ of knowledge and as an object of knowledge. Second, whereas in chapter 3 I considered how humans make machines, here I envisage instead the body as nature's machine. There, the machine was in focus as the artefact, as the expression of a creative human agency. Here instead the natural 'fabric of the human body' (per the title of Vesalius's textbook) is. The tension between the generic body and particular bodies, third, is especially central to this chapter. It serves to reveal how particularities, like gender (here) or race (in chapter 6), were carefully included and excluded in the process of constructing the embodied referent of the human universal, and consequently who could count as the rightful recipient of the political rights that were being attached to it in the seventeenth century, including property.

The Embodied Foundations of Modern Science

By 'modern science' I mean a form of knowledge that broke from earlier sciences in its relation, first, to the authority of the text and its relation to truth; second, to embodied *experiences*; and, third, to *the experiment*. While the terrain I explore overlaps with what is traditionally known as the 'Baconian empirical sciences', tracking the place of the body leads me beyond what historians of science have termed this English 'gentlemen's club' (Shapin 1988, 390; see also Kuhn 1977).[6] I include continental figures like Kepler and Descartes on account of their groundbreaking work on the mechanics of the eye. 'The conduct of our entire life depends upon sense, amongst which sight is the most universal and the noblest' Descartes (2001,65) wrote, and 'there is no doubt that inventions that augment its power are the most useful'. To define it succinctly, modern science favoured the eye over the authoritative text as its primary source of knowledge. To now unfold its three dimensions, first, the text had stood for centuries as the place where truths were validated and securely locked away. The truth was thought to rest, not in the topic under investigation, but in the texts authorised to proclaim it. A classic history of science lore is the tale of the Padua professor who could not trust the telescope Galileo invited him to look into to see for the himself the new moons circumnavigating Jupiter, because neither the technology nor the new astronomical facts it was revealing had received the stamp of the authorities (see Shapin 1996, 72). The 'dull and unintellectual are indisposed to see what lies before their eyes, and even deny the light of the noonday sun', Harvey (1962, 29) wrote. The new science (or 'new philosophy', as it was also called) he helped usher in challenged this unquestioning stance towards textual authority that foreclosed any improvements. Francis Bacon (2000, 70) derided the ways of the alchemist who, when an experiment failed, rather than question the recipe he has followed, 'accuses himself of not properly understanding the words [. . .] and so repeats the experiment indefinitely'. To read directly into the book of nature and describe it as it is was the new scientists' aim. 'Philosophy' for Galileo 'is written into this grand book, the universe, which stands continually open to our gaze' (quoted in Shapin 1996, 69).[7]

Modern science inverted the relation both, second, to sensory data, and to the prolongation and validation of this direct, embodied, experience of the world; third, by experiments. Harvey (1962, 30) 'profess[ed] to learn and to teach anatomy not from books but from dissections'. Pre-modern science was not devoid of empirics, however. In fact, anatomy was one of its more advanced areas on account of its applied nature and its 'social function' (Kuhn 1977, 38). Only experiments remained secondary to the process of knowledge production. Experiments, when they were used, were designed to confirm an already-decided conclusion, hence to validate an existing assumption.[8] The empirical sciences established instead the experiment as the starting point for theory-building.[9] Their proponents, from Bacon to Robert Boyle, all actively promoted the dissections as the model experiment (Sawday 1996, 57). Along with the experiment, instruments took on a new importance. They were the 'artificial Organs [added] to the natural [ones (. . .) to enable] the *inlargement* [*sic*] *of the dominion*, of the Senses', in the words of Boyle's assistant, the experimentalist Robert Hook (quoted in Shapin and Schaffer 2011, 36).

This new trust in the senses was made possible by the revolution in optics. Lenses were not new; they were a medieval technology. The revolutionary gesture was to treat the eye itself as an optical instrument, credit for which is owed to the astronomer Johannes Kepler. His *Astronomica par optića* (1604), also known as *Ad Vitellionem*, is where Kepler turned away from the movements of the stars and the planets astronomers like him had been holding at the end of their long lens, and to the corporeal mechanisms at the other end instead (see Simon 1975; Linnik 1975). Kepler also named the image that was formed on the back of the retina a 'picture' (see Alpers 1983). Descartes (2001) then set out to consolidate Kepler's findings with his 1637 treatise on optics, *La Dioptrique*.[10] Directly observing the mechanics of the eye by, in Descartes's case, experimenting on humans and other large animals, is what enabled the development of a new theory of vision. The revolution, then, was not technological. Lenses came to be trusted, not just because they were greatly improved, nor out of a new-found naivete. Indeed optical illusions were a seventeenth-century obsession. Only they could be accounted for by this new theory of vision. They were a property of this 'picture', caused by the way light was refracted on the retina. The theory both identified the source of error, by locating it on our natural lenses, and how to correct it, with artificial lenses. Apprehending the eye as an instrument signalled the rise of mechanism, that unique ontology of the seventeenth century that underwrote both rationalism and empiricism, and fueled the imaginary of 'the artifice' and the new political agency that was taking shape (see chapter 2). The new confidence in optics, in turn, paved the way for trusting other instruments. The source of change, then, lay in the relations to instruments. It was triggered by turning to the body and by recognising it as the imperfect yet unavoidable, but also rectifiable, starting point for knowing the world. In the second half of the century Robert Boyle, of the air pump experiment and a dissection enthusiast, with this new-found faith in artefacts, could write: 'the informations of Senses assisted and highlighted by Instruments are usually preferable to those of Senses alone'.[11]

Figure 7.1 Frontispiece to Vesalius *On the Fabric of the Human Body* (1543)
Source: n/a

1. Peering into the Body: William Harvey and Francis Bacon

A physician to two Stuart kings (James I and his son Charles I), William Harvey was the early modern anatomist par excellence and the founder of modern medicine (Bayon 1941; Pagel 1951). Locke came of age with the generation of Oxford students that embraced his discoveries and the experimental methods that had yielded it (Shackleford 2003).[12] Francis Bacon (1561–1626), the founder of modern empiricism, was also a patient of Harvey's and a friend of Hobbes's (who was his amanuensis for a time). Lord Verulam (his peerage title) was a powerful statesman with an elaborate vision for the new science (or 'new philosophy') and its role in fostering human progress, which he deployed across an extensive body of work. He was consecrated 'the father of modern science' by the Royal Society upon its founding in 1660. He held some of the highest political offices of the realm, serving as attorney general and as lord chancellor, and he sat on James I's Privy Council. He wrote philosophy 'like a Lord Chancellor', his own doctor, a fine writer himself, despaired; and that 'was not unimportant', as the historian Christopher Hill (1965, 87) put it. Harvey and Bacon exemplify a unique nexus of knowledge and power in this singular crucible for modern statehood, seventeenth-century England. In this section, I use Harvey and Bacon's writings to begin to trace the contours of this new way of looking at the human body that was honed at this juncture.

Circulating between Worlds: William Harvey

'The science of man's body' was, according to Hobbes (*De Corpore*, Epistle Dedicatory) the 'most profitable part of natural science'; and it was 'discovered with admirable sagacity by our countryman Doctor Harvey [. . .] in his books on the Motion of the Blood and the Generation of Living Creatures'. The heart, as the motor of blood circulation, and the uterus, as the site of 'generation', per his term, were at the centre of Harvey's work. His discovery was that blood was not produced by the liver from 'the juice of the food that had been eaten' and then used up by the different body parts, which had been the received wisdom since the Roman physician Galen; the blood's innate heat furnishing the principle of motion (Harvey, cited in Cohen 1994, 190). The blood was, rather, pumped through the body, constantly and in large quantities, by the heart. Like Galileo, Harvey was the quintessential modern scientist, who debunked fourteen centuries of erroneous medical beliefs with a carefully demonstrated scientific truth. In fact, he stood with one foot on either side of the threshold of the scientific modernity he helped craft. His discovery achieved nothing short of revolutionising the knowledge of the body, yet the notion of circulation that inspired it harked back to an old world of correspondences.

Circulation and the Play of Correspondences

Like Descartes's *Discourse*, Harvey's *On the Motion the Blood* as well as his lecture notes afford us a precious vista onto the new science in the making in that he carefully retraces the steps of his discovery. However, the terms he drew upon to formulate it belonged to an ancient world where a macro- and a microcosm endlessly reflected each other. It was the closed cosmos we considered in chapter 3, as yet untouched by the scientific revolution's great wrecking ball, infinity. Knowledge was still a finite accrual of sameness, not yet the open-ended, eventually infinite, measurement of differences it would become in the classical age (see Foucault 2005; Cassirer 2000). At the centre of this world the human being stood, a 'microcosm [through which] all the lines of the macrocosm ran together' (Cassirer 2000, 40). Leonardo da Vinci's iconic *Vitruvian Man (The Proportions of the Human Body according to Vitruvius*, 1490) is the archetypal representation of this androcentric episteme. It features the (male) human figure encased in geometry's two most symmetrical and closed figures, the circle and the square, whose centres cross on the man's navel. This play of cosmic mirroring was expressed in a common motif in Renaissance representations of the public anatomy lesson, the looking glass (Sawday 1996). This world afforded Harvey the terms with which to make sense of a discovery that would contribute to shattering it. Harvey understood movement of the blood in animal bodies as a microcosmic copy of the motions of celestial bodies. The heart, whose true anatomical function he was discovering, was the 'sun' of Harvey's (1962, 85) 'microcosm', the body. The scholasticism's founding figure, moreover, looms large over Harvey's narration of his discoveries:

> I began to think whether there might not be a motion as it were in a circle. Now this I afterwards found to be true; [...] which motion we may be allowed to call circular, in the same way as Aristotle says that the air and the rain emulate the circular motion of the superior bodies. (Harvey 1962, 84)

Harvey understood his findings to confirm Aristotle's assumption about the perfection of circular motion that his fellow scientists were also observing in the celestial bodies. Like Aristotle, moreover, Harvey identified the soul as the body's final cause or *entelechy* (although he disagreed as to which body part was its vector, see Wilson 1987), a perspective that would be shredded by mechanism.

Circulation, however, the passage quoted above shows, before it became settled as the modern scientific notion for which Harvey is remembered, as blood circulation, also played a constitutive role in his thought. It carried metaphors between the different parts of science, but also between science and politics. Unlike Galileo, Descartes, or Kepler, Harvey, who evolved in the close circle of state power, did not shy away from drawing upon the political register to formulate his scientific insights. It was he, rather than Hobbes, who reinvented the medieval metaphor of the body politic for modernity by, literally, fleshing it out—or bloodying it, we might say. The deliciously florid and highly politicised language by which he captured the blood coursing from and back to 'its sovereign', the heart, is worth hearing:

Through the motion of the blood [. . .] the various parts are nourished, cherished, quickened by the warmer, more perfect vaporous spirituous, and, as I may say, alimentative blood; which on the contrary, in contact with these parts becomes cooled, coagulated, and, so to speak, effete; whence it returns to its sovereign, the heart, as if to its source, or to the inmost home of the body, there to recover its state of excellence, or perfection. (Harvey 1962, 85)

'Knowledge of his own heart', the king's physician sagaciously underlined, is necessarily 'profitable to a King', both as medical knowledge and as 'being a divine exemplar of his functions', indeed an 'image' of his own 'kingly power' (Harvey, quoted in Cohen 1994, 190–91):

The heart of creatures is the foundation of life, the prince of all, the sun of their microcosm, on which all vitality depends, from whence all vigor and strength arises. Likewise the King, foundation of his kingdoms and sun of his microcosm, is the heart of the commonwealth, from whence all power arises, all mercy proceeds. (Harvey, quoted in Cohen 1994, 190; see also Harvey 1962, 26)

Hobbes's (*L.* 3) metaphor of sovereignty as giving 'life and motion to the whole body' politic thus had already well-tilled grounds upon which to grow. Remarkably, Harvey's discovery operated like a perfect bridge between the Renaissance and the classical episteme; in a way that, for example, Galileo's was not. It was both formulated within, and held meaning by, the old schemas of correspondence, while being *at the same time* the product of the modern scientific methods, to which I now turn. Harvey's nod, here, to his fellow Padua medical student Galileo's discovery of heliocentrism, is noteworthy in this regard.

Discovering the Fabric of the Human Body in Vesalius's Footsteps: The Dissection as a Modern Experiment

While steeped in the pre-modern episteme, Harvey's discovery of blood circulation was also quintessentially modern in its method and in his emphasis on the visual. I consider these dimensions of his work successively. Harvey the pioneer had little but his Cartesian 'good sense' with which to pursue his groundbreaking experiments in the 1610s (Descartes 2006, 5) He began by questioning the Galenic anatomical model, and his discoveries initially received the same cool reception as those who interrogated ancient truths (Shackleford 2003). Harvey's (quoted in Cohen 1994, 189) mathematical calculations established that 'the abundance of blood that was passed through the heart' was of an order of magnitude altogether inconceivable in the Galenic scheme. The heart, Harvey found, played a far more vital function than it could capture. Harvey (1962, 29) then proceeded to test his calculations on blood flows 'by ocular demonstrations'. As he retraces the steps of his discovery, Harvey (1962, 84), we saw earlier, 'began to think' that the blood's motion was circular, and then 'found that it was true' by opening up all manner of bodies, dead or not completely so. He experimented on the deer from the royal hunt; undertook vivisectional experiments on a variety of small domestic animals, like dogs and monkeys; and excised the hearts of live vipers, which, as cold-blooded animals with a slower blood flow, were easier to handle. Equally modern was Harvey's resort to optical instruments to verify his findings and generalise them across species. 'I have also observed that almost all animals have truly a heart', Harvey (1962, 61) wrote, 'not the larger creatures only', but also 'in slugs, snails [. . .] wasps, hornets and flies [. . .] with the aid of a magnifying glass'. Generalisation through observation, and not just the cosmic play of correspondences, underwrote Harvey's discovery of the workings of the heart.

The model Harvey (1962, 52) did have for his experiments was 'the great Vesalius', the founder of modern anatomy.[13] The Renaissance anatomist Andrea Vesalius had taught just over half a century earlier at the University of Padua, where Harvey had been a student.[14] Vesalius had revolutionised the practice of anatomy in three ways. First, he decisively shifted the locus of scientific authority from the text to the experiment, by performing the dissection himself. This collapsed the medieval division of labour and authority between the physician, the guardian of the text, who stood at the pulpit reading the lesson in Latin, and the surgeons, who dissected and spoke little Latin (Wilson 1987).[15] Second, Vesalius privileged the human body, instead of the pigs, monkeys, and dogs then commonly used for dissections and vivisections. Third, Vesalius visualised (in the sense of rendering visible), the human anatomy in ways in which it had not been before with the publication of his *De Fabrica corporis humani*. While not the first to use them, Vesalius's textbook 'made greater and more effective use of anatomical illustrations than had ever been done before' (Wilson 1987, 69). A woodcut from *De Fabrica* features Vesalius himself staring straight at the viewer, his hand laid upon a flayed arm and hand, distinctly human limbs that express the first two innovations—establishing the human body at the dissection's centre point, and the physician's direct involvement (see fig. 7.2). The forearm and hand are echoed in the single illustration that Harvey included in his *De Motu Cordis* (see fig. 7.3).

Harvey's *Praelectiones Anatomiae Universalis*, the lecture notes he drafted to accompany his public dissections as Lumleian lecturer, illustrate the new primacy of the visual in the making of modern science. Anatomy is defined in the

Figure 7.2 Velius's self-portrait
Source: *On the Fabric of the Human Body*

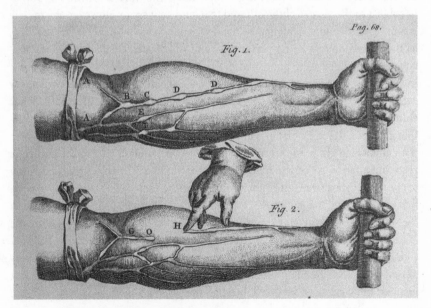

Figure 7.3 From William Harvey, *On the Motion of the Heart and Blood in Animals* (1628)

visual key. It is 'that faculty which through inspection and dissection reveals the uses and actions of the parts [of the body]' (Harvey 1961, 22). Harvey established twelve rules for the public dissection in his Canons of General Anatomy. His seventh canon is *'Not to dispute [or] confute*, other than by visible evidence'. The evidence presented to the view, rather than the text read from the pulpit (and in Latin), is established as the basis for putting forward new knowledge claims and for correcting established ones. His third principle prescribes 'To supplye only by speech what cannot be shewn, on your own credit and by authority'. It reveals the profound reorganisation of the relations between the word and the world that was under way. First, the text is no longer sacred; the unquestionable locus of authority and the fount of all truths. The recourse to a professorial or textual authority (which are coextensive) remains important, in the sense that the anatomist lends credibility to the demonstration, but it remains secondary, a background condition rather than the locus of knowledge production. Second, Harvey's eighth principle recommends to *'Briefly and playnly* [present your case], *yett not letting pass any one thing unspoken which is subject to the view'*. Conversely, his ninth is *'Not to speake anything which with outt the carcass may be delivered or read att home.'* Nothing must be shown which is not spoken of (eighth principle), nor must anything be spoken of during the dissection that directly aids the task of rendering the body's organisation visible (ninth principle). The spoken and the shown are tightly corralled together.

In the medieval anatomy lesson, the body was a prop that served to illustrate the text. Here instead the body is given primacy. The word is subsumed to what is 'subject to the view', tightly tethered to it, and kept spare. However, the merely 'visible' is turned into 'evidence' by the text generated to interpret it—orally, first, as the dissection was being performed, and then in the treatise where the discoveries it enabled were published in *On the Circulation of the Blood*. To put it in another way, the word renders the evidence visible *as* evidence and no longer merely as raw flesh. Only the word has become an epistemological tool. It has shifted from being tightly bound up with, or even constitutive of, the world, ontologically on the same plane as it, to being but an aid to the demonstration, like the magnifying glass. The word is an ordering instrument. His twelfth principle recommended to 'serve' the anatomy demonstration in 'three courses according to the [hour] glass'; that is, to allot a definite time to each part of the body—'in the first day's lectures the abdomen, nasty yet recompensed by its infinite variety. In the second the parlour' (the thorax); and to reserve for the third day's lecture the *'devine banquet of the brayne'*. Rembrandt would represent this divine banquet a couple of decades latter in his second anatomy lesson painting, *The Anatomy Lesson of Dr Joan Deyman* (1656). The primacy of the visual entails, third, not just that the visible is prioritised, but that the place from which it is viewed, the witnesses' point of view is taken into account in undertaking the demonstration. His fourth principle advises 'to cut up as much as may be in the sight of the audience', and no more. This point of view determines how much of the body to open up at the each stage of the lesson.

While Harvey was steeped in a pre-modern world of cosmic correspondences, his experiments broke new grounds for science, methodologically and substantially. His laws of blood circulation drew a bridge between a world where circular motions were sought primarily up in the heavens and one where they would be observed in the human body. With his ocular inspections enhanced by optical instruments, Harvey epitomised the external, distanciated point of view upon the body that would come to lie at the core of the modern episteme. Harvey himself was aware that the path he was charting required breaking with old ways. In opening his *On the Circulation of the Blood*, he wrote that 'true philosophers' do not 'swear such fealty to their mistress Antiquity that they openly, and in sight of all, deny and desert their friend Truth' (Harvey 1962, 30–31). Yet Harvey (1962, 31) was also was cautious: 'I do not think it is right or proper to strive to take from the Ancients any honour that is their due'.

'The Father of Modern Science': Francis Bacon and Modern Science's Corporeal Turn

The founder of modern empiricism had no such qualms where the ancients were concerned. In the 'relentlessly corporeal world of early Stuart London', the dissection loomed large over Francis Bacon's programme for the 'Great Renewal' (his term) of knowledge (Nunn 2016, 1).[16] He may have taken an interest in the public demonstrations that were being performed by his own doctor during the time when he was drafting his project. Whereas Copernicus's system was too 'complex, abstract, and mathematical' to be of much use to Bacon, the biological system that Harvey and his predecessors was laying bear by prying open the body was not (Kuhn 1977, 48; see also Webster 1975). The two components of a Baconian empiricism comprised, first, a science founded in embodied experiences and experiments, and, second, that was useful.[17] I consider each of these successively, before appraising the long shadow he cast over England's 'century of revolution' (Hill 1980). Bacon intended his *New Organon* to be the modern response to Aristotle's *Organon*, the classic scholastic manual of logic. Bacon's new logic substituted the certainty of the syllogism with the approximation of messy empirical verifications, constantly revised, and that sought to question the starting points that the syllogism had fixed. As Bacon (2000, 17) put it: 'we place the foundations of the sciences deeper and lay them lower, and set them further back than men have ever done before, subjecting them to examination'. 'We have committed ourselves to uncertain, rough and solitary ways' because the uncertainty of the senses was preferable to the false comforts of the syllogism, of the kinds that had locked medical knowledge into Galeen's falsehoods for fourteen centuries (Bacon 2000, 11), or of the kind that had Descartes (2006, 51) deplore that 'it is true that medicine as presently practiced contains little of notable benefit'. Bacon's embrace of uncertainty sowed the seeds for the invention of probability in the second half of the seventeenth century that we considered in the previous chapter.

Bacon's 'new' 'organ' or 'instrument' (*organum* translates as both) of knowledge production was the body. Like Descartes after him, he embraced uncertainty as the starting point for knowledge, and the centrality of sight. Only unlike Descartes, he did not look to an inner sense of certainty to counter this experiential uncertainty. He remained resolutely grounded in the messiness of embodied experiences. 'One must travel always through the forests of experience and particular things', Bacon (2000, 10) wrote. Indeed, 'if we prefer not to be insane we must derive everything from natural things', which is to say, for Bacon (2000, 18), from the senses. While 'others merely seem to honour and respect the senses, we do so in actual fact', he remarked pointedly (ibid). What was new, then, in Baconian science was not the instrument he placed at the centre of its development—the body—but a form of knowledge that, for all their flaws, still 'made the senses the sacred high priests of nature', at last (Bacon 2000, 18).

Bacon (2000, 24) recommended 'never to let the mind's eyes stray from things themselves, and to take in images', and presumably, for his physician, smells, 'exactly as they are'. 'We use the evidence of our own eyes or at least of our own perception, in everything, and apply the strictest criteria in accepting things, Bacon (2000, 21) wrote. Carefully designed experiments, then, were the only way to 'meet these defects' in the senses (Bacon 2000, 18). 'We speak of experiments that have been devised and applied specifically for the question under investigation with skill and good technique', such as Harvey's methodical dissections, which revealed the correct laws of blood circulation (ibid). Experiments were Bacon's (2000, 18) primary 'assistants to the senses'. They helped 'bring the matter to the point that the senses judge only of the experiment, the experiment judges of the thing'. Bacon's (2000, 170–71) secondary assistants in supporting the 'direct actions of sense' were instruments. Since 'sight holds first place among senses, as far as information is concerned', it is also 'the first sense for which we must first find aids' (ibid.). Here Bacon (2000, 171) also had Harvey's experiments on fleas, flies, and worms in mind when he referred to the microscope as an exemplary instrument. The second is the 'other magnifying glass', the telescope (Bacon 2000, 171).

A Useful Science: Dissecting and Dominating Nature

Harvey's dissections were the model experiment Bacon sought to generalise in the study of nature. His purpose was to lay the 'foundations of a true model of the world, as it is and not as any man's reason tell him it is' and this required 'performing a most careful dissection and anatomy of the world' (Bacon 2000, 96). Or again the new science:

> instructs and trains the understanding not (as common logic does) to grope and clutch at abstracts with feeble mental tendrils, but to *dissect nature truly*, and to discover the power and actions of bodies limned in matter. Hence this science takes its origin not only from the nature of the mind, but from the nature of things. (Bacon 2000, 219–20, emphasis added)

In an age of 'Anatomies of the World' (the title of Donne's poem cited earlier), dissection afforded the trope with which Bacon, ahead of Descartes and in England, conceived the modern project of subjugating nature.[18] The gratuitous 'contemplation of the truth' could no longer be the aim of nature's study (Bacon 2000, 96). Knowledge had to serve the purposes of 'human progress and empowerment' for Bacon (2000, 13), who was writing at a time of rapid innovations in the crafts (see Hill 1965). Moreover, this scientist-statesman decisively established the parallel between the dominion over nature and over the new world. 'The new world of the sciences and the new geographical world do not agree in the old being more refined than the new', he wrote (Bacon, cited in Weber 1975, 324). 'On the contrary', he continued, the purpose of the advancement in the arts and sciences was 'not only to bend nature gently, but to conquer and subdue, even to shake to her foundations.' Bacon conceived human empowerment as nature's and, as we will see in the chapter's final section, women's subjugation. He even mustered the Word of God to favour the eye over the text:

> For man by the fall fell at the same time from his state of innocence and from his dominion over creation. Both of these losses however can even in this life be in some part repaired; the former by religion and faith, the latter by the arts and sciences. (Bacon 2000, 221, translation slightly modified)

At a time when evangelical fervour ran to fever pitches, and drove people to the battlefield, Bacon cast the improvement of knowledge as a religious duty:

> And therefore it is not the pleasure of curiosity, nor the quiet of resolution, nor the raising of the spirit, nor victory or wit, nor faculty of speech, nor lucre of profession, nor ambition of honour or fame, nor inablement [*sic*] for business, that are the true ends of knowledge [...] it is *a restitution and reinvesting* (in

great part) *of man to the sovereignty and power* [. . .] which he had in his first
state of creation. (Bacon, cited in Webster 1975, 17, emphasis added)

To know nature became, in seventeenth-century England and under Bacon's
aegis, to control it, and peering into the body was the first step towards this divinely sanctioned mastery.

Bacon's Long Shadow and the Birth of an English Empirical Science

Bacon cast a long shadow over the century where England evolved from a scientific backwater to a vanguard of progress. His programme for the advancement of
knowledge was an evangelical call to arms, and it would be heeded, twice—by the
Puritans, the English Revolution's agents of change, and during the Restoration, two
key periods for the institutionalisation of science in seventeenth-century England.[19]
Bacon's vision for a society that granted a central role to a useful, applied science had
been popularised by his utopia, *the New Atlantis*, published just after his death in
1626. 'Baconianism' catalysed the movement of reform that swept through England's
institutions as the Parliamentarians gained ground, including through the universities; such that it 'became the official philosophy of the Revolution' (Webster 1975,
25; see also Hill 1980). The Puritans, who were proudly Baconian, envisaged the
new order that was to be instituted upon the ashes of the old order to be both providential and scientific; indeed, providential because scientific. In the *New Atlantis*
Bacon had dreamed up a state institution to house all knowledge, named Solomon's
House, after the utopic state's benevolent ruler and the biblical king. Parliament's
establishment in 1648 of an 'Office of Address' under Samuel Hartlib's auspices was
the first attempt to realise this vision. It was a national clearing house for collecting
and disseminating ideas and proposals to improve the organisation and governance
in all parts of the realm, from hospitals, to merchant companies, to commerce with
the colonies, and included various experiments in economic planning. It yielded
the Agency for Universal Learning, created during the English Civil War (in the late
1640s), effectively the first state agency for research and development (see Webster
1975, 97–98). The founders of the Royal Society of London for Improving of Natural
Knowledge (1660), however, were those who claimed the mythical lineage (and
denied it their predecessors). 'From These and all long Errors of the Way/in which
our wandering Praedecessors went. Bacon, like Moses, led us forth at last/The
Barren Wilderness He Past' reads Thomas Sprat's preface to the institution's earliest
history (cited in Jardine 2000, xxv).

To summarise, from witnessing Harvey's dissections upon the body, Bacon
derived general principles for a new science that foregrounded the body doubly,
as the site of experiments and of experience. But the body was also the piece of

nature to be conquered as part of a broader project of subjugating a feminine nature and the new world. Bacon catalysed the emergence of a distinctly English science; one that was experimental, empirical, masculine, aggressively self-confident, and doubly grounded in the body. In this section I have shown that this external, detached viewpoint upon the body was defined and elaborated by two powerful figures of early seventeenth-century England who were related by their networks, their status and their intellectual interests. This viewpoint would become progressively entrenched by an institution, the public anatomy lesson, to which I now turn.

2. The Public Anatomy Lesson

Piercing the Membrane of Knowledge

In the seventeenth century, the human body was instituted as the quintessential object of modern science by being, literally, opened up for a very public form of viewing. This transformation of the anatomy lesson from a pedagogical exercise (which is closer to how we know it today) into a large-scale public spectacle began in the late fifteenth century (Ferrari 1987). I will show through the rest of the chapter how this contained important state-building functions. To begin by gauging the cultural shift it represented it is useful to consider how the relations between the visible and the invisible were previously organised around the human body. First, the inside of the human body had marked both the frontier of the visible and the great unknown. Knowledge beyond this limit was possible only by analogy rather than by direct viewing. As Aristotle had put it in his *Historia animalium,* 'the fact is that the inner parts of the body are to a very great extent unknown, and the consequence is that we must recourse to the examination of the inner parts of other animals whose nature in any ways resembles that of man' (quoted in Wilson 1987, 75–76). Human corpses had been used prior to Vesalius, only sporadically and illicitly. In the new regime instead the human body was systematically and ritualistically pried open in order 'to probe the secrets of nature and nature's internal cunning', in the words of one of the earliest works on anatomy by the Venetian physician and Vesalius's precursor Benedictus, who formulated the very first rules of conduct for public anatomy lessons in his 1497 *Historia corporis humani sive Anatomice* (quoted in Rupp 1992, 37).[20] A seventeenth-century invitation to attend a public dissection in Switzerland read:

> Doctors of Medicine and Associates of the Faculty of Medicine, greetings to you all who read this. By the favour of our distinguished magistrates I shall reveal to the sight of any of you who are curious to see what Nature has enshrined

in all of us. Not out of a desire to vent malice on the work of God (the cadaver being that of an evil doer) but so that you may come to *know yourself* (cited in Hansen 1996, 667).

The invitation captures the moment when one regime of visibility around the body was yielding to another. It evidences a new anatomical discourse in the process of becoming institutionalised, yet that was still laced with the scientist's worry that his practices be perceived as violating the very norms that needed to be transformed in order to enable it. To assuage their readers the host-anatomist, like Hobbes (*L.* 3), conjured the Delphic oracle turned motto of the Renaissance, know yourself, to invite his viewers to look into the human body.

The object of the scientist's concerns was a host of religious and social norms that sacralised the human body in pre-modern Europe. Indeed the prior regime was underwritten, second, by Christian conceptions of the body as an inviolable whole. Preserving the integrity of the body was especially important given the belief that the body was integral to salvation (see Walker Bynum 1995). A person of faith could only be saved in his or her soul *and* body, hence dismembering a dead body directly impacted a person's prospects in the afterlife.[21] Body and soul were joined together by the theological concept of personhood, which underpins the Christian doctrine of resurrection. 'God's first care of man was his body, he made that first; and his last care is for the body too, at the Resurrection', John Donne sermoned (quoted in Sawday 1996, 126). Scientific and religious debates remained entwined well into the seventeenth century.[22] These religious proscriptions also shaped the practice of medicine, and sometimes yielded singular associations. For example, as of 1163 the clergy, who had been the habitual practitioners of medicine, were restricted in their practice by an ecclesiastical ruling declaring the Church's abhorrence to the spilling of blood (see Richardson 1988). They enlisted the help of barbers well versed in wielding blades for shaving and cutting hair to perform their surgical operation. This alliance continued until the creation the Company of Barbers and Surgeons in 1540.[23]

Three factors enabled the emergence of a new regime centred on looking into the body. The first was a gradual relaxation in the religious and civic authorities' attitudes towards the utilisation of human cadavers in dissections. In 1315 Modino de Luzzi obtained papal sanction for his human dissection in Bologna (Wilson 1987). The following year the anatomist published his *Anathomia corporis humani*, the manual that Vesalius's *Fabrica* was to supplant two and a half centuries later. The Bologna anatomy lesson was regularly attended by both papal and secular powers well into the eighteenth century (Ferrari 1987). In England, religious and civic authorities were conjoined by Henry VIII, the founder of the first national church. He first granted the Company of Barbers and Surgeons the right to dissect the bodies of four hanged felons in 1540. The shift in attitudes towards dissection was far from linear, however. Benedictus published his rules of conduct, in Venice in 1497, in a context where the public anatomy lesson was not fully accepted (Rupp 1992, 37). In England, the dread of the dissection remained a deeply engrained popular fear and a cause of public riots well into the nineteenth century (Richardson 1988). Jeremy Bentham would bequeath his own body to science in a very public dissection in order to address the enduring apprehensions of his countryfolk.

The publication of Vesalius's *De humani corporis fabrica* in 1543, the same year Copernicus published his *De revolutionibus orbium coelestium,* was a decisive second factor. Copernicus, and Galileo after him, had also been a medical student at Padua. The study of celestial bodies and of the human body was profoundly entwined from the earliest stages of modern science, intellectually and institutionally. Vesalius's manual revolutionised the institutions and pedagogy of medicine throughout Europe. It rapidly became the standard medical textbook; it was Harvey's and Locke's. By 1549 the University of Oxford had adopted statutes prescribing that medical students attend at least two dissections, and perform two more in order to obtain their degrees (Boston and Webb 2016). Cambridge's Caius College was dissecting two bodies a year by 1565 (Sawday 1996, 56). Chairs of anatomy began appearing all over Europe (Harrington 2013). In England the Lumleian Lectureship, which Harvey would occupy from 1616 to 1619, was founded in London in 1582, and in Oxford the Tomlins Readership in Anatomy was established in 1624 (Boston and Webb 2016).

The impact of Vesalius's textbook, which features almost two hundred striking woodcuts of flayed human bodies drifting elegantly across lofty landscapes, reverberated well beyond medical circles, at a time, moreover, where many of the great figures of the seventeenth century had studied medicine (Rembrandt in Leiden, the architect Cristopher Wren and Locke, both at Oxford). For Ruth Richardson (1988, 32), it achieved nothing short of 'revolutionis[ing] Western perceptions' of the body. At any rate, the fabric of the human body was rendered to the view like it had never been before, to a keen and rapidly growing learned audience across Europe. The third factor was the printing press, that crucial technology of the scientific, and in England, the political revolution, whose importance for the establishing 'vision as the master sense of the modern era' has been underlined by cultural historians (Jay 1988, 3).[24] By the late Renaissance, Vesalius's manual had become a staple of any respectable library; Descartes and Rembrandt were known to own copies (Sawday 1996). The circulation of Vesalius's textbook created an audience for the anatomy lesson that extended far beyond those who could attend the public lecture. It also sealed the bonds that were being woven over the human body between art, architecture, and anatomy. Leonardo da Vinci and Michelangelo were constantly seeking bodies to perfect their or their students' draughtsmanship, and they befriended anatomists and executioners. The human at the heart of 'humanism' was acquiring a rather literal and macabre meaning (Sawday 1996; Harrington 2013). Vesalius's frontispiece, which I analyse in the next section, was designed by a student of Titian's (Ferrari 1987).

The *Locus Anatomicus*

How best to present the dissected human body to a growing public became a topic of increasing concern in the second half of the sixteenth century. The anatomy lesson, it came to be thought, required a location of its own. The Parisian anatomist Charles Estienne devoted a chapter of his *De dissectione partium corporis humani libri tres* (written in 1530 and published in 1545) to the organisation and architecture of the *locus anatomicus*, the place of the anatomy. Like 'anything that is exhibited in a theatre in order to be viewed', he wrote, the body appears at its most advantageous when all of the spectators are able to see it clearly, with unobstructed views (quoted in Ferrari, 1987, 85). Estienne, like Benedictus before him (in 1497; see Rupp 1992, 46), offered detailed recommendations for a semicircular building adapted to the requirements of the anatomy lesson. This new edifice was to be based on the Vitruvian ratios, since the perfections of the human proportions demonstrated 'the ingenuity and workmanship of the Great Architect', in the words of fellow anatomist Vesalius (quoted in Sawday 1996, 109). In England the physicians had their hall purpose fit for dissections in 1583, following the creation of the Lumleian Lectureship (Nunn 2016). Padua, however, Vesalius's own university and epicentre of scientific advancement in the Renaissance (Galileo would also teach there), was where the archetype that would be copied throughout Europe was built in 1594. Leiden promptly followed suit two years later with an anatomy theatre that outrivalled its predecessor in both size and stature. Leiden would also be the first university to endorse the discovery made by Harvey, who was a former Padua medical student. In 1636 the Company of Barbers and Surgeons commissioned an anatomy theatre that was to replicate Padua's for their Monkwell Street premises in London (Sawday 1996; Nunn 2016). With no small sense of historical irony, the surgeons augmented their curiosities on display in its adjoining cabinets, which were an emulation of Leiden's, with a bust of the monarch's decapitated father (Sawday 1996, 76). By the end of the Renaissance the public anatomy lesson had thus acquired its own building, a purpose-fit edifice for prying open the human body that was modelled upon its proportions. It was crucial for the making of modern science and, I argue, the state.

The anatomy theatre was, in Holland, France, and England, the first of a wave of scientific institutions built in the seventeenth century that performed distinct state-building functions. It catalysed a sense of national pride within, and stoked a scientific rivalry between these nascent states within the emerging Westphalian state system.[25] In a world undergoing profound epistemological and social transformations, the annual public dissection signalled the public authorities' commitment to advancing the new sciences. Or not. Locally, Amsterdam's and Leiden's anatomy theatres rapidly became emblems of the cities' flourishing cultural and intellectual lives (Hansen 1996). Nationally, in a country in the process of asserting its own statehood in the wake of the truce with Spain (signed in 1609), they served to build the new nation's symbolic capital. The divine George Hakewill, returning from a visit to Leiden in 1627, commenting on the lack of a public anatomy demonstration in Oxford, deplored his own university's tardiness at keeping up with Leiden's forwardness (Sawday 1996, 42).[26] 'Where have we constant readings on either quick or dead *Anatomies*?' complained for his part the poet and Hobbes's friend John Hartlib in 1649, who was frustrated with the ad hoc nature of the demonstrations given at the Royal College of Physician (quoted in ibid.) The public anatomy lesson and its purpose-fit building became landmarks of the nascent modern state's investment in scientific progress.

In England, Harvey's public dissections were inscribed, we have seen, in a broader trajectory of institutionalisation of an English experimental science that withstood the turmoil of the civil war and yielded the Royal Society in 1662 (Hunter 1981; Webster 1975). Its incorporation was one of Charles II's first acts upon acceding to the throne. Perhaps no one better understood the fragility of the restored monarchy than the son of the beheaded king, and how, in an age of rapid scientific development, championing this progress was a way to consolidate both the legitimacy of his personal rule, and the unity of the realm around an English science. Perhaps also Charles II took a leaf out of the book of his powerful French counterpart Louis XIV, who had founded the *Académie Française* in 1635, having had the occasion to observe first-hand during his exile in Paris and under Hobbes's tutorship the importance of this national institution of learning in fostering a sense of national unity. Whatever his reasons, Charles II established himself as both the patron of the science and the sovereign of one of the nascent Westphalian system's first modern states. England and Holland specifically exemplify the extent to which modern science and the state were born hand in hand upon the anatomised body.

The public lesson was the heart of this new regime of corporeal visuality. Anatomy theatres were 'second only to the playhouse' in England in the sixteenth and seventeenth centuries as sites of large-scale public performances (Sawday 1996, 212). They generally counted between three hundred and six hundred spectators who hailed from all ranks of society (Rupp 1992). In parts of Europe, such as Italy, they were sometimes more attended than any other public event in the year, including religious celebrations (Rupp 1992). Admission was free in many cities, notably Padua and Bologna. In Bologna, they blended with the Carnevale celebrations (Ferrari 1987). The demonstration itself was a highly ritualised spectacle, involving one or more lectures, held over several days, generally in the colder weeks before Christmas, and a couple of animals (often a pig, dog, or monkey) being dissected alive. Its pièce de résistance was the dissection of one or several human corpses (depending on the speed of putrefaction), generally that of a criminal or a foreigner. The lesson was often lit by scented candles to augment the dim wintery light, sometimes accompanied by music, and generally followed by a banquet (Hansen 1996). There were also various sideshows, and a range of curiosities of natural history were on display in the cabinets of death that surrounded the theatre (Hansen 1996; Wilson 1987). On the inside the theatres were adorned with paintings and sculptures commissioned from European masters, and indeed of past kings.

Born Hungry for Bodies: Public and Private Demands

The new regime was driven by a seemingly insatiable desire to see the body's insides. The first crisis in the provision of corpses occured in England in the second half of the seventeenth century. It was caused by a rapidly expanding demand for dead bodies, and by a dip in the rates of executions (before their subsequent increase under the effects of the Black Acts in the eighteenth century; see Sawday 1996, 57). In England the demand had two sources, public and private, which I consider successively. From the dissection's earliest regulations onwards and throughout Europe, the scaffold had been its primary source of bodies. The law supplied science its corpses (Rupp 1992). Only England illustrates the profound entwinement of these two early-modern inventions, the state and the public anatomy lesson. It was no mere coincidence that the monarch who broke away from prior modes of a layered, imperial governance centred on Rome to establish the sovereign as the highest point of political-cum-religious power in the realm (Henry VIII) was also the one who first incorporated the professional body that dissected, the Company of Barbers and Surgeons, in 1540. The surgeons were granted four felon bodies per year. Elizabeth I extended this right to claim criminal bodies to the Royal College of Physicians in 1565 (O'Malley, Poynter, and Russel 1961; Nunn 2016). The physicians' demand was new. Their college had been incorporated by her father in 1518. However, before Vesalius, they had looked down on the dissection. This new demand illustrates how the human body had become the front line of scientific advancement, such that opening it up could no longer be left to the lowly surgeons.[27] In 1641 Charles I extended the physicians grant from four to six criminal bodies, and in 1662 the Royal Society was also granted the right to dissect criminal bodies by Charles II (Sawday 1996, 57).

The Tudor penal code, moreover, introduced the use of the dissection as a mode of punishment for egregious crimes of murder (Richardson 1988, 76). From the onset the early-modern dissection was durably established in a central place in the state's punitive apparatus. Its role would be further consolidated by the 1752 Murder Act, which instituted the public dissection as the specific form of punishment for the crime of murder, in addition to the death penalty. In this way the state supplied science with the bodies it required, and science assisted the state in executing the death penalty which, for Locke, was the fount of political power and thus of all law-making (see chapter 4). The relation between science and the state was reciprocal and mutually reinforcing. The public anatomy lesson prolonged into death the state's performance of its sovereign power to kill upon the criminal body. It was both underwritten by a new regime of visuality, and it implicated the two distinct acts of seeing: witnessing and spectating.

In England, this desire to see the secrets nature hides in us fuelled a rapidly expanding 'corpse economy' (Sawday 1996, 58). The commodification of the dead body occurred throughout Europe (and in the United States). Only this macabre market was especially developed in (then) Great Britain, where, outside of these licensed areas where the public dissections took place, and unlike on the continent (see Rupp 1992), the state left the supply of corpses to the anatomist's table largely unregulated. It was driven primarily by a private demand, evincing a widespread desire to see inside the human body. The sources of this private demand were, first, the anatomy schools that mushroomed around England from the seventeenth century onwards to train medical students, but also to satisfy a more nebulous desire to take part in a scientific enterprise perceived as the vanguard of progress. (These anatomy schools were often very wasteful; see Sawday 1996.) Second, the lucrative skills of embalming attracted increasing interest from an ever larger number of corporations and guilds, beyond the professional bodies of 'scientists' broadly writ (the Royal Society, the College of Physicians, and the Company of Barbers and Surgeons); like the butchers, the tailors and the chandlers (see Sawday 1996; Richardson 1988; Harrington 2013). The waxing demand for dead bodies generated or intensified a whole range of practices that developed to diversify the sources of supply (beyond the scaffold), such as snatching bodies out of graves and, in various stages of dying, from hospitals and orphanages, but also in private homes. Unimpeded by a state that was reluctant to interfere with what was perceived as science's needs, this demand expanded exponentially throughout the seventeenth and eighteenth centuries (Richardson 1988). It would drive up the value of corpses to the point that 'the bodies of the poor became worth more dead than alive', which Ruth Richardson (1988, 132) locates around 1827–28. Murders for dissection was the last instalment in the development of this morbid trade. The plundered graveyards, intensifying waves of public panic, and popular riots, which saw anatomy schools burned to the ground (in Aberdeen and Sheffield, for example), eventually led to the passage of the 1832 Anatomy Act, which Jeremy Bentham helped draft. It brought these body-snatching practices to an end by establishing a permanent supply of corpses to satisfy science's demands: the poorhouse and the hospice.[28]

The early modern, public, anatomy lesson was, above all, a spectacle. It was a joint performance by the new science and the nascent state upon the criminal's body, that served to display and reproduce their knowledge and powers. In the remainder of the chapter I will consider successively the work of epistemological and political ordering the public performance achieved. For this spectacle was also amply represented, and these visual materials offer an apt medium for appraising the work of ordering in which seeing played a key role. My primary materials comprise the frontispiece to Vesalius's *On the Fabric of the Human Body* (1943), complemented by additional engravings drawn from the textbook, and Rembrandt's *Anatomy Lesson of Dr Nicholaes Tulp* (fig. 7.4), which I also set into relief with his other paintings in the genre. I analyse the epistemological ordering by considering how the audience was represented in these two sets of materials in part 3. In the fourth and final part, I will analyse the work of political ordering that was wrought by the public performances by turning to the body lying across each of their dissection tables.

3. Epistemological Orderings

Crafting the Audiences: Modern Scientific Subjects-in-the-Making

Vesalius's De fabrica corporis humanis

Vesalius's frontispiece features a rambunctious Renaissance audience closing in on the dissecting anatomist, who is none other than Vesalius himself (see fig. 7.1). Unlike Rembrandt's anatomy lesson paintings the following century, the engraving is executed in a symbolic rather than a realist key. Indeed, the only touch of realism rests in the portrayal of Vesalius himself. Some audience members are naked. A monkey and a dog, which are next in line for the dissection, are running about untethered. The anatomy theatre itself, with its Corinthian columns, is an idealisation, since the frontispiece was etched half a century before this Renaissance building was actually realised. The rowdy rabble represents an audience of subjects who are learning to see for themselves by looking directly into a human body, with all the affective charge that doing so entailed. Anatomy lesson publics were notoriously agitated (Sawday 1996; Nunn 2017). Fittingly for the frontispiece of the first textbook of modern medicine, they are scientific subjects-in-the-making. The importance of sight, of seeing for oneself, is rendered by this lively audience, but also by Vesalius's staring straight out at the readers, inviting them to join in this collective act of looking. They too were modern scientific subjects-in-the-making. They are the designated spectatorship—the Galileos, Descarteses, Leonardos, and Rembrandts who all owned copies of the textbook. Vesalius's frontispiece captures the levelling out of epistemic authority that begat modern science. The anatomist takes centre stage; this is the cover to his textbook after all. Only he is without the main props of the medieval lesson, the text and the pulpit. Earlier physicians would profess anatomical 'truths' remotely, from on high and out of a book, while the body was left to the surgeons to handle. Vesalius lays his hand on the body; he peels back the skin of the abdomen to bear its inner organs to the view. He is teaching his audience to see for themselves, to appropriate some of the epistemic authority that was previously concentrated in the text and jealously guarded by the anatomist. He is instructing them in how to become seeing, thinking things, to paraphrase Descartes: the autonomous subjects of modernity. His relation to the body, moreover, is unmediated; and sight, not a book, is his main pedagogical tool. Vesalius established a direct relation between the subject and object of knowledge. This was the axis of the transfer of epistemic authority from the text and the pulpit to the scientific subject. It is the foundational structure of modern science.

Rembrandt's Anatomy Lesson of Dr Nicholaes Tulp

This subject-object relation is also at the heart of Rembrandt's 1632 *Anatomy Lesson of Dr Nicholaes Tulp* (fig. 7.4). The painting was executed four years after Harvey's *De Motu cordis* and the year before Galileo's condemnation by the Church. It was commissioned by the Amsterdam physician's guild to adorn the city's anatomy theatre and to outdo Leiden.[29] Dr Tulp was both the city's master surgeon and its mayor. His *Observationes medicae*, which were translated into the vernacular, rapidly became a popular medical textbook.

Rembrandt instituted the anatomy lesson painting as a new genre by adapting a classical form of Dutch seventeenth-century painting, the group portrait. At the height of Holland's golden age, group portraits served to project the rising social and economic, but also epistemic and cultural, power of corporations. They traditionally depicted a celebratory banquet that marked an important event in the life of a corporation, such as the review of accounts. Rembrandt replaced the banquet with a corpse, and he made the collective act of viewing the central object of the painting (Hansen 1996). In contrast to the boisterous and very public scene of Vesalius's frontispiece, Rembrandt's is intimate. The theatre, a key feature in Vesalius's engraving, is merely adumbrated in the background. Rembrandt closed in on the subjects' cognitive experience, on the moment when knowledge carries from the teacher to the students, symbolised by the book lying open on the bookstand to the bottom right, possibly Vesalius's *De Fabrica* (Sawday 1996).

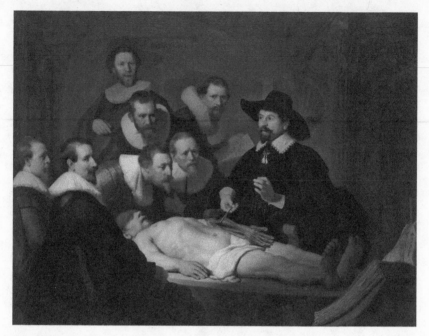

Figure 7.4 Rembrandt, The Anatomy Lesson of Dr Nicholaes Tulp (1632)
Source: n/a

The scene depicts a group of learners tightly gathered around a corpse in whose natural order they are being instructed by the city anatomist, Dr Tulp (see fig 7.4). The audience, to the left, comprises seven clearly identifiable members of Amsterdam's physicians' guild clad in the corporation's uniform and whose names are scribbled on the piece of paper held up by the figure furthest back from the viewer who stares back at her or him to close in the scene. These guild members would have paid for the privilege of being featured individually. The 'evil doer', who did not pay, and whose body was being offered up to science, most likely against his will, given the widespread popular fear of dissections (Richardson 2001), was Adriaan Adriaenszoon, a repeat offender who was put to death for stealing another's property—a coat. The anatomist, to the right, is depicted in full professorial flight, left hand held upright with index and thumb closed. The gesture with which the physician punctuates his scientific exposé illustrates the very movement of the muscles that mobilises the flexor tendons he is pointing to in the corpse's flayed arm; a nod to Vesalius and to Harvey (see fig. 7.2 and fig. 7.3). Two of the learners stare directly at the viewer, drawing them into an intimate setting created by the play of light. With these seven figures, Rembrandt aptly captured the range of ambivalent emotions that discovering the anatomical inside might inspire; from a learner's intense concentration, to an avid curiosity tinged with desire (the gentleman in the middle leaning into the open wound), to wonderment, anxiety, and queasiness. He seized the liminal moment where different individuals, with their idiosyncrasies, were being moulded into modern scientific subjects and taught to see nature's secrets for themselves. The book (but not the pulpit) has reappeared, only it is no longer central; it frames the anatomy lesson to its bottom right. The viewer likely discovers it after she or he has taken in the rest of the scene, where the dramatic action lies. The viewing sequence echoes modern science's process of knowledge production, where the text records what the eye has seen, instead of dictating what it must see.

Sight is the painting's topic. First, it separates out the sight-less corpse from the seeing subjects of knowledge, the semicircle formed by the seven physicians-in-learning and the anatomist. This distinction structures the painting itself. A band of darker light lining the physicians' collars divides it into two panes, an upper two-thirds, where the physicians feature in full formal garb, peering—leering even—into the naked body lying across its lower pane that is being punished once again, in death, and with no small sense of irony from the painter, for the property crime that would have clad it. This spatial division is reinforced by the relations between the two kinds of bodies: upright, clothed and several; supine, bare and singular. The painting's upper two-thirds marks the space of *subjectivation*, where the making of modern scientific subjects out of a range of individual constitutions—of subjectivities—is depicted in the ways we have seen. The lower pane is the space of *objectification*, where science's object, the corpse is being crafted. I will turn to the processes of objectification in the following section. But, second, sight is the painting's topic, not merely as the physical fact of seeing, but as viewpoint—not only as 'vision' but as 'visuality' (Foster 1988). The circle of subjects is completed on its fourth wall, to use a term from the theatre, by the viewer. This is the site of the visual orde*ring*, from which order is seen and for which the painting's composition is ordained.

Notwithstanding the painting's intimate ambiance, third, the type of seeing at work here was not the witnessing conjured in the private theatre of the conscience. It was without the introspective quality that Donne's anatomical poems still evoked, and that the looking-glass motif in Renaissance representations also invoked. This theatre was public. But nor was it an interpreting. The realism of Rembrandt's painting contrasts with the symbolism of Vesalius's engraving, in which a clean skeleton ominously brandishing a staff hovers directly above the dissected body, in an echo of the classic Renaissance *vanitas* (generally a skull) that reminded the viewers of their own mortality. Vesalius's frontispiece, with both its realistic dissection and this *memento mori*, functions like a bridge between a pre-modern world of analogies, and one where the aim had instead become to keep 'the mind's eye' firmly set upon 'things themselves' and to take them in 'exactly as they are' as Bacon (2000, 24) had put it, in order to develop a 'model of the world' based on their 'true appearances'. In Rembrandt's painting, death is rendered eerily tangible; the vibrant hues of the physicians' faces contrasting sharply with the cadaver's grey tones—grey like the paper of the book upon which its anatomy is recorded. Rembrandt has captured death in all its rawness, unsymbolised. Like Bacon's science, he maintained the viewer's eyes upon the thing itself. This new mode of looking, then, is the abstracting, anatomising gaze of modern science, that parses organisms into their constituent parts, and then reconstitutes their order on paper.

Five years before fellow Leiden student Descartes articulated the structure of modern science in his *Discourse on the Method* (1637), Rembrandt captures the act of rending the subjects from the objects of knowledge. But he also complicates the habitual characterisation of modern science's cold 'conquering gaze from nowhere' (Harraway 1988, 581; see also Jay 1988; Bryson 1986). Here the dissecting gaze is still situated; it is incarnated by these living, troubled, desiring perhaps, at any rate, binocular subjects who are processing the complex experience of witnessing a dissection, and with whom the viewer identifies. This is what is so powerful about his painting, and, I suggest, where its subversive potential lies. Rembrandt's is an original scene in the construction of 'natural vision'; only the vision he renders is still two-eyed. It is not the 'lone eye' of modern power (Jay 1988, 7). On the one hand, we are witnessing the formation of the modern scopic regime upon the body. In fact, in offering such finely crafted identificatory points to hook the viewer in, Rembrandt is actively partaking in the making of the modern scientist. On the other hand, he also appears to trouble the epistemic structure he reveals. The boundary between life and death drawn by the line of light and colour is rather thin and vaporous. The forearm and arm of the professor and the cadaver mirror one another uncannily. The line between life and death, between the knowing subject and dissected object, is fine indeed, and could dissipate at any moment, Rembrandt seems to suggest. In these ways he complicates the subject-object relation that the public performance aimed to fix once and for all. Ultimately all bodies resemble one another in the painter's eye. The social relations ordaining who falls on either side of this line are precarious indeed.

Objectifying and Mechanizing the Body and Nature

To know the body was to be able to accurately represent it. This was Rembrandt's and all the other artists scouting the town for body parts' concern. The corpse in the painting is coextensively an object of study and of mastery, which were the two sides of the classical coin, in the arts as in the sciences. The body in the seventeenth century was the privileged site of the two transformations that decisively modified the human relation to nature, objectification and mechanisation. I consider each in turn.

Rembrandt staged in an anatomy theatre the key operator of this objectification, the anatomising gaze. The body, by this gaze, was seized from without, on the mode of the object.[30] By the same token, it became the remainder and the reminder of a nature that was no longer a dwelling-place, that was being set at a remove to be studied and mastered (see also chapter 1). The body in this painting has shed the symbolism that attached to it in Renaissance representations, and become instead a synecdoche for this nature. This, precisely at the time when the relation to it was shifting from a 'lived in' relation, in which nature afforded a reservoir of signs and analogies to be endlessly deciphered, to one where it was but a numbered series of phenomena to be observed, measured, and 'conquered by obedience' (to its law), to add Bacon's (2000, 24) formula to Descartes's. The painting renders the objectification of nature that was under way in its dual dimensions of a distancing and a putting to death (see Merchant 1980). Visuality is this synecdoche's register. In the invitation I considered earlier, the anatomy lessons were justified in terms of the Delphic oracle turned motto of the Renaissance, *Nosce te Ipsum* (know thyself), that Hobbes (*L.* 4) also invoked to open the *Leviathan*. Only here it was rewritten in a visual key. To know oneself had become 'to see what Nature has enshrined in all of us'.

Mechanism, the Body, and State-making

The profound transformation of Western knowledge that began in the Renaissance and culminated with the invention of probability heralded the rise of mechanism. Although this peculiar ontology of the seventeenth century was short-lived, it was, I argue, decisive in is effects, epistemological and political. In mechanism lay the promise of being able to build a world founded in the *mathesis universalis* at last. This was the classical age's ideal of a mathematically expressible matrix underwriting the natural order. The human body played an important yet overlooked part in the broad 'mechanisation of the world picture' (Dijksterhuis 1961). Vesalius had rendered its make up or 'fabric' (*fabrica*) visible to a broad audience.[31] Knowledge of this 'machine (. . .) made by the hands of God', 'incomparably better ordered' and with 'more amazing movements than any that than any that can be created by the hands of man', was nevertheless what would enable humans to make machines, as Descartes (2006, 46) underscored. The body was the principle referent for the clockwork imagery that accompanied mechanism's take-off in the first half of the seventeenth century.

Epistemologically, mechanism underwrote both sides of the rationalism versus empiricism divide (see chapter 3). It contributed to the dismantling of the final cause, because it substituted *function* for *meaning*. Anatomical function afforded an important model for this new way of envisaging causality. To study nature was no longer to appraise how natural beings occupied their places and fulfilled their purposes, both of which were determined by a created order. It was no longer to apprehend their final cause. Its aim instead was to understand the function that the different (body) parts played in the natural clockwork that was to be emulated in building clocks and other kinds of machines, like the state. Function and the final cause are both determinations of what something is for. Only function is without the dimension of meaning that the final cause also vehicled. The final cause had provided the terms for articulating the relations between the body and the soul. The soul was considered to contain the essence or *logos* of a being. It gave significance—a meaning and a direction—to its embodiment.[32] In the body lay its material cause, but the soul contained both its formal and its final causes. It conferred a finality and a direction to material being (including in a developmental sense: a child was a human-in-becoming); its raison d'être. This dimension of meaning inherent to the final cause is rendered by the Christian theology's appropriation of the Greek notion of *logos*, which reconfigures the Christ as the *Logos* bringing meaning and direction to humanity (he offered the prospect of redemption following an original sin). Instead with mechanism, an instrumental, anatomical function came to replace the final cause.[33]

Foucault (2005) granted a minor role to mechanism, which had largely fallen to the wayside by the early eighteenth century. On this, his account is consistent with traditional histories of science and philosophy, which see that century at heralding the ascent of 'life'. Life was also, in fact, at stake in mechanism; the dark underside that the woman on Vesalius' dissection slab serves to reveal, I will show in the chapter's final part. My contention here, however, is that mechanism had largely served its unnoticed political purpose, to help craft the state. Mechanism furnished the imaginary required to make thinkable a different kind of distinctly human, non-natural agency: the modern agency that built the state. By erasing the difference between natural and artificial bodies, it provided a level plane whereon all objects, immobile and mobile, human and non-human, could be apprehended in the same way. As Hobbes (*L.* 3) put it, '[W]hy may we not say that all *automata* (engines that move themselves by springs and wheels as doth a watch) have an artificial life?' With mechanism, we may. It afforded him a solution to the problem, that he decisively shifted from the epistemological to the political level, of how to apprehend moving bodies (see chapter 2). This solution was not straightforwardly yielded by the new concept of space and matter as *res extensa*. For the human body was not just extended. It moved, and was moved by an infinite number of passions. It was the moving, highly volatile, extended thing that needed to be placed within this other extended thing that was also being circumscribed, the state. Mechanism added the *automata* to the grand levelling out wrought by modern space. Hobbes saw the promise it held for the political problem he set out to address.

Whereas geometry's line-drawing afforded the means to conceive (and achieve, see chapter 2) the outward bounding of this new political form, seeing all moving bodies, including political subjects, as *automata* furnished a new way of addressing the intractable problem of how to organise their orderly coexistence within it. Automata could be correctly arranged by building the right kind of machine. To define the problem of war in these terms was to render it resolvable after all. Mechanism enabled Hobbes (*L.* 3) to transform the tragic human problem of how to create a peaceful order into a technical question of how to correctly (re)assemble the different parts of the political machine, in order to give 'life and motion to the whole body'. It made it possible to reduce '*magistrates* and other *officers*' to 'artificial *joints*'; while '*reward* and *punishment*', as this mechanical body's '*nerves*', 'do the same as in the body natural'; its councillors are its '*memory*'; and so forth. Peace-making became clockwork, a complex but not irresolvable engineering problem.

Producing a Human Universal out of Particular Bodies

Knowledge, since Aristotle, was of the universal, as we saw in chapter 3. At stake in the anatomy lesson was the possibility of producing a human universal out of the body lying across the dissection table. The promise the demonstration held was that of revealing the anatomical foundations of a human nature, and thus the physical, visible answer at last to the question that had forever lain at the heart of western philosophy: what is man? A few chosen body parts served to craft the level of generality at which 'what nature has enshrined in all of us' could be laid bare to the view. These were the forearm and arm, featured in the *Anatomy Lesson of Dr Nicholaes Tulp*, the body parts implicated 'artificing' (see chapter 3); and the brain, the container of Descartes's (2006, 47) 'universal instrument', reason, which is represented in Rembrandt's second anatomy lesson painting, the *Anatomy Lesson of Dr Deijman* (1656). Ordering, in this sense, was a process of distinguishing, for the audience's benefit, the markers of this particular body (which denoted a disease, an accident, or a trade) from the generic attributes of the human anatomy. Criminal bodies were favoured by the anatomist because they were generally young. The epistemological ordering that was undertaken upon the corpse, then, was a work of de-particularising, or de-individualising, the dissected subject, in order to expose the general workings of *the* human body.

The anatomy lesson itself thus operated at the level of the universal. However, the criminal body was never fully stripped of its social particulars. It was not anonymised, for one. To the contrary, the corpse's identity, generally that of criminal, was always publicised prior to the dissection. The use of 'criminal corpses' was widespread across Europe since Benedictus, whose rules of conduct (1497) had afforded the template for public regulations (cited in Rupp 1992, 37). In fact, a crucial tension was playing out upon the anatomised body, between this epistemological pull towards the universal and an obverse pull, toward the particular, encapsulated in the need to attribute the body to 'an evil doer'. The body stretched across the dissection slab was both at once a universal human exemplar and a particular criminal body. This body, to which I now turn, helps reveal the work of political ordering wrought by the public anatomy lesson. It also brings class and gender into focus.

4. Inside/Outside: Ordering the Modern Body Politic upon the Body

The work of epistemological line-drawing upon the dissected body doubled up as a series of political boundary-drawings that reasserted the bounded community of white bourgeois male consenters. This was the implicitly designated constituency for and of the nascent state, in theory, as we saw with Locke in the previous chapters, and in practice, I will now show. The body laid across Rembrandt's dissection table illuminates the class elements of this line-drawing, while Vesalius's lays bare its gendered dimensions. I will consider the role of class with Rembrandt in this section, and gender with Vesalius in the next one. I begin, however, by considering the specific form of corporeal violence that the public anatomy lesson brought into play.

Drawing Lines across the Body: The State-making Functions of Corporeal Violence

The annual anatomy lesson was the occasion of another kind of social learning altogether, civic rather than scientific, regarding where the line of the law ran and what were the consequences for crossing it. This instruction in how to become a law-abiding political subject had bodily violence at its core. Or rather, this violence was somatic in its execution (it was deployed upon the body) and symbolic in its effects. Fragmented bodies and body parts were pervasive in early-modern culture, in the theatre as well as in poetry and painting; tokens of old orders that were being dismantled. My contention is that, in its dual dimensions, this violence was properly symbol*ising*, generative of modernity's symbolic order and of the new political forms it sustained. This bodily violence requires being appraised against an epistemic backdrop where the traditional Aristotelian distinctions between 'natural' and 'violent' or 'disruptive' (*to automaton*) movements was collapsing; as was the old hierarchy between (superior) stillness and (inferior) motion (see chapter 1). What was ordering, or disordering, was no longer so set. In fact, for Hobbes, for one, mechanical, automatic motions were less disruptive than the natural human ones. My argument, then, is that, at this unique symbolic, epistemological and political juncture, a specific form of spectacular violence upon the body became the midwife to the state.[34]

This was not the violence of the battlefield that crushed bodies en masse. It was carefully performed upon the single body and dressed in ritual. Nor was it the entrenched, fully institutionalised violence of a more contemporary kind, whose effects are visible but rarely the violence itself. It was not Bourdieu's symbolic violence, for example; which, though also embodied, leaves the body intact, and whose effectiveness rests on remaining unseen. Being widely seen was integral to this violence. Noteworthy in this respect is that not all anatomy lessons were public. The 1606 Amsterdam city ordinances required that 'at least one' dissection be open to the public (cited in Hansen 1996, 665). Something more than the lesson alone was at stake in performing it to a broader public, in the spectacle itself. This is what made it a ready theme for the theatre, where the dissection itself was often staged (in part or in full), in an effect of mise en abyme by which the audience was given to see another audience peering into the human body (see Owen 2005, Nunn 2016).

The public anatomy lesson was a carefully choreographed spectacle of corporeal punishment. It was not the violent spectacle of the Roman games that pitted one man against another or against a beast, for instance. While the games could produce very mangled bodies, their violence lay in the contenders' strength and was proportional to it. It was expended in the spectacle. At play instead here was the collectivised, disproportionate force that Locke defined as political power (see chapter 5). This corporeal violence indexed and conjured a broader apparatus of knowledge and power-in-the-making. The spectacle wrought constitutive effects on both ends of the modern political relation I track. On the side of the state, the ritualized and public deployment of the power to punish upon the body helped perform into being the institution whose power it expressed. This, moreover, at the time when this power was concentrating and the penal apparatus was becoming increasingly centralised (see chapter 4). The two principle architects of this centralisation, Henry VIII and Elizabeth I, were also the first grantors of bodies to the modern dissection. The institutionalization of the public anatomy lesson and of the state thus went hand in hand. In England this process continued in earnest beyond the timeframe I consider in this book. It reach its apex with the 1752 Murder Act, which, by way of the penal dissection, a new form of punishment designed to inscribe a 'peculiar mark of infamy' upon the murderer's corpse, formalized the dissection's role in the punitive apparatus of the state (quoted in Richardson 1987; see also Sawday 1996).

On the side of the subject, the spectacle crafted the publics that the state and the nascent scopic regime required. The dissuasive effects of the penal dissection were aimed at the public rather than at the offender (who was dead). Whether the dissection was witnessed or not, news of it would travel. But the spectacle was also a lesson performed for a large audience of modern learners that aimed to rid them of their superstitions and to teach them to see in a scientific manner. It helped create the modern public of docile scientific-cum-political subjects. On account of the high attendance, especially where admission was free (in Padua and Bologna, for instance), Benedictus recommended the appointment of 'stewards' and 'warders' to 'regulate the unruly incoming rabble' and to shape it into an orderly audience organised by rank and class (quoted in Rupp 1992, 45).[35] A scenography dressed the bodily violence in meanings. The dissection itself was preceded by an opening ritual where the name of the dissected subject was announced; the nature of the person's misdemeanour; the means of his or her execution, and sometimes his or her origin. The words 'our subject for the anatomy lesson has been hanged' often rang loudly around the Bologna anatomy theatre, where this method of execution was favoured because it left the organs intact (Sawday 1996, 75; Harrington 2013). The symbolic apparatus erected around the spectacle thus served the dual functions of integrating it into the penal system and of helping the audience make sense of why this person was punished. It is also the reason Mr. Adriaenszoon's identity and his 'evil deed'—stealing a coat, no less—are still known to us today.

Class: To Be Dissected for Stealing A Coat

Though it was generative of new orders on one level, the public anatomy lesson also effected, on another, a series of boundary-drawings that helped keep the established social order in place. The line of the law was drawn across the body of a person who had crossed it for everyone else to see and to dissuade them from following suit. Locke's (*TT*, II.chap.4[22]284) 'standing Rule' was deployed upon the body of someone who had failed to 'live by it'—and who no longer stood as a result. The dissected body belonged to an outlaw and it served to reassert the limit of the law. Since the fifteenth century Benedictus had prescribed the use of 'criminal corpses' (quoted in Rupp 1992, 37). But Benedictus's other recommendation was to use 'only humble and unknown persons [...] from distant regions' wherever possible (cited in Rupp 1992, 37 and 45). Class and foreignness, in addition to criminality, were thus explicit criteria for selecting the body to dissect from the onset. The Amsterdam ordinances combined these rules. They prescribed that the dissected subject, in addition to being a criminal, must also be someone who was 'not a citizen of the city where the dissection was performed, and had no relatives there' to claim the body (Rupp 1992, 47). The city of Bologna authorised the use of the 'meanest' bodies, of those too penniless to pay for their burial in the city cemetery (Ferrari 1987, 87). Foreignness sometimes also trumped criminality. Dr Tulp's successor, Dr Ruysch, was known to have dissected a non-criminal Italian subject in Amsterdam in 1684 (Hansen 1996).

The dissected body thus belonged, by law, to an outsider. This served to reassert the limits, not just of the law, but of who qualified for inclusion in the ordered polity that was also being reaffirmed by science. The foreigner was an outsider by the law. Per the criminalisation of custom we considered in chapter 5, the poor was increasingly being made a criminal in the law. Locke, we also saw, erased poverty altogether from his picture of political order by casting it as an extra-political threat to be contained by laws (see chapter 5). Instead Rembrandt, in choosing to represent a coat thief, and in the way he staged the relations between the two sets of bodies (the eight upright, formally clad bourgeois physicians who stare down at the supine, naked, single corpse), rendered poverty visible as a motive for breaking the law. Mr Adriaenszoon may have stolen the coat because he was cold. This was, I have suggested, Rembrandt's critical touch. Yet the institution he depicted operated as a site that produced or reasserted the distinction between insiders and outsiders, between those who rightfully qualified for membership in the polity whose boundaries were being reasserted and those who did not. What Rembrandt showed was that, by way of the dissected body (of the specific body that was chosen for the lesson), this political membership was being defined on the basis of class—on the basis, then, of the subjects' social origins, and not strictly of their deeds. Here is, once again, the Lockean bourgeois community of consenters, being delineated in the practice of medicine as the proper constituency for the modern state, just as it would be adumbrated in theory by Locke. The dissected body served to separate out the orderly inside populated by respectable subjects from an outside of undesirables (see chapter 5). The role of the anatomy lesson in the consolidation of class in Great Britain would be ruthlessly confirmed two centuries later by the 1832 Anatomy Act. Designed to allay the growing popular outrage at grave robberies, the act legalised the resort to the bodies of those dying in workhouses, prisons, and hospitals who were too indigent to cover their burial costs. As Ruth Richardson (2001, xv) put it, 'what had for long been feared and hated as a punishment for murderer [per the Murder Act] became one for poverty'.

The anatomised body was a co-creation by modern science and the state that sealed a symbiotic and mutually constitutive relationship. The anatomy lesson prolonged, in a second public performance and into death, the spectacular demonstration of the sovereignty of the law upon the body of an outlaw – of someone who had either crossed the law, as a criminal, or who stood beyond it, as a foreigner. In either case, this person was not a natural member of the polity whose standing rule this law was, in Locke's language. A nascent modern science showcased to an audience of modern political subjects-in-the-making the state's power to kill, while the latter procured the former the bodies it required to pierce the frontiers of knowledge, and a means to legitimise a practice that still stirred stomachs and social unrest. Science did not merely receive the body once the state had expended its lethal power, moreover. The anatomist often chose the means of execution (Rupp 1992). Executions were often delayed until the colder months to suit the anatomist (Shackleford 2003). The relationship was reciprocal. In establishing dissection as the ultimate penalty for those who had dared to appropriate the state's power to kill, the 1752 Murder Act marked the crowning point of this trajectory of mutual constitution of science and the state. The 1832 Anatomy Act showed that this mutual constitution also preserved intact existing social strata. Having considered the role of class, I now locate gender in the public anatomy lesson.

Gender and the Dissected Body

The female body at the centre of Vesalius's frontispiece presents a puzzle. To begin with, female subjects were rarely used for the public dissection (Ferrari 1987; Laqueur 1990; Sawday 1996; Shackleford 2003) and even less by Vesalius (Wilson 1987).[36] The representation of a female body thus confirms that the frontispiece operates on a symbolic rather than a realistic level. It stages a dramatic contrast between a pandemonium of an all-male audience crowding in predatorily on a naked woman rent open on the table at the centre of the engraving, who looks up amorously at the anatomist to her right (and to our left) as he bares her insides to their view—to the anatomising gaze of modern science-in-the-making. The improbability of the situation, which is a vivisection rather than a dissection, serves to drive home the representation's symbolic work, since the subject would not likely still be alive, or not for very long, and surely not enough to fawn at the anatomist in the lively manner she does here, had her womb been opened up as depicted. The woman amorously turned towards Vesalius genders the relation between the anatomist and his dissected subject. This relation encapsulates the gendered dimension of the epistemic violence that lies in the foundations of modern science.

The Emergent Structures of Masculine Science

The woman at the centre of the frontispiece reveals the extent to which modern science's subject-object distinction operated from its inception as a gendered structure of domination. Although it has not been considered in the feminist literature, the public anatomy lesson furnishes, I suggest, the starting point, in modernity, of the long 'construction of masculine science' (Kelly 1985; Hutchings 2008). Vesalius' frontispiece renders how the renting of a subject from an object of knowledge doubled up as a gendered division of epistemic labour, that durably established distinct roles for the knowing male subject and the female object of knowledge. Modern science's anatomizing gaze was thus masculinised from the onset upon the dissection table. Moreover, the body's synecdochic function in relation to a fast eclipsing nature takes on a more precise form with this body. The female subject lay at the juncture of two distinct configurations of the relations between woman and nature, and old and a new: nature as woman, and nature as epistemic object. For she also conjured the ancient trope, of nature-as-woman (see Merchant 1980). She encapsulates how the ancient feminisation of nature was harnessed towards the modern enterprise of objectification. But she also, I suggest, helps navigate the broader transformation that was under way in the human relation to nature. The female body furnished a privileged place where 'to make ourselves as it were the masters and possessors of nature', in Descartes's (2006, 51) words. But it also helped maintain this possessed nature present at the heart of culture.

The new epistemic structure thus reinforced the old political structures of patriarchal domination. In addition, it furnished the axis of their geographical and categorial expansion. The public anatomy lesson shows that modern science's objects, far from being pre-decided on the basis of their biological characteristics, were instituted as objects within a broader structure of knowledge production centred upon the female body. In this way, male bodies too were feminised in a range of rituals through the various stages of the dissection, to produce the female object of knowledge (see Sawday 1996). This extensible circle of objects thus radiated out from the feminised (male or female) body, to nature at large, via animals. The monkey and the dog on the engraving, which stand next in line to come under Vesalius's knife, signify this fungibility of the object. That the feminised object of knowledge was substitutable in this way is what rendered the category apt to encompass the non-white bodies that colonisation would shortly bring into modern science's view. Lastly, the fungibility of the object and the non-fungibility of the subject of knowledge functioned as two sides of the same coin. They worked to secure the latter as being necessarily male, in addition to white (see also chapter 6).

The Female Body as the Location of Life

Above all, the female subject at the centre of Vesalius's frontispiece embodied early modern science's irresolvable puzzle and its ultimate prize. What is bared to the view of this jeering, leering, all-male, and very agitated crowd is the uterus. The body part that was thought to contain the very beginning of life itself exerted a growing fascination upon sixteenth- and seventeenth-century European cultures in general (see Sawday 1996), and on William Harvey. The uterus, its 'membranes and fluids', greatly occupied him throughout the latter part of his life. The man who had uncovered one of nature's best-kept secrets, blood circulation, set out to tackle the biggest of all mysteries. For over two decades he parsed the problem of 'parturition', 'generation', or 'conception', as he termed it interchangeably in the subtitle to his *On Animal Generation*, which was brought to the public, unfinished, in 1651, the same year as Hobbes's *Leviathan*.[37] However, Harvey never achieved his second breakthrough. The uterus would remain early modern science's last, unconquered terra incognita.

The urge to find the principle of life, to *see* it in the body, as Harvey set out to do with his magnifying glass, was the counterpart to the rise of mechanism.[38] Life, generation, was that which eluded it. Mechanising everything was its aim. And it had succeeded to a large extent. It had translated and operationalised the new concept of space. It had established the grand equivalence of natural and artificial bodies whose movements all obeyed the same laws. This had enabled the crafting of marvellous and controllable machines. Life itself, however, still remained stubbornly out of reach. Little surprise then that Hobbes (*L.* 3) felt compelled to reduce this one indomitable force to being 'but a motion of the limbs, the beginning whereof is in some principle part within'. The uterus loomed large; at a time when his hero Harvey, was also busy prying it open. All of motion was coming under mathematical control, of the kind that made it possible to conceive the coexistence of unruly passionate bodies. All, except the minute stirrings of 'this principle part within'. Life escaped this flattening out. The movements of the machine were only ever an imitation of the real thing. Life remained irreducible to mechanism's grand reduction.

This obsession with the uterus was not driven by a desire to locate the difference between the sexes in a material, corporeal basis. This desire only arose in the eighteenth century, once the symbolic apparatus that made sexual difference conceivable was in place. Laqueur (1990, 65) has underlined the dedication with which, for all its 'militant empiricism' and its commitment to sight, for all the scorn it poured on the Galenic anatomy and despite its aggressive exploring of the body, science in the sixteenth and seventeenth centuries continued to account for everything it discovered, including the clitoris, by way of the one-sex corporeal model. The female body was a less perfect and inverted version of the canonical male, which could also account for the clitoris (as a lesser penis). Sexual difference was inconceivable. It was reduced to sameness. The 'perfect animal' that William Harvey (1989, 163) analysed in order to parse the problem of generation could simply not be female, even when it contained the uterus. (For it would not have been so perfect.) The difference between the sexes was written out of the task at hand, even when it centred upon distinctly female body part. On the one hand, then, nature was feminised by way of the female body. On the other hand, this body was denied any ontological distinctness. At stake in this denial was the part it played in generation.

The fascination with the uterus elucidated a desire to control that which, in humans, only the female body could achieve, bearing life. Minimising the role of the female body in procreation was not new. Generation, since Aristotle, was conceived as resulting from a passive female matter being inseminated by the active male seed, properly the life-making ingredient. In this traditional division of corporeal labour, the female body, for all its actual labour, was denied any agency. The principle of life itself, that which injected movement to a passive female matrix, was masculinised by the work of Aristotelian causality. The female body furnished the material cause, while the male brought the efficient cause required to activate it (see Bianchi 2006). The structure of this explanation was kept intact by modern science—this was not the aspect of the classical account of generation it was interested in rectifying. In this it was aided by the one-sex model, which enabled it to patch over, here, the growing cracks in the old knowledge it was so keen to exploit everywhere else, and thus to secure the continuity of this inequality-making epistemic structure.

Instead modern science reconfigured the traditional account of generation into an all-encompassing enterprise of mastery. This was not knowledge for its own sake, or even just to heal, but rather to establish 'The Dominion of Man over the Universe', in the terms of its first ideologue, Bacon (1964). This mastery held the promise of humanity's liberation, for Descartes,[39] for Hobbes, as for Bacon. For Hobbes, it required mechanising nature; for Bacon, subjugating it. Both, I have suggested, were searching for this new kind of human agency, a capacity to craft, that was also political. Bacon reveals the early modern quest's gendered dimensions. In Bacon, and in Baconianism, this mastery doubled up as an explicitly masculine liberation that hinged on controlling a feminine nature. In the words of the Baconian and revolutionary poet Milton:

> He will indeed seem to be one whose rule and dominion the stars will obey, to whose command earth and sea hearken, and whom winds and tempests serve; to whom, lastly, Mother Nature herself has surrendered. (cited in Webster 1975, 1)

Bacon (1964, 62) himself had sought to 'come [. . .] leading to you', the scientist of the future and his 'dear boy', 'Nature with all her children', in order to 'bind you to her service and make her your slave'.[40] His 'only earthly wish', he continued, was to 'stretch the deplorably narrow limits of man's dominion over the universe to their promised bounds' (Bacon 1964, 62).

The public anatomy lesson brought a distinct body part to this conquering quest, the uterus. The life-holding matrix was laid across the dissection slab, ready to yield its secrets, as the compliant and even loving expression on the face of Vesalius's dissected subject suggests. It was open to the view and indeed to the taking. To understand its workings was to be able to imitate, or indeed appropriate, its life-bearing capacities. If this was not explicitly Vesalius's nor Harvey's purposes, who after all were only anatomists, it was built into the structures of the enterprise in which they partook. Bacon conceived his 'Great Instauration' as nothing short of a rebirthing of knowledge itself. It would 'unite' the (male) subject of modern science 'with *things themselves*, in a chaste, holy and legal wedlock' (Bacon 1964, 72, emphasis in original):

> and from this association you will secure an increase beyond all the hopes and prayers of ordinary marriages, to wit, a blessed race of Heroes and Supermen who will overcome the immeasurable helplessness and poverty of the human race. (Bacon 1964, 72)

Bacon thus flushes out any female principle in the future he envisages for humanity. But perhaps where his sense of a threat posed by a distinctly feminine power to his fantasy of mastery surfaces most clearly is in his conjuring of a masculine birth of time. The essay's title bears rendering: 'The Masculine Birth of Time or the Great Instauration of the Dominion of Man over the Universe' (Bacon 1964). If not matter, or indeed life, then time at least could be reclaimed away from a female generation. The threat of the feminine was an ancient one; it was biblical. Only, to the early modern age, the uterus seemed to offer up the biological location, visible at last, of the ungovernable female principle that had once led man to his downfall. In addition to the secret of life, the uterus on the dissection slab thus promised to reveal 'a demonstration of Eve's sin, a reinforcement of those structures of patriarchal control [that] were necessary to avoid a repetition of the first act of rebellion in the garden of Paradise', as Sawday (1996, 224) explained. Short of being able to bear life, Bacon's new science, then, would birth time itself.

*

In this chapter I have traced the emergence of modernity's regime of visuality that durably established the pre-eminence of sight as an ordering instrument, epistemic and political, and that was crafted upon the body in the anatomy theatre by opening up the eye for all to look into it. I began by considering two figures who were key to defining this new mode of seeing, and to orchestrating the passage from a world where the play of resemblances signified cosmic correspondences, to one that sought to cut through these resemblances; from a *seeing* to a *looking* enhanced by instruments. William Harvey, with a foot in both worlds, was a pivot between the two. Francis Bacon marks the starting point for the progressive emergence, over the course of the seventeenth century, of an empirical, experimental English science that was also a hyper-masculinised project of mastery and nation-building. Having considered two of the key actors who shaped the modern scopic regime, I then considered how it was institutionalised across Europe more broadly by the public anatomy lesson. I traced how science and the state co-created the dissected body as an epistemic object, and how this, in turn, supported their own institutionalisation. I showed how the anatomising gaze of modern science was crafted upon the dissection slab of constituting the human body as the object of modern science par excellence. I analysed the role that this performance of corporeal violence played in constituting the viewing subjects this scopic regime beckoned, capable of looking rather than merely seeing. Yet not all qualified. The public performance, both in the ritualised event and in the cultural representations that reverberated its political effects through a wider public (through theatre and print), reaffirmed the difference between those who rightfully looked, the bourgeois subjects of modern rights, and those whose insides were offered to this looking, the poor. In the public anatomy lesson the state-making, exclusionary, and disciplining line-drawing that Locke conceptualised was implemented in practice. Last, I showed how the public anatomy lesson lays bare modern science's deeply gendered structures of knowledge production, beginning with its distinction between the subject and object of knowledge. The early modern obsession with generation and with the uterus revealed that which constantly escaped the modern project of mastery and the attempt to mechanise nature: life itself. The public anatomy lesson shows how, on the one hand, nature was feminised by way of the female body. On the other hand, this body was denied its functional specificities, and specifically its life-bearing capacity. The stakes, political and epistemic, were simply too high. The public anatomy lesson, then, inaugurates the modern battle for the technical control of the female body's reproductive system.

Conclusion

> The thing I am provisionally calling 'collectivity' is not only impossible to think, it's impossible to form in any kind of state in the first place. [. . .] From Aristotle to Kant and on, the ultimate aim and endpoint of political theory lies in the drafting of a constitution.
> —Frederic Jameson, Lecture delivered at the
> CUNY Graduate Centre, 14 April 2014

The body in this book has served to peel back the layers of time and taken-for-granted-ness on the state and the subject of rights, the two political forms that underwrite the contemporary international system, our political lives, our relations to one another, and the demands we make of the state. I tracked their emergence across two revolutions. One, scientific, threw humanity out of the universe's centre, while the other, legal, put it squarely back in it. I showed how the state and the political subject mutually constituted each other all the way down, by going all the way back to their moments of emergence, and by considering them from history's unconstituted, the body. My concern was specifically with the state's and political subject's coming into being, rather than with the myriad ways in which they have evolved over time and across places since then. I tracked how their co-constitutive relation was initially sealed in security, liberty, and property; across different sites of theory and practice; and by taking the body as their referent. A sticky corporeal ontology is the key implication for our times of this originary history. It accounts for the readiness with which many different states today are able to turn to the body to control, surveil, and regulate us. It also explains why these somatic controls are too readily normalised and accepted by citizenries. The body is the familiar terrain of political modernity, the lingua franca shared by states and their citizenries. Hence also why it has yielded such a ready focal point for private corporations deeply invested in the ruthless expansion of surveillance and the technologies designed to enable it, although these were not my primary concern here (but see Epstein 2008; 2009; and Srnicek 2016 and Zuboff 2019 for the broader context).

Birth of the State. Charlotte Epstein, Oxford University Press (2021). © Oxford University Press.
DOI: 10.1093/oso/9780190917623.001.0001

The Body, History's Great Naturaliser

The body was the long-neglected item of Western thought, the scholarship on the body showed. I have sought to draw out, in addition, how this neglect wrought potent political effects. The body was the great naturaliser that helped stabilise and entrench the succession of experimentations, the world-shattering transformations, and dramatic inversions that begat modernity itself. The body has functioned in two different yet complementary ways in this book that I revisit successively in closing, as a referent and as an epistemological viewpoint.

By 'referent' I mean that the body is that which was referred to. It is distinct from the real body. For the referent is also a construct, what Saussure termed 'the signified'.[1] The signified points to, or 'names', in Hobbes's term, the real body; it conjures it, re-presents it, in the sense that it renders it present a second time within the mediated plane of language; but it is not that body. The difference, and the distance between them, encapsulates the entire modern regime of language and representation that first emerged in the seventeenth century. *All* modern (or contemporary) modes of theorising remain tributaries to this regime; whether they are comfortable recognising it, or whether instead they conceal it behind a range of labels, like 'realism' or 'positivism', that largely work to deny that they too use language. The real body belongs instead to the domain of 'the Real'. This is the term by which Jacques Lacan indexed that which stands beyond the referent, towards which it tends, but never, in fact, meets. It is the signified's permanently vanishing anchoring point. While the Real is lived, experienced, in the body constantly, it remains ultimately unsymbolisable, and thus, quite literally, unthinkable. This, moreover, is unbearable to the task of thought; indeed, scandalous to the academic enterprise. The 'scandal of the Real', as Jameson (2016) termed it, accounts for much of the criticism misdirected at the so-called linguistic turn or constructivism, for their purported inability to handle a so-called reality 'out there' (wherever 'there' is), a materiality, or, for that matter, bodies. The charge is moot, insofar as it concerns language itself, without which there is no theorising. This rupture of the world and the word is where we continue to dwell in the twenty-first century. The play of the signifier and the signified this rupture enabled is precisely what we must continue to mine to further theorising (see also Epstein 2013b).

The key transformation I have sought to circumscribe in this book is the moment when the corporeal referent shifted from a metaphorical and collective, to the biological, individual body. The state and the subject of rights emerged from the latter replacing the former as the referent for political construction. It came into view, first, as a function of a new way of conceiving movement and matter, and thus the body as an extended moving thing. Second, opening it up promised to bare human nature itself to the modern scientific eye. To sum up this first sense, I showed how the body qua referent served to naturalise security, to individualise liberty, and to privatise property. Together these three historical processes, that I tracked through the book's three parts, have yielded individual rights as we know and claim them, and the state to guarantee them.

The second way in which I have drawn upon the body has been to turn its 'thereness', its historical ipseity, into a place from which to undertake the work of critique. To rehearse one final time the steps that led me to this place, the body just *is*. This 'thereness' does not of itself yield political, let alone critical analysis. Yet in this ipseity also lies something that precedes political construction. There have always been bodies, before there were states and subjects of rights. I have sought to turn this ontological banality into an epistemological point of view that, moreover, draws attention to the problem of situatedness itself, to the need for the analysis to explicate where it is analysing *from*. That is, firstly, the body in this book has served to displace the habitual starting point of the story of modernity. Instead of an individual springing fully formed out of the seventeenth century, with *his* natural rights restored to him at last, it leaves us with a subject of rights that was crafted out of a series of exclusions that the body serves to draw out. But secondly, attending to this unnoticed 'thing' in that story served to attend to the problem of point of view itself, to the fact that every analysis is necessarily situated in a set of theoretical assumptions, and those claim not to be are worthy of suspicion.

Ordering: Modernity's Epistemological-cum-Political Problematique

This book's central finding is that *ordering* was modernity's defining problematique. At the joint of fundamental transformations in science, the law and in language itself, order was no longer yielded by the world as it had been known. It would need to be crafted, for knowledge and for the polity coextensively. Excavating this problematique has required looking, not just to a collapsing religious worldview, where the roots of political modernity are habitually traced, but to the scientific revolution, that the body, as an extended moving material thing, brought into view. In the seventeenth century, knowledge turned back upon itself to order itself. Descartes's doubting subject, the figure of this re-turn, was made necessary by a world where nothing was the way it used to be; where everything was in flux, open, infinite; where the sun was in the middle instead of the earth; and, above all, a world that no longer furnished ready-made categories to make sense of it. Knowledge required being reconstructed from scratch; starting, no longer from an unruly and unreliable world, but right here: from my sense-impressions and my embodied capacity to seize myself thinking and doubting and rejecting the false categories that dogmatic authorities had plied me with. Just how embodied this capacity was was a matter for debate, but not embodiment as its starting point. Embodiment, a chaotic world, and a widening chasm between them, were the starting coordinates for the epistemological task of ordering that characterised the seventeenth century. In England, in addition, it conjoined with the political work of reordering in the wake of the collapse of the old rule.

This is the context in which the theme of construction at the heart of what we now know as constitutive or constructivist theorising first entered into modern thought, as a problem of knowledge needing to reconstruct itself by creating the categories by which to order and classify. It was bound up with the birth of critique as the work of sorting—knowledge from illusions, categories between themselves, identity from difference, and so forth. Hobbes and Locke each had their own ways of both rendering this chasm, and of negotiating it. Hobbes, by emphasising the disjuncture of the word and the world, along with the contingent, constructed nature of all the norms and values upon which the state is built, starting with good and evil, and therefore justice. These are all founded in a contract, not in nature (chapter 3). Locke drove the wedge still further, and differentiated between forms of knowledge accordingly: an ectypal knowledge condemned to chasing after the originals in nature in order to construct mere replicas, and a knowledge founded instead in archetypes, the mind's true artwork, its proper creations and that also furnish the foundations for collective life. Archetypes, for Locke (*EHU*, II.chap.31[3]250), are 'made by the mind to rank and denominate things'. They are not 'copies' of these things but rather the means of their ordering. They 'cannot want anything' since they already have in them 'that perfection which the mind intended they should' (Locke, *EHU*, II.chap.31[3]250). Locke's ultimate archetype, and indeed his artwork, was 'government' (chapter 5). So, yes, he constantly refers to natural law and natural reason to secure it; only nature has already become but a distant referent in his own epistemological work. His was the business of archetypes and 'adequate ideas', which, for Locke (*EHU*, II.chap.31[1]249) was to say, perfect representations of these archetypes.

Construction and constitution were deeply entwined at this unique historical juncture—as a problem of needing to constitute the categories for ordering knowledge, and as a problem of how to think through how political institutions, like property, first came about. This is how the problem of origins came to be formulated as a political problem, not simply as a matter of birth or generation, but of founding and ordering. The state of nature is but one of its expressions. Autonomy was at stake, or how the subject learned to rely on itself to find its own sources of law (*nomos*) and to wean itself from a heteronomy, a law received and imposed from without, in the dual sense of from authority and from a 'nature' that was fast disappearing anyways. This source was the conscience, for some. It included criteria for what to believe in, but also what to accept as true knowledge as opposed to authoritative opinions, and whom to grant one's allegiances to.

Crafting, Constitution, and Generation

Making, or crafting, as I have called it in this book, was the response to the problem of ordering. It was a matter of building new models for the task of epistemological and political ordering, but also of the human agency discovered in the process of doing so. It runs through Hobbes's artifice, and through Locke's overarching preoccupation with crafting – adequate ideas and the right kind of government. It is the defining theme of the constitutive theorising they exemplified. This was a thought that crafted, constituted, and founded its own procedures, and the world around it. Thought and action were tightly bound together in this age where knowledge turned back upon itself to act upon itself, hence where thought was not just thought; and more specifically in England's revolutionary context, where reordering was both a pressing practical and a theoretical task. Thought and action were conjoined and geared towards crafting. The scientific revolutionaries of the seventeenth century crafted lenses, scientific treatises, archetypes, calculators, submarines, clocks, pocket watches, political treatises, laws, air pumps, utopias, champagne, steam pumps, barometers – and states. This was an age of invention, unconcerned with disciplinary specialisation, obsessed instead with artificing, busy relentlessly deploying the agency that had been unleashed by untying the human polity from God's and by the immanentization of political authority into the state. Fictions were constructions, not just novels or plays; they were no lesser products of this newly celebrated human ingenuity than machines. Hobbes's *Leviathan* was both, as well as a rulebook for political construction. Locke's archetype too exemplified this agency. It required a making that was no longer a copying, but properly a constituting. The first historical form of constitutive constructivist theorising does not just take us back to constructivism's linguistic roots, as I suggested (see chapter 3). It drives home the point that all knowledge is construction. Construction and constitution were exactly coextensive in the making of modernity.

However, the corporeal lens, and specifically the female body in the public anatomy lesson, also laid bare an antagonism buried deep in the foundations of constitutive-constructivist thought and of modernity itself, between constitution and generation. Life itself constantly eluded modernity's crafting grasp. It remained its holy grail. It marked its outer limit, and its failure. Constitution *instead of* generation; and because the latter remained unattainable. Harvey's *On Generation* was published, unfinished, the same year as Hobbes's *Leviathan*, exactly at the mid-century. To craft an 'artificial life', because the real one remained unattainable (Hobbes, *L*. 3). To be sure, Hobbes posited an 'artificer' that stood above humans (God). Ultimately, however, artifice, together with the ontology it exemplified, mechanism, and that also underwrote the making of the state, was lined with a masculinist fantasy of control (chapter 7). This fantasy, which drove the collective pursuit of the uterus's secrets in the anatomy lesson and Bacon's (1964) pursuit of a masculine rebirthing of time, indexes the gendered dimensions of the agency that built the state and modern science coextensively. Moreover, the secrets thus sought in the female organ marked what stood forever beyond the visible for the distinctly early modern scopic regime that, I argued, underwrote both. However often the uterus was peered into, generation itself remain sealed off to this nascent masculinist gaze. To see like the state—indeed, to become one—was to look into the body, and to see in the uterus the promise of holding its most prized possession, the ability to create life itself.

Bounding, Unbounding, and Constructions of Nature

Historians of the nation have showed how boundedness was the condition of possibility of this political form that first emerged a century after the state. 'No nation imagines itself continuous with mankind' in the ways that medieval Christendom did, remarked Benedict Anderson (1983, 16). The nation requires instead 'finite if elastic boundaries, beyond which lie other nations' (ibid.). The nation, and Anderson, thus presume the state, as a bounded, containing space. The crafting of this container has been my focus in this book. I parsed how a new need *to bound* took shape in the context of the scientific revolution, in response to the transformations in the modes of knowing nature and in the kinds of natures that were known. A methodological implication carrying forward is that constructions of nature wreak distinct effects of political constitution.

The crucial transformation that accounts for this new epistemological-cum-political need is that nature was becoming a site of limitlessness in the wake of the discovery of infinity (chapter 1). Hobbes and Locke both invested their respective states of natures with two kinds of limitlessness—an unlimited right to everything, for Hobbes (chapter 2); an uncontrollable natural executive power of punishment, for Locke (chapter 5). The limits of the human understanding were, in addition, a central concern of Locke's epistemological essay. However, they differed, both the Hobbesian and the Lockean state of nature beckoned a limiting, and delimiting, mechanism, the state. Science had discovered infinity to be a wondrous mathematical entity, rather than the unfinished, the formlessness it had previously been conceived to be. However, something was lost for the political: the spatial equilibrium underwriting imperial rule. The open-endedness (but not limitlessness) of empire, the horizon of the universal, was previously counterbalanced by the boundedness of place (*topos*), the locus of particularities. The medieval Aristotelian space inherently contained. The infinite, homogenous space that the seventeenth century was grappling with did not.[2] With this new scientific space, the bounding, the containing was no longer given; it required being deliberately and carefully constructed. The state thus emerged at this juncture as the container, to be later filled by the nation. I also considered developments in the law and in everyday practices where the subject too was detached from the old belonging to place and attached instead to this new form (chapter 4).

Two Dynamics of Political Constitution: Putting Together (the State) and Dividing Up (Government)

Tracking the body in the making of modern politics in the seventeenth century revealed two distinct sets of processes of political constitution that supported either a putting together, or a dividing up instead. The first yielded the state, the second produced the individual as the figure of indivision. The forms of putting together, in turn, were of two kinds, incorporation, and what I have termed corporealisation. Incorporation was the old process, rooted in the Pauline metaphor and formalised by medieval corporation law, 'by which', in Hobbes's (*L.* 3) words, 'the parts of [a] body politic were at first made and set together, and united'. Henri IV, the monarch who set aside his private beliefs in order to take upon himself the interests of the realm, and thereby better achieve France's 'making and setting together', exemplified this process in historical practice. Incorporation continued to afford important symbolic resources for statecrafting well into the seventeenth century (and beyond), that Hobbes, among others, readily tapped into to theorise a new kind of body politic, the state. At the same time, a very different process of corporealisation was taking shape, evinced by the seminal case for the law of naturalisation, *Calvin's Case*. Here the bond between the subject and the state was corporealised, in the double sense of incarnated and realised, in the natural bodies of the monarch and the subject coextensively. This was still a symbolic process, only it has shifted referents, from the body politic to the natural, individual body. I showed in chapter 4 how corporealising the political bond of subjection enabled it to be unhooked from place and attached instead to the space of the state that was being invented, territory. The state emerged at the cusp of these two distinct processes of putting together, incorporation and corporealisation.

Converse processes of dividing up were also taking shape at the same time. These ultimately yielded the individual as the undivided. This was Locke's definition. He arrived at it in the process of defining his principle of identity, by which something remains identical to itself over time. Locke found the basis for this indivision, and thus the foundation for his concept (identity), in the body. This, in turn, enabled him to distinguish between 'human', or 'Man' in his language, and 'person', as the biological and moral (or legal) categories, respectively. The former was corporeally defined: to be a human being is to have a human body. The latter properly comprised the site of identity-making, which Locke conceived as a self-crafting. The body, the natural given, furnishes only the process's starting point, yet it remains nevertheless its anchor, the guarantee of its undividedness. 'The individual' emerges at the end of this process. It is supported by two additional modalities of dividing up, that I termed 'individuation' and 'individualisation'. How to legitimise the individuation of communal rights, or how to rightfully break up collective rights (which were also known as 'properties'; see Tully 1980, 125), into individual ones was the driving concern of early modern natural rights theories of property. The body, via the *suum*, afforded the main instrument for this operation. The psychological process of individualisation proper, where this breaking down of collective rights is tied to the making of a modern 'self' and thereby durably legitimised, is furnished by Locke.

These processes of putting together and dividing up overlapped with distinct political logics, that would yield, respectively, 'the state' and 'government'. In Hobbes, the need to put together and contain, the ongoing necessity for holding the many as one, brought forth the state. It also remained the motor of an ongoing demand for the state. The threat of fragmentation, of which bodies in their sheer multiplicity are a constant reminder, renders the state permanently necessary. In Locke, the need for the state lay instead in the difficulty humans have in reigning in their impulses to punish. This natural desire to hurt back calls for the state as the limiting instance, as the mechanism that institutes proportionality in punishment and holds in check the (for Locke) natural and legitimate power to kill. Conceiving the state in this way opened up the possibility of envisaging other forms of limiting, however, that did not require the state. It placed the prospect of self-limiting on the horizon of thought. It ushered in education and discipline as the means to attain it. These, properly cultivated, ultimately rendered the state redundant. They paved the way for a bottom-up 'government' instead. Hobbes and Locke posited between them the two poles of the forms of power underwriting modern politics, top-down and bottom-up.

An Anatomy of Originary Exclusions

The ordering in play in the seventeenth century presupposed and required an 'outside' against which to contain and to constitute an orderly 'inside'. The work wrought by the antagonism for political constitution was first brought to light by R. B. J. Walker (1993), who drew out by the same token how the spatiality of international relations, as an object of analysis and as a discipline, illuminates the logics of concept formation more broadly. He showed how modernity's universal values, like freedom, equality, or justice, have as their condition of possibility an 'outside', onto which is ejected anything that is seen to vex their realisation or that dares to call their universal reach into question: the enemy, the barbarian, the infidel, the unreasonable; anyone or anything that threatens 'civilisation'. Modern values were born of a profound reordering of the relations between the universal and the particular. Medieval Europe was a mosaic of particularities extending out upon the horizon of Christendom, which was also the space of universality, the *orbis terrarum* (see also Anderson 1983; Bartelson 1995; 2010). It had no outside, or none that mattered enough to wreak constitutive effects. Instead modernity's universal values require an outside to hold the particulars that make them simultaneously thinkable, and unrealisable. That is, their non-realisation is built into the frame that made them conceivable in the first place. It is not a matter of eventually getting there, as, say, democratisation processes take hold in this or that state. It is, rather, that these modern universals are structurally unrealisable; they are necessary promises that cannot eventuate yet keep our democracies ticking. The body in this book has brought into view the crafting of the universal that sustains all others, the 'human'.

I traced how 'the human' was originally constituted in seventeenth-century Europe as the foundational category for individual rights and for modern concepts of legal and moral personhood by excluding a series of inconvenient humans: the poor, women, foreigners, and non-whites. This occurred coextensively in spaces of thought and practice. In practice, this universal was enfleshed by being pinned onto the human body in a key institution of state- and science-making, the public anatomy lesson. The early modern anatomy theatre offered the promise of *seeing* the workings of human nature at last, and this drew sizeable crowds (chapter 7). Only constructing the public lesson as the site of the unveiling of this universal, in all its nakedness, was premised on having an 'outside' built into the performance, onto where particulars of the chosen body were ritualistically expunged prior to the dissection, by announcing the name of the subject and the details of their 'crime'. The body was stripped of its social particulars so as to be crafted into a 'clean' biological universal, a pure receptacle of human nature. At the same time, the fact that it was a criminal, hence these particulars, made the public dissections possible in the first place. In this way, in the choreography of the public anatomy lesson, the space of criminality and poverty was established without, while within was constituted as the site of the construction of a natural human universal. The constitutive exclusions upon which 'this human' was founded were also erased in the process.

In thought, 'the human' as a figure of universality and as the bearer of innate rights was born of a reordering of the relations of the universal and the particular that was evinced by the universality-minus-one logic at work in John Locke's political writings. Locke's 'minus-ones', the criminal (chapter 5) and the slave (chapter 6), embody specific logics of class and race. They also, however, represent the particular that must be excluded to constitute the human as a universal, and in this they are non-specific. Locke's equality argument, in which his human universal is grounded, reveals additional boundary-drawing logics and a distinct spatiality at work in crafting this universal that I now consider in closing.

'There being nothing more evident', writes Locke (*TT*, II.chap.2[4]269), in a manner that typically announces his most dangerous moves, 'then that Creatures of the same species and rank, promiscuously born to all the same advantages of Nature, and the use of the same faculties, should also be equal one amongst another'. Locke's equality argument collapses the distinction between archetypes and ectypes that he was otherwise at great pains to uphold. This, not just in his epistemological work: the purpose of the *Two Treatises* was to design 'the True Original of Government' (per its subtitle), by setting aside the second-rate copies erroneously modelled after a fantasised hierarchical nature, like Filmer's. He takes considerable care to establish his political work upon the terrain of archetypes. This collapse can be shown in two ways, via the ectype and the archetype, respectively. First, Locke suddenly ushers in an ectype, a biological category, 'species', at the heart of his archetypal pursuit. Nor is this just any old ectype. The human species is the example he draws upon throughout the *Essay* to underline the pitfalls of ectypal reasoning à la Aristotle and the intractable difficulties that inhere in trying to fix categories after nature. It is central to his case for the superiority of archetypal reasoning and of the social over the natural sciences. 'Morality is the proper science and business of mankind', for Locke (*EHU*, II.chap.12[11]423). He recounts the absurd case of an ill-shaped French abbot ('Malotru', the ill-shaped) who, as a child, was 'very near being excluded out of the species of man, barely by his shape' (*EHU*, III.chap.6[26]297). This is a mistake, for Locke (*EHU*, III.chap.5[9]286), since the mind, not nature, 'makes the patterns for sorting and naming of things [. . .] [and] the boundaries of the sort or species'. 'There is no such thing made by nature and established by her among men' he added (*EHU*, III.chap.6[27]298). And he drove the point home: 'I cannot see how it can be properly said', Locke (*EHU*, III.chap.6[26]297) wrote 'that nature sets the boundaries of the species of things'. These are, rather, 'the workmanship of the understanding' (*EHU*, III.chap.3[14]276). Locke multiplies examples of deformed bodies, like l'Abbé Malotru's, throughout the *Essay* to underscore the impossibility of drawing 'the precise and unmovable boundaries of that species' (*EHU*, III.chap.6[26]297). The human species is thus a slippery category with a history of unstable limits, Locke cautions.

On one, epistemological, level, this kind of line-drawing that excludes a human being from humanity on the basis of a perceived deformity is simply erroneous. Yet on another, Locke (*EHU*, IV.chap.4[4]383) recognised that it belonged to the kind of necessary human-made, customary, normalising yet contingent, or indeed 'random', to use his word —at any rate, entirely culturally specific laws that constitute a central mechanism upon which social orders rest (chapter 5). Perhaps this is why he was not prepared to relinquish the potent ectype for his own project of political ordering. Instead he recovers it to found his archetype, government by consent. The wearisome ectype appears at a crucial point in the second treatise, namely, when he sets out 'to understand political power right' by 'deriving it from its Original' in nature (*TT*, II.chap.2[4]269). By locating it in the state of nature (in the chapter by this name), Locke signals that he conceived this state, not as an accurate scientific description, a copy of nature as it really is, but as a thought-experiment constructed for normative purposes, building the polity. Locke is perhaps more explicit about this than Hobbes, who sought to track closer to the human matter. In Locke's (*TT*, II.chap.2[4]269) nature, 'a *State of Perfect Freedom*' as well as '*of Equality*' are to be found, which is to say ideal-types or models, or, indeed, in his language, archetypes, for political construction. But Hobbes did not have the same problem as Locke, since he did not seek to carry this natural equality into the state. He readily left it behind, with nature. For his purposes Locke needs to show that *his* nature and the equality he sees in it is not a fantasy, like Filmer's (or Hobbes's). This is where, in a context where the understandings of nature were in considerable flux, the old Aristotelian category of species, upon which he otherwise pours considerable scorn, proves just too precious to forgo. Locke heeded none of his own warnings in his political treatises. He may be just an inconsistent thinker, across his two works published in the same year (1690). Or, more interestingly, this inconsistency owes to and expresses the force of the new antagonism of the universal and the particular that he was both grappling with and helped to stabilise.

However, second, Locke did not just implicitly retrieve the ectype at the heart of an archetypal argumentation, in the way that he had 'the conscience' (see chapter 5). He quite explicitly flanked his ectype 'species' with an archetype, 'rank' ('species and rank'; *TT*, II.chap.2[4]269). Ranking was the mind's craft, we have seen. This was no minor addition; and it did more than just confirm the erasure of the archetype/ectype distinction. It ushered in a distinctly social, norming logic at the heart of his equality argument, that ultimately short-circuited it from the onset. This opens up significant questions regarding the category of the 'human' that it was meant to found. For in the oscillation between the archetype and the ectype took shape, under Locke's own pen, this form of species thinking is what paved the way for the category of 'the human' to become racialised. This was achieved coextensively as the constitution of a non-human 'outside' and the regulation of a gradated, typed 'inside'.

The ectype spatialises the 'human', while the archetype norms, or normalises it. The former delineates the category's boundaries, while the latter ordains its internal space around an archetypal human being: the white male. In order to parse the first, external boundary-drawing process, I propose a diagnostic oxymoron, 'legal speciation'. 'Speciation' is a biological, post-Darwinian concept for 'the formation of a new and distinct species in the course of evolution', according to the *Oxford English Dictionary*. It captures the scientific process of delineating a new species after nature, such that a given individual can then be categorised as belonging to it or not. It is an ectypal practice, not a legal or normative one—hence the oxymoron. The scientist's task is an observing and a naming, not a making of the species.[3] It becomes a political border-drawing as a function of the slippage between types of reasoning. Locke's work of legal speciation thus consisted in establishing the 'human' as the closed, contained space where equality was achievable. Not all of nature's creatures needed apply, however. Here too the limiting condition is operative. Equality cannot be limitless, for Locke. It requires pushing out some differences (or particulars) to be able to level out those within; and perhaps the easiest to expunge are those that are indelibly inscribed upon the body. Internally, this space is further gradated or 'sorted', in Locke's language, by way of the archetype. This is where 'archetype' takes on its full meaning as a model, an ideal type against which all humans are to be measured and 'ranked'. Enter, once again, the white Vitruvian man. All other natural beings who did qualify for admittance—like white women, children, or foreigners—can only ever remain derivatives. And then there are those who do not qualify.

'Race' was a barely adumbrated category in the late seventeenth century, and would only really flourish the following one (see Bracken 1973; Bernasconi 1992). Yet it is easy to see how race would afford a ready means to operationalise this gradating—either to draw the initial contours, or to stake out the internal space thus constituted; or indeed to achieve both depending on the circumstances to hand. As Robert Bernasconi (1992, 315) underlined, 'racism rarely—and perhaps in a sustained form, only much later—took the form of excluding "Negroes" explicitly from humanity'. But 'race' offered the possibility of further refinements in line-drawing both within and on the edges of 'the human'. Ultimately, in the slippage between archetypes and ectypes, Locke recreates at the heart of his human universal a new ordering hierarchy that seriously undercuts his own claims to founding the modern polity in equality. The racialisation of the human was not simply something that happened in practice, as a function of degenerative interpretation of Lockean ideas in the colonies and in the nineteenth century. It was, rather, enabled by the category's original crafting by Locke, amongst others.

Critique as Responsibility and as a Creative Agency

These constitutive exclusions in the making of 'the human' raise two sets of questions regarding what other untold discriminatory epistemological-cum-political orderings have quietly carried forth from this liminal moment in the making of modern science, the state, but also constitutive-constructivist theorising; and what *to* carry forth. To the former, that they are constitutive suggests that these exclusions cannot be simply ironed out of the concept, but likely only displaced. To the latter, however, it is, despite it all, the crucial original insight that humans live in a world of their own making, and therefore that unmaking and remaking it is available to them. The nexus of critique and responsibility was very much at stake for the authors I considered, who both helped hone critique as a duty of deconstruction, and helped hew the biased, gendered, and classed structures we have inherited and that is now incumbent upon us to undo. The purpose of critically reengaging with them was twofold.

It was, first, to rekindle the sense of responsibility that arises from realising that the agency of political construction still lies in our laps or indeed our hands; that we are wielding it all the time, including when we do not attempt to correct these structures; and even if some wield it (much) more than others, of course. Only the 'making' in play in the seventeenth century troubles contemporary thought's habitual ways of conceiving agency. Liberal agency is hyper-individualist, whereas Marxian agency is collective. Both, however, are ultimately founded in material interests—of the individual, or of a class; the one interested in maintaining the status quo, or the one concerned to change it. Performativity does delink agency from interests, to capture its immaterial workings. Insofar as it captures the agency of institutions, starting with language, it is also collective. It too is largely geared towards reproduction, however. All three miss out on the quality of creativity that also inheres in agency. It was on intensified display in the early stages of modernity's making, in what I have analysed alternately as its 'crafting' and its 'constituting'. I have suggested that appraising this creativity required attending to the revolutions in the structures of knowledge and language, not just in the play of class interests, or in the individuals, where the agency of this age is usually sought.[4] That the transformations they wrought endured showed that the agency at work was collective.

Today, in our 'post-revolutionary', 'post-liberation' (pick your label) age, we are of course a far cry from this seventeenth-century crafting, historically and technologically. The world we are in seems here to stay, or fewer and fewer people appear interested in changing it. So why be interested in retrieving an antiquated agency that can do very little for our time? There is one key place where it can, I suggest, and that is in the work, indeed in the obligation of critique itself. What the seventeenth century draws out better than any other age is that there is a fine point at which thought and action, knowledge and practices, necessarily come together to undo and redo existing structures—and must do so for these to be undone. I call this the fine point of critique. It is also necessarily a creative point that implicates invention, finding new ways of disrupting existing circuits – of denaturalising.

If this sounds only aspirational, there is another way in which the point can be put, which is related to my second reason for engaging with the seventeenth century. It draws out the extent to which the juncture of the epistemological and the political is the proper locus of critique. What locks existing political, social, international structures in place are the epistemological schemes that work to render these invisible or indeed 'natural', starting with 'rights' and 'the state'. The failure to dwell at this juncture, in the name of claiming some conciliatory disciplinary middle ground, explains why so many attempts to critique in international relations and in other disciplines have misfired, and particularly the bankruptcy in which IR constructivism finds itself today. It will be evident to the reader by now that my purpose with this book has been to rejuvenate the term, because the insights it holds, and the agency it promises, are too important to give up. Nevertheless, so long as the focus is on actions, behaviours, or practices only, without attending, not just to the political structures, but to the concepts, epistemological frames, and discourses that underwrite them, then the analysis will continue to remain barren.

Notes

Chapter 1

1. Biometrics (such as facial recognition) are technologies designed to identify an individual on the basis of somatic characteristics (like their fingerprints, iris, bone structure, keystroke, or voice) and to track her or him through spaces.

2. Biometrics have also flourished in postcolonial states. Fingerprinting as a mass technology was first invented by the British in Bangladesh (see Cole 2001). South Africa is a highly proficient 'biometric state' (Beckenridge 2014). India's recent turn to biometrics is generating the world's largest citizen biometric database, the surveillance industry's dream come true (since the bigger the database, the more effective the technology, see Epstein 2007). One of the first countries to adopt biometric solutions to contain a pandemic was Sierra Leone, with the 2014 Ebola outbreak (see Counter 2014).

3. 'Extension' (*res extensa*) was coined by Descartes, as the counterpoint to 'thought' (*res cogitans*). Together 'extension' and 'thought' cover the full range of all that is for Descartes: the material and the immaterial, body and mind, and so on. However, 'extension' rapidly travelled beyond Cartesian thought, on account of the key role that it played in breaking the hold of the unitary Aristotelian 'substance'. Even those, like Hobbes, or Spinoza, who rejected his mind/body dualism, retained 'extension', which rapidly became the category for matter at large.

4. This is not to deny, of course, that the state-subject relation has taken on endless variations across time and places since the seventeenth century—not least as it was rinsed through nationalisms of all kinds (see Anderson 1983). However, I contend that, at it is core, it affords the basic structure that is conjured and reproduced by every rights-claim in the contemporary international system, where the state, however undemocratic, affords the basic framework for rights. To put it bluntly, rights as we know them cannot be recognised, let alone upheld, without a state, even if they can also be violated by it.

5. England and France are traditionally considered by historical sociologists to constitute the first two modern states; see, for example, Kiser and Kane 2001; Comninel 2000; Lachmann 1989; Fehér 1989; and Tilly 1989. In France, however, this agonistic relation emerged a century later. Of England, moreover, 'the island famous for so many atrocities and good laws', Voltaire would write a little over a decade before the revolution that would bring it about in his own country that its penal code 'is directed at the citizens' safeguard [. . .] whereas in France [it] is directed at [their] ruin' (1777 Prix de la Justice et de l'Humanité, art. 32, my translation).

6. By 'radical' I mean an enquiry that is centrally concerned with how the structures of power define political actors' understandings of who both they are and what lies in their interests. See Lukes 2005 for a classic exemplar.

7. For example, by the way the child is spoken to in the womb and the monikers it is attributed.

8. An example is the structuring force of taboos; see Butler (1990, 181–82).

9. Benedict Anderson (1983, 15) also captures something of this agency with his analysis of the nation as an 'imagined community', understood as a genuine, collective 'creation', rather than a mere 'fabrication'. I track its initial irruption in early modern Europe. I use 'modern' in the conventional sense that historians do, as referring to the developments that took place in Europe in the seventeenth century and that yielded the state. My use of the term is in no way intended to suggest that other kinds of polities were not being constructed differently, elsewhere and before.

10. The attraction of geometry, for Hobbes (*De Homine* chap.10[5]42–43) lay in that 'we ourselves draw the lines': 'Since the generation of the figures depends on our will; nothing more is required to know the phenomenon peculiar to any figure whatsoever, than that we consider everything that follows from the construction that we ourselves make in the figure to be described. Therefore, because of this fact (that, is, that we ourselves create the figure), it happens that geometry hath been and is demonstrable'. This, unlike 'natural things', which are 'not in our power but in the divine will'. Geometry was to afford the model of a science founded in 'First Principles [. . .] [or] Definitions' These ought 'to contain [. . .] 'the Generation of the Subject'; otherwise 'there can be nothing demonstrated as it ought to be', for Hobbes (cited in Jesseph 2016, 70).

11. See Mathiowetz 2011 for a critique of the hegemony of 'interests' in US political science, and Epstein 2013a for its hold upon international relations.

12. Hobbes stipulated in his will that this representation feature on the front of every edition of *The Leviathan*; see Springborg 1995; Brown 1980.

13. The closest I have found Butler (1988) to have broached this relation is, first, in her 'Performative Act and Gender Constitution: An Essay in Feminist Phenomenology', where she gestures towards another type of constitutive theorising à la Searle, which is off-limits here (and for her) because it exemplifies the hyper-individualistic focus, but which nonetheless envisages how the single act reorders relations. However, she promptly inverts the agentic focus to consider a form of 'constitution that takes the social agent as an *object* rather than a *subject* of acts' (Butler 1988, 519). John Austin's speech act theory might have provided another way forward (see Wæver, forthcoming). Second, Butler's (1990, 186–88) discussion of the subversive potential of 'drag' as a performance that, in denaturalizing the sex/gender distinction, reveals the performativity of gender occurs under the aegis of repetition rather than disruption. I am thankful to Laura Shepherd for our conversations on these matters.

14. Locke is not mentioned in Foucault's 1975–76, 1977–78, as well as his 1972–73 lectures (see Foucault 2009; 2003; and 2013, respectively). Foucault (2008, 91) does note his role briefly in the 1978–79 lecture series *Birth of Biopolitics*, as the successor to the last English theorist of the state, Hobbes, and the producer of the 'first theory

of government'. But Locke is absent altogether from his extensive discussion of 'the enormous literature on government', as he puts it (Foucault 2009, 89); see in particular the 1 February 1978, lecture of *Security, Territory Population*. Hence the relations between Locke's 'government' and his own 'governmentality' are left unspecified.

15. 'Universe' originally derived from the latin locution *summa rerum, universae res*, 'the sum total of all that exists', and it was used to designate the unity of the world (in opposition to philosophers like the Epicurians, who posited several worlds (cf. 'Univers' in Lalande 1926). Francis Bacon considers 'the universe' rather than 'the cosmos' in his *New Organum. The Universe* is how Descartes titled his most ambitious, unfinished project.

16. Descartes's 'extension' set a crucial milestone in the emergence of the modern concept of space, which is the story I tell here, although Descartes himself remained one step short of granting space its separate existence. However, infinity was central to his concerns.

17. Hence Aristotle's concept of space qua place is without a void. Every place contains something. Historians of science have defined Aristotelian space as, in Max Jammer's (1993, 12) terms, 'the adjacent boundary of a containing body' (Jammer 1993, 12) or in terms of the surface enveloping a body (Alexandre Koyré [1966]).

18. *Urbi et orbi* is a type of papal address, pronounced on solemn occasions. It holds the traces of the spatial imaginary underwriting the Christian empire: a stable, geocentric world ordained around an unmoving centre, Rome (*urbi*), and held within spheres of rule revolving around it (*orbi*).

19. The main sources for this all-too-summary account of the passage from 'a closed world to an infinite universe' are Alexandre Koyré's (1958) book by that title, as well as Koyré 1966, Casirer 2000, and Kuhn 1957.

20. Thomas Kuhn (1957, 135) has called Copernicus's *De Revolutionibus Orbium Caelistium* 'revolution-making rather than revolutionary'.

21. Descartes occupies a complex position in the story of the emergence of modern space. He coined the category of 'extension', and formalised this geometric language; however, he fell short of granting space its separate existence. This left him unable to recognise the existence of the vacuum.

22. Aristotle's force (*bia*) is instead disruptive; it hinders or prevents the realisation of impulse (*hormē*) and natural tendency (see Bianchi 2006).

23. One of the fundamental principles of classical physics, inertia was a process of collective discovery that began with Galileo and ended with Newton, via Isaac Beeckman and Descartes (see Koyré 1966). It reveals that any object will persist in its state, of movement or rest, so long as it remains undisturbed (that it does not collide with another object).

24. This was not, strictly speaking, Galileo's conclusion, as he attempted to steer clear of the question of whether the world was infinite, on account of Bruno's fate. But, as the Church was prompt to realise, it was the logical outcome of the moves he was making. See Koyré (1966) for an excellent account.

25. Descartes also conceived the world as 'indefinite' rather than 'infinite' as a result. Hence the universe is an 'indefinitely extended body', for Descartes, who also talks of

'the extended matter that makes up the universe' (cited in Koyré 1957, 132, my translation). Instead he located the idea of infinity in the idea of God, and explicitly not in the material world.

26. In this way, menstruation was conceived as a way of evacuating excess humours and heat, and not something specific to the uterus.

27. Koyré (1966) recounts a delightful medieval Aristotelian theory of seasons as the properties of hot and cold countervailing each other. Cold actualises itself in the winter, and vice versa with heat in the summer. The evidence? That our stomachs stay warm in the winter, as the heat is pushed into them. Conversely the cool in the summer, de-actualised, lodges itself in the belly of fruit.

28. I am not saying that difference was accepted in seventeenth-century Europe, but rather that, in an age of conquest, it was amply seen, experienced. For a masterful account of the ways in which Europeans oscillated between rejection and acceptance in their grappling with the differences they encountered, see Todorov 1982.

29. Strictly speaking, this is the Ancient Greek ontology, particularly the stoic variant. Aquinas in the Middle Ages rendered this correspondence of logos/Logos by translating it as 'word'/'Word', which blended in the scriptures (by invoking the opening of John, 'in the beginning was the Word'). Cf. Aquinas *Summa Theologia*, 1a, 34.1.

30. Article 2 of the 1789 Declaration of the Rights of Man and the Citizen lists 'liberty, property, security (*sûreté*) and resistance to oppression' as the 'fundamental and inalienable rights of man'. For the US Declaration of Independence, 'Life, Liberty and the pursuit of happiness' are the 'unalienable Rights' with which 'men' have been 'endowed by their Creator'.

Chapter 2

1. Security is proclaimed a natural and universal human right by Article 2 of the 1789 Declaration of the Rights of Man (*sûreté*). Security is one of the 'self-evident truths' underwriting the US Declaration of Independence and the positing of 'Life' as the first 'unalienable right' for which 'Governments are instituted among Men'. It is one of the first constitutional rights of many states.

2. The uses and abuses of Hobbes in both international relations and political science have been subject to extensive debate. For recent analyses, see Prokhovnik 2005; 2010; Mathiowetz 2011; and Epstein 2013a.

3. Founding a science of politics is what Hobbes saw himself to be doing. This is my concern here, rather than whether the study of politics is a science, which is a highly contestable and contested claim. For an apt, critical engagement with this question and Hobbes's place in it, see Mathiowetz 2011.

4. Bodin was responding to the 1572 Saint Bartholomeous massacre of Protestants by Catholics.

5. Both Bodin and Hobbes then translated their political treatises into Latin (in 1586 and 1668, respectively).

6. Here is an example of Hobbes's dismissal of the final cause: "The Writers of Metaphysiques reckon upon two other Causes besides the *Efficient* and *Material*,

namely, the ESSENCE, which some call the *formal Cause; and the End*, or *Final Cause*, which are nevertheless Efficient Causes' *DC*, chap.10[7]96.

7. '[F]elicity in the present life' is in Hobbes's Latin translation of the *Leviathan*'s chapter 13.

8. In the Catholic topology, this space of the afterlife of the soul acquired its distinct imaginary with the invention of the purgatory in the Middle Ages, where these departed souls were believed to stand in waiting (see Le Goff 1991). A whole economy of relations with these souls was entertained and regulated by the Church who aided their salvation through organised prayers.

9. By English revolutionaries, I mean, roughly, the 'Puritans' on the battle ground (to use the historians' term) and the Parliamentarians who were taking control of political institutions, starting with the Parliament itself, but also the universities. See Hill 1965, 1980, 1989; Walzer 1965; Woodhouse 1974; Webster 1975.

10. For example, 'the sacred rights of the conscience' was the weapon of choice for contesting the new settlement for the Anglican Church that was being discussed at Westminster in 1643–44 after the collapse of the Laudian regime.

11. Hobbes, who was a tutor to Charles I's son, defended the royalist side. However, this is less interesting to me in this chapter than the broader solution he devised to the problem of war driven by matters of conscience, or what Arash Abizadeh (2013) has called his 'disagreement theory of war', which is not reducible to his historical position.

12. Hobbes (*DC*) also concluded in the same dedicatory epistle that he had in fact succeeded in emulating his model: 'Natural philosophy is but young, but civil philosopher is younger still, as being no older than my own book *De Cive*'.

13. 'Opinion'—*doxa* in Greek, *opinio* in Latin—was a traditional philosophical term handed down from Ancient Greek philosophy via Thomas Aquinas. In these ideational epistemologies, it denoted the lesser form of knowledge and captured the succession of the sensible, the flux of appearances, the phenomenon. Opinions were distinguished from knowledge proper, which aimed at the realm of ideas; at what remained constant and unchanging; at the noumenon (see Cassirer 2000).

  This hierarchy of forms of knowledge was about to be drastically upturned with the invention of probability in the mid-seventeenth century, as we will see in the following chapter (see Hacking 1987; Shapin and Shaffer 2011). Hobbes stands at the cusp of this change, with one foot in the middle ages and the other in the modern era, whereas Locke stands with both feet in the latter (on the latter Tully 1988).

14. '[T]here can be nothing so absurd, but may be found in the book of philosophers. And the reason is manifest. For there is not one of them that begins his ratiocinations from the definitions or explications of the names they are to use; which is a method that hath been used only in geometry'. Hobbes (Hobbes, *L.*, chap.5[7] 24) had in fact a complicated relationship with the scholastics: elsewhere he uses the term 'philosophy' interchangeably with 'science'.

15. Truth, for Hobbes (*L.*, chap.4[12]19), 'consisteth in the right ordering of names in our affirmations'. To be so, affirmations require being anchored in definitions, against which they can be verified. Hence establishing truth and falsity as a general criteria, as opposed to the solipsistic truths of our immediate experiences, harks back to the

business of definitions. Truth and falsity are features of the discursive communicative structure we considered earlier. 'For *true* and *false* are attributes of speech, not of things', including things experienced (Hobbes *L.*, chap. 4[11]19).

16. The *Elements of Law,* Hobbes' earliest political treatise (1640), is composed of a first part, 'On Human Nature', abbreviated as *EoLi,* and a second 'on the Body Politic' (*De Corpore Politico*), abbreviated as *EoLii.*

17. The Hobbesian 'public conscience' is distinct from that of a 'civil society', which only takes shape in the following century. Thanks to Julie Saada for our discussions on this point.

18. The latin version of *Leviathan*'s chapter 46 can be found in the Hacket edition (1994) that I use for quotations throughout the book.

19. Tracy Strong (1993, 138), for his part, has argued that Hobbes's position was that of the 'thnetopsychists, who believed that the soul died with the body, that it was but the animating force, and that it would in turn be resurrected with the body'.

20. Unlike Hobbes, Descartes retained the soul. But he also shirked away from the realm of human affairs. Both, however, wielded the same procedural, causal, and a-telic reason that was emerging with the scientific revolution, as we will see more extensively in the next chapter

21. Here is an example of this strategy: 'We who are Christian acknowledge that there be angels [. . .] and that the soul of man is spirit But [. . .] nowhere does [the scripture] say that they are incorporeal. [. . .] To me therefore it seemeth, that the Scripture favoreth them more, who hold angels and spirits for corporeal' (*Human Nature*, chap.11[5]66).

22. See Sreedhar (2010) for a comprehensive account of the context and just how unique Hobbes's position on resistance was.

23. The extent to which the German Nazi party explicitly drew on the Hobbesian iconography in the 1930s, which is amply evidenced by the permanent collection of the Deustche Historiches museum in Berlin, adds grist to the biopolitics literature's mill.

24. The state of nature first appears in chapter 14 of *The Elements of Law*, Hobbes's first political treatise (1640).

25. As Friedrich Meinecke (1984) has shown, the Edict of Nantes, the first modern treaty of toleration, was the product not of lofty renaissance ideals (as argued by Toulmin 1990), but of raison d'etat, a form of reason that continues but which seems unpopular in our times, yet that evinces a form of interest that troubles the simplistic analysis of interests that prevails in rational choice theory and liberalism more broadly.

Chapter 3

1. See Mathiowetz 2011 and Epstein 2013a for critical engagements with rational choice's misappropriation of Hobbes in political science and in international relations, respectively.

2. The Hobbesian choice is not therefore the choice that features in liberal thought either. As I argued in the previous chapter, and will continue to show in this chapter, the 'individual' at the heart of liberal thought does not feature in Hobbes.

3. Strauss does consider both poles, but he wants no truck with the body and what he considered to be the excessively subjective basis of his thought. My more specific differences with Strauss will be addressed in the course of the chapter.

4. The origins of modern voluntarism are habitually traced back to William of Occam, and to a specific debate on property rights that unfolded in the Church in the thirteenth century (see Villey 1975). Only Occam's was a legal and strategic argument. He never developed a comprehensive ontology that could sustain this voluntarism in the ways that Hobbes did by focussing upon the body.

5. The Levellers, who were common soldiers of Cromwell's army, had tabled for debate within the ranks of the Roundhead army an Agreement of the People in 1647, which contained the idea of a contract between ruler and ruled (see Hill 1989; 1980; Brailsford 1961; see also chapter 4). Political thought and practice were converging here again (see chapter 2), on the figure of the contract in mid-seventeenth-century England.

6. As Meinecke (1984, 208) nicely put it: 'The immense power of the old tradition of Natural Law is shown by the fact that even the most emancipated thinkers of the century lay under its spell'. 'But, being great and profound thinkers, besides imbibing the old tradition', he continued, 'they also mentally digested the living reality of state life[. . .] [and eventually] developed ideas in the process which broke up the presuppositions they had made on the basis of Natural Law'.

7. The 'state of nature' is not, strictly speaking, Hobbes's expression, but rather Locke's (see Prokhovnik 2005; 2010). Locke also added a third state (the state of war), as we will see in chapter 5. However, insofar as Locke merely firmed up the spatial ordering that Hobbes initiated by conceiving it in terms of distinct 'states', I retain the convention of speaking of Hobbes's as the state of nature.

8. The debate, which it is beyond my scope to engage with in any great detail, turns on whether self-preservation in Hobbes consists in a right or a duty. Warrender (1957), who argues that it places an obligation upon individuals to seek peace primarily (and defend themselves secondarily), has stood on the losing side of the debate, but has been rehabilitated by Tuck (1979).

9. Hobbes is a natural rights theorist, albeit a critical one, for Warrender (1957), Strauss (1963; 1965), and Tuck (1979), but not for Tully (1980) or Finnis (2011).

10. The soul was thought to be divided between an appetitive part, which humans shared with other animals, and a superior, rational part, which only humans possessed, such that reason submitted the appetites. Relinquishing the soul left Hobbes without a clear scheme for superseding these appetites or instincts.

11. Although my own reading tracks closest to Flathman's (1993), he too commits this fallacy.

12. This is significant as the Leviathan was written in English. A word search of the text indicates that he uses 'individual' only in adjectival form, and relatively sparingly at that.

13. Descartes's last work, published in 1649, before the Leviathan but after Hobbes had begun mining the topic with his Elements of Law (in 1640), was a Treatise on the Passions of the Soul. Spinoza would further explore the nexus of the passions and the political that Hobbes first problematised.

14. 'It is the case that I tend to refuse to write my thoughts concerning morality' wrote Descartes in an epistle (1 November 1646, cited in Monnoyer 1988, 12). His final work, his 1649 *Treatise on the Passions of the Soul*, is the closest he ventured onto the terrain of the motives for human behaviour, the unsettlingly unscientific grounds (for him) Hobbes was already treading. Even there, moreover, he fell short of applying his analysis to political questions.

15. Michael Walzer (1965, 200) has underscored this instability may have had particular resonance in the seventeenth-century English polity, moreover, where life-worlds were being upturned by profound 'political and social transformations that literally set [humans] moving'.

16. The difference between causation and probability, which belong to two different epistemological categories, is nicely explained by Ian Hacking (1987, 86) as follows: 'the concept of epistemic probability requires us to recognize the difference between what causes things to happen and what tells us that they happen'.

17. This is in another of Hobbes's (*DC*, Chap.1[2] 3) definition of Philosophy: 'such knowledge of effects or appearances, as we acquire by true rationication from the knowledge we have first of their causes or generation: And again, of such causes or generations as may be from knowing first their effects'.

18. 'The definition of the *will* given commonly by the Schools, that it is a rational appetite, is not good' (Hobbes, *L.*, chap.6[53]33).

19. For the importance of language in Hobbes' thought, see also Ball (1985), Flathman (1993), Williams (2005), Dawson (2007) Pettit (2008) and Epstein (2013a).

20. Indeed, for Hobbes, the priest and the scientist (at the time of the formation of the Royal Society) represented a similar danger, that of subverting the authority of the undivided state, insofar as they formed small states within the state based on a claim to a 'segregated area of competence' (Shapin and Schaffer 2011, 284).

21. For Aristotle, the material cause was, literally, the stuff out of which an object is made, the wood of a chair, for example. The efficient cause was what caused the actualisation of the chair's shape (or form) into this matter. To this distinction Hobbes (*DC*, chap.10[3]94) replied: 'The Efficient and Material Causes are severally and by themselves parts onely of an Entire Cause, and cannot produce any Effect but by being joyned together'.

    The emergence of probability, as Ian Hacking (1987) has shown, was a new kind of logic that would eventually entail by the eighteenth century and with Hume, the shift of causation from the realm of knowledge as *scientia* to that of *opinion* (or *doxa*).

22. 'In production, the artist acts with a view to an end; production is not an absolute end [. . .] instead, in action, the act has the end in itself' (Aristotle [1990] VI, 2, 1139 0–4 [my translation]).

23. For classic statements, see Finnis 1998; Gierke 1950.

24. An important and largely unnoticed distinction to emerge from the Hobbesian scheme is that the general and the universal are not on the same level. This opens up the possibility of a wedge existing between the epistemological acts of generalising and that of universalising which, while beyond my scope here, may be usefully mined for debates around the particular and the universal that are currently taking place in postcolonial IR (see also Epstein 2017a).

25. Whether Hobbes's case study, the Amazons, is historically accurate or largely a myth matters less than the fact that Hobbes resorted to it as historical evidence. As Edwin Curley (*L.*, p.129) underlines, Hobbes would have found it in classical historical sources such as Quintus Curtius's *History of Alexander*.

Chapter 4

1. Both poles (of subject and state) are, however, always implicated by each other, since their mutual constitution is the book's starting point. Here I mean simply a shift in emphasis: focusing on liberty brings mostly the subject into view. Security brings both as we have seen, but it is more readily associated with the state.

2. The commercial sense that we mostly associate with the term 'corporation' today is a belated, specifically seventeenth-century development (see Holdsworth 1922).

3. For the role of the city in the development of the state, see Brett 2011; and Canning 1988.

4. One famous case was the king litigating against the City of London in 1682 (Holdsworth 1922, 385).

5. For example, the bishop held rights in common with the churches of his diocese and some additional rights, such as to visit, punish, and claim revenue from them (the *cathedraticum*). Conversely, however, he was obligated to uphold his clergy's (enforceable) right to partake in elections, including of his own office (Frohnen 2005).

6. 'A *polis* consist[s] of a multitude of human beings', writes Aristotle in his *Politics*. And 'just as the multitude becomes a single man with many feet and many hands and many senses, so it becomes one personality' (cited in Turner 2016, 9).

7. On the basis of the principle of *cuius regio, eius religio*, 'to each king their religion', which was first adopted at the 1555 Peace of Augsburg and then reasserted at Westphalia.

8. The distinction does not feature in the founding documents of the Dutch Republic, for example, whereas the Union of Utrecht (1579) guaranteed Dutch citizens their freedom of conscience (see Kaplan 2007, 177–78). Arash Abizadeh (2013) has underscored how Hobbes was one of the first to theorise this distinction between public and private worship (see chapter 2).

9. Whether the constitution of Great Britain was successful or merely attempted at this point, and properly achieved with the 1707 Act of Union, makes little difference to my argument, which engages with constitutional logics, rather than the historical conditions of its success. Note also that I leave out the complex matter of Irish colonisation. To put the matter in another way, I consider only how the island of Great Britain (and not the island of Ireland) was constituted into a unified territory out of several kingdoms.

10. The 'corporation sole' was contradistinguished from the older figure of corporate law hailed directly from Roman law, the 'corporation aggregate'. On this distinction, see Turner 2016. Ernst Kantorowicz's *King's Two Bodies* (1957) played a decisive role in kindling the contemporary interest in the mystical and mystifying legal fiction. See Turner 2016 for a recent overview of the cottage industry it has yielded.

11. Like the 'outlaw', the alien was considered not fully in the law and not entitled to all of its protections (see Kim 1996).

12. Political subjecthood is constituted, for Coke as it would be later for Hobbes, in the very act of subjecting: 'protection draws subjection, and subjection draws protection'. Only this raises the question, what makes it the act that founds the polity: our nature, or its institutionalisation by the law, which it founds? This chicken-and-egg problem would become the defining problem of early modern political thought. It runs in the background of his analysis of *Calvin's Case*, but Coke sidesteps it with a deft common law move, by locating the starting point of his analysis *in* the bond as it exists, rather than returning to its origins, as natural rights theorists would do (see chapter 6).

13. This passage from Coke's 'birth-rights' to our non-hyphenated 'birthrights' is at the heart of this chapter.

14. In fact, the theory of the monarch's two bodies also enabled regicide, insofar as (legally) it separated out the monarch's head from the Crown, such that only the former was decapitated. In this way, the threat to the unity of the body politic was contained.

15. Eric Santer (2011) has beautifully parsed how the monarch's spiritual body continued to haunt the political. The symbolic functions that the monarch's spiritual body performed do not simply 'disappear once the place of the sovereign has been emptied and the principle of sovereignty relocated in the will, life, and fate of "The People"' (Santner 2011, 50)—and in their bodies, I hope to have shown. Santner situates his corporeal lens at the cusp of the Symbolic and the Lacanian Real, the part of the human experience that eludes symbolisation altogether. He uses the body, or rather 'the flesh', to move beyond the Symbolic. My purpose is to show instead the work of naturalisation that the body achieves *for* the constitution of a modern symbolic, as the space of the political but also of the state itself (see also Epstein 2013).

16. I am grateful to Paul Halliday for drawing my attention to this dimension of the case.

17. Officers of the law would typically use it to claim exemptions from duties in other courts. For example, when an officer from one court was being held or sued in another, his own court could issue a habeas corpus to obtain his release; ostensibly so that he may exercise his own duties, but also in the process curbing the other court's powers (see Jenks 1923).

18. Edward Coke, 5 *Reports* 91b, cited in Hostettler 1997, 128.

19. Sir Robert Heath, Coke's successor as the chief justice of common pleas declared that, should the liberty of subjects be dangerous to the state, even if they were innocent, they had, as per 'reason of state', to be kept in prison until the king was ready to bring them to trial (Hostettler 1997, 126).

20. The old English term 'realise', which, in the early seventeenth century, still meant 'to make royal or regal' is worth noting in this context (see Oxford English Dictionary). The English revolutionaries' battle for corporeal liberty inverted this old sense by realising liberty in the body of the subject, I suggest.

21. My claim is not that modernity dissolved all local ties. The contemporary individual undoubtedly has many attachments—local, national, and even supranational, for many Europeans. Only Great Britain, not Lancaster or Camden, is the

territorial referent for the British subject's rights. Moreover, colonial subjecthood and subjectivities have illustrated in the chapter the workings of these attachments to an abstract distant territory mediated by a personal relation to the sovereign.

Chapter 5

1. Foucault's (2005) is a longue durée tableau of the evolution of the conditions of knowledge production, specifically the structures of language. Hence for him, the classical episteme is one among a succession of epistemes constitutive of modernity. For me, the pertinent rupture lies between the medieval and the classical episteme, which begins in the seventeenth century. I am less persuaded by the distinctions he draws for the post-classical age.
2. The *mathesis universalis* was, for Descartes (1998, 97), a 'general science [that] explains all that can be investigated concerning order and measure irrespective of any particular matter'.
3. This does not mean that Locke did not think nature 'existed' out there, or that he collapsed all distinctions between truth and falsity, to address the tired, hackneyed caricature of constructivist theorising that seems to refuse to die. Locke (*EHU*, chap.30[2]248) explicitly defines as 'fantastical or chimerical' the ideas that 'have no foundation in nature, nor have any conformity to that reality of being to which they are tacitly referred as to their archetypes'. A mathematical formula is real. Its application has to conform to the formula, or else it yields a 'chimera'. Archetypes exist, even if they are constructed. They are real constructed things, like language.
4. I use the term 'state' here as it is my object of analysis. Strictly speaking, neither Locke nor Hobbes use the term extensively. Hobbes (*L*. 3) does posit it in opening the *Leviathan* among a chain of equivalent terms: 'that Great LEVIATHAN called a COMMONWEALTH', which is his standard term, 'or STATE (in Latin CIVITAS)' and he also brings in 'body politic' later in the same paragraph. 'The use of the term in relation to Locke is more of a lexical stretch; indeed, his reasons for preferring 'government' are at the heart of this chapter. It is Locke, however, who coins the expression (but not the referent) 'state of nature'. He conjoins 'state' to both nature and to violence.

   Locke, however, does use the term 'state', which, Like Hobbes, he conjoins to nature on the one hand (in the 'state of nature'), and to war on the other (in 'state of war'). My reasons for using 'state' when discussing Locke, then, are twofold: first, because it was the actual political form taking shape with and around him; but second because I contend that the term was achieving considerable conceptual if negative work as foils for 'the state', in both 'the state of nature' and especially (in his case) 'the state of war'. For a similar, more developed, argument in relation to Hobbes, see my Epstein 2013.
5. What Descartes shared with Hobbes, in this age of the machine, was a mechanistic epistemology, but not a materialist ontology. The soul was very real, albeit distinct from the body, for Descartes. He did not, however, carry this epistemology to the realm of politics, which he avoided altogether, as we saw in chapter 3.

6. This is one of the reasons for the enduring debate over whether Hobbes has a substantive theory of obligation. See notably Skinner 2008 and Pettit 2005 for recent expressions of this debate.

7. On the practical conditions of the slave in the Middle Ages, see also Bloch 1968.

8. The inner workings of power have been at the centre of Michel Foucault's and Judith Butler's work. See also Lukes (2005).

9. That the difference resides in the situation does not take away the choice. You can always choose not to contract, for Hobbes, even when you are scared for your life.

10. An influential tradition has insisted on holding the different parts of Locke's thought separate, on account of the circumstances surrounding the *Two Treatises*, which was published anonymously and just as Locke was about to step into positions of power, and of the practical bend to his thought. It is underlined that, unlike Hobbes, Locke did not have a comprehensive philosophical system, but rather a piecemeal, physician's approach to political problems (Laslett 1988). The limits to this way of approaching Locke have already been drawn out in more recent Locke scholarship (Tully 1988; Waldron 1988). In fact, Locke's towering influence on our political modernity makes it urgent to hold no part of his thought off-limits in seeking to account for it.

11. The term 'consciousness' itself was coined by the Cambridge Platonist Cudworth, who was a close friend of Locke's (Balibar 2013).

12. This is the Hobbesian *foro interno* we saw in chapter 2, or indeed, in French, the *for intérieur*, given the French Protestant Jean Calvin's role in articulating this dimension in his 1539 *Institutes of the Christian Religion*, which he translated himself into French in 1541.

13. Locke drafted a first *Two Tracts of Government* in 1660, and then revisited the question (in a very different direction) in his *Two Treatises on Government* in 1690.

14. Early in the seventeenth century, Francis Bacon (1964) already readily spoke of the 'Torch of [the new] Science' he set out to found, as we will see in the following chapter, but it was Descartes, properly, who appropriated the Lucent metaphor for the cognitive activity of thinking.

15. On the importance of the semantic proximity between the conscience as *Gewiss* and *Gewissenheit*, 'certainty', see Büttbinger 2014; Balibar 2013.

16. Balibar's argument is not that Descartes is not the point of origin of philosophies of the subject, only of the concept of 'consciousness'—a significant difference. Balibar takes as his starting point the difficulties encountered by Locke's first French translator, Pierre Coste, in rendering the English 'consciousness' in French, which, he points out, would not have existed if the term had been firmly established by Descartes, and argues that the concept's lineage is more accurately traced to the *Essay on Human Understanding* and to the English language. Locke, at any rate, understood himself to be continuing Descartes's enterprise (see Pringle-Pattison 1924).

17. Descartes defines the experience in the following terms: 'by the word "thought" I understand all that which happens in us that we immediately apperceive or know ourselves' (Descartes, cited in Balibar [2013, xviii]).

18. On Locke as a natural law theorist, see Tuck 1979; Tully 1988; Waldron 1988; Ashcraft 1986; Dunn 1969; Laslett 1988; Simmons 1991; and Buckle 1993.

19. The conscience has not been the focus of this literature on natural law and natural rights, which I engage with extensively in chapter 6, because, I suggest, it is the heir to Locke's solution, which it is my purpose to describe here.

20. On these contradictions, see Laslett (1988, 79–82); and see Buckle (1993, 127–28) for a response. With Laslett 1988, I think these contradictions can be taken at face value.

21. The closest Locke comes to referencing the mechanistic imagery in the *Essay concerning Human Understanding* is a nod to Descartes's clockwork, which we will consider in the following chapter. Locke does not apprehend the state or 'government' as a mechanical construction, as does Hobbes.

22. Hence while I agree with Laslett (1988, 84) (rather than with Buckle 1993) that Calvin's crusade against innate ideas was a 'solvent of the natural law attitude', I question its effectiveness. What it did not dissolve was the knot that bound natural law to a reason steeped in a Calvinist conscience.

23. Locke was not the first to analyse the understanding. It features in Francis Bacon's *New Organon*, which I will consider in chapter 7, and indeed in some of Descartes's own writings (*l'entendement* or *intellectus*). Only reason remains the centre point of Descartes's 1637 treatise, which was decisively influential on Locke. Its full title is *A Discourse on the Method of Correctly Conducting One's Reason and Seeking the Truth in the Sciences*.

24. Locke is concerned with making room for the scriptural (Paulinan) emphasis of the resurrection of bodies, which the Ancient Greek (Platonic) focus on the soul left unaddressed. On these influences and the importance of theology for Locke, see Forstrom 2010.

25. This also enables him to distinguish between a human justice and a divine justice; see Forstrom 2010.

26. Moral matters were both the starting and the endpoint of the *Essay*. They were the topic of the discussions Locke had with his friends that prompted its drafting, according to one of the participants, James Tyrell (see Woolhouse 1997). Locke also returns to them in his subsequent essay on the *Conduct of the Understanding*, which I turn to in the next section. It was initially intended as an appendix to the *Essay*.

27. In the fifth discourse of his treatise on vision, *Dioptrics*, Descartes recommends to 'take the eye of a man freshly deceased', or 'of an ox, or another large animal' and to cut it open in order understand the mechanics of sight in the brain (my translation).

28. I borrow the distinction between 'rational' and 'reasonable' from Carrig (2001), and develop it using a range of critical and feminist Locke scholarships throughout the rest of the chapter.

29. The expression is John Baltes's (2012; 2016). See also Tully 1988; Mehta 1992; Carrig 2001; Hirschmann 2008; and for a critique of this critical scholarship, see Nazar 2017. For Locke on education more generally, see Tarcov 1984, and, to a lesser extent, Josephson 2002

30. To be clear, the figure of the foreigner functions as an ideal type that serves to locate the threshold of political membership, the stage before subjecthood. It does not designate all actual foreigners.

31. Since Walter Raleigh had popularised tobacco early in the century, such claims about the benefits of tobacco were not uncommon, in a time, moreover, that saw the take-off of colonial trade in which Locke held direct (he owned shares in the slave trade) and indirect (he was one of the drafters of the Constitution of Carolina that legitimised slavery, employed notably in tobacco plantations) interests (see Armitage 2002).

32. Locke did venture there, of course, at several points in his life, notably in his writing titled *Questions concerning the Law of Nature*. Only he never intended these to be published. However, the desire to nail Locke's position on natural law began in earnest in Locke's time, with the entreaties of his friend James Tyrell, and has continued in the Locke scholarship ever since; and to it we owe the several versions of these questions (see Locke 1990; 1997). Only, with Laslett (1988), I think it is worth taking seriously his intention not to publish them. For a position opposite to Laslett's, that renders what is at stake in this question for natural rights theory, see Buckle (1993).

33. Marx (1992, II, chap. 27) has underlined the role played by the wool industry in his historical analysis of the rise of capitalism.

34. It matters here that Locke considered education to be a matter for the family rather than for government. This is another difference with Hobbes, who broaches the topic of education via the sovereign's duties.

35. The records of the 1715 session at the Old Bailey show that one offender was put to death for stealing 'one bed, two blankets and a rug' (Linebaugh 1991, 80).

36. Historians have found it in France (Comninel 2000), across Northern Europe, and in Germany, from where it was brought over to England by the Anglo-Saxons prior to the Norman Conquest (Thirsk 1964). The 'vil' was at once a social, legal, and economic unit (Seebohm 1883).

Chapter 6

1. My argument is not that private property did not exist in the Middle Ages, nor that there were no laws for regulating it in practice. It is, rather, that it was not the primary paradigm underwriting property relations, as these authors have also shown. It was modernity's invention, not an eternal truth about human organisation.

2. Behind what may seem like a mere terminological quibble lies both a methodological and substantial point. The 'individual', etymologically the undivided, is not a relational concept. Nor is it primarily a social scientific concept, but a biological and a logical one. Hence, to my eyes, it does not offer a solid enough foothold for critiquing the figure at the heart of liberalism's individualist modes of thought. It risks inadvertently reproducing them. It also holds the risk of perpetuating an implicit hierarchy between the natural and the social sciences. The subject is instead, first, an inherently relational concept that maintains the state and their mutual dependence in focus. It explicitly short-circuits liberalism's ontology. Second, it is more consistent with

my broader commitment to holding separate the realms of the natural and the social scientific, against a contemporary tendency to collapse them. My purpose in this chapter is precisely to show how a biological object, the human body, served to constitute and entrench the taken-for-granted 'individual'.

3. Terminologically, I reserve 'natural law' for the medieval body of thought and refer to early modern theories when I use 'natural rights'. For similar uses see Villey 1975; Arneil 1996; Brett 2011; or Fitzmaurice 2014, for example.

4. Moreover, in medieval Church law, given the Church's charitable mission, one of the most important set of questions concerned the kinds of claims that could be rightfully made by people in need (see Tierney 1997). Hence some of the most important developments in property law turned on the right to use (*domine utile*), rather than own (*domine directum*) (see Fitzmaurice 2014, 37). These sorts of questions were, at any rate, a far cry from the positive claim to occupy and appropriate that took shape in the seventeenth century.

5. The full formula is 'the constant and perpetual will of rendering to each what is rightful theirs' (*justicia est constans et perpetua voluntas, jus suum unicuique tribuiendi*). Aquinas (*Summa Theologia* 2a 2ae qu. 58, p.164) attributes it to Ulpianus, finds it in Cicero, and establishes it to be consistent with Aristotle. Aquinas rehabilitated Roman law by conjoining it with Greek philosophy and Christian theology. His main contribution is to have drawn the classic definition of justice closer to reason, rather than the will.

6. The question as to whether natural rights, centred upon the subject, existed prior to the early modern age has been the object of extensive debate. Michel Villey (1975) traces the origins of subjective rights to William of Ockham in the Middle Ages, whereas Brian Tierney (1997) has sought to refute Villey's classic account by tracking it back to the Romans. There is a difference, in my view, between whether these rights simply existed, whether they could be found in practice in some area of the law to address relations between individuals (who did indeed exist), and how salient they were, how representative they were of the broader ontology where they obtained. I have found this difference to be downplayed by contemporary natural rights theorists in favour of perpetuating the anachronistic translation of *jus* with 'right' (cf., for example, Tuck 1979, 5).

7. The importance of the *suum* to natural rights theorising has been emphasised by recent scholarship, largely building on Karl Olivecrona's (1974a; 1974b) early insights (see Waldron 1988; Buckle 1991; Schmidgen 2002; Mautner 2010; Olivecrona 2010; Mancilla 2015).

8. Hobbes (*L.*, chap.24[8], 162) also provides for the commonwealth 'to have a portion' in the distribution of land it ordains.

9. The *suum* has provided an enduring foundation for notions of privacy until this day. To take a contemporary definition: "The right to privacy is our right to keep a domain around us, which includes all those things that are part of us, such as our body, home, property, thoughts, feelings, secrets and identity" (Onn et al., 2005).

10. A significant episode in the history of property law turned on the attempt, by the Franciscans in the fourteenth century, to separate out use rights from property rights

entirely and to create a new legal form of property-less-ness founded in use (see Villey 1975; Brett 2011).

11. Wolfram Schmidgen (2002, 56) has nicely illustrated the importance of this boundary-drawing for natural rights theories, by showing how it was haunted by the figure of cannibalism. 'The absence of boundary of a boundary between "mine" and "thine" [was considered] the first characteristic of a society that knows no limit', he writes.

12. *Jus* was also different from *lex*. Within this series of subsystems that composed the *jura*, *lex* referred to a specific rule within one such domain, created by an act of legislation or command (see Mautner 2010).

13. In fact, this highly agential notion rights is specific to Grotius. It is relaxed by both Pufendorf and Locke, who both recover the 'passive' dimension of rights (see Tully 1980; see chapter 4). My contention, however, is that the work of establishing the natural *suum* as a pillar of modern natural rights had been achieved by the time of Locke's and even Pufendorf's writing.

14. Recall that the task of justice is, literally translated, 'their own to each to attribute', *suum cuique tribuere*.

15. Stephen Buckle also illustrates this oversight. While he (rightly) notes that private property was 'a late stage in a process of extensions to the suum', again he conflates 'one's due' and 'one's own' (see Buckle 1993, 52).

16. My differences with Esposito, and with the biopolitical scholarship at large, are, first, that what is conjured by way of this 'biological reference' is not a generic 'life', but rather nature, and a particularly one, human nature. Not *bios*, then, nor Agamben's (1998) *zoe* (organic life), but rather a narrowed down, androcentric *physis*. Second, the scholarship has followed Foucault's cue in shifting the focus away from the state (to explore post-statist, bottom-up forms of power centred upon the management of life), whereas I am interested in its constitution.

17. The contract, which Hobbes invents, does not feature as such in Grotius (see Tadashi 1993). However, his concept of property contains a liminal form of the contract, tacit recognition (see Haakonsson 1985; Shimokawa 2013), and in this account, he is generally considered as part of the pantheon (see Tuck 1979; Tully 1980; Buckle 1993).

18. Of course the state of nature is Hobbes's myth. But as I also showed, it is what enabled him to negotiate the broader epistemological break with nature that other natural rights theorists papered over.

19. Strictly speaking, the basis of Grotius's account of private property evolved through the course of his writings. He began with a theory of occupation, in his *Mare Liberium*, written as the twelfth chapter to his *De Indis* (also published as *De jure praedae*) and added the notion of agreement in his *De jure belli ac pacis*.

20. The contract is also what explicitly excludes animals from the realm of justice: 'There is no convention among animals which conferes a special right over a thing to the one that first got it', writes Pufendorf (1934, IV.chap.4[5]538). Therefore 'man is permitted to use creatures which lack reason' (ibid.).

21. This reified, individualised form of property would be handed down to the Enlightenment, surfacing notably in Rousseau, who in his *Social Contract* (I.4.) defines property as a relation between things.

22. Whereas Locke contended that uncultivated land was simply wasteful and could be appropriated, Pufendorf instead claimed that if something 'should be found, which is not ascertained to a private Owner, it must not presently be looked on as *void* and *waste*, so that any one person may seize it as his *Peculiar* (quoted in Fitzmaurice 2014, 114).

23. Politically, Locke's *Two Treatises* was an intervention against Filmer, whose attack aimed at the Whig party, to which Locke's employer, the Earl of Shaftesbury, belonged.

24. Thus for example when he writes: 'such is the constitution of man's body that it cannot live from its own substance, but has need of substances gathered from outside, from which it is nourished and fortified against those things that would destroy its structure' (Pufendorf 1934, IV.chap.3[1]524).

25. Hence Locke also undoes Pufendorf's 'physicalising' of substances, since for Locke labour per se is more than the work of the body.

26. Locke (*TT*, II.chap.5[31–36]290) does consider Pufendorf's objection to Grotius, namely, the risk of an unbridled race to appropriate that inheres in a natural right to property. He addresses it by way of the law of nature or reason, which establishes a natural 'measure' within this right (*TT*, II.chap.5[36]292): to take as much as one can use up 'before it spoils'. This limiting mechanism, in turn, paves the way for the 'invention of money' (ibid.), where interpersonal relations enters into this framework, via exchange. That Locke envisages such a natural measure for appropriation beggars the question as to why he does not do so for punishment (see chapter 5).

27. 'Lives, Liberties and Estates' is Locke's (*TT*, II.chap.9[123]350) definition of property.

28. The question of their emancipation was raised by slaves being baptised, hence in relation to the question of their being admitted into communities of Christians.

29. In the realms of practice they also make things. This work of sorting thus also exemplifies the creative agency at work in Locke's 'making'.

30. Hume officiated for the Empire as Under-Secretary of State, effectively for Colonial Affairs.

31. Once again his purpose in the *Essay* is not to nail definitively the attributes of the (nominal) human essence, but rather to explore the kinds of errors that arise from confusing real and nominal essences, as indeed Hume does.

Chapter 7

1. So significant did Descartes (2006, 39–46) consider Harvey's discovery to be for the emergence of a modern science that he spends a considerable portion of the *Discourse*'s fifth part explaining it. Harvey was appointed 'Physician Extraordinary' by James I and remained the doctor for James I's son, Charles I (see Shapin and Schaffer 2011).

2. Four dissections were required to obtain the medical degree at Oxford.

3. Surveillance studies scholars have extensively studied the explosion of modes of surveillance and the new forms it has taken. For horizontal, 'lateral' or 'social surveillance', see, for example, Andrejevic 2005; and Marwick 2012. See Mann and Wellmann 2002 and Albrechtslund 2008 respectively for 'sousveillance' and 'participatory surveillance', among other modalities of looking back up at the state, broadly writ.

4. Foucault does touch upon the seventeenth century in his 1970s public lectures, which were broad historical overviews, and notably in *Society Must Be Defended*. Only, as I showed in chapter 1, this is also the lecture where Foucault bid farewell to sovereignty. Nor were these where Foucault deployed his careful, extensive empirical analyses. They were indeed lectures, and Foucault had not intended them to be published.

5. My focus on the production of the dead body is why the biopolitical angle is not relevant for my purposes. I will show that it is a necessary moment in the trajectory of the emergence of the particular form of concrete knowledge that concerned Foucault in *Birth of the Clinic*.

6. Tracing the place of the body in the formation of modern science troubles the Kuhnian distinction between 'the classical physical sciences' and 'the Baconian empirical sciences'. Descartes and Kepler, which I also consider here, belonged to the former, for Kuhn (1977).

7. The grand book of the universe is, moreover, Galileo continues 'written in the language of mathematics, and its characters are triangles, circles and other geometric figures without which it is humanly impossible to understand a single word of it', rendering the importance of geometric thinking for the seventeenth century, see chapters 2 and 3 (quoted in Shapin 1996, 69).

8. 'Quasi-deductive' is how Thomas Kuhn (1977, 48) describes a mode of knowledge that did contain some measure of empirical data; the geometers, for example, saw their figures in nature. However, experiments intended either to 'demonstrate a conclusion known in advance', or to 'provide answers to questions posed by existing theories' (Kuhn 1977, 43). They did not lay the foundations for new theories, as they did in the science begat by the scientific revolution.

9. This is where Hobbes broke with Boyle (see Shapin and Schaffer 2011).

10. The (since much more famous) *Discourse* was intended to constitute the introduction to this treatise on optics, which Descartes thus established as the cornerstone of his scientific enterprise.

11. Boyle is quoted in Shapin and Schaffer (2011, 36). See Sawday (1996, 57) for his support of dissections.

12. Harvey published his work on blood circulation in 1628 and his final important discovery, on the generation of life, in 1651, whereas Locke arrived in Oxford a year later, and obtained his bachelor of medicine in 1675. Harvey withdrew to Oxford during the civil war, where he was appointed ward of Merton College in 1645.

13. Histories of medicine tend to attribute the title of founder of modern medicine either to Harvey, on account of his discovery of blood circulation (see Pagel 1951; Bayon 1941), or to Vesalius, on account of his role in establishing the human body at the centre of anatomical practice (see Wilson 1987; Rupp 1992; Steiner 2010).

14. Harvey and Vesalius did not overlap, since Harvey graduated in 1602.

15. This division of labour overlaps with the distinction between 'empirics' and the more theoretical and scholarly dimensions of medicine, known as 'physics' (Richardson 1988, 34).

16. Bacon published his *Great Instauration*, where he deploys this programme, in 1620. It includes the *New Organon*, which is Bacon's better known epistemological treatise and my primary source. *The Great Renewal* is its subtitle.

17. Thomas Kuhn (1977) distinguished between the classical sciences and the experimental sciences (or 'experimental philosophy'), inaugurated by Bacon. Although they developed along two distinct axes (the 'mathematical vs. experimental sciences', in Kuhn's categorisation), the rise of Baconian science marked an empirical turn even in the classical science, like mathematics which were 'radically reconstructed' in his wake (see Kuhn 1977, 40–41).

18. Significantly, the oldest instance recorded by *Oxford English Dictionary* of the irruption of the word *dissection* in common language is from Bacon: 'Thus have i described and opened by a kind of dissection those peccant humours' (1604).

19. I follow the historical convention in using the word 'Puritanism' broadly, as the religiously inspired reform movement that led the charge against the established order, rather than as specific a Protestant sect, hence as the driving force of the English Revolution (see Hill 1980, 26; see also Walzer 1965; Webster 1975). I use 'Parliamentarians' to refer to the the Civil War's wining faction led by Cromwell, and opposed to the Royalists.

20. Benedictus's rules would afford the model, widely used across Europe, for the first public regulations.

21. This belief underwrote the terror that forms of punishment that denied the criminal a burial were designed to inspire, particularly the gibbet, which exposed the bodily remains to be dissolved by the elements.

22. For example, the theological concept of personhood and debates about resurrection were central to Locke's concept of personal identity (see chapter 5; see also Forstrom 2010).

23. One purpose of the creation Company of Barbers and Surgeons in 1540 was to clarify and settle the divisions of labour. It proscribed barbers from undertaking surgery, and surgeons from shaving or cutting hair. Teeth extraction was the only area that remained common to both.

24. The multiplication of political pamphlets, caused both by the drop in printing prices and the collapse of censorship, where new ideas circulated freely, was a defining feature of the English Revolution. In addition and in relation to the body, the Interregnum saw a sharp increase in scientific and especially medical publications, mostly in the vernacular (see Webster 1975; Hill 1965).

25. See Ruth Richardson (1988, 35) for an account of the importance of Louis XIV's much publicised operation for anal fistula in 1687 for the institutionalisation of science in France. The importance of scientific emulation and rivalry for the contemporary state is well known (see Finnemore 1996; Zarakol 2010).

26. This, despite the fact that the Tomlins Readership in Anatomy was established in 1624, although clearly not to our divine's satisfaction (Boston and Webb 2016).

27. The college also issued a series of regulations for the private anatomy schools that were proliferating around the country, which I consider below (see Sawday 1996, 57).

28. Although the 1832 Anatomy Act is beyond my time-frame, in her detailed study Ruth Richardson (1988) demonstrates how it was a deliberate and explicit alliance of the middle and upper classes to sacrifice the English poor, in a way that both protected their own dead, and satisfied science's need for corpses. For my purposes, Richardson's study is useful to evince the exponential demand for corpses from the seventeenth century onwards: Richardson (1988, 87) estimates that dissections were occurring 'in the several thousands' in the early nineteenth century. In 1826, 600 dissections were performed in the London area alone (ibid., 125).

29. Dr Tulp was the Amsterdam city surgeon from 1628 to 1653. Amsterdam had one of the oldest anatomy theatres (since 1555), but it was not as spectacular as Leiden's, where Rembrandt had studied (Hansen 1996).

30. That the corpse was objectified did not mean that it had no agency; it exerted its own, material constraints upon the anatomy lesson (see Wilson 1987). The body-as-object, in other words, has a different kind of agency. Although this agency is not my focus here, it is useful for drawing out that distinction between subject and object does not straightforwardly overlap with that distinction active and passive.

31. 'Fabric', which initially referred to product of craftmanship in early modern English, acquired the additional meaning of 'engine' in the first half of the seventeenth century, the period of mechanism's rise (See Oxford English Dictionary).

32. The co-extensiveness of 'meaning' and 'direction' inheres in the French for 'significance', *sens*.

33. Function, of course, would never fully be capable of replacing meaning; the seeds for a Weberian disenchantment of the world were planted here, although it is beyond my focus here.

34. In a similar vein, Yves Winter (2018) has recently shown how the spectacle of violence performed constitutive functions in the political writings of another founding theorist of the state, Niccolò Machiavelli.

35. Although this was apparently less necessary for the Dutch performances, which were notoriously more orderly (see Rupp 1992).

36. This frontispiece can be considered a cultural artefact, expressive of the broader culture from which it hailed, especially given the iconic status this textbook rapidly achieved (perhaps aided by this frontispiece), rather than as an accurate rendition of Vesalius's conception of the female anatomy (which features abundantly in the book itself).

37. Although the more known section is the one on *Animal Generation*, the full title of the work in which it is published is *Anatomical Exercises on the Generation of Animals, to Which Is Added Essays on Parturition, on the Membranes and Fluids of the Uterus, and on Conception* (1651).

38. Harvey's use of the magnifying glass is thought to account for some of the limitations of his work on animal generation.

39. For Descartes (2006, 51) the 'as it were' mastery and possession of nature would yield 'a host of inventions that [would] lead us effortlessly to enjoy the fruits of the earth' and to the preservation of health, the foundation of all the other goods of this life.

40. The essay, 'the Masculine Birth of Time of the Great Instauration of the Dominion of Man over the Universe', is written in the form of a letter addressed to the scientist of the future.

Conclusion

1. Saussure's 'signifier' is of course a construct as well. My aim here, however, is to draw attention to the signified *also* being a construct, rather than the real thing. This is one of the common misunderstandings of the Saussurean terminology.

2. Hobbes's and Locke's states of nature were not designed to be exact scientific depictions of nature, but rather thought experiments aimed at political construction. They were more archetypal than ectypal, to use Locke's distinction. Nevertheless, by virtue of the fact they took nature as their referent, their status remained ambiguous, hovering somewhere between these two, as I will further show below. My point here is simply that this infinite space loomed large over the imagination of nature in the classical age, including over Locke's and Hobbes's.

3. The etymology of 'species', which shares roots with 'spectacle' and derives from the verb *specere*, 'to look, to see or behold', underlines the observatory nature of the task.

4. The English Revolution occupies an iconic status in both liberal and Marxian historiographies, who see it as a crucible for modernity's individual or collective agency respectively.

Bibliography

Abizadeh, A. 2013. 'Publicity, Privacy and Religious Toleration in Hobbes' Leviathan'. *Modern Intellectual History* 10, no. 2:261–91.

Agamben, G. 1998. *Homo Sacer: Sovereign Power and Bare Life*. Translated by D. Heller-Roazen. Stanford, CA: Stanford University Press.

Agnew, J. 2017. 'Continuity, Discontinuity and Contingency: Insights for International Political Sociology from Political Geography'. In *International Political Sociology: Transversal Lines*, edited by T. Basaran, E. P. Guittet, D. Bigo, and R. B. J. Walker, 49–67. London: Routledge.

Alpers, S.L. 1983. *The Art of Describing: Dutch Art in the Seventeenth Century*, Chicago: Chicago University Press.

Ajana, B. 2013. *Governing Through Biometrics: The Biopolitics of Identity*. Basingstoke and New York: Palgrave.

Albrechtslund, A. 2008. 'Online Social Networking as Participatory Surveillance'. *First Monday* 13, no.3.

Amoore, L. 2008. 'Governing by Identity'. In: *Playing the Identity Card*, Edited by C. Bennett and D. Lyon, 21–36. New York: Routledge.

Anderson, B. 1983. *Imagined Communities: Reflections on the Origins and Spread of Nationalism*. London: Verso.

Andrejevic, M. 2006. 'The Discipline of Watching: Detection, Risk and Lateral Surveillance'. *Critical Studies in Media Communication* 23, no.5:391–407.

Aquinas, T. (1485) 2009. *Somme Théologique*. Édition numérique: bibliothèque de l'édition du Cerf.

Aristotle,1990. *Éthique à Nicomaque*. Translated by J. Tricot. Paris: Vrin.

Aristotle, 2000. *Organon IV: Les Seconds Analytiques*, Translated by J. Tricot. Paris: Vrin.

Armitage, D. 2004. 'John Locke, Carolina and the *Two Treatises on Government*'. *Political Theory* 32, no.5:602–627.

Arneil, B. 1996. *John Locke and America: The Defence of English Colonialism*. Oxford: Clarendon Press.

Ashcraft, R. 1986. *Revolutionary Politics and Locke's Two Treatises on Government*. Princeton, NJ: Princeton University Press.

Ausch, R., R. Doane, and L. Perez 2000. 'Interview with Elizabeth Grosz'. *Found Object* 9, 1–16.

Babot A., A. Boucaud-Maître, and P. Delaigue. 2002. *Dictionnaire de l'histoire du droit et des institutions publiques*. Paris : Ellipses.

Bacon, F. (1603) 1964. 'The Birth of Masculine Time or the Great Instauration of the Dominion of Man over the Universe'. In *The Philosophy of Francis Bacon*. Edited and translated by B. Farrington, 59–80. Liverpool: Liverpool University Press.

Bacon, F. (1620) 2000. *The New Organon*. Edited by L. Jardine and M. Silverthorne. Cambridge: Cambridge University Press.

Bacon, F. (1627) 2009. *The New Atlantis*. Auckland: The Floating Press.

Balibar, É. 2013. *Identity and Difference: John Locke and the Invention of Consciousness*. Translated by W. Montag. London and New York: Verso.

Balibar É. 2014a. SOUL. In *Dictionary of Untranslatables: A Philosophical Lexicon*. Translated by Steven Rendall. Edited by B. Cassin, 1009–1022. Princeton, NJ: Princeton University Press.

Balibar, É. 2014b. 'CONSCIOUSNESS. In *Dictionary of Untranslatables: A Philosophical Lexicon*. Translated by Steven Rendall. Edited by B. Cassin, 174–187. Princeton, NJ: Princeton University Press.

Balibar, É., Cassin, B. and De Libera A. 2014. SUBJECT. In *Dictionary of Untranslatables: A Philosophical Lexicon*. Translated by Steven Rendall. Edited by B. Cassin, 1069–1090. Princeton, NJ: Princeton University Press.

Ball, T. 1985. 'Hobbes' Linguistic Turn'. *Polity* 17, no. 4:739–60.

Bartelson, J. 1995. *A Genealogy of Sovereignty*. Cambridge: Cambridge University Press.

Bartelson, J. 2010. 'The Social Construction of Globality'. *International Political Sociology* 4, no. 3:219–35.

Bayon, H.P. 1941. 'The Significance of the Demonstration of the Harveyan Circulation by Experimental Tests'. *Isis* 33, no.4:443–453.

Beauvoir, S. D. 1953. *The Second Sex*. London: Jonathan Cape.

Beckenridge, K. 2014. *The Biometric State: The Global Politics of Identification and Surveillance in South Africa from 1850 to the Present*. Cambridge: Cambridge University Press

Bell. D. 2014. 'What is Liberalism?' *Political Theory* 42, no.6:682–715.

Benjamin, J. 1988. *The Bonds of Love: Psychoanalysis, Feminism and the Problem of Domination*. New York: Pantheon.

Benjamin, W. 1986. 'Critique of Violence'. In *Essays, Aphorisms, Autobiographical Writings*. Translated by E. Jephcott. Edited by P. Demetz, 277–300. New York: Schocken Books.

Bennet, J. 2010. *Vibrant Matter: A Political Ecology of Things*, Durham, N.C.: Duke University Press.

Berlin, I. 1969. 'Two Concepts of Liberty'. In *Four Essays on Liberty*, 118–172. Oxford: Oxford University Press.

Berman, H. J. 2003. *Law and Revolution II. The Impact of The Protestant Reformations on the Western Legal Traditions*. Cambridge, MA: Harvard University Press.

Bernasconi, R. 1992. 'Locke's Almost Random Talk of Man: The Double Use of Words in the Natural Law Justification of Slavery'. *Perspectiven Der Philosophie* 18, 293–318.

Bianchi, E. 2006. 'Material Vicissitudes and Technical Wonders: The Ambiguous Figure of Automaton in Aristotle's Metaphysics of Sexual Difference'. *Epoché. A Journal for the History of Philosophy* 11, no.1:109–39.

Blits, J. H. 1989. Hobbesian Fear. *Political Theory* 17, no.3:417–31.

Bloch, M. 1968. *La Société Féodale*. Paris: Albin Michel.

Bourdieu, P. 1998. La Domination Masculine. Paris : Éditions du Seuil.

Bourke, J. 2014. *The Story of Pain: From Prayers to Painkillers*. Oxford: Oxford University Press.

Bousquet, A. 2017. 'Lethal Visions: The Eye as Function of the Weapon'. *Critical Studies on Security* 5, no.1:62–80.

Bracken H. M. 1973. 'Essence, Accidents and Race'. *Hermathena* 116, 81–96.

Brailsford, H. N. 1961. *The Levellers and the English Revolution*. Edited by C. Hill. Stanford, CA: Stanford University Press.

Brett, A. S. 1997. *Liberty, Rights and Nature: Individual Rights in Later Scholastic Thought.* Cambridge: Cambridge University Press.

Brett, A. S. 2010. '"The Matter, Forme, and Power of a Common-wealth"': Thomas Hobbes and Late Renaissance Commentary on Aristotle's Politics'. *Hobbes Studies* 23, no.1:72–102.

Brett, A. S. 2011. *Changes of State: Nature and the Limits of the City in Early Modern Natural Law.* Princeton, NJ: Princeton University Press.

Brown, K. 1980. 'Thomas Hobbes and the Title-Page of "Leviathan"'. *Philosophy* 55, no.213:410–411.

Bryson, N. 1986. *Vision and Painting: The Logic of the Gaze.* New Haven, CT: Yale University Press.

Buc, P. 2015. *Holy War, Martyrdom and Terror: Christianity, Violence and the West ca. 70 C.E. to the Iraq War.* Philadelphia, VA: University of Pennsylvania Press.

Buckle, S. 1993. *Natural Law and the Theory of Property: Grotius to Hume.* New York: Oxford University Press.

Butler, J. 1988. 'Performative Acts and Gender Constitution: An Essay in Phenomenology and Feminist Theory'. *Theatre Journal* 40, no.2:519–31.

Butler, J. 1990. *Gender Trouble. Feminism and the Subversion of Identity.* London and New York: Routledge.

Butler, J. 1993. *Bodies that Matter. On the Discursive Limits of Sex.* London: Routledge.

Butterfield, H. 1975. 'Raison d'État'. Martin Wight Memorial Lecture, University of Sussex, Brighton, UK, April.

Büttgen, P. 2014. *Conscienta* and *Gewissen* in Luther. In 'CONSCIOUSNESS'. In *Dictionary of Untranslatables: A Philosophical Lexicon.* Translated by Steven Rendall, Edited by B. Cassin, 178–179. Princeton, NJ: Princeton University Press.

Campbell, D. 1998. *Writing Security. United States Foreign Policy and the Politics of Identity,* Minneapolis: University of Minnesota Press.

Canning, J. P. 1988. 'Law, Sovereignty and Corporation Theory'. In *Cambridge History of Medieval Thought 350–1450.* Edited by J. H. Burns, 454–476. Cambridge: Cambridge University Press.

Carrig. J. 2001. 'Liberal Impediment to Liberal Education: The Assent to Locke'. *Review of Politics* 63, no.1:41–76.

Cassirer, E. (1927) 2000. *The Individual and the Cosmos in Renaissance Philosophy.* Translated by M. Domandi. New York: Dover Publications.

Chamayoux, G. 2013. *Théorie du drone.* Paris: La Fabrique.

Cohen, E. 2009. *A Body Worth Defending: Immunity, Biopolitics and the Apotheosis of the Modern Body.* Durham, NC: Duke University Press.

Cohen, M. 1940. 'Habeas Corpus Cum Causa: The Emergence of the Modern Writ'. *Canadian Bar Review* 18, no.3:172–99.

Coke, E. (1608). 1932. *The Reports of Sr Edward Coke Kt.* Volume 7, Edited by J. F. Fraser, 376–411, London: Lincoln's Inn.

Cole, S. 2001. *Suspect Identities: A History of Fingerprinting and Criminal Identification.* Cambridge, MA: Harvard University Press.

Colebrook, C. 2000. 'From Radical Representations to Corporeal Becomings: The Feminist Philosophy of Lloyd, Grosz and Gatens'. *Hypatia* 15, no. 2:76–93.

Coleman, J. 1988. 'Property and Poverty'. In *Cambridge History of Medieval Thought 350–1450.* Edited by J. H. Burns, 607–648. Cambridge: Cambridge University Press.

Comninel, G. C. 2000. 'English Feudalism and the Origins of Capitalism'. *The Journal of Peasant Studies* 27, no. 4:1–53.

Corpis, D. 2014. *Crossing the Boundaries of Belief: Geographies of Religious Conversion in Southern Germany, 1648–1800*. Charlottesville: University of Virginia Press.

Counter, P. B. 2014. 'The Role of Biometrics in Containing Ebola', on Finding Biometrics, available at: https://findbiometrics.com/archive/the-role-of-biometrics-in-containing-ebola/, accessed 25/07/20.

Crary, J. 1988. 'Modernising Vision'. In *Vision and Visuality*. Edited by H. Foster, 29–50. Seattle: Bay Press.

Dardot, P., and C. Laval. 2014. *Commun: Éssai sur la révolution au XXIe siécle*. Paris: La Découverte.

Dawson, H. 2007. 'The Rebellion of Language Against Reason in Early Modern Thought'. *Intellectual History Review* 17, no.3:277–290.

Derrida, J. 1986. 'Declarations of Independence'. *New Political Science* 7, no.1 7–15.

Derrida, J. 2009. *The Beast and the Sovereign*. Translated by G. Bennington. Chicago: University of Chicago Press.

Descartes. R. (1649) 1988. *Les passions de L'âme*, Paris: Gallimard.

Descartes, R. (1619–28) 1998. *Rules for the Direction of the Natural Intelligence*. Bilingual edition. Translated by G. Heffernan. Rodopi: Amsterdam and Atlanta, GA.

Descartes, R. (1637) 2001. *Discourse on Method, Optics, Geometry and Meteorology*. Translated by P. Olscamp. Indianapolis: Hackett.

Descartes, R. (1637) 2006. *Discourse on the Method of Correctly Conducting One's Reason and Seeking the Truth in the Sciences*. Translated by Ian Maclean. Oxford: Oxford University Press.

Dicey, A. V. 1985. *Introduction to the Study of the Law of the Constitution*. London: Macmillan and Co.

Dijksterhuis, E. 1961. *The Mechanization of the World Picture*. Translated by C. Dikshoorn. Oxford: Clarendon Press.

Dilts, A. 2012. 'To Kill a Thief: Punishment, Proportionality, and Criminal Subjectivity in Locke's Second Treatise'. *Political Theory* 40, no.1:58–83.

Dilts, A. 2014. *Punishment and Inclusion: Race, Membership and the Limits of American Liberalism*. New York: Fordham University Press.

Donne, J. 1896. *The Poems of John Donne*. Edited by E. K. Chambers. London: Lawrence & Bullen.

Dooley, P. C. 2005. *The Labour Theory of Value*. London and New York: Routledge.

Douglas, R. 2014. 'The Body Politic "is a Fictitious Body"'. *Hobbes Studies* 27, no.2:126–47.

Douzinas, C. 2000. *The End of Human Rights: Critical Thought at the Turn of the Century*. Oxford and Portland, OR: Hart Publishing.

Duff, K. 2017. 'The Criminal Is Political: Real Existing Liberalism and the Construction of the Criminal'. PhD Dissertation, University of Sussex.

Duhem, P. 1913. *Le Système du Monde: Histoires des Doctrines Cosmologiques de Platon á Copernic*, vol. 1. Paris: Hermann.

Dunn, J. 1969. *The Political Thought of John Locke*. Cambridge: Cambridge University Press.

Dunn, J. 1984. *Locke*. Oxford: Oxford University Press.

Ekeland, T. 2006. 'Suspending Habeas Corpus: Article 1, Section 9, Clause 2 of the United States Constitution and the War on Terror'. *Fordham Law Review* 74, 1475–1521.

Epstein, C. 2007. 'Guilty Bodies, Productive Bodies, Destructive Bodies: Crossing the Biometric Borders'. *International Political Sociology* 1, no.2:149–164.

Epstein, C. 2008a. *The Power of Words in International Relations: Birth of an Anti-Whaling Discourse*, Cambridge, MA: MIT Press.

Epstein, C. 2008b. 'Embodying Risk: Using biometrics to protect the borders'. In *Risk and the War on Terror*. Edited by L. Amoore and M. de Goede, 178–193. Abingdon, New York: Routledge.

Epstein, C. 2011. 'Who Speaks? Discourse, the Subject and the Study of Identity in International politics'. *European Journal of International Relations* 17, no.1:327–350.

Epstein, C. 2013a. 'Theorizing Agency in Hobbes's Wake: The Rational Actor, the Self, or the Speaking Subject?'. *International Organization* 67, no.2:287–316.

Epstein, C. 2013b. 'Constructivism or the Eternal Return of Universals: Why Returning to Language is Essential to Prolonging the Owl's Flight'. *European Journal of International Relations* 19, no.3:499–519.

Epstein, C. 2016. 'Surveillance, Privacy and the Making of the Modern Subject: Habeas what kind of Corpus?' *Body and Society* 22, no.2:28–57.

Epstein, C. 2017a. *Against International Relations Norms: Postcolonial Perspectives*. Abingdon: Routledge.

Epstein, C. 2017b. 'Why We Need to Decolonize Norms'. In *Against International Relations Norms: Postcolonial Perspectives*. Edited by C. Epstein, 1–22. Abingdon: Routledge.

Epstein, C. 2018. 'The productive force of the negative and the desire for recognition: Lessons from Hegel and Lacan'. *Review of International Studies* 44, no.5:805–828.

Esposito, R. 2008. *Bios. Biopolitics and Philosophy*. Translated by T. Campbell. Minneapolis, MA and London: Minnesota University Press.

Fanon, F. 1952. *Peau noire, masques blancs*. Paris: Éditions du Seuil.

Farr, J. 1986. ' "So Vile and Miserable an Estate": The Problem of Slavery in Locke's Political Thought'. *Political Theory* 14, no.2:263–289.

Farr. J. 2008. 'Locke, Natural Law and New World Slavery', *Political Theory* 36, no.4:495–522.

Federman, C. 2006. *The Body and the State. Habeas Corpus and American Jurisprudence.* New York: State University of New York Press.

Fehér. F. 1989. 'The French Revolution and the Birth of Modernity: Introduction'. *Social Research* 51, no.1:3–4.

Feldman, A. 1997. 'Violence and Vision: The Prosthetics and Aesthetics of Terror'. *Public Culture* 10, no.1:24–60.

Filmer, R. 1949. *Patriarcha and Other Political Works*. Edited by P. Laslett. Oxford: Basil Blackwell.

Finnemore, M. 1996. *National Interest in International Society*, Cornell: Cornell University Press.

Finnis, J. 1998. *Aquinas: Moral, Political and Legal Theory*. Oxford: Oxford University Press.

Finnis, J. 2011. *Natural Law and Natural Rights*, 2nd ed. Clarendon Law Series. Oxford: Oxford University Press.

Fitzmaurice, A. 2014. *Sovereignty, Property and Empire 1500–2000.* Cambridge: Cambridge University Press.

Flathman, R. 1993. *Thomas Hobbes: Skepticism, Individuality and Chastened Politics*. Newbury Park, London, and New Delhi: Sage.

Forstrom, K. 2010. *John Locke and Personal Identity: Immortality and Bodily Resurrection in 17th-Century Philosophy*. London and New York: Continuum.

Foster, H. 1988. 'Preface'. In *Vision and Visuality*. Edited by H. Foster, ix–xiv. Seattle: Bay Press.

Foucault, M. (1963). 2003. *The Birth of the Clinic: An Archaeology of Medical Perception*. Translated by A. M. Sheridan. London: Taylor and Francis.

Foucault, M. (1975). 1995. *Discipline and Punish: Birth of the Prison*. Translated by A. M. Sheridan. New York: Random House.

Foucault, M. 2003. *Society Must Be Defended: Lectures at the Collège de France 1975–76*. Translated by D. Macey. Picador: New York.

Foucault, M. (1966). 2005. *The Order of Things: An Archaeology of the Human Sciences*. London and New York: Routledge.

Foucault, M. 2008. *Birth of Biopolitics: Lectures at the Collège de France 1977–78*. Translated by G. Burchell. Edited by M. Senellart. Basingstoke: Palgrave Macmillan.

Foucault, M. 2009. *Security, Territory, Population: Lectures at the Collège de France 1977–78*. Translated by G. Burchell. Basingstoke: Palgrave Macmillan.

Foucault, M. 2013. *La société punitive. Cours au collège de France (1972–73)* Paris : Éditions Gallimard Seuil.

Frost, S. 2008. *Lessons from a Materialist Thinker: Hobbesian Reflections on Ethics and Politics*. Stanford, CA: Stanford University Press.

Frohnen, B.P. 2005. 'The One and the Many: Individual Rights, Corporate Rights and the Diversity of Groups'. *West Virginia Law Review* 107, 789–845.

Frug, G. E. 1980. 'The City as a Legal Concept'. *Harvard Law Review* 93, no. 6:1057–1154.

Gallup, J. 1988. *Thinking Through the Body*. New York: Columbia University Press.

Gaskin, J. C. A. 1994. Introduction to *The Elements of Law, Natural and Political, I & II*, by T. Hobbes. Edited by J. C. A. Gaskin, xi–lii. Oxford: Oxford University Press.

Gates, K. 2011. *Our Biometric Future: Facial Recognition Technology and the Culture of Surveillance*. New York: New York University Press.

Gierke, O. (1934) 1950. *Natural Law and the Theory of Society*. Translated by Ernest Barker. Cambridge: Cambridge University Press.

Glausser, W.1990. 'Three Approaches to Locke and the Slave Trade', *Journal of the History of Ideas* 51, no.2:199–216.

Glick, M. H. 2018. *Infrahumanisms: Science, Culture and the Making of Modern Non/Personhood*. Durham, NC: Duke University Press.

Goldsmith, M. M. 1989. 'Hobbes on Liberty'. *Hobbes Studies* 2, 23–39.

Gorski, P. S. 2003. *The Disciplinary Revolution: Calvinism and the Rise of the State in Early Modern Europe*. Chicago: University of Chicago Press.

Gould, M. 1987. *Revolution in the Development of Capitalism: The Coming of the English Revolution*. Berkeley: University of California Press.

Graeber, D. 1997. 'Manners, Deference and Private Property in Early Modern Europe'. *Comparative Studies in Society and History* 39, no.4:694–728.

Graf, S. 2018. ' "A Trespass against the Whole Species": Universal Crime and Sovereign Founding in John Locke's *Second Treatise of Government*'. *Political Theory* 46, no.4:1–26.

Grant, E. 1984a. 'In Defence of the Earth's Centrality and Immobility: Scholastic Reaction to Copernicanism in the Seventeenth Century'. *Transactions of the American Philosophical Society* 74, no.4:1–69.

Grant, E. 1984b. 'Were There Significant Differences between Medieval and Early Modern Scholastic Natural Philosophy? The Case for Cosmology'. *Noûs* 18, no.1:5–14.

Grant, R. W. 2003. 'Locke on Women and the Family'. In *Two Treatises of Government and a Letter Concerning Toleration*, by J. Locke. Edited by I. Shapiro, 286–308 . New Haven and London: Yale University Press.

Grasyon, K and Mawdsley, J. 2018. 'Scopic Regimes and the Visual Turn in International Relations: Seeing World Politics through the Drone'. *European Journal of International Relations* 25, no.2:431–457.

Grosz, E. 1994. *Volatile Bodies: Towards a Corporeal Feminism*. Bloomington: Indiana University Press.

Grosz, E. 2000. 'Interview with Elizabeth Grosz'. *Found Object* 9, 1–16.

Grotius, H. (1625). 2013. *On the Law of War and Peace (De jure belli ac pacis)* Cambridge: Cambridge University Press.

Haakonssen, K. 1985. 'Hugo Grotius and the History of Political Thought'. *Political Theory* 13, no. 2, 239–65.

Hacking, I. (1975) 1987. *The Emergence of Probability*. Cambridge: Cambridge University Press.

Hall, R. 2007. 'Of Ziploc Bags and Blackholes: The Aesthetics of Transparency in the War on Terror'. *The Communication Review* 10, no.4:310–347.

Halliday, P. D. 2010. *Habeas Corpus: From England to Empire*. Cambridge, MA: Harvard University Press.

Hampton, J. 1986. *Hobbes and the Social Contract Tradition*. Cambridge: Cambridge University Press.

Hansen, J.V. 1996. 'Resurrecting Death: Anatomical Art in the Cabinet of Dr Frederik Rysch'. *Arts Bulletin* 78, no.4:663–679.

Haraway, D. 1988. 'Situated Knowledges: The Science Question in Feminism and the Privilege of Partial Perspectives'. *Feminist Studies* 14, no.3:575–599.

Haraway, D. 1991. *Symians, Cyborgs and Women: The Reinvention of Nature*. London: Routledge.

Harding, A. 1980. 'Political Liberty in the Middle Ages'. *Speculum* 55, no.5:423–443.

Harrington, J. F. 2013. *The Faithful Executioner: Life and Death, Honour and Shame in the Turbulent Sixteenth Century*. New York: Farrar, Straus and Giroux.

Harris, I. 1992. *The Mind of John Locke: A Study of Political Theory in Its Intellectual Setting*. Cambridge: Cambridge University Press.

Harris, C. I. 1993. 'Whiteness as Property'. *Harvard Law Review* 106, no.8:1707–1791.

Harvey, W. (1615–19). 1961. *Lectures on the Whole of the Anatomy* (Praelectiones Anatomiae Universalis) Translated and edited by C. D. O'Malley, F. N. L. Poynter, and K. F. Russell. Berkeley: University of California Press.

Harvey, W. (1628). 1962. *On the Motion of the Heart and Blood in Animals*. Translated and edited by R. Willis and A. Bowie. Chicago: H. Regnery Co.

Harvey, W. 1989. 'Anatomical Exercises on the Generation of Animals'. In *The Works of William Harvey*. Edited by A. C. Guyton. Translated by R. Willis, 3–586. Philadelphia: University of Pennsylvania Press.

Herman, H. 1985. *Law and Revolution, I: The Formation of the Western Legal Tradition*. Cambridge, MA: Harvard University Press.

Hill, C. 1965. *The Intellectual Origins of the English Revolution*. Oxford: Clarendon Press.

Hill, C. 1980. *The Century of Revolution 1603–1714*, 2nd ed. Wokingham: Van Nostrand Reinhold Co. Ltd.

Hill, C. 1989. *The World Turned Upside Down: Radical Ideas during the English Revolution*. St Ives: Penguin Books.

Hirschmann, N. 2008. *Gender, Class and Freedom in Modern Political Theory* Princeton and Oxford: Princeton University Press.

Hobbes, T. (1640). 1928. *Elements of Law, Natural and Politic.* Edited by F. Tonnies, Cambridge: Cambridge University press.

Hobbes, T. (1651/1668). 1994. *Leviathan: With Selected Variants from the Latin Edition of 1668.* Edited by E. Curley. Indianapolis, IN: Hackett Publishing Company.

Hobbes, T. (1658). 1974. *De Homine.* Translated by P. M. Maurin. Paris: Albert Blanchard.

Hobbes, T. (1679). 1958. 'The Autobiography of Thomas Hobbes'. Translated by B. Farrington. *The Rationalist Annual*: 22–31.

Hobbes, T (1642). 1983. De Cive: *The English Version.* In *The Clarendon Edition of the Works of Thomas Hobbes.* Edited by H. Warrender, Vol. 2. Oxford: Oxford University Press.

Hobbes, Thomas. (1655). 1839. '*De Corpore*'. In *Elements of Philosophy: The First Section concerning the Body.* London: John Bohn.

Hobbes, Thomas. (1658). 1998. '*De Homine*'. In *Man and Citizen:* De Homine *and* De Cive. Translated by C. T. Wood, T. S. K. Scott-Craig, and B. Gert. Edited by B. Gert. Indianapolis, IN: Hackett Publishing Company.

Holdsworth, W.S. 1922. 'English Corporation Law in the 16th and 17th Centuries'. *The Yale Law Journal* 41, no.4:382–407.

Hostettler, J. 1997. *Sir Edward Coke: A Force for Change.* Chichester: Barry Rose Law Publishers Ltd.

Hunter, M. 1981. *Science and Society in Restoration England.* Cambridge: Cambridge University Press.

Hutchings, K. 2008. *Time in World Politics. Thinking the Present.* Manchester: Manchester University Press.

Jagger, G. 2015. 'The New Materialism and Sexual Difference'. *Signs: Journal of Women in Culture and Society* 40, no. 2:321–42.

Jameson, F. 2016. 'An American Utopia'. In *An American Utopia: Frederic Jameson.* Edited by S. Žižek, 1–104. London and New York: Verso.

Jammer, M. 1993. *Concepts of Space: The History of Theories of Space in Physics*, 3rd ed. New York: Dover.

Jardine, L. 2000. Introduction to *New Organon*, by F. Bacon, vii–xviii. Cambridge: Cambridge University Press.

Jay, M. 1988. 'Scopic Regimes of Modernity'. In *Vision and Visuality: Discussions in Contemporary Culture.* Edited by Foster, 3–28. Seattle: Bay Press.

Jenks, E. 1902. 'The Story of Habeas Corpus'. *The Law Quarterly Review* 69, 64–77.

Jenks, E. 1923. 'The Prerogative Writs in English Law'. *Yale Law Journal* 32, no. 6:523–34.

Johnson, W. 1999. *Soul by Soul: Life inside the Antebellum Slave Market.* Cambridge, MA: Harvard University Press.

Josephson, P. 2002. *The Great Art of Consent: Locke's Use of Consent.* Lawrence: University of Kansas Press.

Kantorowicz, E. H. 1957. *The King's Two Bodies: A Study in Medieval Theology.* Princeton, NJ: Princeton University Press.

Kantorowicz, E. H. 1997. *The King's Two Bodies: A Study in Medieval Political Theology.* Princeton, NJ: Princeton University Press.

Kaplan, B. 2007. *Divided by Faith: Religious Conflict and the Practice of Toleration in Early Modern Europe.* Cambridge, MA: Harvard University Press.

Kelly, A. 1985. 'The Construction of Masculine Science'. *British Journal of Sociology of Education* 6, no. 2:133–54.

Kim, K. (1608). 1996. 'Calvin's Case and the Law of Alien Status'. *The Journal of Legal History* 17, no. 2:155–71.

Kiser, E., and J. Kane 2001. 'Revolution and State Structure: The Bureaucratization of Tax Administration in Early Modern England and France'. *American Journal of Sociology* 107, no. 1:183–223.

Koselleck, R. (1959). 1988. *Critique and Crisis: Enlightenment and the Pathogenesis of Modern Society*. Cambridge, MA: MIT Press.

Koselleck, R. (1979). 1985. ' "Spaces of Experience" and "Horizons of Expectations": Two Categories'. In *Futures Past: On the Semantics of Historical Time*. Translated by K. Tribe, 255–276. Cambridge, MA: MIT Press.

Koyré, A. 1957. *From the Closed World to the Infinite Universe*. Baltimore, MD: Johns Hopkins University Press.

Koyré, A. 1961. *Études d'histoire de la pensée philosophique*. Paris: Gallimard.

Koyré, A. 1966. *Études galiléennes*. Paris: Hermann.

Kuhn, T. S. 1957. *The Copernican Revolution: Planetary Astronomy in the Development of Western Thought*. Cambridge, MA: Harvard University Press.

Kuhn, T. S. 1977. *The Essential Tension: Selected Studies in Scientific Tradition and Change*. Chicago: University of Chicago Press.

Lachmann, R. 1989. 'Elite Formation and State Conflict in 16th- and 17th-Century England and France'. *American Sociological Review* 54, no. 2:141–62.

Lalande, A. 1926. *Vocabulaire technique et critique de la philosophie*. Paris: Libraire Félix Alcan.

Langston, D. 2015. 'Medieval Theories of Conscience'. *Stanford Encyclopedia of Philosophy*. Fall 2015 edition. Edited by Edward N. Zalta et al. https://plato.stanford.edu/entries/conscience-medieval/.

Laqueur, T. 1990. *Making Sex: Body and Gender from the Greeks to Freud*. Cambridge, MA: Harvard University Press.

Laslett, P. (1960). 1988. 'Introduction'. In *Two Treatises of Government*. J. Locke, 3–126. Cambridge: Cambridge University Press.

Le Goff, J. 1991. *La naissance du Purgatoire*. Paris: Gallimard.

Leijenhorst, C. 2002. *The Mechanisation of Aristotelianism*. Leiden, Boston, and Cologne: Brill.

Lennon, K. 2014. 'Feminist Perspectives on the Body'. *Stanford Encyclopedia of Philosophy*. Fall 2019 edition. Edited by Edward N. Zalta et al., https://plato.stanford.edu/entries/feminist-body.

Levine, D. P. 1978. *Economic Theory: The Elementary Relations of Economic Life*, vol. 1. London, Henley, and Boston: Routledge & Kegan Paul.

Lilburne, J. (1645). 2015. 'Englands Birth-Right Justified against All Arbitrary Usurpation, whether Regall or Parliamentary, or under What Vizor soever'. In *Tracts on Liberty by the Levellers and Their Critics*. Vol. 2: *1644–1645*. Edited by D. M. Hart and R. Kenyon. Indianapolis: Liberty Fund, available online: https://oll.libertyfund.org/pages/leveller-tracts-table-of-contents

Linebaugh, P. 1991. *The London Hanged. Crime and Civil Society in the Eighteenth Century*, London: Allen Lane.

Linnik, V. 1975. 'Kepler's Work in the Field of Optics'. *Vistas in Astronomy* 18:809–817.

Locke J. (1663–64). 1997. 'Essay on the Law of Nature'. In *Political Essays*. Edited by M. Goldie, 79–133. Cambridge: Cambridge University Press.

Locke, J. (1664). 1990. *Questions concerning the Law of Nature*. Ithaca, NY: Cornell University Press.

Locke, J. (1689). 1924. *An Essay concerning Human Understanding*. Abridged and edited by A. S. Pringle-Pattison. Oxford: Clarendon.

Locke, J. (1690). 1988. *Two Treatises of Government*. Edited by P. Laslett. Cambridge: Cambridge University Press.

Locke, J. (1693). 2013. *Some Thoughts concerning Education*. Edited by J. W. Yolton and J. S. Yolton. Oxford: Oxford University Press.

Locke J. (1697). 1997. 'An Essay on the Poor Law'. In *Political Essays*. Edited by M. Goldie, 182–198. Cambridge: Cambridge University Press.

Locke. J. (1697–1704). 1901. *On the Conduct of the Understanding*. Edited by Thomas Fowler. Oxford: Clarendon Press.

Luban, D. 2018. 'Hobbesian Slavery'. *Political Theory* 46, no. 5:726–48.

Lukes. S. (1974). 2005. *Power: A Radical View* Basingstoke: Palgrave Macmillan. 2nd edition.

Macpherson, C. B. 1962. *The Political Theory of Possessive Individualism: Hobbes to Locke*. Oxford: Clarendon Press.

Magnet, S., and T. Rodgers. 2012. 'Stripping for the State: Whole Body Imagining Technologies and the Surveillance of Othered Bodies'. *Feminist Media Studies* 12. no. 1:101–18.

Maitland, F. W. 1915. *A Sketch of English Legal History*. New York and London: G. P. Putnam's Sons.

Mancilla, A. 2015. 'What We Own Before Property: Hugo Grotius and the *Suum*'. *Grotiana* 36, no.1:63–77.

Manent, P. 2012. *Histoire Intellectuelle du Liberalsime*. Paris: Fayard/Pluriel.

Mann S, Nolan J, Wellman B. 2002. 'Sousveillance: Inventing and using wearable computing devices as data collection in surveillance environments. *Surveillance & Society* 1, no.3:331–355.

Marwick, A. E. 2012. 'The Public Domain: Surveillance in Everyday Life'. *Surveillance and Society* 9, no. 4:378–93.

Marx, K. (1867)1992. *Capital. A Critique of Political Economy vol.1*, translated by B. Fowkes, London: Penguin Books.

Mathiowetz, D. 2011. *Appeals to Interests: Language, Contestation and the Shaping of Political Agency*. Philadelphia: Penn State University Press.

Marwick, A. E. 2012. 'The Public Domain: Social Surveillance in Every Day Life', *Surveillance and Society* 9, no.4:378–393.

Mautner, T. 2010. 'Introduction: A Lawless Natural Law?' *Jurisprudence* 1, no. 2:197–208.

McBride, K. 2007. *Punishment and Political Order*. Ann Arbor: University of Michigan Press.

McQueen, A. 2017. *Political Realism in Apocalyptic Times*. Cambridge: Cambridge University Press.

Mehta, U. 1992. *The Anxiety of Freedom: Imagination and Individuality in Locke's Political Thought*. Ithaca and London: Cornell University Press.

Meiksins Wood, E. 2012. *Liberty and Property: A Social History of Western Political Thought from the Renaissance to the Enlightenment*, London: Verso.

Meinecke, F. 1984. *Machiavellism: The Doctrine of* Raison D'État *and Its Place in Modern History.* Translated by D. Scott. London: Routledge & Kegan Paul.

Merchant, C. 1980. *The Death of Nature: Women, Ecology and the Scientific Revolution.* New York: Harper & Row.

Monnoyer, J. M. 1988. 'La Pathétique Cartésienne'. Introduction to *Les passions de L'âme,* by R. Descartes, 11–31. Paris: Gallimard.

Müller, B. 2010. *Security, Risk and the Biometric State.* Oxon: Routledge.

Nazar, H. 2017. 'Locke, Education and "Disciplinary Liberalism"'. *Review of Politics* 79:215–238.

Neocleous, M. 2014. *War Power, Police Power.* Edinburgh: Edinburgh University Press.

Nietzsche, F. (1887). 1994. *On the Genealogy of Morality.* Translated by C. Diethe. Cambridge: Cambridge University Press.

Nunn, H. M. 2016. *Staging Anatomies: Dissection and Spectacle in Early Stuart Tragedy.* London & New York: Routledge.

Oaks, D.H. 1965. 'Habeas Corpus in The States–1776–1865'. *Chicago Law Review,* 32:243–288.

Olivecrona, K. 1974a. 'Locke's Theory of Appropriation'. *The Philosophical Quarterly* 24, no.96:220–234.

Olivecrona, K. 1974b. 'Appropriation in the State of Nature: Locke on the Origin of Property'. *Journal of the History of Ideas* 35. no.2:211–230.

Olivecrona, K. 2010. 'The Two Levels of Natural Law Thinking'. *Jurisprudence* 1, no. 2:208–224.

O'Malley, C. D., F. N. L. Poynter, and K. F. Russell, trans. 1961. Introduction to *Lectures on the Whole of the Anatomy* (Praelectiones Anatomiae Universalis). Berkeley: University of California Press.

Onn, Yael, et al. 2005. *Privacy in the Digital Environment.* Haifa: Haifa Center of Law & Technology, University of Haifa

Owen, M. 2005. *Stages of Dismemberment:The Fragmented Body in Late Medieval and Early Modern Drama,* Newark, DE: University of Delaware Press.

The Oxford Companion to the Body. 2001. Edited by C. Blakemore and S. Jennett. S. Harvey, William. Oxford: Oxford University Press.

Pagel, W. 1951. 'William Harvey and the Purpose of Circulation'. *History of Science Society* 42, no.1:22–38.

Pateman, C. 1988. *The Sexual Contract.* Cambridge: Cambridge University Press.

Perelman, M. 2000. *The Invention of Capitalism: Classical Political Economy and the Secret History of Private Accumulation.* Durham, NC: Duke University Press.

Pettit, P. 1997. *Republicanism: A Theory of Freedom and Government.* Oxford: Clarendon Press.

Pettit, P. 2005. 'Liberty and Leviathan'. *Politics, Philosophy and Economics* 4, no. 1:131–51.

Pettit, P. 2008. *Made with Words: Hobbes on Language, Mind and Politics.* Princeton, N.J: Princeton University Press.

Pierson, C. 2013. *Just Property. A History in the West. Volume One: Wealth, Virtue and the Law.* Oxford : Oxford University Press.

Pocock, J. G. A. 1987. *The Ancient Constitution and the Feudal Law.* 2nd Edition. Cambridge: Cambridge University Press.

Pollock, F. and F. Maitland. 1898. *The History of English Law. Before the Time of Edward I,* 2nd ed. Cambridge: Cambridge University Press.

Price, P. J. (1608). 1997. 'Natural Law and Birthright Citizenship in Calvin's Case'. *Yale Journal of Law and the Humanities* 9, no. 1:73–145.

Pringle-Pattsion, A. S. 1924. Introduction to *An Essay Concerning Human Understanding*, by J. Locke. Abridged and edited by A. S. Pringle-Pattison. Oxford: Clarendon.

Prokhovnik, R. 2005. 'Hobbes Artifice as Social Construction'. *Hobbes Studies* 18:74–94.

Prokhovnik, R. 2010. 'Hobbes, Sovereignty and Politics: Rethinking International Political Space'. In *International Political Theory after Hobbes*. Edited by R. Prokhovnik and G. Slomp. Basingstoke: Palgrave Macmillan.

Pufendorf, S. (1688). 1934. *On the Law of Nature and Nations*. Translated by C. H. Oldfather and William Oldfather. Oxford: Clarendon.

Ribeiro, R. J. 2011. '"Men of Feminine Courage": Thomas Hobbes and Life as a Right'. *Hobbes Studies* 24, no. 1:44–61.

Richardson, R. 2001. *Death, Dissection and the Destitute*. Chicago: University of Chicago Press.

Robinson, J. 1988. *The Body: A Study in Pauline Theology*. Bristol: Wyndham Hall Press.

Roney, Eileen. 1989. 'In a Word'. Interview by G. C. Spivak. *Differences*, vol. 1, no. 2:124–56.

Roots, I. 1974. Preface to *Puritanism and Liberty*, by A. S. P. Woodhouse. London: J. M. Dent and Sons Ltd.

Rubinelli, L. 2019. 'How to think beyond sovereignty: On Sieyes and Constituent power'. *European Journal of Political Theory* 18, no.1:47–67

Ruggie, J. G. 1993. 'Territoriality and Beyond: Problematizing Modernity in International Relations'. *International Organization* 47, no. 1:139–74.

Rupp, J. C. C. 1992. 'Michel Foucault, Body Politics and the Rise and Expansion of Modern Anatomy'. *Journal of Historical Sociology* 5, no. 1:31–60.

Ryan, A. 1965. 'Locke and the Dictatorship of the Bourgeoisie'. *Political Studies* 13, no. 2:219–30.

Said, E. 1978. *Orientalism*. New York: Pantheon Books.

Sandford, S. 2013. 'The Incomplete Locke: Balibar, Locke and the Philosophy of the Subject'. In Balibar, É. 2013. *Identity and Difference: John Locke and the Invention of Consciousness*, xi–xlvi. London and New York: Verso.

Santner, E. L. 2011. *The Royal Remains: The People's Two Bodies and the Endgames of Sovereignty*. Chicago: University of Chicago Press.

Sawday, J. 1996. *The Body Emblazoned: Dissection and the Human Body in Renaissance Culture*. London and New York: Routledge.

Sawday, J. 2007. *Engines of the Imagination: Renaissance Culture and the Rise of the Machine*. London and New York: Routledge.

Scarry, E. 1985. *The Body in Pain: The Making and Unmaking of the World*. Oxford: Oxford University Press.

Schmidgen, W. 2002. *Eighteenth-century Fiction and the Law of Property*. Cambridge: Cambridge University Press.

Schmidgen, W. 2007. 'The Politics and Philosophy of Mixture: John Locke Recomposed'. *The Eighteenth Century* 43, no. 3:205–23.

Schmitt, C. (1922). 1985. *Poltical Theology. Four Chapters on the Concept of Sovereignty*. Translated G. Schwab. Chicago: Chicago University Press.

Schmitt, C. (1938). 2008. *The Leviathan in the State Theory of Thomas Hobbes: Meaning and Failure of a Political Symbol*. Translated by George Schwab and Erna Hilfstein. Chicago: Chicago University Press

Scott, J. C. 1998. *Seeing Like a State: How Certain Schemes to Improve the Human Condition Have Failed*. New Haven, CT: Yale University Press.

Seebohm, F. 1883. *The English Village Community Examined in Its Relation to the Manorial and Tribal Systems and to the Common Open Fields System of Husbandry: An Essay in Economic History*, 2nd ed. London: Longmans, Green, and Co.

Sennett, R. 1994. *Flesh and Stone: The Body and the City in Western Civilization*, New York and London: Norton and Company.

Shackleford, J. 2003, *William Harvey and the Mechanics of the Heart*, Oxford: Oxford University Press

Shapin, S. 1988. 'The House of Experiment in Seventeenth-Century England'. *Isis* 79, no.3:373–403.

Shapin, S. 1994. *A Social History of Truth: Civility and Science in Seventeenth-century England*. Chicago: University of Chicago Press.

Shapin, S. 1996. *The Scientific Revolution*. Chicago: University of Chicago Press.

Shapin, S., and S. Schaffer. 2011. *Leviathan and the Air Pump: Hobbes, Boyle and the Experimental Life*, 2nd ed. Princeton, NJ: Princeton University Press.

Shimokawa, K. 2013. 'The Origin and Development of Property: Conventionalism, Unilateralism, and Colonialism'. In *The Oxford Handbook of British Philosophy in the Seventeenth Century*. Edited by P. R. Antsey. Oxford: Oxford University Press.

Simon, G. 1975.'On the theory of visual perception of Kepler and Descartes: reflections on the role of mechanism in the birth of modern science'. *Vistas in Astronomy* 18:825–832.

Simmons, J. 1991. 'Locke and the Right to Punish', *Philosophy and Public Affairs,* 20 no.4:311–349.

Skinner, Q. 1990. 'Thomas Hobbes on the Proper Signification of Liberty: The Prothero Lecture'. *Transactions of the Royal Historical Society* 40, 121–51.

Skinner Q. 1997. *Reason and Rhetoric in the Philosophy of Thomas Hobbes*. Cambridge: Cambridge University Press.

Skinner, Q. 2005. 'Hobbes on Representation'. *European Journal of Philosophy* 13, no. 1:155–84.

Skinner, Q. 2008. *Hobbes and Republican Liberty*. Cambridge: Cambridge University Press.

Spitz, J. F. 2001. *John Locke et les fondements de la liberté moderne*. Paris: Presses Universitaires de France.

Spragens, T. A., Jr. 1973. *The Politics of Motion: The World of Thomas Hobbes*. Lexington: University of Kentucky Press; London: Croom Helm Ltd.

Springborg, P. 1995. 'Biblical Beasts: Leviathan and Behemoth'. *Political Theory* 23, no. 2:353–73.

Sreedhar, S. 2010. *Hobbes On Resistance: Defying the Leviathan*. Cambridge: Cambridge University Press

Srnicek, N. 2016. *Platform Capitalism*. Cambridge: Polity Press

Stalder, F. 2002. 'The Failure of Privacy Enhancing Technologies (PETs) and the Voiding of Privacy'. *Sociological Research Online* 7, no. 2:1–15.

Steiner, G. 2010. 'The cultural significance of Rembrandt's "Anatomy Lesson of Dr Nocolaas Tulp"'. *History of European Ideas* 3, no.3:273–279.

Stoler, A. L. 1995. *Race and the Education of Desire: Foucault's History of Sexuality and the Colonial Order of Things*. Durham, NC: Duke University Press.

Stone, L. 2002. *The Causes of the English Revolution 1529-1642*, 2nd ed. London and New York: Routledge.

Strauss, L. 1963. *The Political Philosophy of Hobbes: Its Basis and Genesis*. Translated by E. M. Sinclair. Chicago: University of Chicago Press.

Strauss, L. 1965. *Natural Right and History*. Chicago: University of Chicago Press.

Strong. T.B. 1993. 'How to Write Scripture: Words, Authority, and Politics in Thomas Hobbes'. *Critical Inquiry* 20, no.1:128–159.

Tanaka, T. 1993. 'State and Governing Power'. In *Normative Approach to War: Peace, War and Justice in Hugo Grotius*. Edited by Y. Onuma . Oxford: Oxford University Press.

Tarcov, N. 1984. *Locke's Education for Liberty*. Chicago and London: Chicago University Press.

Taylor, C. 1989. *Sources of the Self: The Making of the Modern Identity*. Cambridge, MA: Harvard University Press.

Thirsk, J. 1964. 'The Common Fields'. *Past and Present*, no. 29:3–25.

Thirsk, J. 1967. 'Enclosing and Engrossing'. In *The Agrarian History of England and Wales*. Vol.4:*1500–1640*. Edited by J. Thirsk. Cambridge: Cambridge University Press.

Tilly, C. 1989. 'State and Counterrevolution in France'. *Social Research* 51, no.1:71–97

Todorov, T. 1982. *La Conquête de L'Amérique : La question de l'autre*. Paris: Éditions du Seuil

Thompson, E. P. 1990. *Whigs and Hunters*. London: Penguin Books.

Thompson, E. P. 1991. *Customs in Common*. New York: New York Press.

Tierney B. 1982. *Religion, Law and the Growth of Constitutional Thought 1150–1650*. Cambridge: Cambridge University Press.

Tierney, B. 1997. *The Idea of Natural Rights: Studies on Natural Rights, Natural Law, and Church Law 1150–1625*. Grand Rapids: William Eerdman's Publishing Company.

Toulmin, S. 1990. *Cosmopolis: The Hidden Agenda of Political Modernity*. Chicago: Chicago University Press.

Tuck, R. 1979. *Natural Rights Theories: Their Origins and Development*. Cambridge: Cambridge University Press.

Tuck, R. 1988. 'Optics and Sceptics: The Philosophical Foundations of Hobbes's Political Thought'. In *Conscience and Casuistry in Early Modern Europe*. Edited by E. Leites, 235–264. Cambridge: Cambridge University Press.

Tuck, R. 1989. *Hobbes*. Oxford: Oxford University Press.

Tuckness, A. 2016. 'Locke's Political Philosophy'. *Stanford Encyclopedia of Philosophy* Spring 2016 edition. Edited by Edward N. Zalta et al. http://plato.stanford.edu/archives/spr2016/entries/locke-political/.

Tully, J. 1980. *A Discourse on Property: John Locke and His Adversaries*. Cambridge: Cambridge University Press.

Tully, J. 1988. 'Governing Conduct'. In *Conscience and Casuistry in Early Modern Europe*. Edited by E. Leites, 12–71. Cambridge: Cambridge University Press.

Turner, H. 2016. *The Corporate Commonwealth: Pluralism and Political Fictions in England 1516–1651*. Chicago: Chicago University Press.

Villey, M. 1975. *Histoire de la Philosophie du Droit*. Paris: Montchrétien.

Wadiwel, D. J. 2014. 'The Will for Self-Preservation: Locke and Derrida on Dominion, Property and Animals'. *SubStance* 43, no.2:148–61.

Wæver, O. 1995. "Securitization and Desecuritization". In *On security*. Edited by R. Lipschutz, 46–86. New York: Columbia University Press.

Wæver, O. forthcoming. 'Speech Act Theories of Securitization: Illocutionary Insistence and Political Performativity'.

Waldron, J. 1988. *The Right to Private Property*. Oxford: Clarendon Press.

Walker, R. B. J. 1993. *Inside/Outside: International Relations as Political Theory.* Cambridge: Cambridge University Press.

Walker Bynum, C. 1995. *The Resurrection of the Body in Western Christianity.* New York: Columbia University Press.

Walzer, M. 1965. *The Revolution of the Saints: A Study in the Origins of Radical Politics.* Cambridge, MA: Harvard University Press.

Warrender, H. 1957. *The Political Philosophy of Thomas Hobbes: His Theory of Obligation.* Oxford: Clarendon Press.

Watkins, J. (1965). 1989. *Hobbes's System of Ideas,* 2nd ed. London: Gower.

Webster, C. 1975. *The Great Instauration: Science, Medicine and Reform 1626–1660.* London: Ducksworth.

Weiss Muller, H. 2017. *Subjects and Sovereign: Bonds of Belonging in the Eighteenth-century British Empire.* Oxford: Oxford University Press.

Weldes, J., Laffey, M., Gutterson, H. and Duvall, R. (eds). 1999. *Cultures of Insecurity. States Communities and the Production of Danger,* Minneapolis and London: University of Minnesota Press.

Wendt, A. 1999. *Social Theory of International Politics.* Cambridge: Cambridge University Press.

Whitehead, A. (1925). 1954. *Science and the Modern World.* New York: Free Press/ Macmillan.

Wight, M. 1992. *International Theory: The Three Traditions.* London: Holme and Meier.

Wilcox, L. 2015. *Bodies of Violence: Theorizing Embodied Subjects in International Relations.* New York: Oxford University Press.

Williams, M. C. 1996. 'Hobbes and International Relations: A Reconsideration'. *International Organization* 50, no.2:213–36.

Williams, M. C. 2005. *The Realist Tradition and the Limits of International Relations.* New York: Cambridge University Press.

Wilson, L. 1987.'The Performance of the Body in the Renaissance Theatre of Anatomy. *Representations* 17:62–95.

Winter, Y. 2018. *Machiavelli and the Orders of Violence.* Cambridge: Cambridge University Press.

Woodhouse, A. S. P. 1974. *Puritanism and Liberty,* 2nd ed. London: J. M. Dent and Sons Ltd.

Woolhouse, R. 1997. Introduction to *An Essay concerning the Human Understanding,* by J. Locke. Edited by R. Woodhouse, 9–24 . London: Penguin Classics.

Zarakol, A. 2018. *After Defeat: How the East Learned to Live with the West,* Cambridge: Cambridge University Press.

Zuboff, S. 2019. *The Age of Surveillance Capitalism: The Fight for a Human Future at the New Frontier of Power,* New York: PublicAffairs.

Index

For the benefit of digital users, indexed terms that span two pages (e.g., 52–53) may, on occasion, appear on only one of those pages.